ST MARTIN'S
TRUE CRIME
CLASSICS

ST. MARTIN'S TRUE CRIME LIBRARY TITLES
BY GREGG OLSEN

Abandoned Prayers
Cruel Deception
Bitter Almonds
The Confessions of an American Black Widow
If Loving You Is Wrong

BITTER ALMONDS

The True Story of Mothers,
Daughters, and the
Seattle Cyanide Murders

GREGG OLSEN

St. Martin's Paperbacks

For Claudia, Marta and Morgan

BITTER ALMONDS

Copyright © 1993 by Gregg Olsen.
"Update: 2002" copyright © 2002 by Gregg Olsen.
Letter to readers copyright © 2006 by Gregg Olsen.

Cover photo of Stella Nickell by Bruce Nickell.
Cover photo of pills courtesy of Graphistock.

ISBN: 0-312-98200-3
EAN: 9780312-98200-3

Printed in the United States of America

Warner Books edition / December 1993
St. Martin's Paperbacks edition / September 2002

10 9 8 7 6 5 4 3

BITTER
ALMONDS

PROLOGUE

Though only half an hour drive away, the South King County towns of Auburn and Kent are worlds away from high-rises that make up Washington's largest and most magazine-revered city, Seattle. Ringed by the Olympics, the Cascades, and the waters of Puget Sound and sailboat-specked Lake Washington, Seattle is as beautiful and as cosmopolitan as the Northwest gets: art galleries, symphony, opera, and Nordstrom's home base.

All of that is glitz and glamour.

The milky, glacial-fed White River roars down from Mt. Rainier to meet the meandering Green River near Auburn and Kent. It is here we find the real Northwest. The real Northwest is pool tables and beer in Kent or Auburn taverns. Mobile homes and hydroplanes. Chain saws and six-packs. Big hair and oil-soaked Levi's, slung low to expose that fish-belly-white strip of skin between back and buttocks. In the real Northwest, pleasures can be small but dreams are big.

The call came in at 5:02 P.M. on June 5, 1986. A volunteer fire department—issued plectron, or radio, announced the emergency. A man was having a seizure at his residence just off of Lake Moneysmith Road. The address was 17807 S.E. 346th, Auburn, Washington. The man's name was Bruce Nickell. His wife, Stella, had made the call.

Lori and Bob Jewett were volunteer fire fighters living at the station, saving for the purchase of a dream home in the wooded hills above Auburn. Lori's younger brother, Eric Oehler, was living with his parents in their home, just a couple hundred yards from the fire station located on the Kent/Black Diamond Road. The tones of the plectron were the jolt that got them going, and they were close enough to respond quickly.

They drove with lights flashing but sirens off. Such a ruckus was often unnecessary in the rural area that made up their district. The Jewetts and some other volunteers led the way in the white and orange aid car. Eric Oehler followed in a yellow fire truck. From Lake Holmes Road, they turned onto Lake Moneysmith Road. Though they were familiar enough with the area, and it was still light out, finding the address proved difficult. No street markers pointed the way and the mailboxes were in a cluster, far from any of the addresses displayed in reflective tape and Magic Markers.

Turning onto a narrow dirt and gravel road, Bob Jewett stopped the aid car in front of a mobile home where he saw a woman peering through the silver mesh of a screen door. Another woman, older and with light-gray hair, was in the driveway and appeared to be calling her dog as she stood in front of another mobile home, set farther back on the property. Neither woman signaled the rescue team.

"Is this it?" Lori asked.

"It didn't seem like the right place," Lori Jewett later remembered. "Usually there is somebody at the end of the driveway waving their arms . . . just can't wait for you to get down the dirt road."

Bob Jewett was also confused.

"What in the hell is she doing?" he wondered out loud, reaching for the PA to ask the woman behind the screen door if she had been the one who had called 911. Before he had the chance, Stella Nickell waved slowly, gesturing the driver into the yard and then into her home.

Bruce Nickell, damp from a shower and clad in a bathrobe, gaped like a salmon on a riverbank as he lay on his back on the floor in front of a living-room couch. His terry robe was smooth and flat beneath him. At their request, Stella ticked off Bruce's health history, telling the fire fighters that her husband was a recovering alcoholic, that he had had no health problems other than some recent headaches.

"After his shower, he went over to the sliding glass door to the deck to watch the hawks," Stella said. "He turned to me and said, 'Stella, I'm feeling light-headed' . . . then he fell."

"Is he on any medication?"

"No. Just aspirin," she answered.

Stella Nickell explained that Bruce had taken a couple of Excedrin and, as had been his custom lately, had gone out on the deck to relax and watch the birds.

Throughout her explanation, Bruce continued to gasp every twenty seconds or so.

It was not a symptom the fire fighters had seen. Neither was the man's two-tone coloration. Bruce Nickell was cherry red from the neck up, white below. It was such a contrast, it looked as though a line had been drawn between the red and white. It was baffling. If this were carbon monoxide poisoning the victim would be red from head to toe.

While waiting for the paramedics, Bob Jewett checked the ABCs—airways, breathing, and circulation. Nickell had a pulse, but he wasn't breathing so they "bagged" him with an oxygen mask over his nose and mouth. This procedure was now preferred over mouth-to-mouth resuscitation.

Eric Oehler took Mrs. Nickell into the kitchen to get the necessary background information away from the hubbub. Concerned about her husband's condition, she looked up frequently toward the room where he was fighting for his life.

"When he fell," Stella said, pointing to a cigarette on the kitchen table. "he was smoking this." The white paper casing has shredded down the center. It did not appear to have been lighted, and there was no ashtray to be seen.

Lori Jewett looked over her shoulder and watched Stella tear up the cigarette further, while telling the young man of her concern.

"She was breaking it up even more," Lori recalled. "It was like she was trying to find something in that cigarette."

Oehler listened; but although Stella Nickell's ramblings were strange responses to a stressful situation, he dismissed them. Most family members are so focused on the immediate health of their loved one, they don't talk about things like cigarettes or a cup of coffee that might be the culprit.

Paramedics Chris Merritt, thirty-one, and his partner Roger Matheny, thirty-six, arrived at the Nickell property just moments after the volunteer fire fighters. Employed by the King County Health Department, the men were summoned from their shift at the Medic 6 unit, housed just behind the Auburn fire station. The call indicated the victim was "an unconscious man, a sudden collapse."

Both men were experienced paramedics, but neither had been prepared for a case like Bruce Nickell's. In April 1979, Merritt became one of eight original paramedics based in the area. Roger Matheny, a former respiratory therapist at Harborview Medical Center, joined the unit about a year later. When they arrived, they sensed immediately that something was different about this call.

"Here is a guy who has just suddenly collapsed," Matheny thought, "just went unconscious. But, he has a blood pressure, and his heart is beating . . ."

The paramedics considered the possibility that something chemical might have caused the fifty-two-year-old man's collapse. Maybe an overdose? Some sort of a stroke? Unlikely. In such cases, victims are usually slightly conscious. Bruce Nickell wasn't. An airway was placed into his trachea.

Stella Nickell came out of the kitchen to repeat what she had told Eric Oehler to Chris Merritt, who was still kneeling next to her husband; that he had taken some Excedrin capsules. She thrust a small bottle into the young paramedic's face. She mentioned the pain reliever several more times. Later, he suggested Stella Nickell did so as many as six times.

"He took these," she emphasized. *"These . . . just before he fell."*

Chris Merritt held the bottle for a moment and handed it back. He figured since it was only an over-the-counter product, it was not likely to be the culprit. He also heard something mentioned regarding a cigarette, but that seemed farfetched as well.

Stella repeated the story that her husband had collapsed after taking several Excedrin capsules, and that before he fell, he had been watching hawks fly over their property. As she spoke, Merritt looked up and saw one of the birds of prey swoop through the sky. The fleeting image stuck with him years later. So did the memory of Stella Nickell.

"She was calm in a way," paramedic Merritt recalled of the woman's demeanor. "She seemed to be more concerned to identify to us what actually happened."

Bruce Nickell's blood pressure began to fall rapidly, although he wasn't bleeding. He was injected with epinephrine to increase his weakening heart rate. Baselpressers were employed to constrict blood vessels in an effort to increase the failing blood pressure. When nothing seemed to work, a helicopter was called from Harborview Medical Center in Seattle.

"We thrashed him all the way to the helicopter," Roger Matheny later said, using the vernacular of paramedic circles. It simply meant they tried everything they could think of to stop Bruce Nickell from dying. He was still gasping when they reached the Red Barn Ranch, where the helicopter landed in an open field.

As they loaded Bruce Nickell on board, Stella Nickell and an elderly woman most assumed to be her or Bruce's mother left the cab of their pickup and stood next to a fence. Tears didn't fall, but Bruce Nickell's wife's eyes had welled up. She stood clutching an afghan that had been used to keep her husband warm. The helicopter lifted and the wind blew her coarse black hair as she watched for a moment before getting back in the truck to make the trip to the hospital in Seattle.

Later that evening at the paramedics' living quarters, Roger Matheny took a call from Stella Nickell. It was around 10 P.M. By the time she called, Roger Matheny already knew Bruce Edward Nickell had not made it. Such a call was out of the ordinary. The paramedic living quarters phone number is not given out freely. Someone had given the number to Mrs. Nickell. It must have been for a good reason.

"Do you have my afghan?" she asked.

Roger Matheny didn't know what she was talking about.

Stella Nickell explained that medics had wrapped Bruce in a knitted afghan from her home and she wanted it back. She wondered if Medic 6 had taken it.

But they had not.

As he hung up, paramedic Matheny interpreted the call as a bereaved spouse calling for a belonging that held sentimental value.

"Maybe it held some memories for her and her dead husband?" he later wondered.

PART ONE

Sue Kathryn

PART
ONE

CHAPTER 1

Sue Snow's free-spirited oldest daughter, Exa, was off at the Pony Soldier Inn with a man she had just met who was going through a drug-treatment program.

"Should I worry about your creepy sister?" Sue asked with a rueful smile when she saw her youngest daughter, Hayley, that morning.

It was true that Exa Snow, always the independent one, could take care of herself—even if she didn't exercise the best judgment. Sue had always treated her eldest more as a friend than a daughter. And because of that, Exa pushed the line to the limit. But when push came to shove, as it often did, Sue Snow was still Mom. And Mom was in charge.

Hayley hugged her mother good morning.

"No, Mommy, don't worry about her."

Even though fifteen, Hayley Snow still called her mother "Mommy." Sue was proud that her daughter had the guts to use the name, when all her girlfriends had switched to the less endearing, albeit more grown-up, "Mom." Yet Hayley's friends understood. To them, Sue really was a "Mommy."

She kissed her daughter and called "I love you" as she went down the hall to her bathroom located off the master bedroom. Hayley closed her bathroom door. As she stepped into the shower she heard her mother turn on the faucet to her sink.

It was just after 6:30, June 11, 1986, when she heard the noise.

"I heard something drop while I was in the shower," Hayley later recalled. "At first I panicked, the first second I heard it. Then I thought, *That's really stupid, she's not going to just fall on her face.* So I ignored it, got out of the shower, and put on my bra and underwear."

Hayley was applying eye makeup when she realized that the water in her mother's sink was still running. She knew her mother's pattern from hearing her every morning through the bathroom walls. Something was wrong. Hayley went to see what was going on.

Then she found her.

Sue, wearing her zippered purple robe with a white stripe down the front, lay on her back. The water was nearing the top of the sink, so Hayley turned the spigot off before dropping to her knees beside her.

Her mother's pretty hazel eyes were fixed, frozen at the corner of the room. Her head rested on the sliding track of the shower door; her hand was across her breast. Her red lacquered nails accented fingers curled backward sharply and unnaturally.

Hayley struggled as she tried to figure out what had gone wrong.

She noticed that the curling iron was by the sink, then checked her mother's head, pulse . . . she tried to remember what she had learned in health class. There was a pulse, but it was faint. She bent her mother's fingers back to a normal position, because it looked as if they hurt.

Then she realized her mother wasn't breathing. Hayley got ready to do CPR when her mother gasped for air. Yet she didn't exhale. Hayley had learned that if a person is breathing on her own, do not do CPR.

She called Karen Inoue, a friend from their old condo complex, just down the road. Karen told Hayley to call 911 and she'd be over right away.

"What's the matter?" asked dispatcher Brenda Deeds, a Valley Comm 911 operator, when Hayley's call came at 6:43 A.M.

"I think my mother fell while I was in the shower . . . and she's breathing and everything, but something's wrong with her."

The dispatcher asked the address and Hayley told her it was 1404 N. Street N.E., Auburn. She calmly provided their phone number.

"Okay. Is she able to talk to you still?"

"I don't know. It's like she's sleeping with her eyes open."

"Is she able to talk to you at all?"

"She's not talking," Hayley answered, her voice now beginning to quaver. "She's lying in the bathtub . . . I mean she's lying in the bathroom . . . and her head is in the shower."

The dispatcher told Hayley to go back to her mother and try to get her to talk. She also told her to check on her mother's breathing.

The receiver picked up Hayley's scared cries as she called: "Mommy, Mommy . . ."

"She's breathing, but it's kind of weird," Hayley answered.

"Is she able to talk to you yet?"

By now the fifteen-year-old was in tears. *"She didn't talk . . ."*

"Did she move at all or do anything?"

"She just took a deep breath."

"I want to make sure she's breathing normally, though. How is her coloring?"

"Um, hold on a sec, okay?"

"Can you hear me?"

"Yeah."

"Shake her hand. Tell her to talk with you. See if she will. Come back and tell me."

"Okay. Hold on . . ."

Again she went to her mother, sprawled out on the bathroom floor. "Mommy, Mommy, please talk to me. Mommy . . ." Her voice got louder as she tried to wake her. "Mommy, won't you please talk to me? Mommy. Mommy, please talk to me."

"She won't talk to me . . ." she cried into the phone.

The dispatcher did what she could to reassure the girl. "We've got the aid car on the way, okay? I want you to keep on the phone with me. What is she doing now? Is she still breathing normally?"

"It's not really normal. It's just breathing."

Karen Inoue arrived and Hayley left the phone for a second to let her in. The dispatcher told Hayley she wanted her to stay on the phone and to check her mother again. Did she know CPR?

Hayley said she did. She had learned it in health class. As she spoke, the doorbell rang and the fire department arrived.

It was 6:47 A.M.

In tears, the girl directed the men to the bathroom, where they found Sue Snow lying on the floor in agonal respiration, a gasping, snorting respiration. Sue's eyes were open, fixed, and dilated.

The firemen attempted to ventilate her by using a bag mask, a device with a face piece fitting over the nose and mouth and a plastic reservoir the EMT squeezes to facilitate breathing.

But Sue Snow was deteriorating.

It was near the end of her shift when paramedic Debbie Ayrs and Medic 6 officer Randy Bellon answered the call of a "woman down" in Auburn. They arrived just after the fire fighters. Hayley Snow took them to her mother, still sprawled on the upstairs bathroom floor. The fire fighters lifted Sue Snow, arms dangling, from the bathroom to the bedroom, where there would be more room to work.

Debbie remembered it all years later: "We started doing our resuscitation, but it wasn't going right. We would give her something to help her cardiac rhythm and it wouldn't help. She was neurologically intact, she was acting like a head injury, but she wasn't exhibiting any of the things that go along with that."

"Has this ever happened before?" she asked the girl.

"No."

"Does she have any history of depression? Suicide attempts?"

"No."

"Was your mother on any drugs?"

"No."

They asked if she thought her mother had slipped while going into the shower. Again, the answer was no. Hayley explained that Sue Snow took her showers in the evening.

Debbie made a sweep through the cabinets for drugs, shaking bottles rapidly to determine if Sue Snow might have overdosed.

Hayley volunteered that her mother took Excedrin each morning, and Debbie Ayrs asked for the bottle. When Hayley brought it out of the kitchen, Debbie shook it, but it was full.

Airlift Northwest was summoned from Harborview Medical Center. Debbie Ayrs and Randy Bellon hadn't a clue about what had caused Sue Snow to collapse.

They put a tube down Sue Snow's trachea.

It was hard for Hayley to watch and at the same time hard not to watch, as the paramedics swarmed over her mother. She went to the phone and called the bank to leave a message that her mother had fallen down and wouldn't be in that day.

She was asked again about possible drug use.

"No. My mother's not a druggie," the girl responded incredulously.

The garbage in the bathroom was examined to see if anything was there. There wasn't.

An unresponsive Sue Snow was loaded onto a stretcher for the ride to the landing zone on a tiny stretch of runway passing for Auburn's small municipal airport. No one thought the woman was going to survive.

Hayley gathered up her math homework for the trip to Harborview with Karen Inoue. Why she brought her schoolwork, or how she ever thought she could even work at it, was something she would never be able to recall.

Seattle's Harborview Medical Center is the Northwest's best trauma center, and the county hospital where the indigent come for care. Gang fights. Knifings. Murder. It is a place where the saddest of stories often end. Desperate measures were used to save Sue Snow's life when she was airlifted there that morning.

Hayley and Karen arrived before 7:30. Clutching her math homework, the fifteen-year-old plainly did not understand the seriousness of her mother's condition. She sat in a waiting area, staring at her book.

She did not know where her sister was; her mother's husband, Paul Webking, was at work and someone had contacted him; and her own daddy, Connie Snow, was on the job at Boeing in Auburn—not the easiest place to track someone down.

A doctor came in and told the girl that something was the matter with her mother's brain. It was swollen, she thought she heard the man say.

A few minutes later, the doctor returned and said Sue was still in a coma.

"We're trying everything we can," the doctor said. "We're going to run some more tests. Is your father coming?"

"I think so," Hayley said.

There is no way to measure time in a hospital waiting room, but a short time later, the man returned.

"I'm sorry," he said. "But your mother is brain-dead."

Paul Webking was loading his truck at Safeway's Distribution Center in Bellevue, just east of Seattle, when a salesman from the Metro Freight office came and told him that his wife had been rushed to Harborview.

He wondered aloud if Sue had suffered some kind of anxiety

attack, caused by the stress of her job as a vice president of the North Auburn branch of Puget Sound Bank.

"Sue has been working so hard," he said.

She had even taken some medication to calm her nerves, though what the pills were eluded him at the time.

Paul and his boss left for Harborview. Their conversation was so unconstrained, they were distracted enough to even lose their way to the hospital. Paul Webking wasn't even close to being worried, and he certainly didn't exhibit much concern. After all, whatever medical problem his wife was suffering was being handled.

Paul entered through the emergency-room entrance. Hayley Snow would later recall that his demeanor seemed casual. She thought she saw him carrying a book, as if he was going to have time to get a little reading in.

"Hey, what's going on?" he asked when he saw Hayley.

"Mommy's brain-dead."

The color drained from Paul's face, and he hugged her.

"I was thinking, *God, would you just let go of me?* I just turned really bitter, but I didn't exactly know why," Hayley later said.

A doctor came and reaffirmed the prognosis. Sue Snow was on life support, but for all intents and purposes she was dead. He indicated they were going to work on her a while longer to see if they could get some kind of response.

Paul went to call Sarah Webb, Sue's identical twin sister, who lived in Denver.

The previous evening, Exa Snow and her mother had discussed having lunch that day. Exa hadn't planned on spending the night at the motel with Jorge Sanchez. Even though she was in her early twenties, she still had the part of her mother in her that cautioned against "sleeping around."

Exa was a bit of a free spirit, but she was not reckless. Her mom knew that.

"It was not like I did bad things, but I was very independent, just did whatever I wanted. I was just kind of inconsiderate. I would tell Mom I'd be home at ten, and come home at one or two o'clock or whenever. That night we went out to Seattle Center. When we came back it was three or four o'clock in the morning, and I said, 'I'm just going to stay here with you instead of going back.' So we stayed there. Nothing happened. Swear to God. I knew I'd never see him again," she later said.

Up before 11 A.M., Exa phoned her mother at the bank, but an employee told her she wasn't in. She had fallen down at home. The woman didn't seem particularly alarmed and suggested Exa call the house. Exa did, but her mother wasn't there either. She called the bank again, and the bank employee told her that it was Hayley who had called earlier with word her mother had passed out.

She must have broken her arm, Exa thought, before calling the family doctor. But his office didn't know anything. She tried Auburn General. They didn't have her mother registered there.

Where could she be?

Not knowing what else to do, and beginning to feel a little panicky, Exa called Auburn General again. The woman who answered said she'd check to see if an ambulance had been called for a Sue Snow. She came back on the line and said, "Your mother was picked up by helicopter and taken to Harborview."

"What's the deal? What's happening?" she asked when she finally reached a doctor at Harborview.

"I have some pretty bad news," he told her. "Your mom is dying."

She got directions, went home, changed in record time, and left for the hospital in Jorge Sanchez's rental car.

Hayley saw her sister coming from down the hall and ran to her. Clinging together, they told each other they had to be strong.

The day before Sue Snow collapsed, Sarah Webb phoned her twin, but Sue never called her back. That was unusual, but Sarah thought maybe something was going on at the bank and she couldn't get back to her. After all, she was a VP.

That night Sarah couldn't sleep. Her thoughts turned to old times, times with Paul and Sue.

The next morning, Sarah was in the bathroom when the phone rang.

"Go ahead and answer it," she called to her husband, Rodney, who was back in Denver after a thirty-day job in Egypt. "It's Sue," she said, "tell her I'll be right there."

It wasn't Sue. It was Paul with the news Sue was in a coma. The Webbs made flight reservations and Rodney threw some clothes together. Their preschooler daughter, whom the family called Baby Dumpling, went around the house saying her prayers. Sarah, in a daze, watered houseplants.

"We were walking out the door to the airport when they called to say she died. I think Paul should have waited until we got there before he pulled the life support. But he didn't. He wanted to be the boss," she later said.

A little after 11 A.M. the doctors asked if they could remove Susan Kathryn Snow from life support. They said it was the family's decision, but there was absolutely no hope for recovery. Just forty, Sue was gone. The family agreed.

Hayley went into her mother's hospital room. The woman lying there no longer looked like her mother. In her hospital gown, Sue looked like an inflatable mannequin. Her fingernail polish had been removed, her toes were swollen and sticking out from under the sheet. Sue's eyes were tiny slits and there was tape and tubing all over her arms. Her mother's chest rose and fell with the machine. It made Hayley ill. She took one look and left.

"I couldn't touch her," she later said.

Exa was even more uncomfortable with going in to say good-bye to the distorted figure in the hospital bed. She looked at her mother's feet, though, and knew it was her.

"She just had these perfectly painted toenails."

Paul stayed in the room for some time. A doctor watched him pat his wife's distended hands as he cried. He wondered how his wife had died. He even made some suggestions. Then he told Sue good-bye.

Connie Snow and some friends from the branch of Puget Sound National Bank where Sue worked had come to the hospital, and Hayley left with her father.

"Let's go by school, it's not out yet," she said. "I need to get some things to study for finals."

Connie figured his daughter wanted to get her mind off of what had happened.

Hayley didn't know what else to do.

CHAPTER 2

For Artesia's Golden Jubilee, a special edition of the *Daily News* boasted: "Artesia today is classed as the most progressive city in the Pecos Valley, and among the leaders in the state . . . and offers much in the way of cultural events."

And Artesia, New Mexico, was on a roll when O. C., "Chap," and Marion Chapman and their children, son Burney and twin daughters Sarah and Sue moved to town. People who scoffed at the cultural wonders of the town obviously hadn't lived in the dusty grab bag of towns in the Southwest that the Chapmans had called home. The girls liked Artesia for its shops, their new friends, and of course, the boys.

The twins were born on April 13, 1946, in Hobbs, New Mexico, though they lived in nearby Denver City, Texas. Sarah arrived fifteen minutes before Sue. It would end up being one of the few times she beat her sister at anything.

While Chap, who worked for Continental Oil, seemed to be liked by everyone, his wife's personality was not enjoyed so widely. Marion Chapman had opinions about the way things should be done, and made them known to anyone who would listen, and to a few who didn't. Sarah always felt that her mother was partial to Sue, and such a feeling was entirely justified. Mrs. Chapman kept little to herself. Chap, however, was more easygoing, and reveled in the fact that he was doubly blessed with beautiful daughters.

Sarah and Sue were inseparable in the way that identical twins often are. Neither could cite a major "I'm never talking to you again" fight. Not since they were fifteen or sixteen, anyway. They had their disagreements as all sisters do, but they were twins, and that always meant that they were closer to each other than anyone would ever be. No man would be as close to either as her twin was.

As alike as they seemed, they were night-and-day different.

Sue was the adventurous one, the girl who would try anything, anytime. Sarah considered herself a "big chicken." When she couldn't muster the courage to get a driver's license, it was Sue who would drive her around, punching the pedal to the metal and sending up a trail of New Mexican dust. The only thing Sarah tried first was smoking, a habit her twin was glad she never picked up.

Where Sue's heart ruled her head, Sarah was the opposite.

The pages of the 1964 *Bulldog*, the Artesia High School yearbook, make no mention of Sue Chapman. Twin sister Sarah smiles sweetly over her shoulder in her senior portrait. Sue never made it that far.

At sixteen, Sue found herself both popular and pregnant. She married her baby's father, Jackie Clayton, and moved onto his farm. Exa Clayton was born June 30, 1963.

Though Chap and Marion were very upset, the girls didn't think badly of the pregnancy. To Sarah, her sister was, as always, cool.

"That was sort of the going thing . . . all the cheerleaders got pregnant. All of the popular girls had to get married. Now it's not cool, but then it was kind of cool—but then it was . . . like smoking," Sarah later said.

Being stranded out on a farm was not cool. Cooking and cleaning, making sure her man was taken care of, was too much for young, cute, and fun-loving Sue. And though she doted on her baby Exa, she found that Jackie Clayton was not the man of her dreams. After barely giving him a chance, she left him.

Sarah, who was always there to listen to her sister's version of the marriage, was glad when Sue left Jackie. She felt that he was too strict with Exa.

The man who next caught Sue's eye was Connie Snow, her brother-in-law, married to Jackie's sister, Kay. The situation was complicated by anyone's standards. Though they had known him for years, Chap and Marion didn't cotton to the idea of Sue's romance with Connie Snow, who was eleven years older than she. Like Chap, Connie's father had worked the oil fields from

Oklahoma to New Mexico. They told their daughter to wait awhile, a year. If she still wanted to marry Connie, they wouldn't stand in her way.

In August of 1966, Boeing was recruiting employees in the area around Artesia and Connie took a job and left for Seattle, to wait out the Chapmans' one-year edict. With little experience but plenty of mechanical ability, Connie, then thirty-one, started work as a structural mechanic on the 727 project.

Sue moved with her baby just north of Artesia to Roswell, New Mexico, where she took a job stitching jeans for Levi Strauss. Though she was self-conscious about her lack of a high-school diploma, she didn't let it get in her way. She moved up from the line to floor manager.

"She was real smart, real ambitious, and she moved up real fast," Sarah later recalled.

A year to the day of her daddy's deadline, and after some good-natured pleading from a lonesome Connie Snow, Sue packed up four-year-old Exa, all the things she could fit into her Corvair, and headed north to Seattle. She was twenty.

Sue and Connie married the following year. At first, the marriage was Connie Snow's version of dying and going to heaven.

"Sue had an ability to make you feel like you were on top of the world. She made me feel like I was the king. She was always saying 'Connie could do this . . . do that . . . ' Not too many women can do that," Connie later recalled.

"Whatever I could do, I wanted to do it for her."

Sarah was always the more demonstrative of the Chapman twins. Dealing with the sudden death of her sister made her even more so. Crying jags and open hostility mixed with the sorrow of losing her mirror image.

Hayley, handling her grief in her own quiet way, was disturbed by so much emotion. When she saw Sarah and Paul hug each other that June afternoon at SeaTac Airport, she wanted to pull them apart and tell them to get a grip on themselves.

Mommy wouldn't have acted this way, she thought.

Auburn friend Kristi Solberg prayed her daughter had made some terrible error when she told her about Sue Snow's death. Sue was so young, so healthy, so vital. Sue was the kind of person Kristi felt honored to call a friend. Sue and Paul had been so good to her daughter Kammi, helping the girl gain confidence. And they truly seemed to like Kammi. Sue used to beg Kristi to allow Kammi to sleep over with Hayley.

"Oh please, oh please let Kammi stay with us Friday night," Sue would say, pouring on her thickest southwestern accent.

Kristi could never refuse. Paul Webking and Sue Snow were right there with all of the love and friendship Kammi needed. Later, she would say her daughter was a better person for having known Sue Snow.

When Kristi Solberg arrived at the Snow/Webking residence on June 11, it was Paul who answered the door. He was wearing a Hawaiian shirt and a pair of shorts. He looked fine. Kristi thought the news had been a cruel mistake.

"He seemed so normal," she later said.

But it was not a mistake. He told her that Sue had died.

The people filling the house on N Street gravitated toward the kitchen, up half a flight of stairs overlooking the living room. Sarah went to the cabinet to get some Excedrin. She knew Sue would have a bottle; she always did. Sarah woke up with a headache nearly every day and took two tablets. Her sister did the same.

In the cabinet to the left of the sink, Sarah picked up a bottle of Excedrin. As her sister always did, Sue had discarded the container's top when she opened it. She hated the child-proof caps that wreaked havoc on her lovely fingernails. Besides, unless Sarah and Rodney's Baby Dumpling was in town, there were never any children in the house anyway.

"Oh my God," Sarah blurted out. "What was Sue doing with these damn capsules!" She held the bottle out for all to see. "This is probably what killed her!"

Some nervous laughter ensued—Sarah later thought it was Paul who laughed the loudest—and she put the bottle up on the third shelf behind some spices and told her husband to go to the Pay 'N Save for Excedrin *tablets*.

"I'm not joking . . . nobody take these capsules," she said.

"Why in the hell take capsules?" she later asked Paul.

"She bought them by mistake one time and liked them because they were easier to swallow. Sue had a hard time swallowing pills," he said.

Sarah didn't agree. She recalled how she had seen her sister swallow pills by drinking from a water fountain. She had no difficulty. And she had been using tablets when Sarah visited in April, just a little over a month earlier.

Why would Paul say something like that? Sarah could only wonder.

When Rodney Webb returned with the tablets, his wife asked if he thought she was being stupid about the whole thing.

"Sue never used capsules," she said. "Never. We talked about that tampering in Chicago. She wouldn't use them."

"I know," he said. "You did the right thing putting them away." He didn't really think the capsules had caused his sister-in-law to die, but his wife obviously needed bolstering.

That evening, hands shaking and eyes rimmed in red, Sarah went through her sister's purse. She found a wallet, makeup, business cards, and a half-full bottle of Excedrin tablets.

Hadn't Paul said Sue now preferred capsules?

A death in the family is uniquely painful. People awkwardly attempt to comfort the bereaved. Even the hugs from strangers can be annoying. Sarah and Paul would later talk about how tired they grew of people patting their heads and telling them they'd be all right.

"I'll never be all right," she told her brother-in-law. He said he felt the same way.

That night, Paul gave up his bedroom to Sarah, Rodney, and Baby Dumpling. The Webbs fussed, but he told them he didn't expect to get much sleep anyway. He went downstairs to the den. Though Paul's influence in decorating was everywhere in the house, that room truly was his domain: Papasan chair, wicker furniture, and safari-motif curtains.

He hauled an air mattress out in front of the fireplace that in winter burned so frequently because his wife complained she was cold. His son Damon, who arrived from his apartment when he heard of Sue's death, came downstairs to comfort his father. Paul held him all night.

CHAPTER 3

Sue and Connie Snow made their home in a mobile-home park in Sumner, a small Pierce County town within an easy commute of the Auburn Boeing plant. Though she had spent her whole life in the desert of the Southwest, Sue adjusted to the Northwest in short order. The green and the rain agreed with her.

It was June 1969 when Sue took a job at the Pacific East Valley Branch of Puget Sound National Bank. She later told people the reason she took the teller's job was that she figured "anybody could do it" and that meant she could. And if her self-esteem was non-existent, it didn't show to others. Sue was young and smart. *Too* smart, some who worked with her at the time believed, to be stuck at the teller's window.

Over the next few years, Sue moved up to credit and later, re-possessions. Sue wasn't thrilled with the repo job, which occasionally involved stealing cars back for the bank, but she knew she had to do it in order to move up. By then she had earned her GED, but the lack of additional credentials continued to embarrass and haunt her. If she didn't have the credentials, she would make up for it with hard work and her personality, which many, especially men, found irresistible.

Sue always liked Hayley Mills, the actress known for her role as a set of identical twins in the Disney classic *The Parent Trap*. When her second daughter was born she named her after the actress.

Connie nicknamed the baby "Hayley Rain Snowball"—since he didn't get to name her Stormy Snow, as he had suggested.

Boeing was suffering its worst layoffs in company history, and two days after Hayley was born on April 24, 1971, Connie was served notice that he was out of a job. Luck intervened and he was reassigned to the paint shop. Needing more room, the Snows moved into a bigger mobile home on Prairie Ridge.

Motherhood the second time around was a special joy. Hayley was an easy, loving baby and toddler. That sweetness balanced Sue's relationship with her tumultuous child, Exa. Connie, who loved Exa every bit as much as if she were his own, recalled instances when Exa and Sue nearly had knock-down-drag-outs over the littlest things. It was true Sue was strict with Exa, but it was only because she wanted to make sure Exa didn't make the same mistakes she herself had. More than anything, she wanted her daughters to go to college.

"It bothered her that she didn't go on to school, missed out on something. She had the brains and the smarts to do things," Connie Snow said.

In the typically independent fashion that the family would come to expect of her, Exa stopped calling herself Clayton and went by the Snow surname. Like her mother, she liked the last name Snow.

And though they were separated by hundreds of miles, Sue and Sarah remained as close as ever. They talked on the phone daily. When Sue made noises that the marriage wasn't working out, Sarah was the first to hear of it—even before Connie Snow. When there were other men, Sarah heard about it. Sarah thought Connie Snow was wonderful, a good husband and father, but still she understood her sister's infidelities. Sue was young and vibrant. And since her pregnancy at sixteen, she had missed all the fun of running around.

"Years later she told me that she was never faithful to Connie. I think she sort of outgrew Connie. She was real smart. She was real pretty. You know, men liked her. She was outgoing. Connie was a homebody. He came home and slept on the couch," Sarah said later.

"If they were fairly serious [affairs] I knew about them at the time. If it went on more than a week, I knew about them. He knows about a lot of her affairs, but he doesn't know about all of them."

As the Snow marriage began to fall apart, Sue and her daughters left Seattle for New Mexico to care for her daddy, who had had a stroke and was in a Roswell rehab center. She enrolled Exa in elementary school and took a job at a Roswell bank. The money was terrible, but it was good to be back in New Mexico.

As her sister pegged it years later, Sue's heart had ruled her head again. She fell in love with a paraplegic Mexican, the victim of a waterskiing accident. Then, as quickly as it began, the love affair was over.

About a year after she left him, Connie sent Sue money to return to Washington, half hoping she'd come back to him. But it was not to be. After she returned, Sue asked Connie to fish some change out of her purse. Inside, he found a love letter his wife had written to a co-worker at the bank.

"That was the beginning of our crumble," Connie later said. Connie knew his wife was a bit of a flirt, but he never expected anything to come of it. She was just being charming . . . and it seemed to be working. Sue had more promotions than anyone else at the branch.

Sue told Sarah she was going to marry the man from Puget Sound National Bank.

"He kept telling her that he'd leave his wife for her, she wanted him to, but he never did. He lied to her a lot. She really thought he loved her. That was the final straw for Connie and Sue."

Devastated, and as if he needed any more grief, Connie continued to put himself in situations that would drive home the point. He would sneak out of the plant during lunch to spy on his wife and her boyfriend. He even drove to the Motel 6, where Sue was living, to see if his car was parked alongside hers. It was.

"I saw her car over there, I saw her car and his car. Just stickin' that old knife in there deeper and twisting it. Why couldn't I just go and say it's over with and forget it? *Can't*. Too many good things happened over all the years," Connie later said.

Stress and a near-ulcer put Connie Snow in the hospital. He knew he couldn't go on; he loved Sue and doubted he'd ever love any woman as he loved her. Their marriage, however, was over.

She asked him to stay, but Connie had more pride and brains than that.

"I just felt like if I couldn't trust her if she was fifteen minutes late getting home . . . And that's not a marriage when you're having to question somebody about where they are all the time," he said.

Sue broke up with her boyfriend a short time later.

"He wasn't the greener pasture on the other side of the mountain that she thought he was," Connie said. "Sue needed attention from all kinds of men. She just had to have that, I think. I'm just the opposite. I've got to be a one-woman man."

Though he hated her at first for what she had done, they remained close because of the girls, and because Connie Snow knew he would always love Sue. She told others she felt the same way about him.

They didn't file for divorce for eight years.

Sue and her girls moved into some apartments in Puyallup and Exa made what she later claimed was the biggest mistake of her life: She introduced her mother to Paul Webking.

CHAPTER 4

Sue Snow's body was under a white hospital sheet when Dr. Corrine Fligner, the Assistant Medical Examiner for King County, and pathologist's assistant Janet Miller went to work. There was a great mystery surrounding the woman from Auburn. She was only forty. She was not a drug abuser. She just got up one morning and dropped dead.

As Janet Miller made her first incision, she got a whiff of an unforgettable scent. It was the same smell she had encountered years earlier when a University of Washington employee committed suicide by ingesting cyanide. It was the smell of bitter almonds.

"I smell cyanide," she said, looking up at Dr. Fligner, who was busy recording findings.

"You know, it might sound crazy, but did this woman take Tylenol?" she added, almost as a joke, referring to the infamous Chicago poisonings.

"There is something that is so characteristic about the smell of cyanide that once you smell it, if you smell it again you know," Janet Miller recalled later. "There was no doubt in my mind that I had smelled cyanide. I just didn't know the significance of it at the time, because she didn't have any of the classic symptoms of cyanide poisoning. She was as pale as a white shirt. The other cyanide case that I had seen, he was cherry red, just like he was supposed to be."

The M.E. offered no comment on her assistant's suggestion of cyanide. And Janet Miller, a technician, didn't press the point. Yet Corrine Fligner, like the majority of the population, was unable to smell cyanide.

Well into the procedure, a doctor came into the autopsy room. He asked if Dr. Fligner had turned up anything suggesting the cause of Sue Snow's death. Like everyone else, he was baffled.

Janet Miller spoke up. She had smelled cyanide, she said.

The doctor became somewhat animated, and obviously relieved. "That might explain why she presented the way she did."

Dr. Fligner made a note to check for cyanide in the toxicology screen.

The day after Sue Snow's sudden death, more family members had gathered at the house. Burney Chapman, Sue's brother, flew in from Lubbock, Texas. Now a widow, Marion Chapman, whom the girls called "Gammy," arrived from Artesia. The house was full, and emotions alternated between fluid and taut.

That morning Paul's son, Damon, had taken a call from the Medical Examiner's office while his father, Sarah, Exa, and Burney Chapman were at the funeral home making burial arrangements. Hayley was at school.

The caller told Damon that he wanted to discuss a possible electrical problem that might have caused Sue's death.

When the family got back that afternoon, Paul returned the call from the kitchen phone and Sarah picked up the receiver in the bedroom.

The technician, a male, focused on Sue's morning routine. He was especially concerned with her curling iron.

"Was the curling iron on and was the water running?" he asked.

"As far as what Hayley told me, yes," Paul answered.

Sarah only listened.

The discussion went on, the technician clearly implying that he felt Sue's death might be attributed to electrocution.

"Hey, this is bullshit," Paul shot back at the caller, his face flushed with tension. "Sue was not electrocuted. We have a ground fault in the bathroom. Nobody reset it, and it still works. If there had been a short it would have shut down the ground fault. There was no way it was electrical."

The caller, clearly not up to handling an angry Paul Webking, put Corrine Fligner on the phone.

The King County Assistant Medical Examiner was polite and
compassionate. But to Paul Webking, her tone seemed patronizing
and evasive. She said her office had not found any discernible cause
of death. She suggested Sue's death might be related to a "heart
rhythm" problem that interrupted the flow of blood to her brain.
But she wasn't certain.

Sarah interjected that her sister had been complaining of stress-
related headaches. She wondered if that might be related to something like a stroke. Dr. Fligner didn't know.

"Could she have died of capsule poisoning?" Paul asked.

"I don't see how," the doctor said.

"We found a freshly opened bottle of capsules in the cupboard,
and Sue obviously took two before she died. Perhaps that's a possible reason," Paul said.

Dr. Fligner dismissed it as being "farfetched."

Hayley Snow went to school because she didn't know what else to
do. At least there she would be rid of all those clingy people back
at the house. She loved them, but everyone seemed so intense. She
heard a cruel rumor that she must not care about her mother because
she went to school the day after she died.

"At the same time," she later recalled, "the same people are
being nice to me so they can say they know the kid whose mom
just died. I had so many thoughts just going on in my head, and I
tried to ignore them all."

When she returned home, electrocution seemed to be the topic
of the day. Hayley remembered the running water, the curling iron
. . . her mother's fall, which she had told no one about. She hadn't
seen any burns on her mother's hands when she uncurled her fingers. She saw no burns anywhere.

Wouldn't there be burns? she wondered.

Hundreds came to Sue Snow's 2:00 P.M. memorial service at Price-
Helton on Saturday, June 14. Sue was eulogized by Tom Nixon, a
longtime friend from the bank. He spoke of her "shocking frank-
ness" and her sense of humor.

When Sarah Webb dressed in one of her dead sister's outfits to
wear to the service, her daughter, B.D., became confused and cried.
She thought her mother was "Auntie Mommy," the name she called
Sue Snow.

Her longtime hairdresser did Sue's hair. She looked pretty, almost as she did when she was alive.

Connie Snow's recording of an old "beer-drinkin' country tearjerker" he had written, called "Darlin' Sue," was piped in after some music by the Judds, Sue's favorite musicians.

> Dark clouds again
> Shadows are falling
> I keep remembering Darlin' Sue.

"It was really hard watching Exa and Hayley. They were standing up there by their mother, not believing what had happened," Connie later said.

After the funeral, one of Sue's doctor friends warned Sarah that her sister's death might have been caused by some hereditary disease or disorder. She was encouraged to have a checkup right away. Though Sarah didn't heed the man's advice, Hayley worried about losing her aunt.

She wrote in her diary:

> One night, the lights in her room were out and Aunt was laying in an awkward position and when I called her name she didn't move, not even her eyes. For one split second, I thought, "Oh no, not again." It's like now I know it's nothing that could happen to her, but I always catch myself checking up on her. I don't feel that way with anyone else so I can't figure it out. Maybe because they're twins. Who knows?

CHAPTER 5

Love him or hate him. Nobody was ambivalent about Paul John Webking. The Bremerton, Washington–born, though mostly South Bay, Los Angeles–raised, long-haul trucker was stretched out down by the pool at the Meridian Firs apartment complex when Exa Snow introduced him to her mother, Sue Snow. He wasn't a tall man, but he still seemed big. His hair was long, scraggly, and blond. His eyes were the bluest she'd ever seen.

He could be both intimidating and gentle.

Over the years, Paul had developed the ability to pull up in anger like a blowfish, but it was all show. Always had been.

"I can make myself pretty scary," he admitted. "So I don't have to deal with a lot of confrontation. Since I was eighteen, I've only had one physical argument."

Paul overcompensated for what he describes as innate shyness by being direct. *Very direct.*

Sue's daughter, Exa, and Paul's son, Damon, were students at Kalles Junior High when she offhandedly told him she thought his father was good-looking and should meet her mother. Though Sue, now a bank manager's secretary, seemed to favor dating doctors and lawyers at the time, she was intrigued enough to agree to meet the man down at the pool.

It was the spring of 1978.

Either by design or by accident, Paul Webking had always been a rover. By the time he graduated from high school, he had attended fifteen different schools. His father wasn't military, but a mechanic, who simply liked to roam.

As an adult, Paul had done everything from digging ditches and handling customer-service complaints for a gas company to tending bar, before he went to truck-driving school in Fresno in 1974. By the time he had eventually found his way back up to Washington in 1976 to take a job as a long-haul driver for Hayes Truck Lines, he had divorce decrees from three ex-wives. It was shortly after his move to the Puget Sound area that he met Sue Snow.

Paul took Sue in his primer-mottled van and went out for pizza the day they met in 1978. He figured they might become good friends, like his son and her daughter. Instead, they started seeing each other romantically.

On the surface, Paul and Sue wouldn't seem even close to a suitable couple, but friends would later say it was easy to see how their personalities complemented each other. Paul was demanding. He was the kind of man who would tell a salesclerk in no uncertain terms that she had better learn the meaning of the word "service."

"I want to speak to your manager!" he'd boom, and then watch the befuddled clerk scurry for the boss.

Sue was taken aback by his outbursts. Paul thought the world was sinking into a dangerous abyss of apathy. He found the human race to be lazy and selfish. Paul shook Sue up—challenged her. Paul found her to be an eager student, to test, to try, to influence.

Sarah, still in conservative Artesia, was in daily contact with her twin, and began to see changes in Sue as the result of Paul's influence.

"We thought alike. Our opinions were the same. She didn't believe in prayers in school later. I didn't have an opinion. She would show me things, to make me have an opinion. Sue was exposed to more of that; this was a dead-end town. She just put a lot of things in my head that would not have got in there. A lot of it was Paul. Sue *became* Paul."

With Paul, Sue could also let her hair down, and set aside the cheerful smile she felt forced to maintain all day.

"Being cheerful requires a lot of energy, and she would get very tired of being cheerful. When I met her," Paul remembered, "one of the things that probably attracted her to me and me to her was that she was not able to go beyond being cheerful. She always had to be cheerful, and she was suffering from being cheerful. She never learned to, you know, to say no. She was able to relax with me."

The next year, Sue and her daughters moved to a town house at 2019 N Street N.E., Auburn, and she and Paul started to date again. By then, things had fizzled somewhat with a doctor Sue had been seeing. As with the man from the bank, the fellow wouldn't leave his wife.

To those outside, the new relationship seemed somewhat strange and certainly unconventional. Sue sometimes traveled with Paul on weekend trips with the truck. For a while, she continued to date the kind of men who fit the plan she had for her life after Connie Snow. Paul was the cook (Sue could cook also, but frequently grew tired of the process halfway through preparation), the house cleaner, the domestic. He and Hayley formed an immediate bond. Exa continued to butt horns with her mother and resented Paul's influence.

When the town house next door became available, Paul and son Damon moved into it. In 1981, after he totaled his Peterbilt and needed some convalescing, they made it official and Paul finally moved in with Sue and her girls. Damon, only seventeen, moved back to Puyallup with a friend, and Exa Snow, who did not like sharing her mother with Paul Webking, soon went off to the University of New Mexico.

Sue's oldest daughter later recalled how her mother handled the idea of Paul's moving in: "Rather than just saying 'I'm the mother and this is the decision,' she probably just tried to ignore me to block it out so she wouldn't have to say anything. She was real sensitive to my criticism. It happened so gradually . . . you could accept it little by little."

CHAPTER 6

At thirty-five, Auburn police detective Mike Dunbar was a quiet man of few words, the kind who commanded attention as listeners strained to hear what he had to say. His blue eyes, blondish hair, and strong jawline gave him the look of a *Downhill Racer*–era Robert Redford.

By his own admission, Mike had never been an outgoing individual. He sometimes wondered if it had been because of his life as a military brat, always moving, never making lifelong friends. The Auburn police detective was the kind of man who says he speaks only when spoken to and was not one to go up and introduce himself to a stranger.

That, of course, was in his personal life. As a detective, he had lots of introducing to do.

It was Monday morning, June 16, when Mike Dunbar got the news from his sergeant that Sue Snow, the pretty bank manager from North Auburn, had been murdered. Even more disturbing, she was the victim of cyanide poisoning.

He phoned Dr. Fligner, who told him they were unable to determine a cause of death during the autopsy, but that a technician thought she smelled cyanide. Toxicology tests confirmed a fatal level of cyanide in the blood.

"Before toxicology results, we believed her death was caused by cardiac arrhythmia," she said.

Fligner went on to explain that cyanide is so fast-acting that it was consistent with the time frame outlined by Hayley Snow.

It was possible, Dr. Fligner said, that Snow had been poisoned with a tainted Excedrin capsule.

"Snow's husband, Paul Webking, told me his wife took two Extra Strength Excedrin capsules the morning of her death," the medical examiner said. "I'm not sure if he saw her take them or if he just assumed she did. He said she routinely took them for chronic headaches."

Hayley Snow had last seen her mother at 6:20 A.M. About ten minutes later—long enough for a gelatin capsule to dissolve—the woman collapsed.

Mike Dunbar knew he would have to move quickly. He hung up the phone and immediately made a call to Paul Webking.

At the Snow/Webking house, Sue's survivors were preparing to leave for her burial at Mountain View Cemetery on the west side of the valley. Though Sarah Webb wanted to help with the decision of what her sister would wear, her brother-in-law had already made up his mind. He selected a black and white checked suit. The rings she had worn at the memorial service on Saturday were removed.

Sarah thought her sister looked lovely, though she felt her twin had been dressed in Paul's vision. Sue had told her before her death that Paul had preferred her to dress in tailored suits.

Most of the dozen or so people were in the kitchen area drinking coffee when Paul took the call from Mike Dunbar telling him that his wife had been poisoned, that an investigation was now underway and that he needed to interview family members.

When Paul got off the phone he was visibly upset, though he said nothing of the poison. He did tell everyone, however, that something had come up and after the service they would all need to return to the house.

Paul Webking would later say he never uttered the word "cyanide" in connection with the phone call.

Just after the lunch hour, detectives Mike Dunbar and John Calkins knocked on the door of what had been Sue Snow's house. Dunbar had expected a somber group returning from Mountain View. Instead it seemed like a celebration.

"Everyone was there for the funeral . . . it was like a party atmosphere . . . 'Hey, I'm going for pizza, what does everybody want?'

Everyone was firing out their orders. It struck me as kind of strange," he later said.

In the center of it all was Paul Webking.

Detective Calkins said hello to Kristi Solberg, whom he had dated previously.

At 12:04, Webking signed a consent to search the residence. Donning rubber gloves, the Auburn detectives went through the house and loaded all prescription and nonprescription bottles into evidence bags. Partial packages and bottles of Dexatrim, various vitamins and antacids, Excedrin P.M. tablets, and some tranquilizers were collected.

"All we had was a bottle with no cap, no packaging. I went through every bit of garbage in the house. They had a trash compactor. They had a garbage can in the garage. I went though it all piece by piece," Mike Dunbar later recalled.

Of the headache remedies, which also included a bottle of Albertson's store-brand aspirin, all were tablets. The detective noted that only the Extra Strength Excedrin bottle Sarah Webb had moved to a higher shelf the day her sister died contained capsules.

Sarah nudged Exa Snow when she heard Paul tell Dunbar: "Sue always bought capsules."

"That was bullshit," Sue's twin said later. "He told some big lie. I knew it wasn't true."

The detectives also searched the garage, pulling anything, such as an insecticide, that might contain cyanide. Paul went with them, pointing things out.

Paul Webking told the investigators that he and Sue Snow had met eight years before, had lived together for the past five years, and married on Thanksgiving Day of 1985.

Hayley was the only other person who lived with Sue and Paul consistently. Exa and Damon were occasionally at the house.

Mike Dunbar asked for an explanation of his whereabouts around the time of his wife's death.

"I left for California on Sunday, June 8, at about one o'clock in the afternoon. I took two Excedrins before I left. I noticed we were getting low, and I mentioned it to Sue. She said they were on her list."

Paul Webking's delivery was unemotional, matter-of-fact. Though it had been five days since his wife died, Detective Dunbar thought it was strange.

He said he returned to Auburn Tuesday evening, June 10.

"On the morning of June 11, before I left for work I took two Excedrin capsules from a nearly new bottle in the kitchen cupboard. The lid was already gone," he told them.

Paul explained that Sue always threw the packaging away—including the cap—so she didn't have to mess with the clutter.

He also said he and Sue took two Excedrin nearly every morning for the caffeine.

"I don't know if she took any on Tuesday, because she was still in bed when I left. She took vitamins every morning, too. But I didn't see her take them that morning."

Paul Webking said he knew nothing more until his boss from Metro Freight told him he was needed at Harborview.

Mike Dunbar asked about their marriage.

"Sue and I had been getting along very well," Paul answered. "We had not argued since September 1985, when I told her about an affair I had with Mary, an old girlfriend . . . on a trip to California."

Later, Dunbar and Webking would offer differing accounts of what was really said during the interview in the basement on N Street.

"When we got home," Paul Webking later said, "Calkins and Dunbar took me downstairs into the den and started questioning me about the house and what I had said on the phone. Dunbar kept accusing me of saying 'cyanide.' 'How did you know it was cyanide that had killed her.' If I had said cyanide, I would have said it from what has been going on the past five years, what I read in the papers, that would have been the word that would have came out of my mouth—not because of prior knowledge. 'No, you said cyanide. I want to know why you said cyanide.' I said look, if I would have said cyanide in front of twelve people, everybody would have turned their heads around. I don't remember anybody reacting."

Later, Kristi Solberg couldn't recall Paul's mentioning cyanide before the police came, but she could never forget Paul Webking's reaction after he emerged from his interview with the Auburn detectives.

"I'll never forget the look on his face. He was just red. He was enraged. I could just see this look on his face. I thought, *What on earth did they say to this man that has got him so upset, as if he's not upset about having to bury his wife?* He came upstairs and he said, 'They think *I* did it.' "

Detective Dunbar left the house on N Street wondering about

Paul Webking's statement. The Medical Examiner had said the man's original story was that his wife suffered from "chronic headaches" and took Excedrin "every morning." Now he was saying he and his wife both took it for the caffeine.

By the end of the afternoon, most family members had given statements either at the house or down at the police station. There had been some jockeying about what was personal and what wasn't.

Exa didn't want the family to mention her friend Jorge Sanchez. "He's having enough trouble right now. He's got nothing to do with any of this," she told Sarah.

"I already told them about him," Paul said.

Sue Snow had been the one to hold the family together, to calm the storms. She had been dead only five days, but loyalties were crumbling and fear was spreading. Hayley felt it first.

"Right after they told Paul it was murder, he pulled me aside," she later recalled. "He said, 'Get ready. They are going to think it was either you or me. They are going to consider us the prime suspects. You were here; so was I.'

"It scared me. It was like maybe I *did* do it . . ." she said later, recalling her confusion and fear.

CHAPTER 7

Midway through the year before her murder, Sue Snow learned her husband had had a fling with Mary, a high-school girlfriend from California. It broke her heart. Paul insisted it meant nothing when he finally told her. Sue wanted to believe him.

The couple saw a counselor to sort things out and, after a while, it seemed to work. On Thanksgiving Day 1985, Sue and Paul surprised everyone by going to Reno in the truck and coming back husband and wife.

Sue called Sarah with the news. There was no doubt by the sound of her voice that she was elated. No matter what he had done, she knew her sister loved Paul Webking.

While going through her sister's clothes after the funeral, Sarah Webb found evidence that Sue's jealousy hadn't completely faded. She found an old notebook scribbled with an angry hand: *"Fuck Paul! I hate Mary! I hate Paul!"*

Sarah left the notebook where she found it, and never told anyone it existed.

The discovery, however, started her thinking. She thought about the last months of her twin's life.

"When she called, sometimes she was mad. Sometimes she was devastated. She thought she was losing him. She did love Paul. *I can't have him, so I really want him.* I know you are that way in high school, but you are supposed to outgrow it."

Sarah just listened. She never encouraged her sister to leave her husband. She knew Sue didn't want to leave him.

During one of their marathon phone calls, Sue told her Paul had claimed he had slept with Mary only once.

"Sometimes I don't believe the son of a bitch," Sue said between tears.

"Sue thought that it was only once, and that was real important to her. It wouldn't have made a difference to me—one or a thousand times. It was important to *her*. It really was," Sarah recalled later.

As she had even in childhood, Sarah supported her twin. Sometimes that meant keeping her mouth shut. She saw her brother-in-law as a master manipulator and controller. She wondered how Sue had fallen for a man like him in the first place.

When her answer came, it was from a television program.

"About the time Sue and Paul were having that trouble with Mary there was a show on *Donahue* that we all watched: 'Women Who Fall for Shitty Men.' One point they made was that the way we are raised, we don't feel like we are worthy of accepting our success, so we fall for some man who will bring us down a notch or two."

Sue Snow had not kept Paul and Mary's affair secret from her daughters, either.

One time she pulled out a photograph of Mary that she kept in a kitchen drawer.

"Look at this bitch!" Sue raked her nails across the photo's glossy surface.

Hayley Snow stared at the blond woman with the thick eyeliner and agreed. How could Paul have done this?

One time Sue and Hayley considered gathering all of Paul Webking's belongings and piling them out on the front lawn. He'd get the message when he returned home. In the end, neither could quite bring herself to do it.

Heated arguments, which had never been the norm between Sue and Paul, ensued during that time.

"I remember her being very, very upset and they would fight a lot," Hayley recalled. "I remember hearing them yelling at each other, which is something they never, never did. The only time I was really scared, they had a big fight and Paul threw the phone."

The young girl's diaries documented the ups and downs after the other woman entered their lives:

Jan. 6, 1986
Monday

Mommy and Paul are getting along real good, which is a relief, it makes a lot of difference around here if they don't.

Feb. 5, 1986

I guess Mommy and Paul got in a hurkin' fight tonight for some reason, I don't even want to know about. Paul was yelling so loud in the kitchen . . .

March 17, 1986

Lately the whole family has been getting along great. I love it. Especially when I feel like I can really talk to Mommy and Paul, and Ant Sera [sic] really feels comfortable around them. It's so cool.

April 28, 1986

Mommy and I have been getting along a little better the past couple of days. Talking more easily but I don't know. To me, it seems she's too, way too, strung up on Paul. That *really* bugs me! I suppose I gotta live with it!

Sue Snow refused to let Paul's little girlfriend shanghai her man, and she wasn't the type to let things run their course.

Hayley witnessed her mother's determination to keep Paul.

"I think my mother and Mary had it out on the phone. My mother—she has a mouth on her when she's mad—I think she called Mary every name in the book. I saw her do the whole thing. At least one phone call, I was there listening in the room."

Exa Snow, who was away at college during most of it, had ideas of her own as to why Paul would have played around with Mary.

"Because my mom loved Paul so much, he might have felt like he was controlled a little bit. Maybe there was just a little escape for him. For a brief time he went back to his past with no responsibilities," she suggested.

Paul's affair with Mary changed Sue Snow. For months it was all she could talk about. She complained of stress, and had bouts of irritability that some didn't think were like her at all. She suggested her bad moods were the result of the demands of her job.

She told people she wanted to hate Paul but couldn't.

*   *   *

It was a little after 8:00 P.M., June 16, when the FDA completed their analysis of the Excedrin capsules recovered from Sue Snow's kitchen. Depending on the number taken by the victim, either nine or eleven of the capsules had been tainted with potassium cyanide. The sixty-count bottle had fifty-six remaining.

Sue had been murdered, of course, but the horror of the discovery was that there could be other bottles of tainted capsules in area stores, or worse, in the medicine chests of local residents. The city of Auburn had no blueprint, no information manual on how to handle a product-tampering murder. With the exception of Chicago, where seven had died of tainted Tylenol, it was doubtful any other place would either. The seizure of bottles was the next life-saving step.

Mike Dunbar returned to N Street to confirm the tainted-capsule news to Sue Snow's family.

Paul Webking was not surprised.

"That's what we expected," he said.

The detective was put off by the response.

Could it be that he put it there, so he already knew what the results of the tests would be?

Other aspects of Paul Webking's statement continued to bother Mike Dunbar. Paul said he took two capsules out of the same bottle that held the tainted ones that killed his wife. Nobody had seen him do that. The police had only his word.

"He takes the first two, she takes the second two off the top, and she drops dead. Do you believe it or not? It's suspicious," he said later, back at the station.

Further, Paul Webking had told the Auburn detective he had mentioned the possibility of tampered Excedrin to a doctor at Harborview, and he had suggested the prospect to Dr. Fligner after his wife's autopsy.

And there was the question whether Sue Snow had taken the Excedrin for headaches or as some kind of a caffeine upper. Paul had suggested both reasons. Which was the truth?

As the hours and days passed, Mike Dunbar became more and more convinced Paul Webking was his wife's killer.

That evening, while Auburn police began to plan the seizure operation, they did not know the FBI had jurisdiction over consumer-product tamperings, the result of a federal law passed after the 1982 Chicago Tylenol murders. In fact, the FBI had already been notified of the case by the FDA.

*   *   *

The Auburn City Council was meeting in their chambers in the building adjacent to the police headquarters. As was his custom, J. D. "Jake" Evans, Auburn Police Chief, sat in on the meeting. He, Mayor Bob Roegner, and City Attorney Jack Berieter had all been advised of the possible tampering case. How they could have focused on the city business at hand will never be known.

Just after 8 P.M., a messenger alerted the chief that the capsules had, without any doubt, been laced with cyanide.

"I didn't feel comfortable, based on the telephone call we took in the morning, that we had a cyanide case and a possible tampering case in doing a seizure operation, but I sure as hell planned for it," Chief Evans later recalled.

The mayor, the city attorney, and chief of police retreated to the mayor's office, just behind Council Chambers. When they returned moments later, Mayor Roegner declared a state of emergency for the city and ended the council meeting.

To recall or seize all bottles of Excedrin capsules was a tough decision to make. After all, Chief Evans and Detective Dunbar knew it could ultimately cost manufacturer Bristol-Myers millions of dollars. And it was entirely possible that Sue Snow's murder was an isolated incident.

"But we can't take the risk," Mike Dunbar said. "If there's another bottle out there, it might wipe out a whole family."

In the end, it was the only decision to make.

Though stores were all closed and nothing more could be seized, work continued on the tampering case. Around midnight, an FDA investigator with the tainted capsules boarded a plane at SeaTac bound for the FDA labs in Cincinnati. There, with any luck, chemists would be able to determine the source of the poison.

Digital calendars on wristwatches had already rolled over to the next day when Mike Dunbar tried to sneak through the lobby past the press that had swelled around the justice center. He was grabbed by a patrol sergeant who knew that Dunbar's least favorite duty was speaking to the press.

"Here's the guy you want to talk to," the sergeant said.

A reporter's microphone was jammed into his face. "How do you investigate something like this?"

Mike Dunbar gave his standard response: "You knock on a lot of doors and ask a lot of questions. . . ."

The next day, *Good Morning America* aired his comment, but the detective didn't catch the show. He had more pressing things to do.

CHAPTER 8

Once it had been confirmed that Sue Snow had died of another deadly product tampering, the FBI went into breakneck action. Though all cases were important, none had affected as many as the rash of tamperings that had followed Chicago's case. The public was in a panic, because no one had caught any of the tamperers.

As it was that first day, and as it would be until nothing more could be done on the Snow case, a podium was wheeled into a conference room in the Seattle FBI field office. Supervisory Special Agents Mike Byrne and John Detlor led the All-Agents Meetings. "First office" agents, or rookies, were given bottle-seizure duty; "second office," or the more seasoned, were assigned administrative duties and responsibilities reflecting individual expertise.

Close to a hundred agents packed the conference room as SSA Mike Byrne reviewed case facts, scant as they were. Here was where the game plan for each day was worked out. The case agent from Chicago's Tylenol killings flew in and lent his expertise and ideas on classifying the various aspects of a tampering case. Briefings addressed extortion calls that might be made by the perpetrator. The Seattle case was what the organization calls an "office special," a case that absorbs everyone's attention and leaves the other cases a little breathing room.

Everybody had his or her own idea about who did it. Random killing or intentional murder scenarios were batted around. Maybe a stock manipulator was afoot, as in the Smith-Kline case when a man had tainted over-the-counter products with a rat poison to send the manufacturer's stock down the tubes.

For many, Paul Webking seemed a likely suspect. A family member is often the culprit in a murder case.

Special Agent Jack Cusack was in Phoenix running a polygraph on a source who contended he had information on a terrorist neo-Nazi group when he got word he'd be needed back home in Seattle on the cyanide case.

At forty-three, SA Cusack embodied the classic veteran FBI agent. Jack Cusack was nearly TV-star handsome enough to cause some women to think he was too good-looking to be trusted. But the genuinely unaffected man didn't seem to be aware of his looks.

He ignored the attentions of his interested seatmate on the plane home as he considered his new assignment. The unsolved Chicago Tylenol murders had been a major disappointment and a public-relations nightmare for the FBI. The thought of investigating another tampering was like diving into a black hole. There was no telling if they'd find anything, and if the deaths were truly random, how could they link them to the killer?

CHAPTER 9

Early the second morning of the investigation, the Seattle office of the Food and Drug Administration went public with the announcement that Sue Snow's death had been caused by cyanide-laced Extra Strength Excedrin. Investigators from several jurisdictions continued their sweep of South King County retail stores, pulling Extra Strength Excedrin bottles, with particular attention being paid to lot #5H102.

Excedrin manufacturer Bristol-Myers initiated a nationwide recall, though the FDA stressed that the tampering was the only known incident.

"Only one bottle involved," a spokesperson emphasized, unaware that hours later a second tainted bottle would be recovered from Johnny's Market in Kent.

Exa Snow was the kind of drop-dead gorgeous young woman that surely must have given her mother plenty of cause for concern. The twenty-three-year-old had perfect skin, blue eyes, and light-blond hair she wore past her shoulders. Though she was beautiful, she was also smart. When she gave her statement to Mike Dunbar at police headquarters, she said she was finishing up a tax-law degree in New Mexico.

Exa told how she and Jorge Sanchez had stayed at a motel the night before her mother died. She came home that night to get some things, and then left. Everything was fine. She dispelled any notion of a disturbance at the house that night.

"Paul barbecued . . . everyone was just having a good time. We used the hot tub. There was no drinking."

She said that after shopping her mother routinely would set out an empty grocery bag and fill it with the wrappers and containers not needed from the things she had just purchased.

"The garbage man comes on Tuesdays," she said.

Great, the detective thought, *the day she died, the packaging was sent to some landfill.*

"There's another thing I want to tell you," she said just before leaving. "Mom never used capsules, she always used tablets. I have never seen her use capsules in my entire life."

Just after noon on June 17, an employee from the bank called to say she had seen a box of Excedrin in the garbage at work. The timing was lucky. By now the packaging had become critical, for a couple of reasons. First it might lead to where Sue Snow had purchased the capsules—if indeed she had purchased them. (Detective Dunbar and others considered the possibility that the tamperer was a disgruntled employee who had sought revenge.) Second, investigators needed to either verify or disprove Paul Webking's statement.

An interview with the employee suggested that Sue Snow was a bright, attractive, and extremely popular woman. Although the women employees and customers had nothing but glowing things to say about her, her real success was with men.

"A lot of our customers liked to deal exclusively with Sue. They liked the way they were treated," she said.

Mike Dunbar understood. *If it takes a little harmless flirting to drum up a little business, then what's the harm?*

The woman was unsure about where she had seen the Excedrin box. She thought it might have been in the employee break room's garbage, but of course, it was long gone.

The detective was told about a man Sue had enraged when she turned him in for embezzlement some six months earlier. *Sure, he had motive,* the detective thought. *But what about opportunity?*

There was something else, but it happened so long ago that the woman said she was reluctant to bring it up. Several years ago someone had left a nasty note for Sue Snow.

"It read, 'To the whore of Puget Sound Bank.' "

For the next several hours, Mike Dunbar met with some of Snow's admirers, all prominent members of the Auburn community. All were adamant that they had dated Sue *before* she was married to Paul.

Detective Dunbar ended the afternoon of the second day of investigation on an odd note. During her interview, he had asked Exa Snow to return to the station for further questioning and was on the phone when she arrived—with an attorney.

He wondered what was going on that she thought she needed an attorney. Even more peculiar, Exa refused to wait for him to get off the phone. She just left.

"I was only on the phone a minute or so," he recalled later.

Back on N Street, neighbors jumped into the fray. One man recounted a secondhand story of screaming and crying heard at the Snow/Webking house at 3:00 A.M. the morning Sue Snow collapsed.

Mike Dunbar followed up on that one himself. The neighbor who had originally told the story cleared it up: it was a cat that was yowling early that morning that woke her. Like the old game of "telephone," the story had become so twisted that the cat had turned into Sue Snow and she was screaming for her life.

Everywhere he went, he learned a little bit more about Sue and Paul's relationship.

Another neighbor told him Sue Snow had said, "Paul wouldn't let her talk to anyone. Paul was jealous."

Paul Webking was not a popular guy.

By the end of the day, the FDA's testing of the Excedrin bottles removed from Auburn store shelves showed no others laced with cyanide. The FDA had also informed Mike Dunbar that of the nine contaminated capsules, six had been passed on to the FBI for latent-prints examination.

CHAPTER 10

The FBI sent a busload of agents to Auburn, enough men and women flashing badges around town that it was obvious to Mike Dunbar that working together would serve everyone's purposes. He knew that with the FBI would come manpower and federal money. When and if the product tamperer was identified, Auburn would have its murderer. It was a big "if." So far none of the product-tampering murders had met with a single arrest.

FBI Special Agent Ike Nakamoto told Detective Dunbar the FBI would need fingertip prints for comparisons on capsules—if they received any latents from the lab.

"We'll need to start eliminating those who might have had legitimate access," he said.

That meant Hayley, Exa, Sarah, Sue, and, of course, Paul.

At five feet six, King County police officer Edward Sexton has had his share of short jokes. When he was on motorcycle detail, if he parked on an incline he had a tough time getting the kickstand down. Yet Sexton, thirty-six, had a good sense of humor and could laugh it off.

"Dynamite comes in small packages," he'd say.

Assigned to the patrol unit based out of the South East Precinct off of the Maple Valley Highway, Officer Sexton was on meal break at a fellow officer's house just off the Kent-Kangley Road when he was radioed that a hysterical woman had called in to report that her husband had recently died and she had discovered a bottle of Excedrin capsules that matched the lot number of the one that had killed Sue Snow.

The dispatcher said that the woman was so upset, she was nearly unintelligible.

It was around 5:30 P.M. June 17, when the officer left in search of an address off Lake Moneysmith Road, just outside of the Auburn city limits. Though he hadn't been involved in the capsule-seizure operation, he was well aware of the Snow case. Anybody who could read or slump in front of a television set knew of it.

Forty-five minutes later, when he finally found the place, he parked by a work shed next to a Honda Goldwing motorcycle. A woman came out of a wooded area just behind the mobile home to meet him.

Years later, Officer Sexton fumbled trying to describe Stella Nickell. "Real nice-looking. Had nice slacks on. I believe she was dressed mostly in black, a black top on, kind of a sports jacket on."

If she had been in a panic when she called, that had passed. She was calm as she introduced herself.

Ed Sexton suggested they go inside where he could listen and take notes on what she had to say.

"I'm sorry I sounded so hysterical on the telephone," she said as she led him to the trailer's back door. "I was watching the news report on Mrs. Snow. . . ."

Inside, over the din of the television, Stella Nickell drank a Coke and recounted how she had heard about Sue Snow's death and the lot numbers of the tainted Excedrin capsules. Her husband had taken Excedrin capsules with the same lot number two weeks before—and he died at Harborview.

"Did they do an autopsy to determine the cause of death?" Sexton asked.

"They did, but it isn't finished. They gave me a preliminary report, but not a final one," she answered, adding that the preliminary report stated Bruce Nickell had died of emphysema.

She doubted their findings.

"He was healthy . . . he had a checkup . . . there wasn't any emphysema."

Ed Sexton requested the names of Bruce Nickell's doctors at Harborview and said he'd contact them.

"Sometimes when people die you get a report, but you don't know it is the final one."

"Will you call me and let me know what you find out?"

"As soon as I do, I'll let you know."

Stella went to the kitchen cabinet near the sink and returned with a nearly empty bottle of Excedrin. Only eight capsules remained.

"Bruce had been complaining of bad headaches lately. He was taking three or four capsules a day for pain for a little over a week."

The officer commented that the cap came off easily when he opened it to look inside.

"Bruce had a hard time taking the tops off, so I trimmed it so it would be easier for him."

Stella handed over an additional bottle, still in its original box, with a price sticker of $3.39. "You might as well take these, too," she said. "I don't want any of these around the house."

The cap was loose on the second bottle, but it was practically full to the top.

The black-haired woman sipped her Coke and said she had purchased the bottles two weeks apart. The first somewhere in Auburn, the second at Johnny's on the Kent East Hill.

As the officer was leaving, he noticed a man and a woman pull into the Nickells' gravel driveway. He set the Excedrin bottles on the passenger seat.

"Do you know these people?" he asked Stella, more out of kindness than anything else. He didn't want to have a new widow bothered by some strangers.

"No," Stella answered.

"Do you want me to tell them to leave?"

"No," she said. "They're here to look at the motorcycle. My brother knows I want to sell it, and he probably sent them over to look at it."

"It struck me kind of funny to have a relative suggest that. For one thing, all property has to go through probate after anybody dies. Probate can take months," Ed Sexton later said.

He returned to the precinct and told his supervisor what he picked up from the kitchen of the Nickells' single-wide mobile home. The bottles were to be entered into evidence, or disposed of under the the guidelines established since the Snow case broke. Since he didn't really know what he had, Ed Sexton put them in his locker.

He phoned Harborview, but none of the doctors who worked on Bruce Nickell were available.

Ed Sexton called in sick the next morning, but he still kept his commitment to that nice lady from out by Lake Moneysmith. He called Harborview again.

"We closed that case two days after Nickell died," a doctor told him. "Mrs. Nickell knows the results."

He wondered why Stella Nickell had said she received only a preliminary report.

"Did you test for cyanide poisoning?" Sexton asked.

"No. Why would we? There was no reason to suspect foul play."

"Are you going to?"

"He's dead and buried."

Frustrated, Sexton made another call, this one to the King County Medical Examiner's office. Dr. Fligner got on the line and told the officer that she understood a tube of blood from Bruce Nickell's eyes was available at the eye bank.

"I wouldn't say she was interested, but she seemed open to the subject of testing to see if there was foul play," Ed Sexton later recalled.

CHAPTER 11

King County officer Ed Sexton's bout with a flu bug kept him home again on June 18. He was called from his sickbed to talk with an FDA supervisory investigator named Kim Rice. The FDA man wanted to know the whereabouts of the bottles of Excedrin.

"Apparently on TV there was a report another tainted bottle had been found. I didn't see TV," the officer recalled later, "but evidently Stella Nickell had, and called Precinct 3 wanting to know about the tainted pills. She called the detectives downtown; they said they didn't know anything about it. They called the precinct. They looked in the log for evidence, but didn't see anything. Somebody said it was Officer Sexton who made the call. Why she thought it was her bottles, I don't know."

He told the FDA investigator the bottles were in his locker, safe and sound. Reluctantly, he pulled himself from under the covers and drove to Maple Valley to hand over the bottles.

Hours later, preliminary FDA lab tests showed that both bottles contained cyanide-laced capsules. It was likely that Stella Nickell's husband was actually the first of the two known victims.

And the woman had two bottles of the stuff!

Ike Nakamoto, a "first office" special agent with only two years with the FBI, was a huge Hawaiian fellow. Mike Byrne assigned SA Nakamoto to join the FDA's Kim Rice, who planned to head out to interview Stella Nickell. SA Larry Montague would go along to conduct a search of the premises. Nakamoto and Rice discussed the interview the afternoon before at FDA offices, and, in what was a breach of good investigative work, called Stella Nickell to let them know they were coming the next morning.

The woman was the widow of a tampering victim. SA Nakamoto and investigator Rice agreed that sympathy and a gentle touch were warranted.

Sandy Scott was oddly jolted by a news report that a second cyanide death was being investigated by federal and county authorities. Across the road from the five-acre spread where she lived with her husband Harold, a King County police officer (nicknamed "Scottie"), and their adopted son Brandon, was the Nickell place. She recalled Bruce Nickell and the emphysema ruling that didn't make sense to her or to his widow. Rather than mull over the possibility that Bruce was the reported victim, Sandy Scott cut to the chase. She reached for the phone and called Stella Nickell.

"I just heard on the news . . ."

Before she could finish, Stella answered the question she must have known was coming.

"It is Bruce," she said.

Sandy offered condolences again and wondered out loud how something like that could happen in the first place. Did Stella need anything? No, she said she'd be all right.

But later that day, a rambling Stella Nickell phoned her neighbor saying she had changed her mind.

"The FBI and FDA are going to come out tomorrow morning, and the Medical Examiner is going to announce Bruce's name to the media this afternoon. They told me reporters will probably show up, and I don't want to see anyone. Will you come down and stay with me?"

Sandy said she would. She made arrangements for her son to spend the afternoon with a friend, who was renting the Scotts' camping trailer. It was between three and four in the afternoon.

A reporter purporting to be with a big-time news agency had wormed his way into Stella Nickell's mother Cora Lee's trailer under the pretext of using the telephone. He was already asking questions when Stella sent Sandy over to ask him to leave.

"I'm worried about Mother's heart," she said.

Stella needn't have worried. Cora Lee, whom Sandy thought of as a hard-boiled Ma Kettle, was giving the reporter a piece of her mind. *A big piece.* The reporter seemed glad to leave.

The fence and Joe, Bruce's Labrador, fended off more of the media as they lined the narrow dirt road in front of the Nickells' property. Three Seattle TV stations and one from Tacoma overloaded the lane.

"You can't trust me with the press if Ted Koppel shows up," Sandy joked.

Stella laughed. "If Koppel shows up, you can talk to him."

While asking the local media to leave, Sandy repeated one of Stella's lines. "Please go away. Mrs. Nickell doesn't want to see anyone. No pictures. She feels like her husband has died all over again."

When it looked as if she'd be spending the night, because Stella didn't want her to leave, Sandy asked her husband to bring her pajamas down to Stella Nickell's trailer.

"By the way, bring my makeup. The press will be here," she said.

Until that evening, the two women had been hardly more than neighborly acquaintances. Yet Stella had asked Sandy Scott to come down and help her in her hour of need, and Sandy, always eager to get involved in something interesting, did so gladly.

In the end, Sandy Scott got more than she bargained for.

Stella passed the evening slamming down iced-tea-sized glasses full of Tanqueray gin and 7-Up. If it had been she who was drinking, Sandy knew without a doubt she'd be under the table. The booze didn't seem to affect Stella in the least.

The two women talked and watched the news, flipping the channels for more information on the cyanide murders.

Stella said she had put two and two together when a news report broadcast Paul Webking's description of his dying wife's symptoms.

"They matched Bruce's," she said.

Stella was concerned the news media would show pictures of Bruce or herself on TV. She told her mother to stay in her trailer and not to answer the door again. Stella was afraid TV people would find out she had been videotaped at a mobile-home-park rent strike centering on cable-TV charges a couple of years before.

"I know they got pictures of me," she kept repeating. "I'm just waiting for them to dig that footage out and show it."

"She had an absolute hemorrhage that night when they showed her mailbox on TV. I had to call Channel 7 and ask them not to show it. They said they could if they wanted," Sandy said.

She called her husband and asked him to remove the Nickells' name from their box up on Lake Moneysmith Road.

When another station showed an old photograph of Bruce, Stella questioned where the producers got it.

"I didn't give them permission to use that picture," she said.

The answering machine was left on automatic as the media called one after another. Stella told Sandy not to bother answering it. The only person she picked up the receiver for was a friend named Jim McCarthy.

Sandy was surprised by who *didn't* call. Stella's daughter Cindy had certainly been out to the property plenty of times. Sandy thought it was odd that Stella had asked *her*, and not her own daughter, to be there. The girl didn't even call.

As she fooled around with her gin bottle, Stella discussed Bruce's winning battle against alcoholism.

"She got almost defensive as she poured herself another drink. 'We kept the booze here because he wanted to be strong enough to have it in the house and still not drink it,' " Sandy recalled Stella saying.

Stella admitted that her first marriage had problems from the start. It made sense; after all, she was pregnant with another man's child. She said her daughter Cynthia Lea had been conceived during a rape. It was her mother-in-law who told the little girl that her daddy wasn't really her father.

"She's been nothing but problems since then," Stella said.

Sandy felt sorry for her neighbor. How could all this happen to one person?

Just before taking a sleeping spot on a couch around 3 A.M., Sandy made a trip to the bathroom. She noticed that the roll for the toilet paper was empty.

"You're out of TP!"

"Oh, it's under the sink," Stella called from the kitchen.

Sandy opened the cabinet under the sink and saw a bottle of Extra Strength Excedrin capsules. Right in front. Surprised, she picked it up and examined it. It was full of red capsules. As she put it back, she wondered if it was the deadly lot number. A twinge of panic set in.

The FBI is coming tomorrow, and . . . Oh God, I touched it!

She set the red and white plastic bottle down and decided not to mention it.

CHAPTER 12

Media attention frequently unleashes the 220s—police code for crazies. Sometimes it is the crazy who calls in; many times it is someone calling about a crazy. Mike Dunbar had never seen anything like the national media attention that the product tampering produced. While the FBI agents were gearing up to see Stella Nickell, the widow of victim number two, Detective Dunbar went to work, sifting through the deluge.

As with the Green River serial-murder case, some called to finger one who might have been the tamperer. Many left a specific name. Others said they saw someone acting strangely at the grocery store.

One man contacted the police to say that on June 1 he had purchased a bottle of Excedrin capsules in Ellensburg, a town just east of the Cascades. En route to Spokane, he was repeatedly passed by a driver who somehow seemed suspicious.

"While I was in Spokane a second bottle of Excedrin showed up in my car. I think the killer might have followed me, because he saw me buy the capsules in Ellensburg."

As off the wall as it was, Detective Dunbar still notified the FDA's Kim Rice, who could make arrangements for the recovery of the mysterious bottle.

At the Snow/Webking house, it was a repeat of more questioning, but this time it was the FBI asking Paul, Sarah, Hayley, and Exa the questions. The special agents took each person into a separate room. Hayley and Paul added little, if anything, to what they had told Mike Dunbar.

Sarah Webb learned more by the agents' questions than she would have guessed.

"Was your sister a nymphomaniac?"

Sarah blinked at the stupidity of the question. She wondered who would have said something like that about her sister.

"No. Sue was just normal," she answered. "She could make you feel like you were the only person in the world. She loved to flirt . . . she'd say to you, 'Let's do *it* . . .' but she would not mean it. She could make you believe anything she wanted you to—you really turned her on, she really wanted to go to bed with you, when in fact, you were just like everyone else."

Years later, Sarah put it all in perspective: "I bet five thousand million dollars whoever said it was someone who never went to bed with her."

A special agent named Randy Scott sought insight into Paul and Sue's marriage.

"Were they getting along?"

"It seemed better," Sarah answered somewhat cautiously.

He also wanted to know about Paul's personality.

"Was he violent?"

She shook her head. "He just screamed and hollered a lot."

Throughout the interview Sarah Webb spoke softly. She was afraid her voice would carry into the room where Paul was being questioned. She didn't want him to hear anything she had to say.

When SA Randy Scott concluded the interview, he warned Sarah not to disclose what they had discussed with anyone.

"Especially not to Paul," he said.

That same day, Auburn police detectives conducted more interviews with employees of the Auburn North branch of Puget Sound National Bank.

A loan specialist told detectives that within two days of Sue Snow's murder, Paul Webking had asked for the "entire contents of Sue's desk." Other employees complied with the request.

A woman who had worked with Sue for several years emphasized that Sue carried a large bottle of Excedrin tablets in her purse at all times.

"Never capsules."

The two employees agreed that, at least professionally, Sue had been on top of the world. She had just closed a deal on a $5 million account with a local trucking firm.

Just before lunchtime, Mike Dunbar and SA Sid Rubin met with a woman who worked with Sue at the bank. The woman was deeply troubled by what had happened to Sue, whom she considered a good friend.

She said Sue was a flirtatious woman with a bit of a hot temper. She rattled off a list of men she had known. All were customers of the bank.

"Sue only went to lunch with customers—never dinner. She did have a lot of lunch dates, but that was business. Sue always was a flirt, but not serious. Sometimes people took it serious, but it wasn't meant to be," she said.

She also stated that Paul and Sue frequently fought over his trips to California. Sue was still angry about Mary.

The woman knew plenty, Mike Dunbar thought, *maybe even more than Sarah Webb.*

"People want people to think the best of them. You want to be held in high esteem. [The woman] was just a friend, not a relative," he later said.

She also talked about Paul Webking:

"Paul thought that money was important. . . . It bothered Paul that Sue made more money than Paul, that she was more successful."

Further, she described Paul as a very jealous man, which seemed to fit what the detectives had been hearing.

As far as the Excedrin was concerned, the woman insisted that Sue always kept a bottle of tablets in her purse and she took them for menstrual cramps or headaches associated with stress.

She knew nothing of a caffeine habit.

"She took the cap off with her teeth," she said, faintly smiling at the memory.

Details like that made Detective Dunbar think that this woman knew Sue Snow very well. It was clear she knew about the problems that Sue and Paul had, at least Sue Snow's version. She seemed to suggest that it was a possibility that Paul had reason to kill his wife.

Detective Dunbar and SA Rubin met in the yard at Webking's employer, Metro Hauling, in Kent. SA Rubin had the search warrant allowing them to examine Paul Webking's 1985 Kenworth.

A trip log seemed to back up the man's account of his whereabouts the days before his wife was murdered. His truck was fueled in Kent on June 6 and three days later in Redding, California.

They found some pills—vitamins and maybe an amphetamine or two—but nothing to move the investigation any further. "Maybe he cleaned it out before we got here," Mike Dunbar said.

They returned to N Street to talk to Paul Webking anyway.

By now Paul Webking was letting his feelings show.

"I had a lot of vitamins in the truck, in a baggie, rather than take the bottles in the truck. I put the baggie in the ashtray. They got it. They called me downstairs and tag-teamed me," Paul said later.

"You want to explain this?" one of them said, holding the plastic bag.

"What are you talking about? Hey, I'm a truck driver. I've taken bennies . . ."

Paul, his blue eyes bugging out, identified the pills. "The red one is a One-A-Day and the others are vitamin C."

After the investigators left, Paul turned to his sister-in-law.

"They didn't find the Excedrin," he said.

Mike Dunbar did a little checking on Paul Webking's story that Sue bought the capsules because they were easier to swallow, when everyone else said she used tablets.

A visit to the Albertson's store where Snow shopped confirmed that both tablets and capsules had been available when the bank vice-president did her shopping. It was possible that she might have picked up the wrong bottle, but the Auburn detective didn't think so.

Nobody could accuse trucker Paul Webking of being stupid. If he had an inkling that FBI agents and Auburn police had suspected he had been the tamperer, by the time Sid Rubin and Mike Dunbar left after discussing the baggie in the truck, he was totally convinced.

"I have some Excedrin in there and they didn't find it," he finally told Sarah.

Paul's brother, a professor from Canada, was there, and Paul spent most of his time with him. Understandable as it was, it hurt Sarah. When Paul announced he was going to his truck to look for the capsules, she thought he would take her along. But it was his brother who went.

When the men returned a short time later, Sarah met them at the door.

"Did you find it?"

"Yeah," Paul answered. "They weren't hidden, Sarah. They were in a pocket in the truck. They should have seen them."

Sarah Webb didn't really care where the capsules had been. She just wanted to see what it was that Paul thought so important to retrieve.

"I want to see them, Paul, I want to see what they look like," Sarah said. She had never taken a good look at the capsules she moved in the kitchen. She wanted to know what they smelled like. Capsules had killed her sister, and she wanted to know why Sue had taken them in the first place. Shouldn't she have noticed something?

Years later, Sarah could never really be sure if she saw them— Paul flashed something by her face so quickly. She would say it was her understanding that he had thrown the actual bottle in the Green River before bringing its contents home. That night was not a time for logic.

"He went straight into the bathroom and locked the door and flushed the toilet immediately. He did not have a bottle in his hand. What I really think he did is throw the bottle in the Green River and looked at the capsules and then flushed them down the toilet. But he didn't tell me that."

Paul later would insist he had disposed of the red capsules by grinding them in the garbage disposal.

"At this point, I didn't want . . ." he said later, his voice trailing. "I had had enough and I knew where everybody was going. So I had this bottle of Excedrin in the truck and they missed it in the search. Or they did see it and didn't care, I don't know."

"I really don't care to involve myself in it anymore. If you guys think they [the recovered capsules] are important, take them and give them to the police," Paul said to Sarah and his brother. They couldn't agree either, so Paul Webking, looking every bit a guilty man, trashed them.

Sarah still wrestled with one more question: what really made Paul throw away the bottle of Extra Strength Excedrin?

*   *   *

The house on N Street had been split in two. Since the FBI investigators and the Auburn detectives had centered many of their questions on Paul and Sue's relationship, it was clear where the investigation was headed.

Whenever Paul left the house, Sarah and Hayley and Exa—while she was still in Washington before returning to college in New Mexico—spent hours trying to decide whether to tell the FBI about Paul's trip to the truck for the Excedrin. If he did the crime they sure as hell wanted him to pay for it, but if he was innocent and was only trying to take unnecessary heat off himself, they didn't want to add to his troubles.

Finally, Sarah and Hayley mustered the courage to call the FBI. Afraid to use the telephone with Paul around, they waited until he left the house. Sarah asked for Randy Scott, but he wasn't in. He called back two hours later.

"By that time we really lost our nerve. I think maybe we chickened out. I don't remember if we told him."

Sarah, more than Sue's daughters, contended Paul had killed her sister. She *wanted* to believe it. Guilty of the tampering or not, Paul had been the one who told her sister to use capsules. Sue did not use them. Sarah kept going back to the *tablets* in Sue's purse and the fact that Paul had *capsules* in his truck.

They all knew Paul claimed to have taken two capsules the morning Sue died. Sarah considered that another big lie.

"He might have chucked them," she told her nieces, "or maybe he knew which ones to take?"

Hayley didn't know what to think. In many ways she loved Paul. Though Connie Snow was only a few miles away, and had been a good father, Paul was the one she had lived with. She could see so much of Paul in herself: his sense of humor, his way of battling for what was right.

Hayley could see Sarah's unique loss, but she had lost her mother too. The idea of Paul killing her was inconceivable. Yet Aunt Sarah kept pushing it whenever they were alone.

Sarah considered Paul's affair as part of the motive, but she didn't think that was as viable as another, more obvious one—money.

To her way of thinking, Sue and Paul spent like there was no tomorrow. Sue earned just under $40,000 a year, her husband less, yet they never went without. Paul had even gone out on a financial limb and purchased a new Kenworth.

"They were spending money like they were rich . . . took their credit cards to the max. Sue had been buying all those new clothes at his request," Sarah said later.

"He did it for the money, because everything was Sue's."

Even though her sister's suspected killer slept in the bedroom next to hers, Sarah stayed in the house. Sarah never thought he'd kill her too. He didn't have anything to gain, and Paul was not one to waste the effort on something that wouldn't benefit him.

Only once, however, did doubt creep in.

One night Paul offered Sarah a tranquilizer to help her sleep. A half hour later, she stood woozy and dizzy in the kitchen.

"You guys . . . I swear to God, I think I'm dying. . . ."

"How much did you take?"

"Just one," she answered.

"Sarah," Paul said, narrowing his eyes, "you're supposed to cut it in half. . . ."

Why hadn't he told her that?

CHAPTER 13

Stella Nickell was ready for the FDA and FBI by 7:30 A.M. on June 19. Though she could have scarcely slept more than a few hours and had downed more than her share of gin, she seemed refreshed, eager to get on with it. She dressed in her best jeans and a western-style shirt. Her makeup had been applied with a light hand. She looked good. Her long black hair was clipped back with a girlish barrette. Stella Nickell and her neighbor Sandy Scott drank coffee, smoked cigarettes, and filled the hours with small talk. After the night of revelations, what more could they talk about?

One person got through on the phone. It was Anna Jo "A. J." Rider, a friend and co-worker from SeaTac Airport where she and Stella screened passengers for Olympic Security. A. J. had called from her mother's in Yakima after hearing a news report that Bruce was a possible cyanide victim.

"Stella, did Bruce die of cyanide poisoning?"

"Well, that's what they're saying."

"How do they know that?"

"I had an autopsy of Bruce," Stella said. "They didn't throw out a specimen, and when they retested they found cyanide."

SAs Ike Nakamoto and Larry Montague and the FDA's Kim Rice arrived at the Nickell mobile home about 9:45 A.M. Though neighbor Sandy felt she would be a nervous wreck in similar circumstances, Stella was calm and had her wits about her. She an-

swered the agents' background questions with a directness that
Sandy had come to know from the previous evening. Stella was
one self-assured lady.

The five of them took seats at the Formica dinette table, and
with the speed and frequency that had come from years as a "stew"
for United, Sandy Scott poured coffee.

Stella told the investigators that on June 5 her husband had gone
to work as usual and returned at 4:10 that afternoon. She was making dinner when he took a shower and came out to watch TV.

He took four Excedrin capsules and went into the den. Later,
Stella said she saw him walk to the deck, go outside, and return to
the area in front of the couch. He collapsed, and she called 911.

"During that time she said his breathing either stopped or nearly
stopped," Nakamoto later said. "After giving the information to the
911 operator she went back, found he was still breathing, although
in a funny, strange manner, I guess a deep type of breathing, waited
for the aid unit to come, which they did, and basically the aid unit
took over from there and worked on Bruce for about an hour. He
was then transported to the Red Barn Ranch, where he was airlifted
to Harborview."

"Bruce had been suffering from recurring headaches for a couple
of months," Stella explained, adding later that Excedrin was the
only pain reliever Bruce took. He usually took four. She kept all
of her medicines in the kitchen cabinet above the sink.

While discussing the two cyanide-laced Excedrin bottles she had
given to King County officer Ed Sexton, Stella remarked that she,
too, had taken some of the capsules from the very bottle that poisoned her husband.

"I came home from Bruce's funeral with a horrible backache,
and I took two capsules. My God, can you believe it? I could have
taken some with cyanide in them too," she said.

Stella Nickell admitted she had a difficult time accepting that
her husband had died of emphysema—the pathologist's initial ruling. She even called the medical examiner's office twice—June 7
and 13. There had been some kind of a mix-up, she told Nakamoto.
She never got the final results.

A third phone call was made, she said, after she heard the news
of Sue Snow's death.

Though the investigators were concerned with the source of the
poisoned capsules, Kim Rice, in particular, wanted to pinpoint
where the bottles had been purchased.

"Where do you do your shopping?" he asked.

She answered Auburn's Albertson's North, Pay 'N Save South, and at the Johnny's Market in Kent.

"Any idea when you bought the bottles?"

Stella said it was likely she purchased them on one of her days off from her job at the airport.

In all likelihood, she said, the opened tainted bottle had been purchased two weeks prior to her husband's death, either at Albertson's North or the Johnny's Market. But Stella Nickell said she couldn't be certain.

The unopened bottle, however, had been purchased at Johnny's in Kent, a couple of days before Bruce died.

They also talked about Bruce Nickell. The Nickells had first lived together in 1974 and married in 1976. At the time of his death, her husband was a heavy-equipment operator for the State Department of Transportation. He had recently passed a state physical examination in order to become a permanent employee.

SA Nakamoto, who had been a police officer and an investigator for the state, asked about insurance.

As far as Stella knew, Bruce was covered by a single policy, a policy from the state. She went to the desk under the fish tanks and produced a statement from the State Employees Insurance Board. She gave it to Nakamoto and he took notes.

She was uncertain about its value.

Later, SA Nakamoto recalled Stella Nickell's saying her husband had applied for an additional $100,000, but since he had not taken a mandated physical or missed an appointment, or there had been a problem due to delayed delivery by the post office, he was turned down. Bruce had been depressed about that.

The policy indicated that state employees had $5,000 basic life, $5,000 accidental death and dismemberment. Optional coverages were available, including optional life for $25,000, and there was an additional $100,000 accidental death and dismemberment, for a total possible coverage of $135,000.

Stella said she did not know the full amount.

Ike Nakamoto asked if there were any other policies on Bruce's life.

Stella told him that she and Bruce had both applied for an additional $20,000 from Bank Cardholders of America, and that due to a clerical error at the insurance company, she herself had received the $20,000 coverage but Bruce had not.

Stella produced a wallet card from her saddlebag-style purse. It had her name as the insured. She said she had called a toll-free number for the insurance company but learned that through a clerical error her policy was the only one issued—not one for Bruce. Her attorney, Bill Donais, had the certificates at his office in Auburn.

"Ike, I've got something you need to see," an agent called from the hallway near the bathroom.

It was the sixty-count bottle of Excedrin capsules that Sandy Scott had seen the night before.

Kim Rice recognized the lot number immediately—5H102, expiration date August 1988—as the same as that on the bottle recovered from Sue Snow's kitchen.

Kim Rice asked Stella what she knew about the bottle.

She just looked completely blank. "I've never seen it before," she said. She had no idea how it got there.

Sandy Scott blurted out that her fingerprints were on it.

The FDA investigator would later say Stella Nickell's surprised reaction seemed completely genuine.

He put the bottle in an evidence bag.

Next Kim Rice asked if Stella had any grocery receipts from May or June that might help determine where bottles were actually purchased. Stella wasn't sure, but she said she and Bruce saved receipts for income-tax purposes. She went to her desk in the living room and pulled out various drawers and a shoe box trying to locate receipts. An Albertson's receipt included an item for $3.39, the same price as the one stickered onto the forty-count bottle Ed Sexton had taken to his locker.

Although minutes before Stella had said she purchased the bottle at Johnny's in Kent, the FDA man didn't ask about the conflict.

Just as the FBI seemed to be finishing up, Stella's daughter Cindy Hamilton and a trucker boyfriend pulled onto the property. Since the door was locked, Sandy Scott got up from the kitchen table to let them inside. Sandy had met Cindy only a couple times before, but she recognized her immediately: the young woman's photograph was displayed prominently in the den.

"How could they suspect my mother of killing Bruce? I don't understand," she said, angrily pushing past her mother's neighbor.

"Nobody's accusing your mother of anything," Sandy replied,

not knowing what to make of the comment. Why would Cindy have thought anyone was accusing her mother of murder?

Stella went to her daughter, and for the only time during the morning, became teary-eyed. A few words were exchanged, and the widow took her place back at the kitchen table.

In the midst of all of this, Cindy's boyfriend asked to use the telephone so he could check on a battery for his truck.

His attitude galled Sandy Scott.

"I mean, we're talking about a major criminal investigation with the FBI. Cindy's father was murdered in a case that was making national and international headlines, and he interrupted them to use the phone to call about a truck battery!"

Sandy noticed Stella's muscles tighten as the agents swept through her trailer, her mother's trailer, and Bruce's work shed looking for evidence. The woman was under an incredible amount of stress, and Sandy Scott felt sorry for her.

Sandy cornered Cindy in the kitchen.

"Your mother hasn't eaten anything since yesterday afternoon. She's looking tense and not too well. Why don't you try to get her to eat something?"

Cindy shrugged. "She's a big girl. If she wants something to eat, she can get it herself."

Sandy Scott's jaw dropped. She couldn't understand Cindy's apparent lack of concern for her mother.

"The animosity in the retort was so out of character for what the circumstances were," she later said.

The agents involved in the search did so meticulous a job, it even impressed Sandy Scott, whose husband was a cop, and who had read her share of police procedurals. An agent brought out the laundry detergent and sifted through it for some hidden evidence.

Another agent said someone might have gained access to the Nickells' house and planted poison there.

When some powder in a sandwich bag taken from one of Bruce's tool kits was shown to Stella Nickell, she wasn't able to identify it.

"It might have some use in welding," she offered, getting up from her chair to examine it.

Later, out of earshot of the FBI, she turned to Sandy and said, "I hope it isn't drugs. Cindy's boyfriend borrowed the tool kit recently."

The Nickells' coffee table had small cupboard-like compartments on each end. Inside, an FBI agent found some Rainier beer cans filled with a grayish powder.

Stella chortled at the discovery. "That's Mount St. Helens ash," she said, referring to the Cascade volcano that had erupted in 1980.

Agents also took statements from Sandy and Cora Lee Rice, neither of whom knew anything other than what Stella Nickell had told them about her husband's death.

SA Cliff Spingler seated Cindy Hamilton in the Nickells' spare bedroom, where she talked about family history, including Bruce's battle with the bottle.

"Bruce was a weekend alcoholic, and several years ago my mom gave him an ultimatum—either her or the bottle. She took him into treatment, and he hasn't had a drink since."

Though her stepfather had a high tolerance for pain, Cindy Hamilton said he suffered a bout of headaches after he was laid off from his job at McDonald Industries in Kent some time ago. He used Excedrin exclusively.

"He figured if two was the recommended dosage, then four was better."

The same thing Stella had said.

Cindy said there were no problems with the Nickell marriage, and if there had been any financial worries, those had been behind them for better than a year. Her mother loved her stepfather. There were no extramarital affairs.

The agents' train of cars left around the time family friend Jim McCarthy and attorney Bill Donais arrived on the property to help Stella.

Slightly winded from the walk up the hill, Donais stood on the roadside and spoke to the media.

"It's been a real shock to her. If it hadn't been for the unfortunate aspect of Mrs. Snow dying, Mrs. Nickell would be dead."

A reporter asked why.

"Apparently they found cyanide in the last four or five capsules in bottom of the bottle, and both Mr. and Mrs. Nickell used it. If she hadn't been warned, she might have very well taken it herself."

By the end of the day, FBI investigators had also paid a visit to Bruce's place of employment in Seattle. His toolbox was searched for evidence, the idea being it could have been a disgruntled co-worker who spiked Nickell's Excedrin with poison.

By then, the FBI also had a code name for the case: Seamurs, for Seattle murders. The Chicago Tylenol case had been known as Capmurs, for capsule murders.

CHAPTER 14

The morning nine days after Sue Snow died was filled with helpful tips and useless leads. A Pay 'N Save clerk called Mike Dunbar with the sketchy description of a man who tried buying cyanide in the pharmacy some weeks before.

Another caller offered information indicating that the embezzler Sue Snow had turned in might have had access to cyanide.

An officer who had worked the Diane Elsroth case in New York phoned, but he couldn't really help. The February 1986 case, like other product tamperings, remained unsolved.

The greatest part of the day was spent going through canvas bags full of the stored garbage from Sue Snow's bank office. No evidence of any Excedrin was found during the three hours Detective Dunbar and FBI agents pawed through the material in a department conference room.

By the end of the week, the FDA lab in Cincinnati had determined that the cyanide contaminating the Snow and Nickell bottles had come from the same source. In a way, that was good news. At least a copycat wasn't at work. Not yet, anyway.

The King County Medical Examiner's office began to reevaluate nine recent deaths to see if cyanide had been involved.

The Seattle Times published a story headlined:

ALERT WIDOW AVOIDED FATE OF HUSBAND

The same paper ran an article announcing a $300,000 reward offered by the Proprietary Association, a consortium of the drug companies that had been bruised and beaten by this kind of a maniac more than a dozen times. But the rewards offered had been no help in solving the other tamperings.

Drug companies continued the withdrawal of capsule medicines. Datril and Bufferin were withdrawn by Bristol-Myers, along with Extra Strength Excedrin capsules.

The Webking/Snow house got its share of calls from crazies too. Some were just weirdos calling only to say that they had seen the articles; others called with a purpose.

Paul Webking took a phone call from a Colorado man who said he wanted to join in a lawsuit with Sue Snow's estate. He said he had proof that X rays can convert acetaminophen, one of the ingredients in Excedrin, into cyanide. He had even written a paper on it.

Paul's brother listened in on the extension.

"It occurs when they X-ray bottles for consistency in packaging," the man said. "There is a possibility that the radiation emitted from Chernobyl caused the conversion. . . ."

A call from the household's second phone line was made to the police regarding the man with information on the tamperings. An Auburn police officer responded at 10:25 P.M. The officer stood in the hallway, while Paul Webking tried to keep the caller on the line in an attempt to get as much information as possible.

The officer's radio irritated Paul Webking.

"Turn the fuckin' radio off," he whispered, his hand over the receiver.

The officer shrugged. "Just give me the phone, and let him talk to a real person."

"Why don't you get the fuck out of here!" Paul bristled.

The officer left, telling the family to "have Mr. Personality call me when he settles down."

Later Paul Webking reported the call to the FBI, but he felt they dismissed his information. He told family members that if the authorities were looking for Sue's killer, they were looking for him on "their time—not on the killer's time."

The Auburn officer who responded to the harassing call was one of the first to have a run-in with Paul Webking, one of the first to see "Paul the hothead" for himself. As the days passed, others would experience it for themselves.

Mike Dunbar later put it this way: "Paul has the type of personality that doesn't endear him to you. Some people might be guilty, but you want to believe they are innocent. You look for the good, the positive, because of personality. Paul didn't have the kind of personality that made you want to help the guy out. Given all the circumstantial evidence, there wasn't a lot of motivation to want to try and clear the guy."

Anyone who knew Paul Webking wouldn't have been surprised he wanted to control the information doled out to the press about his wife's murder.

Control was one thing, but to Sarah, Hayley, and Exa, it seemed Paul wanted to be the *only* one who spoke to the media.

When a Tacoma reporter inquired about writing a story about Sue and Sarah, Paul told Sarah not to talk with the man. Sarah did it anyway—over the telephone. She was too scared to let the man come to the house when Paul had told her not to.

"I'll do all the talking," he said.

His attitude miffed her.

"Now I look back and think, why'd I listen to him? I wasn't married to him," she said years later.

While local news cameras recorded the awkward moment, one afternoon Hayley, Sarah, and Paul accepted a plaque from a long-time bank customer. It had been inscribed with a tribute, and a photograph of Sue Snow.

The fifteen-year-old girl with cropped blond hair and a set of light-catching braces looked and sounded very much her age.

"Thanks a lot . . . I mean, it's really nice and neat that you've done this for us . . . and you remember her . . . everyone will remember her in this way."

A store off Auburn Way North was one of two Pay 'N Save drugstores located in Auburn. It was next door to the Albertson's grocery store where investigators believed Sue Snow might have purchased her tainted bottle of Extra Strength Excedrin.

Around noon on Tuesday, June 24, 1986, store manager Jim Nordness, his staff, and two FBI agents continued their examination of inventory to ensure the removal of the banned capsules from the shelves.

A bottle of Maximum Strength Anacin-3 quickly became the

subject of great interest. It had been found earlier in the day sitting on a can of peanuts, two rows from where it should have been in the pharmacy's over-the-counter medications display. Not only was it in the wrong section, but further examination showed it was in the wrong store. It had been price-stickered on the end flap with a red "As Advertised" label over an orange price tag not used by Pay 'N Save.

And there was more. After going through store inventory schematics, Nordness discovered that the Pay 'N Save store didn't even carry the fifty-count size in the first place.

The FBI took the bottle off to the lab. By the end of the day the flames of panic were fanned again as the word got out: *The tamperer had struck again—this time it wasn't Excedrin.*

CHAPTER 15

Within a day or so of the FBI search of the Nickells' place, the friends from the couple's days at White River Estates, a mobile-home park in Auburn where they lived before moving to the five-acre property, heard from special agents doing follow-up interviews. Most of the men and women working on the seventh floor of the Federal Building stuck with the idea that Paul Webking was the most likely suspect.

"Stella Nickell had called the authorities herself."

"She turned in two bottles."

"If she was the killer, all she had to do was keep her mouth shut!"

On Friday, a special agent drove across the bridge to Lincoln Mutual in toney suburban Bellevue to meet with Dee Rogers, a sparkly-eyed pistol of a woman with a way with a one-liner that could get her a spot on late-night television. But this was serious stuff. Dee and Stella had been friends for years, and in fact, Stella's daughter Cindy Hamilton lived with Dee and her children in a Kent apartment.

"We're contacting all the people who know Bruce and Stella Nickell, and your name has been mentioned," the SA said. In fact, Dee Rogers's name had been on the top of the list.

If White River Estates ever had a "life of the party" squirreled away in one of the trailers that lined the grid of the neighborhood, it had been Rogers. Sharp-witted and streetwise, Dee Rogers was a transplanted New Yorker—hardly the type to end up in a trailer park outside Seattle doing Christmas-themed ceramics. But she had, and thankfully was now on to other things.

Like Stella Nickell, Dee Rogers, the mother of two boys and a girl, was on her second marriage when she moved into White River Estates. By the time the FBI came to see her, she had wrapped up a third marriage.

"At that time," Dee recalled years later, "I was a little Dotty Domestic. I took care of my own home, own business. I didn't really give a rat's ass what was going on in someone else's household."

Dee told the FBI agent she'd be glad to help, but, as she said, she didn't know anything.

She couldn't think of anything negative to say about the Nickells. They had been friends and neighbors at White River Estates but had drifted apart a little then.

"Bruce and Stella had a close, loving relationship. Neither had anyone on the side," she said between puffs of her cigarette. "Bruce was a homebody and Stella took care of all his needs. Any fights they had were insignificant."

"What about financial problems?"

"There weren't any that I ever knew about."

The agent asked if Stella Nickell had access to cyanide.

"Not any that I would know about," Dee replied, her characteristic certainty intact.

"Do you think Stella could have killed Bruce?"

"No," she answered. "Stel's capable of the mechanics of tampering. She's a very intelligent woman. . . . But, no, she'd never do anything like that."

FBI Special Agent Roger Martz, a chemist in the chemistry-toxicology unit of the Washington, D.C., forensic laboratory, was left with the five tainted bottles from South King County. The latent-print examiners had come up with only one unknown latent on all the bottles, and none on the tainted capsules themselves.

It was a good bet the tamperer had worn gloves.

SA Roger Martz, a young man with bright dark eyes and a thick mustache, had been an FBI chemist for four years before earning his agent's I.D. He was no lab boy lackey—Martz taught forensic chemistry at Quantico. Now it was his task to find out where the poison had been manufactured and where it had been sold.

The information concerning each bottle was recorded in meticulous detail.

Bottle No. 1, from Sue Snow's kitchen, had no outside wrappings, no box, not even a cap. Of the sixty Excedrin capsules purported to be inside, fifty-six remained; nine contained cyanide. Of the nine, four contained green specks.

The second bottle, a sixty-count Excedrin, was from Johnny's in Kent. Though in a box, its safety seal around the neck of the bottle had been cut. Of fifty-six capsules found in the bottle, four contained cyanide mixed with little green specks.

Bottle No. 3 was the forty-count Excedrin from Stella Nickell's home. The lip of the bottle had been pared, making it loose. It contained seven capsules, two with cyanide, and one of those had the foreign green material.

The fourth bottle had a box, though no safety seal around the bottle neck. It was the second one turned in by Stella Nickell, and like its companion, was a forty-count. Only thirty-five remained. Four capsules contained cyanide, all of which were mottled with green specks.

The last bottle was the Anacin-3, found at Pay 'N Save. The bottle was in a box, but the box, SA Martz determined through chemical analysis, had been reglued. Martz also noted that the box had two price stickers, one red, the other orange. The aluminum safety seal on the top of the bottle had been partially removed, as had the polyethylene heat seal. Of the fifty capsules supposed to be inside, only forty-five remained. Four capsules were tainted. All four had the green material.

The sixty-count Excedrin bottle retrieved from under Stella Nickell's bathroom sink was completely clean, and was not considered evidence.

While the source of the potassium cyanide had yet to be determined, one thing was clear. With the capsules averaging 700 milligrams of cyanide, they were lethal.

SA Martz, of course, hadn't been the first to notice the green specks in seventeen of the twenty-three tainted capsules. But it was his job to determine what those particles were.

Fifteen members of the Auburn police gathered in Conference Room #3 at headquarters at 9 A.M., Wednesday, June 26, for what had become their answer to the FBI's daily briefings.

Chief Jake Evans reviewed what was already known: five tainted bottles had been recovered in South King County. Two people were dead—Sue Snow and Bruce Nickell. There was no known link between the two victims.

A preliminary psychological profile—gleaned from FBI work on the Chicago case—suggested the tamperer was a person who lived locally, might visit the stores to check on the sales of the tampered bottles, and finally, in an act of ghoulishness, might even visit victims' graves.

One officer recalled a phone call from an individual who linked the tamperings to the Green River Killer.

Anything was possible, but the crimes were not even remotely similar.

Detective Dunbar told the group about a disgruntled Pay 'N Save employee who was being investigated by the FBI. He also reported that federal chemists were trying to "fingerprint," or determine the source of, the cyanide.

"It's contaminated with some green crystals of some kind," he said.

The investigators had learned how easy it was to purchase a poison as lethal as cyanide. Chemical-supplies stores sold it, high-school chemistry classes used it, so did photographers and jewelers.

The FBI knew the tampering had been done after the bottles left the manufacturing plant, and that the case appeared to be local.

Officers went over the victims' files. Very little time was spent on the Nickell case. It was true that Stella Nickell was being investigated, but she didn't seem as viable a suspect as Paul Webking.

"Snow was a tablet user . . . Webking said he took two capsules before he left . . . Mary . . . an ER doctor said Webking suggested cyanide-laced Excedrin as the cause of death . . . How could Webking know Sue had taken two capsules when he wasn't even there . . . Webking's conversation with Dr. Fligner . . ."

The circumstances piled up.

"Webking has a double-indemnity life insurance policy on his wife. . . ."

The fact that the Anacin-3 had two price stickers—one from Pay 'N Save, the other from Associated Grocers—was mentioned.

"A truck driver would have easy access. . . ."

Paul Webking, of course, was a truck driver.

An officer wondered if it had been a coincidence that Sue Snow had died on garbage-pickup day, leaving no evidence in the home.

The Auburn officers even batted around the idea of a family conspiracy. The quack caller had been from Colorado; Sarah lived in Colorado; they mistakenly believed Exa attended college in Colorado . . .

SA Randy Scott phoned Paul Webking for a list of the people who attended Sue's funeral. The FBI planned to review it for possible leads. Though he didn't say it, the implication was clear: Sue Snow's killer might have been at the service.

When the agent showed up later, however, he didn't mention the list.

"You know," he told Paul Webking as he took a seat in the living room, "we can stop bothering you. I know you're innocent. We *all* know you're innocent. We could really put it to bed if you took a polygraph."

Paul's face grew red and the veins in his neck strained at the surface of his skin. Sarah had seen the look before, as had Hayley. Usually he directed it at some kind of incompetence that frustrated him to the point of an eruption. Be it a clerk at a fast-food place, the school board, or anyone else. *Look out!*

But this was an FBI agent investigating his wife's murder. Paul Webking was about to earn his reputation.

"You're telling me all this bullshit, then you talk about something else? I've never refused to talk to you people yet. You're beginning to piss me off. So if you continue to come back like this I am not going to talk with you anymore, I'll talk to somebody else."

Randy Scott tried to defuse the anger.

"I know you're not guilty, but if you take a lie-detector test it will free us up to pursue others. I just want you to know that in another case there is a person who refused to take a lie-detector test and we still suspect him as the person who did it."

"Why did you have to come out here under the subterfuge of wanting to look at the funeral list? I've been racking my brain thinking about the people who were at the funeral. Here I am trying to help you, and you're trying to bullshit me."

With or without a polygraph, some at the FBI office weren't convinced of Webking's guilt. One of the doubtful was Special Agent Ron Nichols.

A mechanical engineer in his forties, Nichols was a by-the-book Annapolis man; he was a "tech" and computer expert who enjoyed the challenge of the paper chase. He could organize information in a system that worked, not only for himself, but for others. No small achievement.

As the end of June approached, SSA Mike Byrne assigned Nichols the task of taking all case 302s—or interview reports, teletypes, and memoranda—and organizing them in a way to ensure every detail had been covered, nothing missed. Byrne knew Nichols was the right one for the job—they had worked on dozens of other cases, including "Norjack," or the D.B. Cooper case. Nichols was the case agent in charge of the still-open skyjacking case.

For the Snow-Nickell murders it was time to regroup.

Paul Webking might be a dead point; at least SA Nichols thought so. There was talk and worry on the seventh floor of the Federal Building that the FBI was going to be left with yet another unsolved product tampering. Neither Byrne, Cusack, Nichols, nor any of the other scores of agents on the case could live with that.

Ron Nichols gathered the cache of five-hundred-plus Seamurs documents and retreated to his desk.

CHAPTER 16

When it came to the polygraph, Jack Cusack knew firsthand how it felt to be in "that little room with all the guns of accusation pointing at you." When a student at Loyola, he had been accused by a student residence manager of tossing a box of ignited cherry bombs from a window, startling a driver and causing a crash and injury. The residence manager thought the school might get sued, and in order to deflect some of the possible liability, pointed the finger at Jack Cusack. Jack said he was innocent.

Yeah, right.

No one believed him, and the situation grew uglier and more desperate when the residence manager pushed for expulsion. The young man requested a polygraph to prove his case, and he passed.

Few FBI polygraphers have such intimate experience with the machine they use so routinely on others. Sure, they know subjects—innocent or guilty—are nervous. But to actually sit in the chair for more than an FBI training exercise is another story. Jack Cusack saved the dean's letter of apology for the next twenty years. It was at Loyola that Jack Cusack became a believer, and in 1978 he joined the elite squad of special agents in the FBI polygraph unit.

SSA Mike Byrne told Jack Cusack it was time for him to start eliminating some of the people in Sue Snow's inner circle as possible suspects. At the top of the list was Paul Webking.

Jack Cusack regarded the preparation and the strategy of the interview as critical, and he spent his time accordingly. He wanted to know Paul Webking inside out before he took his place in the black chair. He wanted to walk in Webking's footsteps, see how he lived, where he went, what others thought of him.

One of Paul Webking's ex-wives told the FBI that her former husband was innocent.

"He doesn't kill his wives, he just divorces them," she said.

After SA Randy Scott had ticked off Webking with his maneuvering to get the polygraph, Jack Cusack stepped in to fix things up. SA Cusack made Paul Webking his business. He talked with everyone from the Medical Examiner's office, doctors at Harborview, agents who had interviewed other family members. There were plenty of people, like Sarah Webb, who were sure that Webking was the killer.

Though Webking looked promising, Cusack had long since learned it was a mistake to allow one statement to sway an investigation. He knew that trap can lead to the wrong conclusion. Only one statement is worth hanging everything on: "I did it."

Paul Webking insisted he *didn't* do it.

SA Cusack drove down to 1404 N Street N.E. in Auburn wondering if Webking was going to be openly hostile. After all, he had made it clear for days that he was tired of the FBI "fucking with" him and should get on with the case and find his wife's killer. From the foyer inside, Jack Cusack saw Sarah move from the kitchen to the dining room. He knew Sue had an identical twin, but he hadn't counted on seeing her. The image was startling.

Paul Webking employed an unusual directness in everything he said. He was blunt. His eyes didn't dart. And his answers were always given with a somewhat reserved hesitation. Some might have found it to be the way of a man who just carefully thinks out what he is going to say; others found his style of delivery suggestive of a man giving calculated responses.

The FBI agent did his best to smooth out any ruffled feathers Randy Scott might have left behind. Cusack told Webking he would be handling him from now on; he would be the one to administer the polygraph.

"We'd like you to come downtown for a polygraph, so we can eliminate you as a suspect."

"I'll think about it," he said.

SA Cusack thanked him and left, feeling fairly certain Webking would come around.

"From that first meeting, I couldn't say he was or wasn't the guy," Cusack later recalled.

A short time later, Paul Webking called and said he'd do the polygraph.

Paul Webking was in true form when he showed up at FBI head-quarters. Though he was there voluntarily, he was still mad at Randy Scott.

"Randy Scott is a weasel, and I really don't want to deal with him," he said.

"You won't have to," Jack Cusack promised.

As they talked, SA Cusack told Paul Webking about the poly-graph, and how by taking the test, he'd be "able to put all of this behind you."

They talked for an hour or so. It is the subject's chance to ex-plain why he's there, or how it is that he fits into the chronology of what happened. Sometimes all the suspects want to talk about is how useless, how *inadmissible* a polygraph is anyway.

Throughout a pretest interview, SA Cusack always simply ob-served. Did the subject try to steer him away from critical areas? Was he omitting facts from his statement? Was he being evasive?

Paul Webking was not trying any evasive tactics.

Just before sitting the man down in the chair and attaching the components, a telephone call about the case came in and Jack Cu-sack left the room to take it. He took his coffee with him. When he returned, he noticed that Paul Webking hadn't touched his Sty-rofoam cup at all.

"Paul, something wrong with your coffee?"

"My stomach can't take it today."

He reached over and took Paul's cup and started to drink.

"You're a lot more trusting than I would be in your position," Paul Webking said with a smile.

Components attached to Webking's fingertips, tubes around his chest, and a blood pressure cuff on, SA Cusack went on with the polygraph. Paul sat stiffly in the chair.

"Did you cause the death of your wife on June 11, 1986?"

"No."

"Did you put any cyanide in any Extra Strength Excedrin cap-sules?"

"No."

Several questions later, and after some analysis—not much was needed—SA Cusack could see what the results indicated.

"Paul, it is my conclusion after this examination that you're not involved in the cyanide product tampering in any way."

Paul looked satisfied and relieved. After they talked a bit more, he rose to leave.

"I only have one thing to say about this case," he said.

"What's that?"

"You guys will never solve this case."

Fleetingly, SA Cusack wondered what he could have missed during the polygraph.

"Why?"

"I'm just telling you . . ." His voice trailed off. "You guys just won't catch the guy who killed Sue."

When her brother-in-law returned to Auburn and announced he had "passed" the polygraph, Sarah Webb embraced him as though she was glad for him, sorry for what he had been through. Inside, however, she still had her doubts.

"I thought he was so manipulative that he could lie during a polygraph," she later said.

When Auburn detective Mike Dunbar heard Jack Cusack's news, he couldn't believe it.

"There's got to be something wrong," he told colleagues at the department. While he had no doubts about Jack Cusack's ability as a polygrapher, he was convinced Paul Webking had been his wife's killer.

The morning after Webking's polygraph a familiar face stared out at Jack Cusack through the glass of a *Seattle Times* vending rack.

DISMAYED AT QUESTIONING: SPOUSE OF CYANIDE-PILL VICTIM FELT LIKE TARGET IN POLICE PROBE

The special agent had thought Paul Webking was squared away when he left. Even a polygrapher from Peoria can't figure everybody out.

But in reality, Paul Webking had no problems with Jack Cusack. "He treated me like somebody he was curious about, not nosy,

just curious. Just wanting to know the truth. There was something
about Cusack that was likable. There was something about me that
he liked. He accepted my anger more, my directness, whereas most
people are offended by it."

CHAPTER 17

The chemical analysis to establish exactly the source of the poison was a major disappointment for the Seamurs team. Following the cyanide from its source to its distributor ultimately could lead to the tamperer. Though only three manufacturing sources of potassium cyanide were available to the American consumer—Du Pont, DeGasa, and ITI—sodium from the irksome green specks made it impossible to "fingerprint" the manufacturer. Sodium found in potassium cyanide was the trace element FBI chemist SA Roger Martz used to determine the poison's source of manufacture.

The FBI was out of luck. Chemists could not even determine if all the capsules had been tainted by the same batch of cyanide.

Nevertheless, special agents armed with photos and questions visited northwest chemical-supply outlets, both small and major. Profiling done by the FBI suggested the tamperer was probably from the area, and a local source for the poison would seem likely.

Emerald City Chemical, a distributor on Seattle's Capitol Hill, was unique in that it sold to customers, not only chemical companies. Since there were no restrictions, no procedures, it was possible the tamperer acquired it there. And cyanide was cheap. Eleven dollars and a purchaser could walk away with a pound of it to use in electroplating jewelry, photography processing, killing yard pests or people.

Among other things, Paul Lindgren handled front-counter sales

at Emerald City. When federal agents showed up requesting samples, it was the boyish-faced young man's job to put them together.

Agents showed a photo lineup, but the chemical salesman
couldn't identify anyone, at least not conclusively.

Years later, Paul Lindgren summoned a vague recollection of a
woman asking for cyanide, possibly to exterminate garden moles.

"I remember a woman . . . I can't remember much about her,
other than that she looked and acted kind of weird. I remember she
had a lot of rings on her fingers. At least three or four fingers,
multiple rings.

"And as I recall, there might have been other attempts of people
trying to buy cyanide at the same time. I almost wonder if someone
tried to solicit somebody else to buy it. I seem to recall shutting
down some people around the same time."

More than ever it looked as if Paul Webking was going to be
right after all. The death of his wife would be another in the string
of unsolved tampering murders. No one at the Seattle office would
say it, but many thought so, too.

If FBI chemist Roger Martz had done anything for the case at all,
and he most certainly had, it was his analysis of the green specks.
Chemical analysis determined they were made up of monuron, cemazin, and atrozin. All three were algicides—chemicals used to kill
algae.

Sodium chloride was merely yellow and blue dye used to make
up the green color.

After a battery of tests, Martz determined that the green specks
were an aquarium product called Algae Destroyer. No other such
product used by tropical fish fanciers held the exact same chemical
makeup.

The word was passed on to the Seattle Field Office.

"You know," a special agent offered when he heard the news,
"out at the interview at Mrs. Nickell's, I noticed she had a couple
of fish tanks."

SA Cusack's polygraph of Paul Webking had essentially cleared
Sue Snow's husband and sent investigators digging deeper into the
other likely suspect—Stella Maudine Nickell.

SA Nichols was the first to be convinced that the Auburn
woman's story needed further scrutiny. He flat out said she was
guilty. But the agents who went out to Nickell's place for the in-

terview said she seemed believable. She had nothing to hide. If she
was confused about things, it was understandable and hardly a reason to suspect her of the crime.

"Why would a woman who killed her husband come forward if
she was home free?" one asked. "She had the goddamn death certificate stating natural causes *before* Snow's death."

Among the materials piled on Ron Nichols's desk, he found a
newspaper clipping that started him thinking. It stated that Stella
had purchased the two tainted bottles at different stores and at different times.

He grabbed a pen and wrote *What?* in the margin.

"I won't buy that," he later said to Mike Byrne and Jack Cusack.
"How can that be?"

It was true, it didn't make sense. But the information was also
reflected in Ike Nakamoto's report.

"If Stella is to be believed, she purchased the only two forty-
count boxes of poisoned capsules. No one could be that unlucky,"
Nichols said.

The only possibility to explain it away was if SA Nakamoto had
gotten it wrong or, worse, unwittingly prompted Stella Nickell with
store names. That, too, was taken into account.

SA Cusack met with King County officer Ed Sexton at the precinct in Maple Valley to learn if the officer had detected any hesitation when Stella Nickell told him where she had purchased the
capsules.

"She struck me as a woman who knows where she buys," he
said.

There were other things about Stella that worried the investigators.

As the agents understood it, Stella Nickell would inherit about
$135,000 from her husband's death if deemed accidental, only
$5,000 if he died of natural causes.

Investigators thought it odd that if Bruce Nickell had been taking
handfuls of capsules for severe ongoing headaches, his wife would
purchase the smallest, forty-count size.

Stella Nickell said she purchased the forty-count size because it
did not have the plastic wrapping that her husband found bother-
some.

But it also could have been for another reason. A tamperer might
consider the forty-count's plastic wrap hard to reseal. The sixty-

count size did not have a wrapper, so it would be easier for a cunning job of tampering.

Sue Snow's bottle was a sixty, as was the one under the sink in the Nickell bathroom. Was the one under the sink an extra no longer needed by the tamperer?

SAs Cusack and Nichols also discussed the possibility that Stella Nickell kept the poisoned open bottle and wanted an unopened box to show police officers.

"Maybe she was afraid that when the police came out to see and she showed them the nearly empty bottle, they'd say, 'You put those pills in that bottle!'

"If she had another bottle, she could say, 'No, I didn't. In fact, I have another bottle here in the house.' "

"She kept the second to cover any suspicion on the first?"

"What the hell? It could be."

FBI agents speculated that Stella Nickell called 911 for two reasons when she heard of Sue Snow's death. One, she knew there were three more boxes and others could die, and two, she possibly would get more money if her husband died an accidental death.

Could it have been that after Stella Nickell identified all three stores in which she placed poisoned capsules, she returned to Pay 'N Save and moved the Anacin-3 to the peanut aisle so someone would find it?

If it had been there from the beginning, Jack Cusack figured it would have been discovered sooner. It had the wrong price tags. It was in the wrong place.

Maybe Stella Nickell—if she was the killer—had felt guilty and moved the bottle because she didn't want someone else to die?

No one was looking for Anacin, only Excedrin.

The FBI report from the Nickell search indicated that the agents had found a bottle of Maximum Strength Anacin capsules in the kitchen but didn't seize them.

In another conflict with the widow's story, A. J. Rider told the FBI, "No one but Bruce took any Excedrin caps." Stella Nickell had claimed to have taken at least five from the bottle that killed her husband.

None of the people close to the Nickells could confirm that Stella routinely trimmed the bottle tops to make it easier for her husband to open them. In fact, some suggested that Stella Nickell gave medications to her husband.

"Maybe she altered the cap on the opened bottle to remind herself not to take those particular capsules?" an agent suggested.

It was more of a question than a theory. It joined dozens of others, all in need of an answer.

Had Stella Nickell ever used Algae Destroyer? Did she have access to cyanide? Could store inventory records prove she bought two bottles of forty-count Excedrin on two different days at Johnny's?

Finally, SAs Nichols and Cusack knew getting personal with the suspect might answer the most critical question of the case: Why? The logical place to start was a review of her marital life. Such investigations are conducted carefully—friends might tip her off.

"Is she an alcoholic, too?"

"Does she gamble or have debts?"

"Does she have a boyfriend?"

"Could Bruce have started drinking again?"

PART TWO

Stella Maudine

CHAPTER 18

On June 5, 1986, Stella Maudine Nickell was on overdrive without any fuel. She and her mother sat in a waiting area at Harborview Medical Center. Both seemed anxious, ready to kill for a smoke. Stella Nickell resembled a kind of Annie Oakley, rough and tumble in westernwear, yet somehow little-girlish at the same time. Cora Lee Rice, her Indian braids streaked with gray, sat stonily with her daughter, the very picture of the tough bird her family always said she was. Her last name was the only thing she had from her fourth and final marriage to a Las Vegas man named Hank Rice.

"You got that right, lady," was one of her favorite catchalls.

While her husband Bruce lay unconscious, Stella excused herself to make a phone call and sneak a cigarette. Cowboy boots clacked on the scuffed linoleum floor as she strode away.

Glen and Kathy Strand, friends of the Nickells from a CB radio club, were shocked when Stella called from the hospital.

"It's about Bruce," Stella said softly. "He passed out at the house. It might be food poisoning."

Before hanging up, Kathy Strand told Stella Nickell to call back with any news. Neither of the Strands got the impression Bruce Nickell was seriously ill. Stella said that it might be food poisoning; at least she thought so.

More than an hour later, the Strands' phone rang again with another call from Stella Nickell.

"Now we don't know what it is," she said.

At 8:45 P.M., Bruce Edward Nickell was pronounced dead, and without hesitation, his wife released his body to hospital pathology for an autopsy.

The two women returned to Stella's pickup, its plates reading TP 4 2, for the drive home to Auburn. The next morning there would be places to go, people to see. First on her list were Bruce's adoptive parents, Walter and Ruth, over in Wenatchee.

Bruce's cousin and his wife, Dick and Patty Nickell, built their Wenatchee home out in the country, before the town crept up to it. When they had built years before, the place seemed way out of town. But the Valley Mall went in, and the country life went out. Dick, now retired, had served twenty years as Chelan County Sheriff. If Bruce's life had wavered over the line of stability, his cousin's had been the opposite. Dick Nickell and his redheaded wife were as solid as the mountain range that splits Washington in two.

The light of day had barely nudged at the window shades when Dick Nickell was forced to drag himself to the front door to answer a knock. It was before 7 A.M. On the doorstep was Bruce's wife, looking tired—maybe even in shock. Her eyes were red and her dark hair hung lank.

"I've been waiting for you to get up. I've been here for about an hour," Stella said. "I've got some bad news about Bruce. He died."

She slumped to the davenport. Patty emerged from the bathroom in time to hear Stella begin to cry.

"The doctors don't know what the cause is yet. I ordered an autopsy."

Weeping, Stella asked Dick if he would help her break the news to Walter and Ruth. She said she was worried how they'd take it at their age.

Dick agreed and hurried on ahead.

Next, Stella phoned her husband's boss, Dick Johnson, at the Dept. of Transportation office in Seattle.

"Bruce won't be in today. He died."

The man offered condolences and asked as many questions as he could to show concern and to satisfy curiosity. When he hung up, he was still struck by the way the wife led off her conversation. *"He won't be in today. He died."*

The words and delivery were peculiar. It was not unlike calling in sick for someone. But this was a wife calling to say her husband wouldn't be in because he was dead.

Why didn't she have someone else call in for her? he wondered.

Patty Nickell finished dressing and rode with Stella in her truck to the elderly couple's apartment, only a few miles away. Bruce's parents were in their nineties and would surely be shocked by the news of their only child's sudden death.

Walter Nickell's eyes were bad. But surgery had repaired his eyesight enough so that after hearing the news he went into a back bedroom to study photographs of his only son. . . . The memories and disappointment came back. So did the tears.

After fourteen years of trying to conceive, Walter and Ruth Nickell, an apple farmer from Winthrop, Washington, and his second-grade-schoolteacher wife, adopted a boy from a Seattle maternity home. They named the week-old baby Bruce Edward, and brought him home in June 1934.

Many years later, Walter Nickell remembered his wife's joy.

"She was real happy with him. He was a beautiful baby. Actually, I think he was the prettiest baby I ever did see."

Since the new baby was allergic to cow's milk, Walter happily took up the chore of milking a goat every day. He and his wife never wanted anything so much as that little baby. They tried to give the boy everything they could.

Bruce grew up on a twenty-acre Red and Golden Delicious Apple orchard in arguably one of the prettiest spots in a state known for its unsurpassed rugged, natural beauty. Young Bruce had a collie, a horse, and a cow.

Though he had the kind of childhood Norman Rockwell portrayed on canvas, Bruce started drinking at fifteen.

"I never accused him of it, but he knew how I felt about drinkin'. It was something I didn't do. I never have. Don't say I'm a teetotaler, but drinkin' is something I didn't do," Walter said.

Alcohol seemed to be the cause of nearly every misstep their son made in life. Before he met Stella, he had married Ruby, Linda, Mary, and Phyllis. None had worked out. He had two sons by his previous wives, but became completely estranged from both boys. He did a stint in the Marines, but was discharged without honor after going AWOL.

Walter and Ruth never talked to Bruce about his drinking. They didn't figure it would do any good.

*   *   *

On June 6, 1986, at SeaTac International Airport where Stella Nickell and her daughter Cindy Hamilton worked security, A. J. Rider learned Stella had called in the night before to say she wouldn't be in that morning to open the concourse gate.

A. J. told an employee she had been over to the Nickell place the day before to pick up her daughter, whom Stella and her mother Cora Lee had baby-sat.

"Something must have come up," A. J. offered, "because she didn't say anything to me."

When Cindy Hamilton didn't show up that morning either, another employee asked A. J. if the mother's and daughter's absences were connected.

A. J. only shrugged.

Finally, midmorning on the sixth, Stella phoned A. J. on the concourse. She was in Wenatchee.

"Is something wrong with Bruce's mom or dad?" A. J. asked.

"That's where I'm at right now. I'll tell you later, but something *is* wrong. I'll be home later on, and we'll talk then out at the house."

Cindy called A. J. moments after she had finished her call with Stella.

"Has Mom called you at all?" she asked.

"Yeah, she said she'd be back tonight."

"Did she tell you anything?"

A. J. said Stella really hadn't said anything specific. "Something is wrong, and she said she'd tell me when she got back."

The next call, the third in a bizarre, rapid-fire row, sent A. J. Rider into an airport rest room to get a grip on herself.

Her foster son had been out to the Nickells' place to feed some rabbits when Cora Lee saw him and shared some bad news.

"Are you sitting down?" the young man asked. "Grandma came over the hill and called to me that Bruce is dead."

Bruce, dead? A. J. wondered what in hell was going on. Why had Stella been so cryptic in her phone call? They were better friends than that.

Late the afternoon of June 6, after returning from Wenatchee, Stella Nickell arrived in Sumner, at Glen and Kathy Strand's mobile home—the same mobile home for which Bruce Nickell had helped lay pipe. Friends Shirley and Don Webbly were also there. Even before the words came, it was clear something was terribly wrong. Stella's green eyes again were rimmed in red.

It was as though Stella Nickell's legs could barely support her.

Fighting back the tears, she put her arms around Glen Strand's shoulders.

"He's dead. He's gone. The doctors don't know what he died from."

What could the Strands say? When Stella had called the evening before, she had told them Bruce was the victim of food poisoning. To die so suddenly, a man so close to their own age, was a shock beyond belief.

"Stella said he came home from work, had a headache, and she was preparing dinner. She said, 'Bruce took a couple of Excedrin, walked out . . .' She called someone right away, but they lived quite a ways out. Then they called a helicopter," Shirley recalled later.

"I didn't want you to read it in the papers or hear it on the radio. I wanted you to hear it from me," Stella said, hugging her friend.

Then she climbed into her truck and left. She had more people to tell.

CHAPTER 19

Like a noose-knotted necklace, some have suggested the ties that bind choke. It was that way from the very beginning with the Stephenson clan.

Before she was known as Cora Lee, the Stephenson matriarch was called Alva Georgia or "Jo" Duncan. Jo and her husband George Stephenson had a son and three daughters before Stella Maudine was born in Colton, Oregon, in the summer of 1943. She was a beautiful baby with dark hair that curled in ringlets like rain-soaked poodle's fur. Stella looked like her father, a tall, swarthy-complected lumberman with more dark curls than any man had a right to. He had the big, dirty hands of a main sawyer who made his living off timbers felled in the forests of the Pacific Northwest.

Texas-born Jo Duncan was not a beauty, not even close, but nevertheless she was a striking woman with a strong jawline. She told her children she had some Cherokee and Apache blood, and the braids she wore in her hair backed up her contention—at least her children thought so.

Jo was every bit as tough as her husband, and when need be, showed it.

George Stephenson knew little other than how to work the saw-mill and drink until he dropped. Jo chased after him as he chased the bottle. Sometimes she brought the children along, leaving them in the pickup while she went after her obstinate and wayward man.

Eldest daughter Georgia Mae would never forget the routine that often left her in charge.

". . . My dad would come home from work and he'd want to go, and my mom would want to go with him. I took care of the kids and done the chores," she later said.

The Stephenson home was neither the best nor the worst of the places Stella Maudine would call home. They did not have hot and cold running water—fifty-five-gallon oak barrels and a stove did the job. Even so, Jo Stephenson cooked not only for her family but for a mill crew of seven.

Around the time of Stella Maudine's birth, Jo's sister, Hazel, asked to adopt the baby, sight unseen. She and her husband couldn't have children of their own, and her sister's baby would be, at least partially, of the same blood.

"You already have so many children anyway," Hazel pleaded.

"I don't have children just to give them away," Jo fired back. Anyone who knew her, believed it. Her kids were *hers*. Not hers and her husband's. Hers alone.

She had lost one baby—Frankie Gene at eight months—the same year Stella Maudine was born.

Jo was cooking for the mill crew when the baby boy fell from his high chair and landed on his head. The next morning he was found dead in his crib, blood around his mouth. The doctor said the baby died of pneumonia, but Jo and George Stephenson knew it had been the fall that killed Frankie Gene. Jo was devastated, but as she always could, she pulled herself together.

By the time Stella Maudine was born, the household had fallen into a vicious pattern of abuse and neglect, and possibly molestation. Georgia Mae later claimed her father sexually abused her from age six to nine. She never told anyone about it. No other children ever made similar claims, at least not publicly.

The last fight between their mother and father any of the Stephenson children remember resulted in the kind of shock and fear they had grown used to.

"Dad got drunk, been out playing poker with the guys, and he came home and had a big fight with mother. He grabbed a shotgun and mother told us kids to run, and we ran to the neighbors. Mother took off out of the house and Dad shot a couple of shots at us with the shotgun. That was the final blow," Berta, the sister closest to Stella's age, later remembered.

Georgia Mae remembered her final look at her father.

"They drained the millpond. And the last time I seen my dad he was laying facedown in the puddle where they drained the millpond," she recalled. He was drunk, but very much alive.

Stella Maudine would have no memories of her father, only what Jo Stephenson thought was important enough to pass on.

When it was time to leave Oregon, George, Jo, and her children caught a servicemen's boxcar for Leadville, Colorado. World War II was just ending.

Jo told her children she took them to Colorado to keep them away from their father. He threatened to take the kids and run. Jo didn't doubt it, though if she had thought about it, she'd have realized there was no way any of those kids would stay with their father.

So she scattered her brood among her sisters—Hazel, Lucille, and Dorothy—and her parents, and returned to Oregon to divorce George.

For Stella's sister Berta, Colorado was a nightmare. The young girl couldn't convince Aunt Dorothy that she appreciated her home cooking. When her aunt became angry, she booted Berta outside to eat on the porch with the dogs. She was allowed no silverware.

When she felt it was safe to do so, Jo Stephenson and her children returned to Oregon and moved into a tent house just below a sawmill. Jo hired on as a mill worker, the only woman among them. She told her kids she could do the job as well as a man.

In 1948, while mother and son were gathering wood for the mill, the girls were left to build a fire. Mary Belle, the second-oldest girl, was unaware that the jug that held the kerosene for the lanterns and a coffee can holding coal oil had been switched.

"Mary poured what she thought was the coal oil but happened to be the kerosene in a small can and carried it to the stove to start the fire for dinner. And when she did, it exploded. And it was a large *whoosh*. And she carried the can back out of the house and threw it on the porch. As she threw the can down I had just come up one side and run across the porch. And it splattered all over my pant leg, just like liquid fire," Stella Maudine later recalled.

Jo heard her daughters' screams from up at the sawmill, and she and Georgia Mae tackled little Stella as she ran in terror, the left leg of her jeans ablaze.

Stella Maudine Stephenson was admitted to a Portland hospital, where she received skin grafts over a two-month period.

Her stubborn nature was evident even then.

A nurse sat the burned five-year-old, whose leg was in a cast, in a chair in her room so she could make up the bed. When she finished, she told Stella to get back in bed.

"I'm waiting for you to come and get me."

"You can do it. It's time to get back on your feet," the nurse told her.

"*I can't.*"

"Yes, you can."

Years later, Stella didn't know how she got from the chair to the bed, but she did. Even at five, she wasn't about to have that nurse tell her what to do.

By 1949, Jo Stephenson had found what she thought was her saving grace. She answered an ad for an assistant to a logging truck driver placed by a Molino, Oregon, man named Colver "Dewey" Kelly. She was hired, and a short time later married her boss. He was not the answer to her prayers. Jo Kelly ended up with a repeat of her marriage to George Stephenson—abuse and drunken rages.

Dewey's sister, Dorothy Hawes, later remembered the relationship.

"They liked a good time—drinking. Both of them. They liked to dance and party, let's put it that way. He was a hard worker. He loved Harley motorcycles; I'd say he was a little on the wild side. They both liked the motorcycles . . .

"I just could never understand Jo, just between you and me. She was a hard woman. She had nerves of steel. She didn't let anything bother her."

Jo and Dewey—when he was sober enough—worked the pea harvest, cutting and driving trucks in Eastern Washington from Walla Walla to Wapato. Jo was every bit as good a driver as the other men—in fact, so good that few even knew she was a woman. She wore men's clothing and kept her hair hidden in a dirty old bandanna. Tucked over her truck's sun visor, she kept a Coke bottle handy to wallop any man who made an inappropriate advance toward the only woman running a pea truck. And she used it only once, she told her daughters.

Following promises of work, the family moved to the Anacortes and La Conner area on Puget Sound, north of Seattle. While Jo and Dewey looked for work, the children moved in with Dewey's sister, Dorothy, at her place near Anacortes. Dorothy Hawes would never forget the children, especially Stella, whom she considered especially sweet and adorable. The girls sometimes came into her kitchen to ask for food. Dorothy always had something for them.

On New Year's Day, 1952, Little Joe Kelly was born. By then, the family of eight lived in a two-room house below a rendering plant near La Conner, Washington. The children slept in the bedroom, and Dewey and Jo slept in a double bed adjacent to the kitchen stove.

The eldest, Georgia Mae, was long gone by then, having left home at fourteen, but the school-aged Stephenson kids—son James, daughters Mary Belle, Berta Ann, and Stella Maudine—settled in at Fidalgo Island School. Friends teased them about living so close to the foul-smelling plant that turned dead animals into dog food and soap.

It wasn't so bad, Berta would tell them.

"When the wind blows, it blows right over us!"

Berta and Stella, being the nearest in age, were the closest of the sisters. Both enjoyed school, though Stella Maudine was a far better student. Their real love, however, was the wildlife that lived in the forests and on the shore around them.

One time while the girls were hanging out wash, they found an injured great blue heron. When it was apparent the bird wouldn't be able to survive with a mangled wing, Stella held the bird down on the chicken chopping block while her sister severed the broken limb. The next morning the girls got up to find that the bird had died.

In the battles between Jo and Dewey Kelly, the smart money would likely have been on the lady, though her children probably saw it as an even match. She didn't drink to excess, and she could swing a fist when called for. Dewey had a mean streak, and whenever it struck him, he'd show it by beating his wife.

Stella recalled one fight.

"I remember the side of the refrigerator was bloodied where he hit her in the mouth. He broke her front teeth; she had on dentures, and they went through her lower lip. And she leaned up against the refrigerator and just laid her head on her arm for a minute and the blood just drained down the side of the refrigerator. And when she come away from the refrigerator, she laid into him."

Dewey Kelly didn't stick around Anacortes. He told Jo he was going off to make some real money in Alaska. Later, Stella and her sisters heard Kelly got an Eskimo pregnant and was forced into staying up there. But none of that mattered. By the time Jo divorced him, the family was scarcely getting by on welfare and living in a little place on 16th and B streets in Anacortes.

Spring along Puget Sound takes its time. Often, mornings stay cool right through July, with the hottest weather coming in August or September. It was cool enough the morning of June 18, 1953, that lighting the kitchen stove was needed to warm the Kelly home in Anacortes.

It was a good morning for berry picking, which was reason enough for Jo and her daughter Georgia Mae, visiting from her home in Bremerton with her five-month old baby Wilma Mae. The two women left for the fields, leaving behind oldest son James, Mary, Stella, Little Joe, and Wilma.

Stella and Berta attempted to build a fire in the kitchen stove, while James, Mary, and baby Wilma went about the morning in the other room. Little Joe was having breakfast in his high chair when the girls discovered they were out of what their mother called "presto log oil"—the fuel she used to start the stove.

Stella remembered seeing a three-pound coffee can out on the closed-in porch off the kitchen. She had opened it earlier, and thought it contained fuel for the wood stove.

It didn't.

It was one of those things witnesses like to say "all happened so fast," as if there is a different measurement of time for tragedy. When the liquid ignited, it exploded. Berta pushed her screaming sister out of the way.

Then the girls heard baby Little Joe cry.

"She followed me through the flames," Stella said of her sister Berta years later. "And then we tried to get back in the kitchen to get Little Joe, and even James couldn't get in. And he went out our bedroom window and went around and got the garden hose and was putting the fire out before he could get Little Joe out of the house. And Bert and I went out the window. I didn't have to, but as we went through the living room, we headed to the bedroom to go out the window, I stopped, went back, and got Wilma because James had laid her down on the couch. And we took her outside through the window. I had her outside and she was safe."

Family legend later had it that Lady Luanna, the family's collie, found Wilma Mae outside by the corner of the house and dragged the baby to a neighbor's for safety by pulling the pillow or blanket she lay on.

By the time an aid car came, it was too late for Little Joe. Berta was burned badly, and Stella also suffered burns. Both were admitted to Island Hospital, where Berta would stay for several weeks, Stella much less.

As she had at the first fire, Stella later recalled an incident with one of the nurses.

"And when they started to bandage me, I can remember the dispute the nurse and I had. She was going to cover my nose, and I told her I couldn't breathe. She said, 'Yes you can.' She was rubbing me with the gauze bandages soaked in Vaseline—or whatever they soaked them in—and she got to my face and she was gonna rub it across my nose. And I know, of course at that particular time I didn't reason it out, but when I think about it in later years, I know to this day that woman snuck some ether in on me to knock me out so she could get my face bandaged. Because the last thing I remember was fighting with her about my nose, and when I woke up I was in bed. I do not remember in between. And I know she snuck some ether on me somewhere."

The Anacortes *American* played the story in a banner headline:

BURNS FATAL TO LOCAL CHILD
TWO SISTERS INJURED IN MID-MORNING FIRE

While the girls recovered in the hospital, their mother was left to deal with a dead baby.

"They wrapped Little Joe up in newspapers, and Mother had to drive home with that little baby in the backseat. I know I would have lost it, but Mother didn't," Berta recalled some years later.

The Anacortes fire was one of those tragic lifetime events that either pulls people together or hopelessly divides them. Berta blamed herself. She was thirteen; she felt she should have known better.

"When I ran through that fire from the kitchen to the living room, I could have grabbed that baby. I could have dragged the high chair, but Stella was out of my sight, and that's who I was after," she said.

There was no funeral for Little Joe. He was burned beyond recognition. To outsiders, even those who were part of the family, it seemed as though the mother who lost her baby took it all in stride.

Dorothy Hawes, for one, later remarked that she never saw tears.

*   *   *

By 1955, it was clear Jo Kelly was going nowhere fast in Anacortes. She had moved the kids twice since the fire, first to a little place on Sunset Beach, and after that to a house near Dean's Corner. She finally figured the small town held few opportunities for a single mother. The winter months, when field work was not available, were especially hard. When son James enlisted in the service, she knew it wasn't going to get easier.

She packed up her three girls and moved into the North Star Motel on Seattle's Aurora Avenue N. The room had a kitchenette, making it seem more like an apartment than its name implied. Jo found a job waiting tables; she told the girls the tips weren't half bad.

CHAPTER 20

Early on the afternoon of Friday, June 6, 1986, Bonnie Anderson planted herself in a kitchen chair at Cindy Hamilton and Dee Rogers's two-bedroom apartment on Smith Street in Kent. Cindy had promised Bonnie, a co-worker from the airport, a home perm, and this was the day. Though Bonnie's dark-brown hair was short on top, it was past her shoulders in length. It took Cindy nearly two and half hours to do the job, but Bonnie didn't mind. Cindy was abuzz with stories of her love life. She was more interesting than television.

After she finished Bonnie's hair, Cindy changed into a pair of black spandex pants, a khaki sweater, and pumps. She never went out without her pumps and spandex. She told Dee she and Bonnie were going down to Borders, on Central Avenue, for margaritas and tequila shooters. This was also the place where Cindy's boyfriend of the moment tended bar.

Barely into their drinks, Cindy got up from her bar stool to answer a call.

"Dee said my mom's coming over. We have to go home."

"Okay," Bonnie said. "What's going on?"

"Dee wouldn't say. All she said was, 'Your mom's coming over and she wants you here.' "

Cindy mused whether it was a family emergency or something of that nature.

"It's either my dad or his parents," she said.

Ten minutes after Cindy and Bonnie returned to the apartment, Stella arrived. She looked as if she hadn't slept all night. She was drawn and worn out.

Stella Nickell directed her words toward her daughter. "He's gone. Bruce is dead."

Cindy nearly collapsed. Dee looked equally overwhelmed. The three women took chairs at the dining table in the alcove off the kitchen. Dee poured some liqueurs. Feeling out of place, Bonnie retreated to the living-room couch, about fifteen feet from where the other women huddled in shock and grief. She could hear most of the conversation.

Stella said she had driven over to Wenatchee to tell Bruce's parents. She sent Bruce's cousin to break the news.

Bonnie thought she heard Stella say she hadn't gone in to tell the folks, she had waited in the car. If she had heard right, it was a strange remark.

Why go all the way over to Eastern Washington and not go inside to do what you came for?

She clearly couldn't hear everything being said, but a few phrases would register later.

"I know what you're thinking. The answer is no," Stella said, her eyes fixed at her daughter's.

Cindy didn't say a word; she couldn't. She seemed out-of-control, grief-stricken.

After about ten minutes, Bonnie, realizing she was an unnecessary interloper in a tragic family affair, hugged the tearful, hysterical Cindy Hamilton good-bye. She got in her Sunbird and drove home to Bellevue.

Stan Church, a crew-cut-topped machinist at Foss Shipyards in Seattle, had met Bruce Nickell over the CB radio three years before. He and his wife, Laurie, and their three daughters—Kimmie, Krystal, and Karan—lived on 12th and D in Auburn, not far from the White River Estates mobile-home park that had been the Nickell home before Bruce and Stella moved onto the acreage east of Auburn.

Stan Church, whose radio handle was a fitting "Preacher," worked swing shift. Shortly after Stan met Bruce, his family found the two friends monopolizing the airwaves starting as early as 5 A.M. on Saturday mornings.

"Whether I had a Coffee Royale or not, I'd start to slur my words and old Bruce would say, 'Stan's in his cups again. Better get him off the two-way before he says something he shouldn't.' "

Even though they'd all laugh, Stan Church never returned the barb. He knew of his friend's recovery from alcoholism, something Bruce made a point of in many things he said and did.

"He had one whole wall in his den full of booze bottles of all sizes where the seals had never been broken," Stan Church recalled.

"Why do you keep them?" Stan asked one day over at White River Estates.

"Just to remind me," Bruce answered.

Laurie Church was a solitary woman, and with three daughters and a husband as outgoing as Stan, it was easy for her to stay in the background. Although Stella was flashy, with her penchant for tight jeans and stylish western garb, and Laurie was a conservative homebody, the two women clicked. Soon, whenever Stan and Bruce got together, the ladies would get to talking over a card game, often playing solitaire in tandem.

When Cindy Hamilton and her boyfriend traipsed into Kimmie Church's wedding at Auburn's Presbyterian Church, on Saturday, June 7, they were alone.

"Where's Stel?" the mother of the bride asked.

Offering an ambiguous excuse, one that years later no one could readily recall, Cindy indicated Bruce and Stella had something else to do.

It was clear, however, something was off kilter. The Nickells were practically family. Kimmie wanted them to share her special day, as did the rest of the Churches. Neither Bruce nor Stella would rank something more important than the wedding.

All they got was Cindy and some guy. Even worse, Stella's daughter seemed drunk, though she admitted only to a hangover. It was embarrassing.

"She showed up at the wedding on a three-day drunk. She looked like hell and she reeked of alcohol," Laurie Church recalled later.

Laurie told the young woman to tell her mother and stepfather to join the family at their home on K Street S.W. after the reception.

She promised she would.

Later that night, after nearly all the wedding well-wishers had left, Stan and Laurie sat at the table in their breakfast room, when Stella Nickell finally came calling alone.

"Where's Bruce?" Laurie asked.

"That's what I have to tell you," Stella said, tears beginning to fall. "Bruce passed away."

Dizzy with shock, Laurie Church reached out to her friend.

"We held each other for a little while. We sat down, and I gave her a cup of coffee. Then she told me he had died two days before, but she wasn't going to tell me 'til after the wedding, and after Kim and Dan had gone on their honeymoon. She didn't want to ruin their day."

Stella downed a stiff drink and after a while hurriedly got up to leave.

"I've got to go. . . . I'll talk to you tomorrow."

Stan Church took his best friend's death especially hard. Racked with grief, he barely said a word for the next three days. It seemed inconceivable that his friend was gone so suddenly.

He had seen Bruce on his birthday, June 1. They had talked over coffee at the house, and he seemed perfectly healthy. He had straddled his motorcycle, waved, and gone home.

Karan Church called from her boyfriend's the next morning and her mother told her to get her tail home pronto. Stan Church was crying when Laurie told their daughter that Bruce had died on the fifth.

"How?"

Laurie said the doctors didn't know. "Maybe an aneurysm."

"Why didn't Cindy say anything?"

Laurie didn't know. She had assumed Stella had told Cindy to not say anything.

"But why would she bother to show up at the wedding? Wouldn't it have been better not to have shown up?"

Later, when Laurie asked Stella about it, her best friend seemed surprised. Stella said she didn't know Cindy had even gone to the wedding.

At some point during the weekend following her husband's death, Stella Nickell drove to Spokane, three hundred miles east of Auburn, to tell "adopted" son Jerry Kimble the bad news. The drive didn't really seem out of the ordinary to Jerry Kimble. He and the Nickells had remained extremely close since he joined the Air Force. In fact, when he got into trouble over some bad checks, it was Stella, not his own mother, who bailed him out.

When Stella told him Bruce had died suddenly at home, she did so without tears. Jerry Kimble could have predicted a lack of emotion. Stella had always been a good one to hide her feelings.

"She was handling the situation real well. She looked like she was in total control to me. She can fight it for herself," he said.

That night Stella camped along the Spokane River. The next day, she was on her way. She had more people to tell.

It was June 8, Sunday evening, when Stella Nickell returned from Eastern Washington and phoned neighbor Sandy Scott, who had known something was wrong when the Airlift Northwest helicopter and medic units came through the area.

"Did something happen to Cora Lee?" Sandy asked, fearing the worst for Stella's elderly mother.

"No. It's Bruce. He's dead."

The words dazed. Sandy never considered that Bruce Nickell had been the one who was taken away by helicopter.

"What happened?"

"We don't know; we're still in the process of trying to figure it out. The autopsy results haven't come back."

Stella repeated the story of Bruce's collapse and her frantic call to 911.

"Oh, good heavens, that's such a shock! I was just there the other night."

"Yes, I know, and he was just fine."

Sandy didn't dispute Stella's remark, but Bruce Nickell *hadn't* seemed fine to her. He didn't even look up at her when she came to pick up papers for the road committee. Though usually quite friendly, Bruce just sat there in a stupor. Maybe he was just engrossed in what he was watching on TV?

"When's the funeral?"

"We already had it," Stella said, finishing the conversation by asking a perplexed Sandy Scott to let the other neighbors know.

Already had it? That sure was fast.

Sue Ford could tell by her husband's consoling tone that something was wrong and that the woman on the other end of the line was in dire straits. When Jeff Ford hung up, he told his wife Bruce Nickell had suddenly passed away.

"Bruce had told her that if anything had ever happened to him, he wanted Jeff to have first choice of his tools."

Jeff had frequently borrowed the tools after they became friends while working together at McDonald Industries—Bruce had the

best Snap-on and Mac tools sold—that the offer made sense. Jeff
Ford knew he could use them in his Kent shop.

If selling off her husband's tools seemed sudden, it was because
Stella Nickell said she needed the money, "for attorney's fees."
Some of the tools were at work.

Jeff Ford recalled Stella's words: *"If we don't go up and get
them soon, they'll put a lock on them and we won't be able to get
them out."*

"So we acted on them pretty fast," he later said.

They finally agreed on a price of $7,000 for the whole shebang.
Stella probably could have gotten more, and she knew it. She said
the Snap-on man couldn't get to Auburn anytime soon, and she
didn't want to wait for him.

Having barely returned to Houston after a two-week dream vacation
to England, Stella Nickell's niece, Wilma Mae Stewart, now thirty-
four, hadn't even unpacked her new Royal Doulton tea set when
she was awakened by the telephone. It was around 4 A.M. on Sunday, June 8.

On the other line was a very depressed-sounding Aunt Stella.

"I need you. Your uncle Bruce is dead," she said.

In shock, Wilma pulled herself straight up in bed. Her deep
voice croaked with emotion. She asked when the funeral would be
held.

"Tuesday at eleven."

"I'll be there," Wilma promised.

CHAPTER 21

Stella Maudine Stephenson grew up fast. Georgia Mae, who had been away from home for years, once suggested that her baby sister was sexually active before she finished grammar school.

"I know it sounds cold," Georgia Mae later admitted. "Stella seemed to be mentally and physically five years beyond her normal years. Sometimes a girl grows up faster mentally and physically than her years say she is."

By the time Stella Maudine hit her teens, she could play the part. Her back might have been as straight as a yardstick, but her hips rotated like an LP. Well-developed for her age—one sister suggested the youngest Stephenson daughter had a bustline before she was twelve—Stella Maudine had lovely long legs. She never went through a gawky age.

Even Stella considered herself mature for her age.

"I could not stand to be around boys for very long at a time who were my same age. Or even one or two years older than I was. They were childish. And there was absolutely no way that I could even think of going out with one of them."

Missouri-born farm boy Ricky Slawson was one of the guys who liked what he saw when he first laid eyes on Stella Maudine Stephenson. He was staying with family in Seattle.

"She was a beautiful young girl. Had nice tits on her, nice body on her."

Though he was seventeen and she was only thirteen, he didn't pay that any mind. Stella was more a woman, he figured, than a girl.

"She was hotter than a firecracker, I'll tell you," he told his brother.

The two went roller skating around Seattle's Green Lake and hung around the Northgate area. For a time, Stella's mother seemed to like Ricky enough to lend him her 1950 Chevrolet so that he could take her daughter places.

After moving out of the North Star Motel, Jo and daughters Mary, Berta, and Stella lived in a house at 9025 Corliss in Seattle. Jo Kelly hooked up with a couple of men after Dewey, but none were marriage material. And though they sometimes lived with her, she never depended on them. She never asked for anything for herself or her daughters.

Georgia Mae, with her flaming red-rinsed hair, was the pretty one; Berta at six feet was the sensitive and gentle giant; and Mary, with love of caring for the kids and cooking, the little mother. Stella was the one with a wild streak running from head to toe.

One time when Berta wouldn't get off the telephone when Stella decided it was her turn, Stella grabbed her sister's arm and bit hard enough to draw blood.

"It was summer, but I put on a sweater to cover my arm," Berta recalled. "I didn't want her to get in trouble, but Mother heard about it and asked me to roll up my sleeve. I did—the other one."

"Okay, let's see the other one. What happened to you?"

"I'm not telling. If you want to know, ask Stella."

Jo Kelly never did find out what happened.

And though she was running around with boys, Stella dreamed of being a veterinarian, a nurse, or a model.

None of those dreams would come to pass. At fifteen Stella Maudine Stephenson, a student at Woodrow Wilson, found herself pregnant.

How it happened, and just exactly who was the father, would be the subject of much family discussion over the years.

Stella claimed she had been gang-raped.

She said it happened while she was visiting a boyfriend named Russell. His mother left the two alone to do some grocery shopping, and Russell got on the phone.

"He told me he had a friend that he'd like me to meet. So, fine, he wanted me to meet one of his friends. Well, when his friend came over, they proceeded to carry me upstairs. And Russell had tied my hands behind my back with his belt while the other kid held my feet and he raped me."

At least one sister believed the story, because a similar attack had happened to her. Berta and Mary were leaving a Seattle skating rink when two men jumped out of a car and went after the girls.

"Mary turned around and seen this. She said, 'Run!' When I turned around and seen them, I was grabbed. It was too late. They had used a knife and cut my throat and raped me."

Nine months later, Berta gave birth to her first daughter.

Stella Maudine was four months along when she determined she was pregnant, and like many young girls, tried to hide the pregnancy as long as she could. Finally she told her mother. Jo's solution was for her daughter to marry the baby's father.

"I won't marry him if he's the last man on earth," Stella told her.

"He has a right to know," her mother said.

Years later the memory would be so foggy, Stella couldn't recall if it was she or her mother who had broken the news. It would have been just like Jo to have done it. She didn't wait for anything or anyone. Russell showed up on Stella's doorstep. By that time they were living in a duplex in Edmonds, just a few miles farther north. He had come to see how Stella was doing.

"I told him I was just fine, thank you, he could be on his way. He said he heard that I was pregnant and it was his child as much as it was mine. I said, 'I don't believe so.' Well, he decided that being that I was pregnant, I would give in to his wishes and give him what he wanted," she recalled years later.

"Don't lay any hands on me!"

"You're carrying my child. You're my woman. If you don't go to bed with me, I'll attack you again."

"You lay a hand on me and I'll scream this place down around your ears. The woman next door already told me that if I needed any help to holler; she would be able to hear me."

The man put his fist at the base of her stomach.

"If you yell, I'll hit you right here and that'll hit the baby in the head and kill it."

She looked him right in the eye and said, "Go ahead. It's your little bastard, not mine."

Stella never saw him again.

Stella Maudine Stephenson wanted her baby to have a name, so she enlisted Ricky Slawson in a charade.

"She never wanted him. She wanted a name. She used him," Berta recalled.

Ricky, however, never saw it that way. He told people the baby was his.

"I don't know how Ricky could think he was the father. He didn't go with her until *after* she was pregnant. He's either being very naive or out-and-out lying," Berta said later.

In late summer of 1959, Stella and Ricky showed up at Georgia Mae's Holly Park housing-project apartment in Seattle looking for a place to stay. Single after a failed marriage, Stella's big sister was working several jobs, though mostly as a meat wrapper at a grocery. She knew nothing about any rape. She thought Slawson was the baby's father.

Stella said their mother had thrown her out but Georgia figured Stella had probably just run away as she had before. The first time, when she was ten years old, she ran off somewhere, and her mother went and got her. Every time Jo turned around, Stella was gone.

Living with her big sister wasn't the best solution for either party.

Georgia whipped Stella after accusing her of stealing a silver dollar and a wedding ring.

"She never even cried when I took a belt to her, and she was six months pregnant," Georgia said years later. "She stole my one-carat engagement ring, and my 1934—year I was born—silver dollar. I think my mom gave me that silver dollar, and I took a belt to Stella Maudine. She didn't deny it. She battled me. I turned her over on my bed and spanked her worse than my own kids."

"I was afraid I had injured the baby, but I was so mad at her. I was so upset."

Stella didn't stay for another round. She and Ricky left the next day and moved in with Berta and her husband, south of town, until the baby was born.

Stella Maudine gave her last name as "Slawson" when she had her baby girl on October 23, 1959. Ricky wanted to name her Cynthia, and Stella chose the middle name Lea.

By the time Stella Maudine was making her a grandmother again, Alva Georgia "Jo" Duncan Stephenson Kelly had married for the third time, to a retired Navy man named Bill Street. The new couple took off south and moved into a small house in Stanton, Orange County, California.

Stella's mother now felt she was in the position to do something for her daughter. She wanted to adopt Cynthia Lea and raise her as her own.

"Stella, you aren't ready for this," Jo told her daughter. "I want you to have the life of a teenager."

Stella wasn't sure. She and Ricky still planned to marry. Jo didn't wait for an answer. Stella's mother went to work on gathering the information needed for adoption. But when she sent for her own birth certificate, the name that came with it was Cora Lee Duncan—not Alva Georgia.

From that day forward, she adopted her original name, a name she never knew.

"I'm Cora Lee," she'd correct people over and over.

It was as if Alva Georgia or Jo never existed.

When it came time for the wedding, Berta told would-be brother-in-law Ricky that courthouse employees wouldn't ask for I.D. and he should tell them he was twenty-one.

"That way you won't need your parents' permission to marry."

Ricky couldn't do it—or rather, wouldn't do it. He chickened out at the last minute. He later said he was too "goddamn young" to be tied down.

"I can see how much you want to marry me," Stella told him in a fit after he refused to lie.

"We'll wait until I become of legal age, then we're gonna get married."

Stella shook her head later, musing over her baby's father's promise to marry.

"OK, I'm gullible. This isn't to say that my temper was cool, but I'm gullible."

Around Christmas 1959—the same holiday her family gave Stella Maudine a Bible embossed with her name that she would keep with her and read for comfort many years later—Stella's mother called asking her daughter if she would move to California and live with her and Bill Street. She told her she could help with the baby and Stella would be able to learn a trade, and maybe with a little hard work she'd even get her GED. Stella agreed to go.

"Ricky tried to talk me into staying and I told him no, I was going down to California with my mother, because it seemed like the only way that I was going to be able to get any support for myself and my daughter. I said, 'You kinda blew the chances of us getting married.' He says, 'I love you and I wanna marry you,' and I said, 'If you love me and want to marry me all that much, I'll see you in California. When I see you in person on that doorstep, I'll know how you feel.' "

Cora Lee came for Stella and the baby just after New Year's Day 1960. She moved them down to her little house at 7220 Syracuse in Stanton.

Tough bird that she was, Stella's mother was not the type to talk trash about her husbands. No matter what they did to her. Cora Lee Street had enormous pride. She didn't want her children to feel as though she made a mistake in marrying a man. And she didn't want her kids to feel badly about her men, in case the damn marriage didn't work out. She was always hopeful.

She would not complain about her men, and she taught her girls to do the same.

Stella saw evidence of a battering.

"From her waist to her knee and from about her hipbone in the front to just about halfway around in back was nothing but a black mass. You couldn't even hardly see blue in it, you couldn't really call it black and blue. Bill Street had knocked her down on the floor and kicked her with his service shoes on, and they were very hard-toed. When I saw the bruise, I got out of her what happened. Mother would tell me a lot of things that she wouldn't tell the other kids because I kind of take them in my stride. I don't get all bent out of shape like the other kids. They would just as soon he kick the bucket immediately than wait. With me, I knew there was two sides to the story and I hadn't gotten the whole thing yet. I also knew my mother well enough to know that she gets pretty mouthy sometimes. It's no reason for anybody to break her arm, but they had been drinking. He may not have realized how hard he had grabbed hold of her arm, what her age was. Mother may have, as soon as he grabbed her, she may have twisted her arm just right and it snapped; it could have been an entire accident. It could have been intentional, I don't know. I wasn't there."

Instead of coming to get his woman and baby in California as he had promised, Ricky Slawson mailed a letter. Hell hath no fury like Stella Stephenson, and Ricky Slawson should have known it. As Stella saw it, Ricky had made the threat that he was going to get custody of Cynthia by taking Stella to court and prove she was unfit to raise the girl. Cynthia had his name and, therefore, belonged with him.

"And I wrote back to him and told him that he knew that Cynthia wasn't his daughter even though she carried his name. We both agreed on that, that she was not his blood daughter, he was not going to get her," she said.

Later, she recalled a letter:

> Go ahead and try to prove me an unfit mother, try to take my daughter away from me and I'll see you behind bars for 20 long years, because I'll nail you for statutory rape because I was only 15 years old when we started getting together. And I turned 16 a couple months before Cindy was born.

Ricky never contacted Stella Maudine again.

"She really done me wrong," he said years later, still not believing Stella's story that Cindy wasn't his baby. "Stella was a goddamn liar, I'll tell you that. She became the biggest damn liar in seven states."

As hard as they had it—at times on welfare, abuse from Cora Lee's drunken husbands, the house fires—there was extraordinary family loyalty. No one would sell the other out. Punishment was handled by the family, not by outsiders. And they were private, reticent to discuss any family problems.

Cora Lee had taught the girls that "you never, ever, air out the family laundry in public!"

They had nothing but each other. Even so, sometimes they kept secrets.

CHAPTER 22

Stella Nickell and daughter Cindy Hamilton checked into room 241 at the Orchard Inn in Wenatchee on Monday, June 9, 1986. The new widow had originally reserved the room for the night before, but had canceled the reservation for some reason. She paid cash—$38.65—for the room. "Adopted son" Jerry Kimble also stayed at the Orchard Inn.

Most of the funeral arrangements had been made by Dick Nickell, Bruce's cousin. Stella seemed to go along with his suggestions, including the selection of the burial site in Winthrop, an hour from Wenatchee.

Walter Nickell paid for his only son's casket. He asked his daughter-in-law if she had a decent suit for Bruce to be buried in.

"No," she said, "he's gonna be buried in jeans and sport shirt. That's the way I want it."

The ninety-four-year-old man accepted her wishes, though he had hoped for something a little nicer for his boy.

It was not a time to argue. For Walter, it was a time to cry. He lost his fragile composure in the slumber room at the Jones and Jones Funeral Home. The tears came and they wouldn't let up. His son was supposed to outlive him. It hurt to say goodbye. Ruth Nickell didn't cry; she knew her husband could shed enough tears for the both of them.

Stella, Cindy, and Jerry Kimble also visited the slumber room. Jerry thought Bruce looked pretty good.

"But he didn't look like my Bruce. Nobody looks the same when they are laying there all white," Kimble later recalled.

Stella left Dick Nickell with an uneasy feeling at the funeral home. In the car on the way there, she complained of a headache.

"I've got a bad one," she said, "just like the ones Bruce used to give me all the time."

The comment was colored with bitterness from a woman who by all rights should be grieving. *She was a new widow, for god-sakes, why would she say something like that?* Dick Nickell couldn't put it out of his mind.

South Seattle Community College motor vehicle maintenance instructor Jim McCarthy was the only one of the deceased's friends to make it to the funeral. He was big, dark, and boasted of Indian blood, an attribute not lost on Stella Nickell, who, like her mother, prided herself in her Indian heritage. At fifty-four, Jim McCarthy was a three-time divorcé when he met the Nickells through an Auburn CB radio club in late 1983.

He told people that losing Bruce Nickell was the shock of his life. They had so much in common. Big Mac, as he was called on the radio, was the estranged father of two sons. The men shared a fanatical interest in electronics. Though Jim McCarthy's young—and latest—wife made the considerable trip to Winthrop, she refused to go to the funeral. She stayed and shopped the Old West-themed main street.

McCarthy later said his wife didn't go to the service because she didn't like Stella Nickell.

"That was carrying it a little too far, I think," he said.

Wilma Mae Stewart had arranged a flight later on the same morning that she had spoken with her aunt. Mistakenly believing that the funeral was in Wenatchee, she booked a flight from Houston to Pasco, where she had family. She had Bill Johnson, her "adopted dad," and Mel Stewart, her ex-husband, drive her to the service. By the time they arrived at Sullivan Cemetery, the service was just about over.

A couple of rows of folding chairs had been set up on the lawn before the casket. Stella and Cynthia Lea, both dressed in black, occupied two seats in the front row. The widow's face was ashen and her eyes were covered with dark glasses.

But it was Stella's daughter, sobbing uncontrollably, who made the greatest impression on some who attended the funeral.

"If I didn't know better, I would say Cynthia Lea was the widow, not Aunt Stella," Wilma told Bill Johnson.

"It really struck me, the role she was playing," she said later, "a very well-rehearsed, complicated role that Cynthia Lea was playing. Dabbing her eyes with no tears with the hanky, struck me as being very phony. I took offense at it, which is why I remember it so well. All you needed was a camera and a director and it would have been a great shot for *The Omen*. She'd have been perfect in that."

Dick and Walter Nickell noticed it too.

"Look at Cindy and look at Stella," Dick Nickell whispered to the old man. "Cindy's sitting there bawling her head off, just crying and crying like she can't hardly take it."

The funeral director had a different take on Stella Nickell's behavior at her husband's funeral.

"I thought she was rather angry at the time," he said some years later. "I don't know if it was a deep anger kind of grief or what."

Dick Nickell didn't mince words with the funeral director.

"I think she killed him," Nickell told the man, just as the service finished.

Shocked at the very idea of murder, the funeral director asked why and how. After all, didn't the autopsy indicate natural causes?

Nickell shook his head. He didn't have the answer.

"I don't know how. . . . She tried to make this look like an accident," he said.

The funeral director returned to the funeral home in Wenatchee.

"You won't believe what Dick Nickell said to me after the service today," he told a fellow employee.

After the service, the family, including Stella's sister Mary, Cora Lee, Cindy, Wilma, Mel Stewart, and Bill Johnson, went for coffee at a tiny Winthrop café. Dick Nickell had asked Stella to join the Nickells at a relative's place in Twisp, but Stella declined, saying she was too upset and needed to get home.

Wilma was glad that she could spend a little time with her grieving aunt. She had to fly back to Houston the following day.

Her aunt Stella was doing her best to maintain composure, but something was disturbing about her first cousin's behavior.

"It was like 'cut, director's gone on break, let's all be ourselves, let's all be natural.' And Cynthia Lea cut up and played and joked and carried on. There would be times when she would be like, 'wait,

I got to put it back on, the director's coming.' She was bouncing between this 'Oh, woe is me, I lost my daddy,' or whatever."

Wilma thought her cousin was ecstatic because she was the center of attention. She even sat at the head of the table.

On the way back to Pasco, Mel Stewart shook his head about what he had seen and heard in the little café.

"That girl belongs in a truck stop," he said.

Everyone agreed: Cindy Hamilton was as tough as they come. After listening to her talk about beating up some girl at a bar, Wilma, who wasn't exactly a shrinking violet, felt intimidated by her cousin.

"A lot of Cynthia's talk was about physical violence, being in the bar and getting in a fight with that girl and that girl hitting her and knocking her through the doors and underneath the car in the parking lot and how Cynthia got up and went back in there. . . ."

Cynthia Hamilton moved back into her mother's mobile home immediately following her stepfather's funeral. Stella told others that it was unnecessary, but Cynthia said it was something she wanted to do. It was a way she could help.

Mother and concerned daughter paid a visit to their family doctor on Friday afternoon, June 13. The doctor prescribed Valium and Dembutol for the widow, who seemed shaky. Cynthia was there to help, but her concern was short-lived. That night she had a hot date. And as far as Stella could tell, it must have been a doozy.

Cynthia Lea never came home.

Neighbor Sandy Scott was out working in the yard when Stella Nickell drove up in her green pickup after retrieving her mail. She waved her husband's death certificate in Sandy's direction.

"They said it was emphysema," she said, shaking her head. "He just had a physical with the state. He was told he probably would develop it, but he didn't have it then. Does it happen that fast?"

"Not from what I have heard," Sandy said. She told Stella she had friends who had developed emphysema, and in both instances it had been a slow and enfeebling disease.

"For the last year and a half, they could sit up on the couch, but they couldn't walk to the bathroom. You don't go to work in the morning and come home and die of emphysema," Sandy said. "There's no way. How can that be?"

*   *   *

Stella's niece, Wilma Mae, was certainly pretty and smart enough to have been anything she wanted. If only she had been born into a different family. Wide-set eyes and a clear-around-her-face smile were the exaggerated good looks that make run-of-the-mill pretty girls into models. But Stella's niece held no such ambitions.

Her mother was Georgia Mae, Cora Lee's oldest. And if Georgia had been beaten and raped as once she claimed, she had passed on her anger.

Wilma didn't know about her mother's past, only her own torment. When Georgia wanted to go out, she locked Wilma and her brother Bill in the closet.

When the kids sassed her, Georgia Mae would slap and whip until they stopped.

And when she couldn't take the responsibility anymore, Georgia would pawn her brood off on her husband's folks, her mother, or even little sister Stella when she was older.

When Wilma was twelve, her mother left her with her alcoholic paternal grandparents in Snohomish, Washington. It was March 1965.

Wilma later recalled: "I slept in the basement downstairs, and my father smoked Raleighs. Shoe boxes of coupons. I was downstairs counting the coupons, trying to see what I could get for my dad. I was counting them and my grandfather came downstairs with a cat-o'-nine-tails. I was supposed to be in bed sleeping. A wooden handle . . . six- to nine-inch leather straps, twenty straps. To a kid there were two hundred. I got beat with the cat-o'-nine-tails because I was in my father's stuff. Grandfather was very drunk."

Another time, the kids lived on Gravy Train dog food when their grandparents left for an extended drunk.

And yet none of that was as painful as the year-long abandonment by their mother.

During that time, Cora Lee drove up from Orange County, picked up the kids, and drove straight through back to California. A few months later, Cora Lee sold her house and returned to Seattle. At age thirteen, Wilma had to move in with her mother and her new husband. It was all she could do to count years until her eighteenth birthday and the freedom it would bring.

The beatings continued; only the pretexts changed. When Georgia saw Wilma dance with her stepfather at a Rough Riders Club dance, she became bitter and angry.

Wilma later remembered what happened that night: "They got

into a big fight. They sent me to bed. I had got up in the middle of the night to go to the bathroom, and my mother and father were sitting on the couch. My mother looked at me. 'You see, you little bitch, you can't break us up.' "

And so it went. Beating, running away, repeated over and over. The police would bring Wilma home, and Georgia would beat her for it.

It culminated with Wilma's theft of her stepfather's saddle. Georgia told the police she couldn't handle her anymore. A defiant Wilma Mae was sent to a juvenile facility in Tacoma, followed by almost two years at the Maple Lane School for girls. It was there she discovered she was pregnant, five months along.

"My school counselor, Mrs. Tidman, called my mother. She came down and said she wanted nothing to do with me, the child belonged to my stepfather. She based [her story on how] in October, she allegedly found a wet wash rag in the bedroom. My father never touched me. But that's what she claimed."

On June 26, 1970, Wilma Mae, seventeen, had a baby boy at Centralia Hospital. She gave him up for adoption.

"My mother came in the hospital after the baby was born, screaming at the doctors that she had to see this baby because her marriage depended on it. She was sure it belonged to my stepfather."

A year later, Wilma Mae, on a three-month parole, elected to live in a foster home rather than with her mother. She couldn't stand being under the control of a parole officer and told the woman to jam it. A few months later she married her first husband, a trucker. Then, in nine months, she had a son, Danny, and the cycle of abuse recommenced.

"That was an abusive marriage from the get-go. He knocked me out the first time he ever hit me. When I came to, he was on the floor crying about what a terrible person he was. I felt sorry for him, stayed with him. It went on and on."

The young mother passed on her anger.

"I look back at the point where I struck my son with the belt and he turned on me as I struck him and I caught him across the face. I put makeup on it to hide it from his father."

She tried to get help. She wrote a letter to Parents Anonymous but received no reply. She didn't know what else to do.

Two more sons couldn't save the marriage, and by 1978, Wilma had left her husband and her four children.

"I never knew my mother to say 'I love you,' but backhanding me was something that she did. The world says you have to love your parents. I hate my mother. I do have a reason to hate her," she said some years later.

The closest Wilma Mae ever came to a real mother was her aunt Stella.

CHAPTER 23

Cora Lee's suggestion to adopt Cynthia Lea to allow Stella some teenage fun had apparently been taken to heart, and Stella Maudine ran wild in Southern California. She left her daughter with her mother whenever she stumbled across some distraction, some man. By her own admission later, she was a "little promiscuous" then, but she never kept more than one man on a string at a time. Problem was, she had more strings than a loom.

As she had in Seattle, Stella continued seeing older men. Men her own age lacked the maturity she felt she possessed. She, after all, was a mother. A grown woman. This reasoning was lost on Cora Lee. She told her daughter her men were no good and they were looking for only one thing.

And Stella was good at that. In fact, she became pregnant in the summer of 1962.

There was no eenie, meenie, mynie, moe about the baby's paternity.

"I know which one it belonged to, because I only believe in dating one person at a time, believe me," Stella said years later, tears falling. "More than one of them's too hard to keep up with. You can't remember which days you made a date with who."

The baby's father, a former Air Force enlistee, was five or six years older than Stella Maudine. Besides the fact that he said he didn't want to get married—even though Stella claimed he had given her an engagement ring—she caught her beau in bed with another woman.

"I about shoved the engagement ring down his throat and told him to take it and take a hike. And then, when I found out I was pregnant I told him. He was one of the people I thought I was madly in love with. In fact, he was one that Mother and I had a lot of fights over. 'Cause he was 'too old' for me. Of course, at the time she probably suspected, but she didn't know that I was going to bed with him. It was just one of those things that happened."

If the truth were known, Cora Lee must have had an out-and-out fit when her daughter shared her news. If she had a chastity belt, she'd probably have walloped her daughter with it before soldering it in place.

Not another one, Stella!

Cora Lee had bailed Stella out of her "rape" and pregnancy with Cynthia. She had put up with Ricky Slawson and his threats to take the little girl. But another baby, another illegitimate birth, was too much. Cora Lee was working on the assembly line at Hughes Aircraft and trying to keep her jobless, wild daughter and granddaughter in food. The house was another matter. With Bill Street finally gone, Cora Lee didn't have anyone to help her with the mortgage. The baby had to be given up for adoption.

Stella went along with it, partly because, at eighteen she really didn't want another child, Cynthia was enough of a handful. But also, if she was ever to find a man decent enough to marry, supporting two kids was asking too much of him.

Later, Stella would say she held some regret for giving up her baby.

"This was before a whole lot was known about child abuse and all of that. If I'd have known about that at that particular time, I'd have had two children. . . . So, in mulling it over in my own mind, I had made it up that it was probably the best thing for the child. I knew it wasn't the best thing for me."

For some in the family it would be hard to fathom Cora Lee's giving away one of her grandchildren. She was a woman who had lost two children to tragic childhood accidents, and as one daughter later claimed, suffered at least two miscarriages. But according to Stella, it was her mother who pushed for it.

They kept the arrangement secret.

March 10, 1963, was a date that would play in Stella Maudine's head each year after her baby boy was born in an Orange County hospital. What he looked like, Stella never knew. She never laid eyes on him.

"I could have seen him," she said later. "I chose not to. If I had seen him, I would not have signed the papers. And Mother knew this. She told me it would be best if I didn't see him."

When she returned from the hospital, Stella called Berta, who was still living in Seattle. She had some bad news.

"My baby was stillborn at the hospital," she said. She seemed a bit distant about her loss.

Berta broke down. Her heart ached not only for her sister, but for her mother. It was another boy that had been lost to the family. First Frankie Gene, Little Joe, and now the baby Stella had said she had wanted to name Brent.

Nearly thirty years would pass before Berta would learn the truth. When she did, it left her to wonder how well in fact she really did know her closest sibling. She couldn't imagine Stella's giving up a baby and not telling her about it.

"As close as Stella and I were, and as many times as I told her that the reason I didn't give up my daughter is that I would have spent the rest of my life wondering what I had, the way she was, or he, what they were doing, what they grew up to be like."

Georgia Mae had no recollections of Stella's son. She never knew her sister had been pregnant in the first place.

Later, friends would argue that things would have turned out differently if Stella had given her firstborn away as well.

Though he had been stationed north of the 38th Parallel during the Korean War and was one of only two of the ten in his unit to return to the States, Robert Warren "Bob" Strong was no match for Stella Maudine Stephenson. He found her what-the-hell attitude dangerous and appealing. She could alternate between sweet concern and the rage of the most foulmouthed of sailors. When Stella slammed the drinks down, it was with the gusto of a man.

For the thirty-one-year-old who wore heavy, black-framed glasses and spoke in a slow, nearly southern drawl, it was lust, if not love, at first sight.

Stella had been dating an acquaintance of one of Strong's model-airplane hobbyist friends in Garden Grove. Bob Strong saw another side to the raven-haired woman that those merely looking for a good time usually missed. He saw a sweet girl, trying to make something of herself. He figured if she were given a reasonable chance, she really could make it.

"I won't lie," he said years later. "I fell in love with the woman."

Initially, there was The Walk. Stella Stephenson would stand straight as a poker, and swing her shoulders a little bit so her full breasts would move to and fro and catch eyes. Other women might have thought they knew The Walk, but they were amateurs compared to Stella's gait, bobbing breasts, and swaying wave of black, wavy hair. Everything moved and worked together. It got her noticed.

Bob noticed that Stella's four-year-old daughter mimicked her mother. Cindy followed her like a miniature Stella, walking The Walk.

Stella also had a way of talking that was different from any woman Bob Strong had known. She was direct and tough.

"For a female she wanted to be macho. She wanted to give the impression that she was as hard as carbide steel," he remembered.

Cora Lee wanted Stella to be that way.

"She raised us to be strong, independent, to take care of ourselves, because she had to work, so she couldn't be there.

The night Cora Lee learned Bob Strong intended to marry her headstrong daughter, future mother-in-law and son-in-law sat in her car in front of Stella's apartment at 10615 Dorothy, Garden Grove, and talked all night. Cora Lee held hopes that mild-mannered Bob Strong, so respectful and sweet, would somehow tame her daughter and, equally important, provide some stability for her granddaughter.

"Man, is this a relief," Cora Lee told him. "I don't have to worry about that one anymore."

Robert Warren and Stella Maudine were married on June 3, 1964, in Garden Grove. The new couple and Stella's daughter moved into a $115-a-month ranch house at 20392 Acacia Street in Santa Ana. Twenty-foot-high yuccas framed the small patio by the front door, and a picture window faced the street. Out back was a detached garage used as a shop, with doors that slid open like a dairy barn's. Hibiscus blooms and the neighbors' fragrant orange trees competed with the acrid odors of the Orange County Airport just down the street.

Being the old-fashioned type, Bob did not want his wife to work, so Stella stayed home. She remained close to her mother, and even formed a slight friendship with Pat Bilderback, the wife of an alcoholic womanizer who lived across the street. When she needed to shop, Stella left Cindy with her neighbor.

At home, Stella expected things to be just so. Manners were critical. If she caught Cynthia with her elbows on the table, the preschooler got a quick, sharp jab with a fork.

When she felt it was warranted, her husband got similar jabs too.

"She poked my arm one time and I about slapped her ass. 'It smarts! You don't have to poke that hard,' " he recalled.

The little girl was not allowed to get out of bed in the morning until she heard her mother's feet hit the floor.

Lois Schaefer met the Strongs through Pat Bilderback, who was Stella's Avon Lady. An obese woman with minor agoraphobia married to a man twenty-eight years her senior, Lois took an immediate disliking to Stella Strong. She was pushy and defiant. All the men paid attention to her, and she seemed to court it. Stella had few, if any, women friends.

Bob Strong thought his wife didn't like women because she figured all of them were just like her and did the same things she did. Since Lois was heavy and Pat was married with children, it might have been that she didn't view them as threats to her role as the tough-talking, sexy queen bee.

Stella was better than any of them.

"She always wanted to be above herself. She always wanted more than she could afford," Lois said later.

While her friends were on welfare, borrowing from each other and trying to scrimp out a life, Stella was always able to come up with new things, clothes, furniture. No one could figure out where she got it all.

Pat and Lois got their shoes from K mart or Goodwill. Not Stella.

"She didn't care if [Cindy] ate, as long as she had what she wanted. Whatever she could take, she did. It was for her," remembered Lois.

Not long after the wedding Stella Strong was running around and bedding every man in Orange County. At least, that's how Bob Strong saw it.

At first, Stella would just leave the house for destinations unknown. But as time passed and as Bob looked the other way, she grew bolder. Once he caught his wife in a negligee on the couch with another man. Stella said the man was a friend of her cousin's.

"A week later she denied she was ever on the couch in a negligee in the first place," he said.

Bob wasn't the type to fight about it.

Let her do what she's going to do, and I'll go do what I'm going to do, he thought. *It'll keep the peace.*

One time Stella showed up at her husband's job site, where he was installing cabinets at a doctor's office in Garden Grove. Bob took a break to talk with his wife. While they stood by the side of the car, another construction worker approached and he and Stella engaged in pleasant conversation.

"All of a sudden her blouse was standing open and you could see her boobs," Bob recalled. "I was standing there talking to her. And she had nothing on her."

Bob Strong didn't like what his wife was doing, but by then it had become so familiar. The woman always used sex to get what she wanted. Bob felt Stella lived by some sort of Stephenson-gal philosophy that a woman can get anything she wants out of a man if she takes him to the bedroom.

Sometimes Bob would wake to find Stella sitting up watching movies on TV until two or three o'clock in the morning. Since he had to be at work at 6:30 A.M. there was no way he could stay up late. Other times he would awaken and find the TV turned off and Stella gone.

"I knew she was running around," Bob said, though he refused to really press her for an explanation. He figured she'd lie.

Stella liked freedom and she liked to drive. Wherever it was she went was her business. Later, she'd suggest she was off shopping or at a girlfriend's. But Bob Strong knew better, and for a time didn't care. Sometimes a jumbo-sized drink helped him look the other way.

One time he saw her driving down the road in a little convertible Chevy. She had told him she needed to get out by herself. She needed to think. While driving down the coast highway, she later told her husband, she stopped to give a couple of sailors a lift and ended up taking them all the way to San Diego.

"This is what she said," Bob said, shaking his head in disbelief at his wife's story. "The gal had a problem, and she didn't want to get it fixed.

"No one man could ever satisfy her. I don't give a damn what kind of man. He could be the stud of studs and be able to stand forever and never fall and be fourteen feet long and seven inches across, and she'd still want other men. It didn't make any difference about size or nothing. She told me one time she couldn't stop herself. I have the feeling she was more or less a nymphomaniac. No matter what you do, they're not satisfied."

"I'm the only one in Orange County that hasn't been to bed with her yet, and I'm her husband!" Bob told a friend at the time.

Later, even Stella conceded she might have taken advantage of Bob's less-than-forceful personality.

"Sometimes when family life would start to get to me and he and I had been yelling and screaming at one another too much and I'd be ready to pull my hair out, I'd just up and 'see you later' and I'd be gone. Being as young as I was, I probably did take advantage of it quite often."

On November 4, 1966, Stella Strong gave birth to a second daughter, Leah Ruth, at Hoag Memorial Hospital in Newport Beach. The sweet baby girl was blue-eyed and blond, but for some reason never found the place in her mother's heart that her big sister held. Friends suggested the little girl reminded Stella too much of Bob Strong.

A short time later, when Stella found herself pregnant again, she opted for an abortion. She said she didn't want any more kids. Bob didn't care. He didn't think the baby was his anyway.

CHAPTER 24

Dee Rogers told friends she went out to spend the night at Stella Nickell's place after Bruce died because she didn't want her friend to be alone. Others suggested Dee was the type who coveted the good vantage point. Either could be true. The fact that reporters were as thick as the mosquitoes from the runoff below the trailer, and even the national media was pounding on the Nickells' aluminum door, unquestionably made it all the more interesting.

After what was expected to be a short stop at the FBI offices so Stella could be fingerprinted, they'd be on their way camping for a few days. It was late June 1986. Stella had all the things they needed in the back of the truck. Dee thought camping was a good idea. Stella, who couldn't be more angry, could use a break.

"Someone is going to have to pay for this!" she told her friend. "You can bet I'm going to jump on the bandwagon and sue somebody for this!"

Dee understood her sentiments. She felt the same way.

The next morning, they stopped at Stella's doctor's and lawyer's offices, before heading to the FBI and then on to the campsite in Eastern Washington.

Stella Nickell and Dee Rogers parked under the Alaskan Way viaduct, Seattle's ugly double-decker thruway that barricades the city from the spectacular waterfront, and hiked up the hillclimb to the Federal Building. Dee was left to read plaques—"Fidelity, Brav-

ery, Integrity"—in the reception area, while her friend went inside
to be inked and printed. When she emerged a short time later, she
seemed very concerned, almost frightened, though fear was something Dee Rogers had never associated with either Stella or her
daughter. Fear didn't run in the family.

"They want me to take a lie-detector test," Stella said on the
way back to the truck.

The idea of a polygraph had never entered Dee Rogers's mind.
She was just as incredulous about the whole thing as Stella Nickell.

"Why?"

"I have no idea. But I told them I'd talk to my lawyer."

Stella Nickell cracked her truck window and smoked all the way
to Stevens Pass, and just beyond.

Dee Rogers didn't have any idea where they were going, just a
place in Eastern Washington Stella said she and Bruce used to go.
Eastern Washington was one big, hot, dry spot on the other side of
the mountains. Cindy had been left in charge of Dee's sons and
daughter. As much as Dee knew Cindy liked her kids, the prospect
was risky. If Stella's daughter got it in her mind to do something
else, most likely with some pickup from Gee Gee's Truck Stop,
then *adios*. The kids would have to fend for themselves.

Stella pulled into the Squirrel Inn near Leavenworth for a pit
stop. It was the place where she had first met Ruth and Walter
Nickell. The women guzzled a couple of drinks before returning to
the highway, then down a side road to the campsite.

They stayed for almost a week of drinking, talking about the
FBI and the damned lie-detector test. When they grew tired of
drinking McNaughton's, they switched to Wild Turkey. And then
they talked some more.

When booze threatened to run dry, Stella hopped in her truck
with the vanity plate TP 42 for a liquor store in Leavenworth. Dee
lolled on their raft and sipped the last of the Wild Turkey.

Stella was gone for quite a while, longer than Dee thought it
would take to get to the liquor store and back. Maybe she had run
into somebody she knew? Maybe she had gone to see Bruce's folks,
who lived barely more than a half hour from town? Stella never
said where she went.

She made a similar trip a day or so later.

When she returned, she was cool and confident, her old self.
Dee, on the other hand, was so drunk she could barely paddle her-

self to shore. She lay in the river raft on the icy water until Stella bailed her out.

Stella broke out the bottles she had purchased and gave Dee a romance novel she had picked up in town. They were there to get away from the media, but also to have a good time. This was a vacation.

Stella talked about the polygraph and her fear of taking it.

"I feel guilty," she said. "I could have done more for him . . . I wasn't always the best wife."

"Come on, Stella. For Christ's sake, Bruce was a goddamn pampered asshole! He couldn't even wipe his ass. He couldn't find the refrigerator unless you pointed him in the direction. He was spoiled rotten!"

"I don't know . . ." Stella answered. "I also feel responsible because I was the one who bought the Excedrin and brought it into the house. It's my fault. I don't know how it's going to come across on the lie detector."

"Then don't take it. Just don't do it. Talk to your lawyer."

As she had with Sandy Scott, Stella shared more true confessions. She told Dee about the son she had given up for adoption. Though Dee was drinking a bit during the trip, and later couldn't be sure, she thought Stella had said she had recently met with the young man.

"He works at Boeing," Stella said.

On the surface, it was emotional stuff, even for Dee. And though it was true there were tears over Bruce and she said she was a wreck, Stella never appeared to be stressed.

"She was probably one of the coolest people I've ever seen. She carried herself high. You could have just got done reaming her up one side and down the other. She never appeared happy. She didn't appear sad. She just appeared cool, cold, and straight. That was Stella," Dee said later.

"She never had any problem going to sleep at night."

Stella would say later that Dee Rogers had been an uninvited guest on the camping trip to Red Rock Mine. Stella only wanted to be alone, to be with the memory of her late husband. She had grieved in her own way—alone.

"Dee insisted she come. She knew I wouldn't tell her she couldn't come. I'm not the type," she said.

*   *   *

Cora Lee stomped up the hill to the Scotts' place, asking if Sandy had a clue as to where in the hell Stella and Dee had gone off camping. By then, Cora Lee had shifted her hard-boiled but friendly Ma Kettle veneer for a face full of anger and bitterness.

The Nickells' neighbor didn't know anything.

"I wonder if I should file a missing-persons report," Cora Lee said.

Sandy didn't think a call to the police was necessary, at least not at that juncture. She promised to ask her husband, a King County Police deputy, when he got home.

"Why is Stella out with Dee?" Cora Lee wondered. It was so out of character, it confused her. "Stella's mad at her for letting Cindy stay with her."

Sandy, who had heard a little of Stella's ire toward Dee during the night she stayed with her, made no comment, other than to reassure the woman everything was probably fine.

It was so odd that Stella Nickell would go off with Dee Rogers. Sandy Scott thought Stella made her feelings quite clear. She didn't trust her old friend.

For the next few days, Cora Lee continued to call Sandy to see if she had heard from Stella.

Always an outsider when it came to her mother and older sister, Leah, almost twenty, hadn't known the seriousness of the goings-on in Auburn. Her heart skipped a beat when the FBI caught up with her and requested that she come to the field office in Jackson, Mississippi. They had questions about the cyanide poisoning death of her stepfather.

The agent on the phone tried to calm her. "Don't worry. We always investigate matters like this."

Leah was confused by the agents' queries.

"They were asking me kind of odd questions. Did I think he [Bruce] was cheating on my mom? Did my mom cheat on him? Asking me if he ever tried anything with Cindy?"

Leah drew a blank. "I did not live with my mother."

The young woman was trembling when she left, the experience had shaken her so. She wondered what had really happened up in Washington—and who was involved.

"The way they asked me, I thought, you know, it was my sister and my mom," she said years later.

*   *   *

Although Cindy Hamilton had pretty much moved on from her circle of pals, as she tended to do, she sporadically kept in touch with some of them.

A short time after Bruce Nickell's name appeared in every newspaper in the country as a product-tampering victim, an incensed Cindy called her friend Bonnie Anderson and told her the FBI had been harassing her mother about the Auburn tamperings. They had asked her to take a polygraph, but she had refused.

Bonnie was incredulous. "Cindy, they think that your mom killed Bruce?"

"Yeah, that's what they think! I know she didn't."

Cindy didn't pussyfoot around about anything. She let Bonnie know she was absolutely convinced her mother hadn't killed anyone.

"No way."

CHAPTER 25

The photograph album was white vinyl, trimmed with a stripe of gold filigree and a regal script spelling out "Our Family." It was the kind of compendium of memories a mother assembles with great care and love for her children. Two children were listed in the family-tree overleaf: Cynthia Lea and Leah Ruth. As in most families in which there is attention and enthusiasm for chronicling the joys of childhood, emphasis was placed on the firstborn.

In studio portrait after portrait, a little girl with clusters of brown curls and lovely, dark eyes smiled for the camera. The California sun had brought out freckles, and baby teeth had given way to permanent ones. Smile after smile, page after page, until it stopped . . .

Cynthia Lea had always bruised easily. Her mother and father both said so.

"She had a hell of a lot of bruises on her, but on the other hand you could thump Cindy and she'd get a bruise. She could even think something hit her and she'd get a bruise, that's how easy it was for Cindy. She didn't necessarily have to be beat hard to get all of those bruises. I'm not saying that she wasn't," Bob Strong later said.

When Bob come home from work to the little house on Acacia, Stella would sometimes meet him at the door, her voice surging with anger.

"Robert," she said, using his more formal given name as a mother addresses a child in trouble, "you come in here. I want you to punish your daughter. She's in her bedroom now."

Bob went to the bedroom down the hall, but he was torn.

"I mean, the little girl only did what she sees her mother doing—lie, steal, cheat. I could not see going in there and beating her ass with a belt for something she'd seen mother doing," he said later.

Sometimes he would close the door and tell Cindy, "When I pull out my belt and I lean you across my lap and you hear this belt snap, you better yell."

Cynthia Lea Strong was a student at Bay View School in Costa Mesa. Her second-grade class picture showed her leaning forward in the third row, straining for the lens to catch her happy smile. Of the twenty-six faces, hers was the only one the camera seemed to notice. Paper snowmen, the only snowmen the students in the class were ever likely to make, hung on the wall. The chalkboard read "January 17, 1968."

The fourth-graders' class picture also made the family album. She was now in the back row, her smile dimmed and her pose more weary, even grown up. She was not the same girl. The date was January 27, 1970.

The third-grade class picture never found a place in the family album.

In tears, Stella Strong made a phone call to her sister Berta. It was January 12, 1969. Stella said she had tried everything she could think of to stop Cindy from using her makeup or taking her things. The spanking, as she called it, had been a last resort. And it had left a bruise.

"It was on the leg, because I missed," Stella wept into the phone. "I was just giving her an old-fashioned spanking."

Berta hung up the phone feeling upset. She knew how hard it was to discipline kids, how she felt when she spanked her own for misbehaving.

"I knew how she felt," Berta later said, full of compassion for her sister, yet aware a parent can go too far. "My kids got spankings, but I never used a belt. I used my hand."

When Cynthia Lea showed up at school with bruises, a teacher and a nurse questioned her. She said her mother had beaten her with a wooden pole. The Costa Mesa police were notified, Cynthia was taken to a hospital and a youth-protection center, and Stella Maudine Strong was arrested on suspicion of the felonious beating of her daughter. She spent a night in jail and was released on her own recognizance.

Bob Strong confronted his wife about the beating. Stella told him the girl had stolen some crystal earrings and makeup and had given them to another schoolgirl. She had been warned repeatedly to stay out of her mother's personal things. Bob hoped reports of the injuries had been exaggerated.

When he saw the little girl, he knew otherwise.

"It looked like Cindy had been beaten half to death," he recalled.

Years later, Stella's version of what happened was a story of a daughter so desperate for attention, she would turn against her own mother. Stella would not deny that she spanked her, never denied that there were bruises.

"Cynthia had bruises on her because Cynthia bruises very easy. You can walk up and grab ahold of her on the arm and you will leave your fingerprints."

Her daughter had wanted sympathy.

"She had went to the nurses' office complaining that she was sick. And she noticed the bruises on Cindy's butt and she had a couple on the top part of her thigh just below her panty leg. And the nurse asked her what happened, and she said her mother beat her. So the nurse kind of perked up her ears and got to talking to Cindy about it. This was the attention Cindy was looking for. So Cynthia went all out and she said that I had beat her with a stick about the size of a fifty-cent piece and three foot long. It was three foot long because it was meant to go on our doorway. Robert had put some braces in the doorway up against the door frame and that piece of wood hooked in it because that's what I used to do sit-ups with—it held my feet down. Cynthia said that was what I beat her with, was this three-foot-long log that I had in the house."

The day after her release, Stella and Bob went to see Cindy at the center. The little girl, who had survived the handiwork of her mother and the reported three-foot pole well enough to make it to school, was now in tears. But it wasn't the beating that made her cry. She had been hit with the news Bob Strong was not her father. During the admitting process, someone had told the girl that her real last name was Slawson, not Strong.

The child hadn't actually been lied to about her parentage; it was simply a case of her assuming Bob was her daddy and no one having the heart to correct her. She used the name Strong in school.

"And like I say, shit hit the fan as far as Cindy was concerned. She wouldn't even talk to me," Bob said later. "Here's this little kid who finds out that I'm not her real father and she don't even know who he is . . ."

Life on Acacia Street improved somewhat in the weeks immediately following Cynthia's return from the children's protection center. The courts put the battered girl under Bob's supervision and Bob felt his wife had cooled down, "sort of like a person does when they go and rob a bank, they kick back and just lay low until the heat goes off."

Stella was ordered into group therapy.

Though his wife later denied it, Bob Strong went to a couple of the counseling sessions in support of her, but he felt the whole thing was a farce. The therapist let Stella run the meeting—and she was good at it. It was Stella who asked the questions of the group.

One little lady stood and said to Stella, "If you were my mother, I'd be scared shitless of you."

"I about cracked up," Bob said later.

After two or three sessions, Stella later said, the psychologist wanted to know what she was doing there and she explained that she had been required by court order.

"He said I had no business in that class. I did not need to be there. I had a very good grip on my life and reality. And he said, 'If you like, I'll write a paper for you to the judge stating that you do not need to be here.' And I said, 'Well, you can do that if you wish, but I enjoy the classes.'

"It taught me a lot about how I could look at Cynthia, and I think that's the reason that I know so well how her mind works."

When Stella's cousin, Bonnie Shields Hickson—Cora Lee's sister Dorothy's daughter—needed a place to figure out what her struggling family was going to do next, Stella readily offered her a place to stay. The first week in May 1970, Stella and Bob went up to Ukiah to move Bonnie, her husband, Wendell, and their three children down to Santa Ana.

On May 15, Bonnie and Wendell made arrangements to have their welfare checks and food stamps transferred from Mendocino to Orange County.

But before the transfer was complete, their plans changed again and the Hicksons decided to head for Texas, where Wendell could likely get work. A car accident in New Mexico, however, forced them to return to Northern California. Back in Mendocino County, they reapplied for welfare.

Orange County, however, didn't get notice of the change in plans. Welfare checks of $119.50 made out to Wendell Hickson were sent to the Acacia address, the first arriving in September.

Stella Strong cashed them.

Robert Strong told his wife he wanted nothing to do with it. She should send the checks back to where they came from. Stella wanted the money and blew him off.

Stella later said she did it to feed her kids.

"Robert had injured his back for several months—longer than he should have—and his unemployment was not enough to pay the bills and keep the family in food."

If, in fact, his wife had been cashing the checks to put food on the table, Bob Strong never saw any evidence of it. Even the neighbors who knew Stella had been cashing them wondered where the money was going.

Cynthia, now a fifth-grader at Bay View School, and her little sister Leah still didn't seem to get enough to eat.

On January 5, 1971, Stella Strong signed over one of the checks to pay a little more than half of what she owed to a Carnation Milk driver. She told her milkman Wendell Hickson had given her permission to countersign the checks.

The following month, the Hicksons paid the Strongs a visit to retrieve belongings they had left behind. Wendell's health had improved, and Bonnie was grateful. Money, however, was still tight.

"If it wasn't for the welfare department," she told Stella, "we never could have made it down here."

"How long have you been back on welfare?" Stella asked.

Bonnie said they had never been off the program. Their case had never been transferred to Orange, because they returned to Ukiah in time to stop it.

Stella told her that checks had been coming to Acacia.

"I hope you've been sending them back," Bonnie said.

Knowing her cousin as she did, Bonnie likely wasn't surprised by Stella's story that she had a man forge Wendell's name, then countersigned and cashed the checks. Stella also admitted using the Hicksons' food stamps. She showed Bonnie an ID card she used for the stamps.

Bonnie told her she was going to report her to the welfare department and Stella begged her not to—after all, she was family.

"I'm your blood cousin," Stella pleaded.

Two days later, Bonnie made good on her threat and the welfare departments of Mendocino and Orange counties began a joint investigation.

Stella was off God-knows-where when Bob Strong answered Cora Lee's phone call from up in Ukiah, where she now lived. The old woman was hotter than a Santa Ana sidewalk in August. The family gossip line had leaked some news about Stella Maudine.

"Stella better watch her back," Cora Lee seethed. "Bonnie turned her in for welfare fraud and forgery. They're gonna get her good for this one."

When Bob finally told Stella, she seemed to pay it no mind. The threat of an investigation and an arrest just seemed to roll off her back. But that was Stella. She was too tough to let Bob think she was worried.

On the day of her arrest, Stella and her neighbor Pat Bilderback spent the afternoon looking at used cars. Stella was in the market for a car, and she wanted Pat's advice. Where she would come up with the money for a down payment—Bob still wasn't working—was apparently of no concern.

When the women returned home, an Orange County investigator was waiting.

Bob watched his wife protest and deny her involvement in any wrongdoing.

You have the wrong person. You've made a mistake. Someone else must have done it. Bonnie is flat-out wrong.

Then she sat calmly with the investigator at the kitchen table.

"My heart's jumping . . . and what the hell, she's just sitting there as cool as hell. He just looks at me and looks at her," Bob said later.

The investigator tired of her stories. He knew she had cashed those checks, and he had the affidavits to back it up.

"As far as I'm concerned, you did it. Now, unless you come clean right now and tell me the truth, you're going be put away for a long time," he said.

Stella broke down and cried. She admitted she had done it, and that she had done it alone.

"My husband had nothing to do with it," she said, weeping. "He didn't even know about it."

The investigator believed her.

"She knew she was nailed," Bob recalled some years later. "She was making sure that I was clear so that I could take care of the kids. The kids were first, nothing else. Not the husband. She'd lay her life down for her kids, but her husband can go to hell."

Stella saw Bob's role differently.

"Him and me agreed ahead of time that he would plead ignorance. I wasn't about to lose my children and have them taken away from us by having Robert go to jail too. I told him to keep his mouth shut," she later explained.

In a plea bargain Bob Strong thought took into consideration her two little girls, Stella Maudine Strong was convicted of a single count of forgery and was sentenced to six months in Orange County Jail.

Cora Lee drove down from Ukiah to help take care of Cindy and Leah while their mother was in jail. Almost immediately Bob started seeing newly single neighbor Pat as the woman of his dreams. She didn't cheat, lie, or steal.

Stella saw what was happening.

By mid-August 1971, she had written the last of three letters to the court, in an attempt to get the judge to take pity on her and release her.

"I desperately need to get home to my family . . . my problem is very serious at home."

She even suggested he could change her probation from three to five years. Whatever it took, she needed out. She worried that Cora Lee was going to take her girls and leave California.

". . . I've been trying to stop her any way I know how. I know how she thinks. . . ."

While Cora Lee's taking the girls to Washington might have been a possibility, the truth was that Bob Strong was slipping away. No man had ever left Stella Maudine before. Especially to a dowdy lady like Pat Bilderback.

Bob visited the jail every day and even did Stella's laundry. He made sure the girls saw their mother each Saturday. But the marriage was over. The forgery conviction had been the last straw. Friends urged him to divorce her while she was in jail, but he refused to slap her down that hard. She was the mother of his children.

Stella asked Bob if he was going with Pat. He didn't deny it, but he asked her if it was Cora Lee who had been talking out of school.

Stella scoffed. "Mother wouldn't discuss that with me," she said. "It's my own business."

Later, Stella said she had a "feeling" the two of them had been seeing each other.

"It's one of those feelings a woman has inside, you know what's going on."

Later, as though she needed to justify why she and Bob hadn't worked out, Stella suggested the split had been mutual.

"He was spineless, no backbone. I thought it over and I knew what I was letting myself in for to stay with a man like Robert. I loved the man, but he wasn't the right one for me in the long run."

Later she even attributed part of the reason her marriage failed to the circumstances of Cynthia's birth.

"I didn't have a young life, a childhood life. And anger that somebody could do something like that to me like when I was raped. Instead of this coming out as anger, it was basically just always there, so it was a part of me. And I took it out on the closest person to me, which happened to be Robert."

Good behavior set Stella free in October 1971, after she had served only four months. By then Bob had asked for a divorce so he and Pat could marry.

Shut out, with no place to go, Stella was furious.

There is no way, she thought, *that another woman is going to take my place. No way am I going to allow it.*

Bob, who could no longer afford the rent on the Acacia home, moved the family into Pat's new place at 234 Victoria in Costa Mesa. He was beside himself with confusion on the best way to handle his wife. He allowed her to move in for a couple of days. Pat, figuring Stella and Bob had plenty to talk over, slept in the workshop.

Stella Maudine would never forget her plan for revenge.

"The night I was released from jail I slept with Robert. I was determined to see that no woman would take my husband from me. My way of getting back was action. Taking him to bed was what I did."

Bob saw it all a bit differently.

"She figured when she got out she could take me away from any female with no problem."

After seven years, four months, and twenty-one days of marriage, the Strongs officially separated.

For her twelfth birthday Cynthia asked for a parakeet, and Stella got her one. The girl was overjoyed, and even more excited about spending the day with her mother. But Stella had other plans. After she gave her daughter the bird, she went off somewhere.

A couple of days later, Pat and Bob dumped Stella at the Sunny Acres Motel in Costa Mesa. The situation at Pat's place had been rough. Stella had put the moves on Bob, and a wised-up Pat could no longer risk having the woman in the same house.

Stella called Lois Schaefer and sobbed into the telephone.

"I don't know what I'm going to do. They left me at this motel. Bob doesn't want me . . ."

Lois felt sorry for the woman. "Bring the girls and come stay with us for a while," Lois said. She later wondered what had made her make that offer. She didn't even like Stella Strong.

Never did.

CHAPTER 26

By early summer 1986, special agents had begun the process of trying to scrape up anything and everything on Stella and Bruce Nickell. Stella Nickell gave the appearance of being cooperative, but insisted doctor's orders had kept her on tranquilizers, and therefore away from Jack Cusack's polygraph unit. The agents who had met with the woman seemed to buy her story.

Ron Nichols, who left on vacation after announcing that Stella was the likely tamperer, returned to find the investigation had produced little more in the way of evidence against Bruce Nickell's wife.

He couldn't let go of the idea that she had produced two of the five bottles of cyanide-laced painkiller. She told SA Ike Nakamoto she had purchased them at two different times.

Two of the five known tainted bottles out of 15,000 bottles scanned by the FDA and FBI were turned in by Stella Nickell!

"She's the tamperer," Ron Nichols repeated. "It all points to Stella."

SA Cusack thought Ron Nichols's declaration was useless. His memo was fine analysis, but what good did it do? It was easy to say someone was the culprit, harder to prove it.

"Goddamn it, Nichols. We need proof. Evidence. Something."

Who knew what really was going on in the Nickell marriage? A. J. Rider? Dee Rogers? Cindy Hamilton? Cora Lee Rice? Any of them might. All were independent, denim-strong women. If a wagon master were looking for pioneer women, Stella Nickell, her family, and her trailer-park cronies were the type.

Sam Masterson was one of those big grayish-blond fisherman-looking type of guys many assume are typical of Seattle. At six feet four, he was taller, bigger, and better-looking than most of the fellows that considered Kent taverns a second home. Sam Masterson was no drifter, but he was trying to come out of the biggest slump of his life. He didn't have money, a car, or a job.

Then he met Stella and Cindy playing darts at Walt's Inn shortly after Bruce's murder.

"God, she sure moves fast," one observer said to one of Stella's neighbors after he saw the new widow in a bar with Sam.

As Sam observed it, though Cindy lived with Dee Rogers, Stella and her daughter were as close as two could be—laughing, joking, sharing dates with men they met in the bar.

The first night they paired off, they parked along Green River. Sam Masterson knew what he liked, and it was Stella Maudine Nickell.

"She had a unique way about her. And her daughter's the same way, but more aggressive. Her daughter wanted to screw my buddy the first night that we met; she goes and climbs in the back of the truck."

While Cindy crashed on the mattress in the back, Stella and Sam downed a few beers. His friend made a play for Cindy, but she had passed out.

"You're gonna have to go," Stella told the other man as the hour grew late. "Sam and I are going home."

With her husband gone the lady is ready to get laid, he thought.

"I know I was the first one," he said years later. "You can tell by a woman's actions. I think I stayed there for about twenty-four hours. I didn't get out of bed very often, except to take a shower every once in a while and get something to eat, then go back to bed.

"This lady wanted to make love. She was starving for love, and I happened to be the man she took it out on. Oh, God, it felt good. Let me put it this way, I've been laid a whole lot, and that lady wouldn't stop. I mean, she was horny."

Over the next few weeks, when Stella wanted Sam Masterson, she'd go pick him up. He was never disappointed. The woman from down in Auburn was something special.

CHAPTER 27

Stella Strong and her young daughters moved in with Lois and Russell Schaefer, forcing Lois, already shakier than the San Andreas Fault, to tread lightly between Stella and her best friend Pat Bilderback. The fact that Pat and Bob were now a couple only exacerbated the situation. Lois had felt sorry for the new couple, but after Stella told her side, she felt Stella had been the maligned party.

One afternoon the Schaefers were discussing food stamps and Lois asked Stella about the application process.

"You should ask Bob," Stella said. "He's the one who did it, and I took the blame because I figured Bob could be out working and take care of the girls and I'd just do the time."

Lois was furious. "How could a man let his wife go to jail for something he did!"

But that wasn't the worst of Stella's lies. She said Bob had sexually abused the girls and that was the reason she didn't want them over at Pat's house.

Lois couldn't believe it. Later, when she asked Cindy if the story was true, the girl denied it.

Cindy and Leah shared a room with the Schaefer children and Stella slept on the living-room hide-a-bed. Almost immediately, a pattern was established with Stella leaving at night and returning in the morning. When Lois asked her where she went, Stella was evasive.

Stella wasn't the best of guests, either. Since she had no money when she moved in, she paid for nothing. The Schaefers were trying to get by on welfare.

Stella told Lois that she was going to be better off than she and Pat. She didn't like to live down. She wanted to live high. She was going to have things.

The talk hurt Lois.

Lady, I'm letting you live here and you're not paying for anything, and you're saying things about my house, she thought.

Whenever Stella needed something, she somehow got the money.

When the water company threatened to discontinue the Schaefers' service, Stella said she'd take care of it. After being out all night, Stella returned the next day with a receipt from the water district. Lois was so touched—so *impressed*—she saved the receipt for more than twenty years.

When cookies were all they had to eat, it was Stella who went to the store and returned with enough groceries to fill the cabinets and refrigerator.

Where she went at night, where she got the money, remained a mystery.

Lois called Pat about it.

"You know what, Pat, I have a feeling she's either prostituting or she's in drugs. I don't know which."

While Stella was out on one of her night runs, Lois, brushing out Cynthia's hair, saw what appeared to be a bite on her shoulder.

"Cindy, what happened to your back?"

"Oh, the dog bit me."

"The dog bit you? Did your mom report it?"

"No, mom beat it with a wooden spoon."

Lois didn't believe her. The bite was human.

Just after Thanksgiving—four or five weeks after she had begged Lois to take her in so she didn't have to live at the motel—without warning, Stella moved again. Around ten o'clock one night she came to get her girls.

She and a boyfriend had rented a motel room, and she would take Cynthia and Leah there.

"It's been too much for you and Russell," she explained. "I've decided to get out on my own."

Stella woke the girls and told them to pack their things. Lois didn't see them again for a couple of months—until Stella showed up with some man in a Cadillac, looking for her girls' boots.

She said she had rented a little apartment up on El Camino in Costa Mesa.

Lois Schaefer got on the phone to Pat. She didn't think much of Stella Strong's boyfriends.

"The men she picked up, honest to God, to me they looked like they had been in prison. She never had a nice boyfriend. They looked like bikers."

Because they were.

For a time following her release from jail, Stella Maudine Strong partied with the Hessians, a bad-ass motorcycle-gang rival of the Hell's Angels that had been running around Orange County at the time. She hooked up with Eddie "Butch" Jones.

Eddie Jones was a fiberglass man who spent his days customizing Corvettes and evenings and weekends on his bike with his "old lady," Stella Strong. Jones was a bit on the old-fashioned side too. By the time he met up with Stella, he had married four times.

"For a biker's old lady, Stella was a neat person, she took good care of herself. I wouldn't say she was pretty, but there were a lot of men that would take a second look. After you got to know her, her disposition was a little bit on the off sides. That kind of scared a lot of them away. She's very outspoken, and she didn't hide her feelings too well," remembered a woman whose daughter ran with the Hessians.

Word came from the Hessians that Stella Maudine Strong had offered money to someone to kill her ex and his squeeze. Bob Strong called the Costa Mesa police and they promised surveillance. Fortunately, nothing came of the threat. Obviously drunk, Stella called Bob late one evening and kept him on the phone for more than two hours. She admitted she had, in fact, hired a Hessian to kill him and that no-good woman who had taken her place.

Later, one of the gang members told Bob Strong that Stella's motorcycle-gang boyfriend had been told "they didn't want this damn bitch around here anymore because she was nothing but trouble." She had been kicked out of the gang.

"When the Hessians don't want you around, you're pretty bad," Bob later said.

After Butch, Stella settled down with a man named Steve at a rented house on Sungrove. Years later, she fumed when she recalled him.

"Oh, I remember him, all right. I put him into a mental institution. The man was not quite right. One night when I was in the living room he pinned me down on the couch and started choking me. He said he was going to kill me and burn down the house and kill my girls. This didn't set well with me.

"When I managed to get him off and down onto the floor, I ran down to the service station at the corner. Two young men were working there, and I told them, 'My girls are in the house with this man!' One of the kids had a gun and fired shots into the air to scare off Steve."

That was the last of that man.

Years later, Leah Strong also shared her memories of Steve.

"There was one time I had told her about someone touching me and she didn't want to believe me. All I remember is Steve. It was when we lived in California over on Sungrove Street. I remember telling her and she didn't want to believe me, she thought I was lying. She just blew it off."

Stella could never recall any such conversation about Leah's being molested.

"I do not recall her telling me, no. I also think that it's possible she remembers this happening because she probably heard Cynthia talking about it. Cynthia tried to tell me some time later that he would not keep his hands off her, and when I asked her why she didn't tell me at the time. And she said no because she didn't want to cause me any trouble. I said, 'I told you from the time you were little, nothing like that causes me any trouble.' I said, 'You are my girls and I will not allow anything to happen to you.' And as she grew older the doubt started to enter my mind as to whether this was true or not."

No matter what her mother said then or years later, Cynthia Lea stuck to her story that one of her mom's boyfriends bothered her. She was just fourteen at the time.

"He'd, like, want me to sit in his lap, and I didn't like this, and my mother always raised me openly. I mean, I knew about sex, I knew how babies were born, I was not ignorant of any aspects or phases of the human body, and I was very uncomfortable with this man, and I told my mom that I felt that he was making passes at me, and I didn't like it, and she hauled off and she slapped me dead across the face, bounced me off the refrigerator and called me everything but a white girl, and said that if I hadn't been asking for it—Well, I didn't feel that this was necessary, and I did rebel.

"I told her if she ever, ever hit me again, it would be the last time, and she never did strike me again after that. That was the first time I had ever really stood up to my mother."

Stella would punish Cindy and Leah to get back at Bob and that Avon Lady, Pat. Bob gave Cindy a fish tank, and Cindy told him her mom flushed the fish down the toilet. When he gave her new inner tubes for her bike, Cindy said her mother threw them in the trash.

Bob frequently told Leah how much he loved her beautiful, curly hair.

"Stella cut it right at the growth line. I imagine what happened: Leah went home and said, 'Daddy thinks my hair is pretty' . . . and she cut it."

As hard as it would be for Bob to imagine, things got worse.

The Sin-Not was a beer joint off Westminster in Garden Grove. It was a "membership" tavern. If someone asked a patron if they were a "Turtle," they were to reply, "You bet your sweet ass I am." Those who messed up were required to buy a round of beers. Stella Maudine's hanging around the place was one thing, but Bob and Pat heard she had brought Cindy inside with her.

"Cindy was in love with a boy named Willie. She wasn't even thirteen. To be with the older boys like she was, I'd have to say yes, she was sexually active," Pat said.

Later, Bob Strong refused to soften his words. Although Stella denied it, Bob always speculated that Stella had brought Cindy to the bar for one reason.

"To make money," he said.

At the time, it seemed Cindy and Stella were headed for the same fate.

"Her feet are coming down in her mother's tracks so close that you can't tell there are two sets of tracks."

Bob Strong couldn't handle just sitting by and watching his ex-wife self-destruct and take Cindy and Leah down the tubes with her.

Besides the men coming and going, school authorities reported that the girls had missed more than a month of school and Stella didn't seem to care. Even the neighbors on Sungrove noticed that the girls were left to her own devices.

Bob filed for custody of Leah, and not surprisingly, Stella became outraged. She had been forced by her mother to give up her son; she was not about to lose her youngest daughter. Stella tried

to gather support that she was a fit mother. She went to see Lois
Schaefer to make sure she wasn't going to get in her way.

"You better not show up in court to testify against me, or you're
gonna pay for it, lady," Stella told her.

After she left, Lois called Pat in tears.

"I think I'm gonna get done in, and I want you to know who
done it."

After Steve came Harold, known as "Bull." Bull, a carny worker
from Long Beach, moved into the Sungrove address. Stella didn't
love him, but she needed someone to help her out. She now changed
the girls' last name to match Bull's. The changes were confusing.
Leah told her father that she didn't know who her real dad was.

The pressure of dealing with Bob and Pat had worn thin, and
the only relief was to leave. Stella didn't have a reliable car—the
old Packard kept dying—so she enlisted Bull.

"It kept losing the transmission," she remembered of the car she
got from Bob. "We worked on his car and got it up. He was tired
of going through the carnival scene. I wanted out of California. I
had not liked California since the day I set foot in it when I was
sixteen years old. I was divorced and I had my two kids; I had
nothing to hold me there. One day I just packed up and left."

The first week in November 1973, Stella, Bull, and the girls
drove up to Washington to put some miles between them and Bob
Strong, who had petitioned the court for custody of Leah. He would
have taken Cindy, too, but he had no blood claim to her.

They stopped at Stella's sister Georgia Mae's place near Tenino,
Washington, with sights set on Kent or Auburn.

Bob Strong learned some of Stella Maudine's stuff was for sale at
the Sungrove house and went over to have a look. Everything she
owned had been dumped on the front lawn. He bought back a roll-
away bed that he had purchased for the girls, and a few other odds
and ends, including Leah's baby book.

Among the ruins, he found some baby shoes.

Stella had kept the pair of baby shoes, which had belonged to
Little Joe, the baby brother who had died in the fire. She had
guarded them with her life. Cora Lee wanted the shoes, but, for
some reason Stella refused to give them up. In fact, it was Bob
Strong's feeling, Stella didn't want her mother to have them—ever.

"I spotted the shoes, and bought 'em and gave them to Cora.

She cried when she got them. These little shoes . . . why would they be such a big thing?" he wondered later.

December in the Pacific Northwest is a far cry from the sunny warmth of Orange County: rain, followed by more of the same. After living out of the car, Stella Strong and her daughters moved into a one-bedroom Kent apartment, though the girls would later remember it as more of a garage or storage building. If Leah would later had any good memories of her sister Cynthia, they were made there.

Though she was only seven years older, Cindy made sure Leah was dressed and fed before school. Their mother seemed only a visitor.

"My mom would come once in a while in the morning to make sure we had money for lunch. She'd come by and make sure we had groceries and that's about it," Leah recalled years later, still unsure if her mother ever lived with them. It seemed she lived with some man down in a nearby trailer park.

Since Leah didn't have anything to play with—all of her toys had been left on their front lawn in Garden Grove—Cindy waited until dark one night and climbed into a Goodwill depository and emerged with armloads of toys. Cindy also set up shipping crates in a field behind a bakery near their apartment to create a playhouse for her little sister.

"We'd build a house, and she'd set a crate down and it would be a couch, set another as a door. She used to do things like that."

On the weekends or when they missed school, the girls went downtown and window-shopped. One time Cindy saw a two-piece bathing suit that she simply had to have. She gave the suit to Leah and told her to hide it in the folds of her doll's blanket. Leah complied, only happy to help her sister.

"She really, really wanted that suit," Leah later recalled.

Cindy saw that she and Leah never went hungry, even if it meant going to a house next door to ask for something to eat.

No little girl thought her big sister was smarter, prettier, and nicer than Leah Strong did. She was the luckiest little girl in the world with Cindy as her protector.

Leah went to Cindy when carny man Butch messed with her.

"He just . . . touched me in a place he shouldn't touch a little girl. I just didn't like it. I went and cried. Mom didn't believe me. I guess she didn't want to believe it."

Stella Strong and her girls did not stay with the carny man long after that incident. Stella later recalled coming home to find everything littered all over the apartment.

"There was food in the middle of the floor, my clothes were pulled out of the closet and strewn all over the bedroom, the bed was tore up, some of my clothes were even tore up. The man had gone totally berserk," she remembered.

Stella found the boozing troublemaker in a Kent bar and told him never to set foot back in her place again.

Armed with custody papers, Bob and his new wife Pat Strong made the trip to Washington to get Leah. When they finally found her, she was at Stella's sister Mary's house in a suburb outside of Seattle.

Mary stood in a state of shock when she answered the door. Stella had told her Bob was dead. Stella was trying to find someone—anyone—to take Leah in.

"If you tell her I told you," Mary said, "I'll deny it."

By now, such a response didn't surprise Bob Strong. The Stephenson sisters, whether they loved one another or hated one another, were fiercely loyal.

"They are very protective of their own. It's like a Mafia, that family. I don't know how else to put it. They'd lay down their life for their own," he said.

Leah went home to Garden Grove, with her mother's promise she would be down to see her little girl in a few weeks.

Leah wouldn't see her for nearly four years.

Cindy, running back and forth from Cora Lee's place in Ukiah to foster homes in the Seattle area, never made it down to see her little sister either.

CHAPTER 28

Phyllis Cordova nearly died one rainy Seattle night when her car collided with an abutment near the Spokane Street Bridge. Phyllis was pitched through the windshield. The soon-to-be-divorced mother of four lay in a coma for eleven days. When she awakened, she learned the horror of what happens when flesh presses through glass shards. Her face would never be the same.

By the time she returned to her home in Wenatchee, she was a physical and emotional wreck. Nothing but her singing voice was the same. One night at the Columbia Hotel where she worked, she noticed a man over by the jukebox. He was celebrating his birthday.

He introduced himself as Bruce Nickell. It was 1967.

"I had been in an accident in March, and I met Bruce in June. I lost my teeth . . . I was self-conscious, but he never made me feel that way. He made me feel like a million dollars and he introduced me to everyone as his southern belle."

The man Phyllis Cordova fell in love with was a loner who liked to drink to get drunk, sit in bars, shoot pool. He moved from job to job. He told Phyllis he got bored easily. Yet there was also a gentle side. When Phyllis Cordova had plastic surgery, it was Bruce Nickell who stayed with her.

One day he just left Wenatchee for the Seattle area. He didn't say anything, just left. Eventually, he contacted Phyllis and she moved over, too, Bruce was working for the Des Moines Water

Department and living in an apartment near Kent, just behind a bar. It was convenient for a man who drank as much as he did.

In the summer of 1971, Bruce Nickell's alcoholism finally caught up with him. After Phyllis Cordova got home from work one evening, Bruce called her from the Country Fair Tavern on Pacific Highway South.

"Babe, I'm here with an eight-pack of screwdrivers in front of me. Come and get me out of here!"

She thought he was joking. When she arrived, she knew she was wrong. He had emptied most of the glasses put in front of him.

Phyllis tried to get him into her car, but he insisted he could drive his pickup just fine. A mile from her duplex, Bruce was stopped by an off-duty officer out with his family.

"Let me take him home," Phyllis pleaded.

Bruce Nickell was arrested, and since it wasn't his first DWI, he was sentenced to serve four months at Cedar Hills, the county drunk farm near Maple Valley.

Phyllis drove her '64 Ford Galaxy to see her man twice a week. He seemed to be improving. A.A. was even taking hold; at least, she thought so.

"He seemed all right. Joking. Playing cards. He made me a beautiful leather-tooled wallet while he was there," she later recalled.

He also divulged things she hadn't known.

Bruce said he was sixteen when he discovered he was adopted. He overheard his father talking about it. Bruce became bitter and resentful at the woman who gave him up.

Whoever she was. Wherever she was.

Phyllis later wondered if Bruce's relationships with women were affected by his mother's abandonment.

"I kind of feel that he couldn't continue relationships with women because he was feeling so badly about his birth mother."

Walter and Ruth Nickell gave their son a little thirteen-foot travel trailer they had used on a cross-country vacation, and Bruce was glad to get it. He rented space #52 at the Valley Mobile Home Park on South Central Avenue in Kent. It, too, was convenient. The White Spot Tavern was next door.

Every night after work Bruce Nickell hit the taverns, usually downing a half-dozen beers at a sitting. He generally hung out at a place for a few weeks, got bored with the crowd, and moved on. Since he often got mouthy and physical when he drank, sometimes he was thrown out. For a while it was the Red Baron, the cocktail lounge at the Coachman, and the White Spot.

"We spent all these hours sitting in a tavern talking. We talked about everything. He played pool, but I didn't. I'd sit there and gnash my teeth and twiddle my thumbs. A good percentage of the time I was just bored," Phyllis Cordova later recalled.

Though their relationship was on and off, Bruce and Phyllis married before a Federal Way justice of the peace in September of 1972.

In January, only four months later, Bruce changed his mind.

"I think it's time for us to split the sheets," he said.

Phyllis had no idea it was coming.

"Why?"

"I just think it's better. It's time we did."

"I didn't get married to quit," she said.

"I'll meet you after work," Bruce said, not really listening, "and we'll talk about it."

There was another woman on the scene at that time, though Phyllis didn't know it. Her name was Stella Strong. She had just come up from Southern California, and in no time was the talk of the taverns.

It was Bruce Nickell's pattern in dealing with women. He told Phyllis repeatedly she didn't do things the way he wanted. She didn't raise her children right. She was too easy, too soft. Not smart enough. He tore her down, and then, when he felt like it, flicked her a bone.

"I've thought about this situation a lot with him and Stella, and I can understand that if a person had a nature like that, and how he can make them want to kill him," Phyllis said years later.

Stella Strong met Bruce Nickell one afternoon in a tavern in Kent, not far from his little trailer. He walked in and sat down at the bar next to the new girl in town.

"Of course, I'm used to this," Stella said later. "I have been all my life. I ignore things like this, I *learned* to. He ordered a beer and started trying to talk. If he made some remark or asked me a question, I would answer it, and that's all. I was not getting into a conversation with him. And I was about ready to finish my beer and he asked if I wanted another one and I said, 'No, I have to go home.' He says, 'You can stay and have another beer.' I said,

'Nope. I have got to go home. I've got two girls waiting for me.'
I got up off the bar stool and walked out."

A week later, while her girls were down at her sister Georgia
Mae's place, Stella Strong ran into Bruce Nickell again. After that
meeting, she told Cynthia Lea, "That man is mine, and I'm going
to marry him."

Bruce was "perfect-looking" and "he talked very educated, he
was intelligent, he didn't make an idiot of himself . . ." He was tall,
slender, and combed his dark hair back from a high forehead. Stella
wanted him, and the fact that he was married was only a slight
complication.

His heavy drinking didn't dissuade her either. She had been
raised around alcoholics, but didn't think Bruce Nickell fit the mold.
He drank real hard only on weekends.

"He had enough sense to know that it would jeopardize his job,
so he would stay sober throughout the week. But Lord, when Friday
night came, from the time he hit that door he'd start getting ready
to go out, and when we'd go out we'd stay until the bars closed.
And then we would start in Saturday morning at six in the morning.
He knew every bar in South King County that was open at six in
the morning."

Stella went along for the ride, her mother's advice playing in
her head: *If your husband goes out drinking and he wants you to
go with him, go with him. Because then you know where he's at
and who he's with.*

Her man's favorite mixed drink, vodka and grapefruit juice, soon
became her favorite. For a while, she tried to drink one-for-one
with him, something he insisted on. Though she could hold her
liquor, she was no match for his endless capacity.

"I finally told him that there is a pace and a limit for everybody,
that he drinks at his pace and I drink at mine, we're not drinking
drink-for-drink. We tried that for a short time, because he didn't
believe in spending more money on himself than he did on whoever
he was with. And I said that makes no never mind. I said, when
I'm done with my drink, I'll let you know, then we can order another one. Because just sticking with him one-for-one was . . . it
would have killed me before the year was out."

While Bruce was living at Mobile Manor, he arranged for Phyllis
to meet him at a tavern. He wanted to talk about a new girl he had
met. Phyllis, who still loved him, listened.

"He said he had been there a night or two before, and she was there and this guy was knocking her around," Phyllis reminisced some time later. "Beating on her. And so she didn't have anywhere to go, and it was like they were living in this car they had from California. They were living in the car with her clothes. The guy knocked her around and left her there. So Bruce said she could stay at his house."

He said he was in love with Stella.

"I was crushed, but I knew it was coming. She was there. I knew it. And he had her there. He didn't have time for somebody unless they had something he wanted. I think he really fell in love with her—in a way he hadn't been with me."

By March 1974, Stella and Bruce had moved in together. Stella had found her man, and Bruce found a woman with a nice body, brains, and, best of all, a wanton temperament to match his own.

Phyllis Cordova started seeing Stella and Bruce regularly at Walt's Inn in downtown Kent. Stella was warm, funny, and kind-hearted. Though it hurt, Phyllis could see why Bruce liked her.

On Wednesdays, between work appointments as a house-cleaner, Phyllis would stop down at Walt's and there would be Stella—without Bruce.

"Stella would come in and she'd have a stack of books from the library and she'd sit them on the bar. She always wore those short, short skirts. She had long legs, and they were pretty. She'd sit at the bar and we'd talk sometimes."

Phyllis noticed that men liked Stella.

"These guys would buy her drinks. She was an attractive woman. She's slender. She'd sit there and play dollar liar's poker with the guys, taking money from them."

I don't know how she gets away with it—free drinks, too.

It was around that time Stella started phoning Phyllis to get together for coffee or drinks. She wanted to talk, usually about Bruce. Phyllis was skeptical. She suspected Stella was just using her.

Stella insisted later that she felt being friendly with the woman who loved Bruce too might make it easier for her than being ignored.

"I could understand why she loved Bruce, because I did myself. I didn't want her to feel that she was being pushed off to one side. That's where my kind heart comes in. Sometimes it gets me in trouble. I wanted her to know that she could still be friends with

Bruce, that I wouldn't mind. But friends was it—keep your hands to yourself."

It was clear something was wrong with Bruce and Stella's relationship. One time at an Auburn Denny's, Phyllis watched an older fellow climb all over Stella. She couldn't believe Bruce was at home while his woman was out running around like this. Phyllis watched the man fondle Stella's legs.

Another time when she and Bruce were on the outs, Stella called Phyllis and, like the good sport that she was, Bruce's ex-wife picked her up and chauffeured her from bar to bar.

Since she had to work the next day, Phyllis Cordova couldn't make it a late night. Stella was sitting there with another man, and she didn't want to leave.

"Stel, I'll take you home."

Stella didn't want to go, she didn't have any place to go. She didn't have any money.

Phyllis waited a bit longer before leaving—alone.

Four days later, Bruce called.

"Have you seen Stella? Do you know where she is?"

Phyllis said she didn't.

Stella called her a short time later and told Phyllis not to tell Bruce where she was.

"She was living in some southeast Auburn apartments. She said this guy had bought her an old clunker and that she was getting around. She had a job she was gonna start and not go back to Bruce," Phyllis Cordova later recalled.

Bruce, beside himself with worry, enlisted Phyllis in trying to find Stella by driving around South King County. For a couple of weeks, no one knew where she was.

A bartender at the Coachman had one theory. He told Phyllis Cordova that Stella was "prostituting herself up in North Seattle."

Phyllis didn't know if it was true, but it made some things make sense.

"That's what she was doing that night when I left her in Auburn. I left her back in the New Moon Cocktail Lounge. I knew they were closing. I told her, 'You're gonna be stranded here. She said, 'Don't worry about it. Go ahead.' I knew that this old guy had some place where she could crash or something.

"The way she acted with this other fellow, letting him rub her legs just to get him to buy her drinks."

A little while later, Phyllis ran into Bruce at the Eagles Club in

Kent. Her ex-husband confided that he and Stella had problems in the bedroom.

"He said he had tried everything. That she's cold to him. That he couldn't satisfy her in bed. He said, 'I've done everything I know how to do. She has no interest. There's nothing there.' That hurt him, because he and I had a good relationship that way. It was hurting him because he cared for her."

Later, tears came as Phyllis agonized over why Stella ended up with Bruce and she was left alone.

"I made myself too available for him. I let him run over me. Too comfortable for him. She didn't, and it kept his interest."

CHAPTER 29

As Paul Webking gathered his wits for SA Jack Cusack's poly-graph, Stella Nickell wrote out a lovely thank-you card and mailed it to Jones and Jones Funeral Home in Wenatchee. She signed it "Bruce and Stella."

Her husband's amended death certificate was issued. Acute cy-anide poisoning was now listed as Bruce Nickell's cause of death.

Stella's niece, Wilma Mae, and her ex-husband, Mel Stewart, rekindled the flame during the drive to and from Uncle Bruce's funeral. Wilma had been absorbed with thoughts of Mel and the jarring revelation that her favorite uncle had been poisoned by tainted Excedrin capsules.

Throughout the weeks following her husband's death, Stella phoned her niece at her Houston home every few days. She seemed to border on suicidal. The FBI wouldn't leave her alone. They had asked her to take a polygraph.

"Don't do it," Wilma begged. "Please do not take the polygraph. I don't care whether you did it or not, do not take the polygraph. After you take it they are going to crucify you if you fail it. I know what I'm talking about. I work for attorneys!"

She also knew firsthand. She had been given a polygraph for a job interview.

"They asked, 'Do you have any children?' "

"I said, 'No.' "

It was a lie, of course. Her ex had custody of her three boys, and there was also the matter of the baby she gave up when she was in Maple Lane.

"I passed that part of it," She told her aunt. "If you can lie to a polygraph and pass, you can tell the truth and fail it."

Stella said she had no intention of taking it; she was too upset. Trying to come to grips with Bruce's death was extremely difficult.

"They keep saying it will relieve me of all this," Stella told her niece.

"We'll know that you are innocent. And we'll leave you alone."

"Typical governmental lies, that's the bottom line," Willie came back.

Over Fourth of July weekend, Stella's niece flew from Houston to Seattle to take in the World's Fair in Vancouver, B.C., with Mel Stewart. When she returned to Texas and discovered she was pregnant, the couple decided to make another attempt at marriage. There was another plus. Moving back to the Northwest would also put her close to Aunt Stella, who desperately needed her.

It was hot and dry the day Stella Nickell needed a ride home from Sue and Jeff Ford's Kent transmission shop. The truck was giving her fits again. Sue Ford, who put up with the ribbing of employees who had taken to mimicking Marlon Brando in *A Streetcar Named Desire* whenever Stella showed up, agreed to give her a lift back to Auburn.

"Stelllllllaaaaa! Stellllllllllaaaaa!"

They drove south along the Valley Highway, Mount Rainier looming high above warehouses and apartments. Stella was calm, but she had some disturbing news. The authorities had suspected her of killing Bruce. Now they were trying to gather evidence to indict her.

"There's not enough evidence. I didn't do it. I don't know what they're looking for."

The FBI had been pressuring her to take a polygraph.

"My lawyer has advised me not to take it, but I want to. I know I'll pass and it will exonerate me. I don't know why my attorney doesn't want me to take it."

Sue Ford was all ears as Stella told her story over the two hours they spent running around Auburn, even stopping at a drugstore.

I don't want to say anything to this woman to get her upset. I

*don't know if she did it or not. I'm alone with her headed out to
her place in the back forty,* she thought.

Sue Ford didn't ask Stella if she had done the crime. She didn't
want to be the person she might say "yes" to. Since there were no
tears from Stella, only bravado and unlimited confidence in her
exoneration, Sue Ford didn't feel the need to console the woman.
She just listened and wondered.

As July heated up, Sue Snow and Bruce Nickell's survivors filed
separate lawsuits against Bristol-Myers. Such legal action had been
expected. The capsules, despite safety seals and warnings, were
simply too easy a mark for a crazed killer—random or otherwise.

Paul Webking had become an effective source for news reporters
needing a quick quote on areas concerning product safety. To
Webking it was not just pain-medication capsules that should be
banned. He pressed for the discontinuation of all capsules. Drug
companies, he said, were more concerned with profits than with
public safety.

"There are no need for capsules, period! There is no medical
reason for them, and they don't speed up the effects of medication.
Tablets work just as quickly."

In July, Hayley Snow was fingerprinted by the FBI. Agents told
her that a single latent print remained a mystery. The girl hoped
the print would lead to her mother's murderer, and not back to a
family member who might have innocently handled the bottle.

When Sue's daughters talked about the mysterious fingerprint
and suggested a family friend should be printed—since she had
been at the house the morning the paramedics came—word got back
to Paul, who was in the dark on the subject. Paul had words with
Hayley over it.

In her diary, Hayley wrote:

> Paul was mad because I'm supposedly supposed to tell him
> everything if I expect him to be the parent . . . He got mad be-
> cause it was a good idea and he hadn't thought of it first. I'm
> suppose to check with him first! HA! . . . He never even called
> or checked up on me once . . .

During this time, the family discussed the lawsuit against Dr.
Fligner and the Medical Examiner's office for negligence. Their

lawyers discouraged it. The drug company was at fault.

Yet Paul Webking couldn't help but reiterate the obvious. If Bruce Nickell's death had been autopsied properly, Sue would still be alive.

CHAPTER 30

A working-class mother of five, Josephine Nelson was holding down three jobs when she met Bruce Nickell in the early seventies. She was hopping tables at the White Spot in Kent at the time.

Though Bruce Nickell was a foulmouthed rowdy drunk who got along with few, he warmed up to Josephine, whom he quickly and affectionately called "sister."

"He tried to make out like he was a hard-nosed guy, and a bad guy, a mean guy. But he wasn't. He was a Caspar Milquetoast, really," she later said.

Whatever his faults, Bruce was a bunch better than some other barflies that lit on the local tavern scene. At least he went to work every day. His word also stood for something. And if he told someone he was going to do something, he did it.

With all the b.s. permeating taverns, such traits were refreshing.

It was after Josephine took a job tending bar at Walt's Inn that she became close to Stella Strong. She liked the woman. She was an original.

No one in Kent had seen the likes of Stella Strong. She burst on the scene like a scotch-and-water tsunami. Her clothes alone guaranteed her some looks when she entered a bar. Her skirts were just short of being wide waistbands. Sometimes she wore a black fall, to add to her already massive cape of black hair. An absolute knockout, she had the body of a teenager.

Yet there was a dichotomy of sorts at work. Though Stella's pumps and short skirts sent a message of availability, she also presented a more demure image.

"She was like an old-fashioned girl. She'd come in a lot of times dressed in a miniskirt and a big brimmed hat, sun hat," Josephine Nelson recalled.

Stella could drink with the best of them. Sometimes she'd come into Walt's Inn at 7 A.M. and drink all through Josephine's shift.

"She drank Bourbon 7, Vodka Squirt; in between she always had drambuie or crème de menthe. After she ate lunch, she had a double shot of drambuie or crème de menthe or something like that. Then she'd go back to what she might be drinking," the bartender friend remembered.

Only one or two times did the bartender see Stella Maudine stagger, and even then she couldn't be sure if it had been the booze or the high heels that caused her missteps.

When she first considered the idea of Bruce and Stella as a couple, Josephine felt it wasn't a good match. Bruce was a True Honest Person, she thought, and Stella was never faithful. Stella liked other men too much to be devoted to Bruce.

"I always knew she was kinky as far as men go. I used to think she was a nymphomaniac," Josephine said some years later.

"Are you actually telling me that you need 'it' to survive?" Josephine asked Stella one day at Walt's Inn.

"Yeah, I do," she said, the look on her face leaving no room for doubt.

Josephine told her friend she didn't like the way she ran around on her man.

"She had her sad stories. He drank . . . she didn't get her sex because he wasn't able to. That's why she told me she always went with these guys."

At the same time, Stella Maudine always had cash in her purse. It surprised Josephine to see someone like Stella flashing hundred-dollar bills around the bar.

"She always liked to have money. She liked to dress in her fancy little clothes. She bought clothes that were too small for her, the buttons always gapped. Her clothes were always tight," Josephine recalled.

Stella had a sugar daddy somewhere in Auburn, though Josephine never knew who the man was. As she had with Phyllis Cordova, Stella refused to tell her bartender friend where she lived at the time. Whatever was going on, money was not a problem. When Stella wanted to go somewhere, she did. She often paid Josephine's way, too.

"Where are you getting your money? You're not getting it from Bruce. He isn't going to give you that kind of money."

Stella wouldn't answer.

"Where are you living?"

Stella wouldn't answer.

Josephine wondered if Stella was a prostitute. She acted like one, even dressed like one. She dismissed the idea, though.

"The guys she went with didn't have any money to give her," she said.

Josephine's son, eighteen-year-old Tommy, carted a couple of Walt's Inn drinking buddies around town when they were too soused to drive. He was glad for the job.

Sometimes Stella went along. At the time, she was seeing one of the men behind Bruce's back. Tommy didn't like being caught in the middle, because Bruce had always been good to him. Still, he needed the money.

"I'd run them to the motel and have to come and pick them up the next day to give him his car. He'd always give me money and have me go fill it up with gas and go have fun, and come and pick him up. They always went to Don's Motel."

In the morning Tommy would pick up Stella and the man, drop her off at the Coachman, where she kept her car, and take the man back to his wife.

Stella would act like it was no big deal.

"She'd go in and have a few drinks, just like she'd been out partying all night."

It bothered Josephine that her friend didn't have her daughters with her. Stella's story didn't seem true. She claimed her ex-husband kicked her out without so much as a suitcase of clothes. He took the girls to California without her permission. Stella said she didn't have the money for a court battle.

Bruce also wanted the girls. He told Josephine having them up in Washington might help his woman settle down.

"It might stop her from flittin' around so much," he said.

All agreed it was a shame Stella didn't have Leah and Cindy.

"Stella always wanted to be close to her kids. But she couldn't get close to Cindy. Cindy wouldn't let her," Josephine Nelson said.

*   *   *

One morning in the summer of 1974, Bruce woke up with the idea that South Seattle was too big, too noisy, and too crowded. He and Stella packed up his travel trailer and drove east. They stopped in Spokane and stayed for six weeks, camping on the Spokane River, before moving on to look for work at a sawmill in Idaho. When that wasn't suitable—there were only one or two bars in the entire town—he and Stella took jobs at the Sno-Kist Apple Co. in Yakima.

They stayed at the Trailer Village in Yakima until the spring of the following year. Then it was back to Kent.

CHAPTER 31

In 1974, Cynthia Lea Slawson moved into Bob and Pat Strong's home on the corner of Fairview and Trask in Garden Grove. She was more than just a restless teenager. Her mother said she couldn't handle her—she was incorrigible, truant, deceitful—and put her into foster homes. Cindy figured it was because her mother didn't want her in the way of her own good times. So she ran away, another foster home, and another escape.

And though only fifteen, the girl had more miles on her than the trucks she hitched rides on to return from Washington to Southern California. Without question she was following in what Bob Strong knew to be her mother's well-trodden footsteps.

The phone calls would come in the early morning.

"Do you have a daughter named Cynthia?"

"Yes," Bob Strong would answer, because as far as he was concerned, she was his daughter.

"We found her in an off-limits part of the base. Will you come and get her?"

And so he would drive his pickup to Camp Pendelton or El Toro.

Sometimes it would be Cindy's voice on the other end of the line.

"Daddy, come and get me. I'm at the Candy Cane Motel."

And so he would go.

"I didn't think she should be out there doing what she's doing—chasing men. Not boys, *men*. We're talking Marines. Harbor and Katella is a hookers' hangout. That's basically what she was running around with was a bunch of hookers."

As far as the Strongs could see, Cindy was self-destructing before their eyes. The girl seemed to be on the edge of a breakdown.

"I don't want to be like this, but this is the way I was raised. I want to stop, and I can't," Cindy told her stepfather one time.

The words were heartbreakingly familiar.

Stella had said the same thing.

"She used to cry and tell us that she wished she could stop having sex with men frequently," Pat Strong confided years later.

If he had any doubts from the first time he saw Cindy mimic Stella's walk as mother and daughter walked across Acacia Street in Santa Ana, they were laid to rest: Cindy *was* Stella.

Bob Strong agonized over Stella's influence on her oldest daughter. He had some responsibility in it, of course, but Cindy truly was her mother's daughter. He wondered what was missing in the girl's life.

"It's like the stray dog that comes down the street looking for somebody to care for it. The stray dog will bite you if you try to do anything for it, 'cause he don't trust anybody," he said later.

When he told her she was behaving like Stella Maudine, Cindy would lash out in a fit of defensiveness.

Her eyes grew cold and full of anger. "I am not my mother!!!"

There was no disputing; Cindy was indeed searching for something. For one thing, when she got calls at the house, the young men who called asked for "Mandy."

The first week in February 1975, "Mandy" wrote a love letter to a Marine at Camp Pendelton. She told how she had gone dancing with an old boyfriend.

"He kindled an old flame. But I wouldn't let it start. I was waiting for you."

The odd thing was, the letter was written to a *woman* private.

The letter had been returned to sender, addressee unknown.

When the Strongs finally accepted that they had no control over Cynthia Lea, they turned to their last resort and reported her to the police as a runaway.

The teenager had been gone for several days when the Strongs decided to go over to the hamburger place on Katella and Harbor in Anaheim. The place was a hangout for Marines, and they knew

Cindy spent time there. They waited in the truck for their wayward girl to show up.

And she did, looking at least five years older than her fifteen years, wearing hot pants, a vest, and calf-high boots. She looked like some kind of a junior streetwalker. The hamburger place was so notorious, it might have been called "Hookers' Hamlet." But Cindy never said she was a prostitute.

"Cindy, come over here," Bob called across the parking lot. "I want you to get in the truck."

"No."

"Cindy, I told you I want you to get in the truck. I don't want you just running around."

"I don't want to and I'm not going to."

"I could just throw you in the truck and take you home."

"You do and I'll just crawl out the window and be gone again," she said, turning her back. She was calm. She would only do what she wanted. Bob and Pat's rules were a big joke.

For Bob, the whole business in the parking lot was like talking to Stella. Trying to *make* Cindy do something she didn't want to only fueled her determination.

I'll show them.

Cindy called from some man's apartment the next day, and while she was talking to her stepmother, Pat scribbled a note to a visiting friend:

"Go to the pay phone at 7–11 and call the police. Ask for Officer Owenby. Cindy's on the line now. Have them tap the line so they can find out where she's at."

The police instructed Pat Strong to stay on the phone until they got to Cindy's hideout: She did.

"Somebody's at the door," Cindy said, "hold on."

A moment later, an officer got on the line.

"We're taking her to Juvenile Hall," he said.

Cindy stayed in detention for a week during mid-February 1975. Authorities attempted to contact Stella, but she apparently had other concerns. A photograph saved in her scrapbook shows that while Cindy was waiting for her mother to come and get her, Stella was drinking at the Coachman in celebration of a girlfriend's birthday. The icing on the cake read: *"Get your ass out of the saddle, I can't fuck you flying."*

The only other option was her grandmother, who had already taken Cindy in on many other occasions.

Cora Lee drove all night from Ukiah to get her troubled grand-daughter. She didn't even sleep after the Strongs called her to come. She loved Cindy and wanted to take care of her.

"Cora wanted so much for Cindy to be different than her mother," Bob Strong said later.

But as Bob Strong saw it, there was a difference.

He didn't worry that some man would really take advantage of the girl; he knew Cindy could handle herself. Cindy could be colder than Stella.

"She would be more ruthless. She would be more apt to do something with her own hands. When it comes right down to it, blood and guts, she'll stand toe to toe with you and fight it out," he said later.

CHAPTER 32

The Church family had never known Stella Nickell to hit the bottle as hard as she did in the days following Bruce's death and the FBI's probe of the tampering case. Once when Stella was drunk, Laurie and Stan were afraid she was a danger on the road, and they tried to take her keys.

"You touch my butt and you're dead," she said, refusing to hand over her keys, which always jangled from a ring on her back belt loop. "This truck knows the way home."

When Stella got to drinking, she got to talking. One time she told of the 911 call she had made when Bruce collapsed.

Tears came as she told the story:

Bruce had been down the hillside at the shipping container. He came inside, took the Excedrin capsules, and after stepping outside on the deck for a moment, collapsed. Joe, their Labrador, was not allowed in the house, but the dog had followed Bruce in from behind the mobile home.

"He would not leave Bruce's body," she told Stan and Laurie. "The dog would not move."

She could hardly get past him to Bruce. The dog, she said, knew something was terribly wrong.

"He sensed it."

Stella cried when she talked about Joe's devotion to his master. Laurie cried too.

The phone in the den was hooked up to Bruce's electronic gear, so Stella said she went to another room—the kitchen or the den—and dialed 911.

"Is he breathing?" the dispatcher asked.

"I don't know. I can't see him."

She kept trying to get off the phone, but the dispatcher insisted she keep talking.

Stella said she was forced to drag the dog outside and chain him up when the paramedics arrived.

But hadn't volunteer fire fighters Bob and Lori Jewett seen a seemingly disinterested Cora Lee and the dog outside between the mobile homes when they arrived with the fire truck?

Another time when Stella tipped back too many, Karan and Crystal followed her, as if tailing the truck could prevent an accident. When they got to the property, they learned Stella had been drinking more than they had imagined.

"She had bought a case of liquor, which I just couldn't believe she had bought. That's just not Stella. She had whiskey, vodka, rum . . . a big box full. It was like she went to the liquor store and whatever she saw, she threw into a box. It was like she wanted to drink herself to death," Karan Church later said.

The mobile home was a mess, again totally out of character. Even Stella's fish tanks weren't kept up.

It bothered Karan and her younger sister.

"It was like she just didn't care anymore. She didn't care if she wrecked her truck. She didn't care if she lost her house. She didn't care if she lost her job. She didn't care if her dog died. She loved her animals. She just didn't care."

Hayley Snow was wavering on the brink, alternating between showing no emotion and unleashing a deluge. Most of her time was spent alone in her bedroom.

Her family was disintegrating before her eyes. Sarah had returned to Colorado, Exa was gone, and she was left with her mixed feelings for Paul Webking.

On Sunday, July 13, 1986, she wrote of her mother and Paul:

It's so hard to just stop and think and realize that she'll never be here to give me advice I think I'll need or to even talk to me. It's painful not even seeing her take off her jewelry and hearing her bitch about work . . . Paul pisses me off. I like him, love him, but he's trying too hard for the limelight and for a position as head-honcho. He'll never boss me around too bad. . . . I feel stubborn and sort of ornery toward Paul. If something goes wrong, let's say he tries to collect my social security after I turn 16 when it should be mine, I'll let him know how he's being and gather my stuff and walk. I know I have places to turn to and I'll also protect what should be mine even if I do have to piss him off. It's a delicate situation. Very delicate.

Stella Nickell made her last appearance at SeaTac a month or so after Bruce's death. She sauntered up to the security checkpoint at the concourse with a man co-worker Becky Williams understood was a boyfriend. That didn't jar her as much as the way the woman had changed in her appearance.

Stella wore a skintight miniskirt and had put her makeup on with a palette knife. Williams thought she looked like an old street-walker.

Stella was in a great mood, all smiles and "how ya doings?" for everyone.

She told the security firm's president, Mark Vinson, that she was going out dancing.

Her husband just died, and she's going out dancing? Vinson thought.

Shortly after Stella's last visit to the concourse, Cindy Hamilton told co-workers that her mother's life had fallen into a dangerous disarray after Bruce's death. She said her mother had been hitting the bars every night.

CHAPTER 33

Jeff Ford ended each phone call to his wife with an "I love you." And those who knew his wife could see why. Just five feet tall, freckle-faced and green-eyed, Sue Ford was as pretty, sweet, and smart as they come. Jeff was a mechanic at Paul K. Haggard in Tukwila, and after Bruce Nickell was hired in March 1975, the two became friends.

When Jeff Ford got home after putting in a hard day, he often came home with stories about the guys. Bruce Nickell's name came up more often than a sidewalk weed.

Jeff Ford learned quickly that if Bruce was drinking his lunch down at the Golden Nugget or the Coachman, he'd best find another place to go eat.

"There wasn't a foul word in the book that he didn't use, and if you got anywhere near him, you were part of it. That's the way he was. He was an asshole and a jerk."

When he wasn't drinking, Bruce was an everyday guy, a good welder, and at times he had a great sense of humor.

Stella didn't get belligerent or obnoxious when she got drunk, which seemed as often as her "husband," which she called Bruce after moving in with him. If Bruce flipped her any grief, however, she'd push it right back at him. Jeff Ford figured Bruce Nickell had found the perfect woman.

When Bruce's former tough-gal, biker chick Stella came into

the picture, her name was mentioned around the Ford household too.

Sue Ford would never forget the first Stella story she heard.

"Jeff ran into Stella when they were downtown in Kent. I don't know how to say it," she said years later, searching for polite wording. "Bruce lifted Stella's sweater and exposed her breasts. He was very proud of them."

"My gosh, what did she do?" Sue had asked her husband. Jeff shrugged. "She just stood there."

Later, when Bruce brought Stella to the Fords' home, it was hard for Sue to look the woman in the eye. All she could think about was the story of her exposed breasts on a Kent sidewalk in broad daylight.

Though Sue Ford grew to like Stella, she never considered her a close friend. The black-haired babe on the back of Bruce Nickell's motorcycle was hardly anyone the Kent homemaker would invite along for a trip to the mall. Yet somehow Stella intrigued her. Bruce's woman was a creature of habit, decked out in tight jeans, gewgaws, even a bell jingling from her purse. Sue Ford wondered why she would want to call so much attention to herself.

By day, Stella Maudine, who now used Bruce's last name, wore man-tailored western shirts, the collars always turned up and sleeves rolled in her best tough-girl look. Her blue jeans were boot-cut. At night, she wore spiked heels and skintight miniskirts—though other women were wearing skirts midknee. The look might have worked for her in the past. The fact that most women were wearing longer skirts was no matter.

Bruce and Stella spent the spring and summer months of 1975 and 1976 on weekend camping trips.

In June 1975, the couple spent their first overnighter on the beach at Ocean Shores in a camper stocked with a couple of racks of beer. Stella was now nicknamed "Indian," and Bruce was "Bruno." Bruce fished and Stella worked on her tan, her lean body burnished like the color of a Reinlander bottle.

Stella documented each trip with photographs: *"Bruno fishing at Riverside State Park in Spokane." "Bruno fishing on Canyon Rd. outside of Yakima."*

Stella Maudine could be sentimental, too: She pressed a forget-me-not spray into an envelope she marked *"Camping beside a lake."*

And on April 12, 1976, "Indian" presented Bruce with an over-size cardboard placard proclaiming him "The World's Greatest Lover."

Stella told people she had fallen for the hard-drinking mechanic from the apple orchards of Eastern Washington. She refused to allow Phyllis Cordova to weasel back into Bruce's life. She told the lady to back off.

Phyllis responded with a scathing letter to Bruce in July:

"I'd like to straighten Stella out, too. . . . I've been in Kent a long time . . . so maybe she better go somewhere else if she's that worried."

A month later, Stella had made up her mind to at least try to be solely Bruce's woman. She sent a "Dear John" letter to a trucker named Harry Swanson. Swanson had been head-over-heels in love with Stella when she first hit the Kent tavern scene.

"I know you'll understand," she wrote.

Harry Swanson cried when he got the letter. Stella Maudine was one incredible woman, and damn if Bruce wasn't lucky to have her. Swanson tucked the letter into a drawer.

There was little advance notice. Bruce, as he often did, got up with a hangover and his mind made up. He wanted to marry thirty-three-year-old Stella Maudine. On September 11, 1976, the couple drove to the Coeur d'Amour Wedding Chapel ("No Appointment Necessary") in Coeur d'Alene, Idaho, just east of Spokane. The bride wore a brown miniskirt and matching vest, set off with a sheer white blouse. White sling-back sandals with three-inch heels made her statuesque. Her forty-two-year-old groom wore a darker-brown leisure suit with a turtleneck.

When Stella and Bruce returned home to their new 1976 Kit Companion, eight-by-thirty-two trailer, on blocks at Valley Mobile Manor, the bride mailed out pretty blue announcement cards: *"We would like to tell everyone we have joined hands and become as one . . ."*

In December of the same year, Stella Nickell acted as a driver for a tavern friend on a trip to Southern California. She called the Strongs and told them to get Leah ready—she was going to pick her up for a day at either Disneyland or Knott's Barry Farm. The little girl sat by the window waiting for her mother for two days.

Finally, Pat Strong phoned a Costa Mesa motel where Stella had said she'd be staying, only to learn that Leah's mother had checked out and gone back to Washington.

Though there seemed to be no time for Leah, Stella, Cora Lee, and Cindy celebrated Christmas together a few weeks later. Mothers and daughters gathered in the trailer, faces frozen forever in happy smiles bound for the photo album.

Violence and murder shook the Stephenson clan the same year Stella and Bruce made marriage plans. A. C. Duncan, forty-eight, Cora Lee's brother, was shot by his second wife a half-dozen times in the bedroom of his mobile home at the Camelot Trailer Park in Federal Way, Washington. The family rumor mill had it that one of the Stephenson girls was having an affair with her uncle and the wife wouldn't put up with it.

Bob Strong heard the news down in California. He wasn't surprised.

"Those girls are jealous of each other when it comes to their men. They're jealous of their own mother. When you mess with one of those Stephenson girls' men, you're flirtin' with death."

CHAPTER 34

In the bullpen back at the Seattle FBI office, agents bounced around different theories about why Stella Nickell would drive all the way to Wenatchee to tell the Nickells that Bruce had died, then have cousin Dick Nickell do the job.

"Here's a woman who committed murder and needs time to get herself together. The trip was an excuse that bought her some time," an agent suggested.

SA Jack Cusack wondered if Stella might have used the trip as a way to get rid of some evidence.

"She could have stopped at any rest stop or park and dumped the cyanide. It would have been so easy for her to do so."

It was also possible that she wanted to solidify her bond with Walter and Ruth Nickell.

"She wanted to stay in the will, which was a real plus to the whole murder plot . . . getting a fat inheritance."

Up in the polygraph room on the seventh floor of the Federal Building, there was no doubt Stella Nickell was the tamperer.

As the weeks passed, SA Cusack played Stella Nickell's first call to 911 a hundred times. Over and over. What was she saying? How did she say it? Were her responses genuine?

Her voice was calm. Oddly so. There were delays in her responses to the dispatcher.

"I don't know, my husband's gone into some kind of a fit. He's breathing extremely hard, his eyes are rolled back, he told me he was gonna pass out . . . I tried to get him on the couch and he hit the floor . . ."

She gave the address and told the dispatcher her husband had just turned fifty-three.

"Is he conscious?"

"I don't think so, his breathing has slowed down . . . I can't see him . . . I couldn't get to the phone . . . I'm not in the same room he's in. He's in the den."

The dispatcher asked if there was a history of heart problems.

"No, uh, I don't think so. He's had a physical by the state. Works for the state . . ."

Jesus Christ, "he works for the state . . . just had a physical . . ." She was pressing again. . . . Did she go in the other room to file her nails or smoke a cigarette to wait for Bruce to slip closer to death? Maybe she didn't want to watch.

SA Cusack wondered about it all.

But over time the FBI man came to the conclusion that a tape was not enough in and of itself to discern if a person is truly calling for emergency help or if she is doing what she thinks is expected of her. Was it guilt or concern in Stella Nickell's voice? Maybe neither. Based on the tape alone, he could never quite decide.

Airport security supervisor Bobby Bediones was glad to comply with boss Gerry McIntyre's request to compile Stella Nickell and Cindy Hamilton's time sheets from hire dates to last shifts worked. By then, both women no longer worked at the airport.

Gerry said SA Cusack wanted the information.

In circling the dates, the thirty-seven-year-old Filipino made an intriguing discovery: Mother and daughter had missed many of the same days.

"Most of the time when Stella's not coming into work, Cindy's not coming into work too," he said later.

It started to make sense. Up to that point, Bediones had presumed the investigation focused solely on Stella Nickell as the killer. Could Stella and Cindy have masterminded and executed the crime as a team?

CHAPTER 35

If Bruce Nickell had thought marriage would have reined in his wife, or even slowed her down, he couldn't have been more misguided. Stella Maudine continued nuzzling up to any man with a buck for a drink. Friends thought she couldn't help herself. In the spring of 1977, the inevitable occurred and the Nickells separated. Stella told fellow barflies she had rented an apartment in Kent, but again, wouldn't say exactly where it was. Walt's Inn bartender Josephine Nelson wondered if her girlfriend was up to her old tricks.

Yet true love, or the fact that the couple were well suited for each other, kept them from staying apart for very long. Three months after their split, Stella gave her husband another chance.

By October of the same year, Bruce had moved on to a new job as a mechanic at McDonald Industries, a heavy-equipment rental outfit based in South King County. Jeff Ford, a co-worker and sometime buddy from Haggard, later joined his pal.

As the New Year came, the Nickells struggled to make ends meet yet still do all the drinking they wanted. Fittingly, Stella named her cat Smirnoff—after Bruce's favorite brand.

At the same time, across the county, Paul Webking and Sue Snow met by the pool at Meridian Firs Apartments.

In Ukiah, Cora Lee Rice had fallen for a man she thought would make a terrific husband, her fifth. Stella Maudine thought her mother would be better off if she just lived with the fellow.

"Mother shouldn't have married half of her husbands," she told a friend some time later.

And Cynthia Lea became pregnant. She and her trucker boy-friend lived in Willits, not far from Cora Lee's place. Over the Fourth of July, Stella, Cynthia, and Cora Lee gathered for a week-end reunion. Again, Leah was left out.

Pat Strong recalled Stella Nickell's reaction to Cindy's news.

"When Stella found out that Cindy was pregnant, she got real upset with Cindy and said, 'I'm not ready to be a grandmother.' It really hurt Cindy's feelings."

Just before Christmas 1978, Cynthia, now nineteen, delivered a baby girl in a Ukiah hospital and had a tubal ligation. One kid would be plenty.

Though her oldest daughter would later say Stella gave Bruce an ultimatum—either her or the bottle—it wasn't so simple. Stella not only professed her love for Bruce, she also didn't have anywhere else to go. She told friends her mother reinforced the idea that the wife can't make her husband quit. She had tried to slow him down. But Bruce didn't want to, and more than once they separated. But Stella always came back.

"He kept asking me to come back, and I said, 'I told you, when you slow down and you decide that what you want is a good solid marriage,' I said, 'you've got to slow down on your drinking.' I said, 'I didn't say *quit*, I'm not asking you to do that. But you've got to slow down.' "

There were other considerations. Stella worried her husband would wreck their truck, hurt himself in a motorcycle accident, or maybe even end up back at Cedar Hills in rehab. It was also a matter of money. Bruce Nickell's drinking cost them $250 a week.

Stella once tried to convert Bruce to an at-home drinker.

"There was one day we were fixing to go out, and I think it was just before his birthday. I had gone uptown to do the shopping during the day on Friday. I had bought him a bottle of Smirnoff. In fact, I even bought the hundred-proof. And when he came in and decided to start getting ready to go out, I had made the suggestion, 'Why don't we stay home?' And I gave him this bottle. He says, 'Why don't you fix me a drink,' and he says, 'As soon as I get ready, we'll go out for the evening.' I said, 'Why don't we stay home for the evening?' He says, 'No.' We didn't sit at home and discuss it, but it was kind of discussed throughout the evening. And that's how I came across the fact that he couldn't stand to sit at home and drink. Not even beer," she said some years later.

By the first of the year, 1979, it was time for Bruce to get on the wagon. One evening while drinking at Walt's Inn, he admitted he needed "the cure."

Professional help, Stella told him, was the answer.

"I can stand by you, but I can't help you in the ways you need help."

Bruce asked her to do whatever she could. Since they didn't have a phone at their trailer, Stella used the bar's pay phone.

"I made some calls, and the easiest one you might say that I run across was they wanted twenty-seven days as an in-patient, and I knew he wasn't going for that. I knew it in the bottom of my soul. But I relayed the message to him, I said they had some open beds. I said, 'But it's going to require twenty-seven days as an in-patient' and he said, 'Nope.' I said, 'Okay, you don't want help very bad, do ya?' And dropped the subject."

Bruce guzzled for two weeks solid. He didn't go to work. He took off without a word as to where he was going. Stella would wait a bit, then go after her man to find out if he was still alive.

The trail usually ended at Walt's Inn, with a drunken Bruce Nickell at the bar talking with bartender Josephine Nelson.

Bruce ordered Stella a drink, and without any kind of warning turned and said, "Okay. I'll do it."

"Do what?" she asked.

"I'll become an in-patient."

Stella said she'd make the phone call, but Bruce wanted her to do it immediately.

"Make it right now," he said, "because I'm ready for it now."

Not about to take the chance that in his stupor Bruce would change his mind, Stella dialed the number for Schick Shadel in Seattle. She spoke with a counselor.

"And he said," she later recalled, " 'And I can tell you when he leaves here he will not want to drink, and he will not have any desire for drink and he will not be able to drink.' That's the words that hooked me. He says *he won't be able to*."

Bruce Nickell was admitted to the program the same day his wife made the call. Stella visited every day. Her man didn't look so good, but she knew the cure wasn't an easy one. After ten days of aversion therapy and counseling, Bruce Nickell walked out of the place sober and never drank a drop again.

And though Stella had wished for it, even prayed for it, it might not have been what she wanted. As his life changed, so did hers. And after a while, some would later insist, Stella didn't like it.

Bruce showed his appreciation by giving his wife not one, but two valentines the year he became sober. One was a photograph of a bleeding-heart blossom: *"I love you, just wish you knew how much. All my love, Bruce."*

Then a second one: *"Just a little extra for you. Love, me."*

Life seemed to be calming down for Stella's daughter since the birth of her baby girl. Cindy and her boyfriend rented a small house in Willits. If, as her friends would later say, Cindy had wanted to live the life of a stay-at-home wife and mother, this was her chance.

On February 21, 1979, Cindy wrote her mother about her baby's delivery—C-section because of an active herpes virus—and to let her know that she was proud of Bruce for quitting the booze.

"Also tell him I think it took a lot of courage," she wrote.

There was bad news for Cora Lee, however. Her beau died when a piece of World War II shrapnel moved to his brain. The old lady went into a tailspin.

"She really loved that man," Cindy wrote.

Cora Lee packed away a pretty dress she had selected for the wedding that never was. She told her daughter Berta that if she never met another man, she'd wear it for her own burial.

A thirteen-year-old with pretty, dark-blond hair and clear blue eyes, Stella's daughter Leah took the bus to Northern California for a two-week visit with her sister and grandmother in the early summer of 1979.

Cindy was living with her baby's father in the little house across the street from a trailer park. She called him her "husband," though as far as Leah knew there had never been a wedding. During at least a portion of her time with her sister, the man was off driving a truck.

Late one night the sisters went out for a drive. Twenty-year-old Cindy parked in front of a tavern and told her sister to go ahead and fall asleep in the car—she was going to be a while.

And she was. Leah and the baby fell asleep. Several hours later, Cindy returned.

"Don't tell him about this," she ordered.

Leah promised she wouldn't. She looked up to Cindy who was pretty, brave, and tough. Leah wanted to be like her. When Cindy talked about "doing hair" and going to beauty school, Leah even considered the same career.

Yet Cindy was acting more like a mother than an older sister. Or at least more like Stella Maudine.

"She strives to have authority. She likes to be in charge," Leah recalled years later.

Leah wasn't the only one who admired Cindy. Stella, inspired by the beauty and tranquility of Cindy's aquariums, set up her own fish tank. She documented each fish and bubble with blurry photographs. In time, she would add two more aquariums to the Nickell household.

CHAPTER 36

When the assignment came across Equifax insurance investigator Lynn Force's desk at his Kent office, the thirty-eight-year-old former naval communications man was only vaguely aware of the Auburn cyanide murders. The Seattle native had worked SIDS, shootings, drowning cases, but never one like the one on his desk. It was July 18, 1986, when Force got the request from the Minneapolis-based Northwestern National Life.

Stella Nickell's claim was considered contestable because the Northwestern accidental-death policy was only six months old when her husband died. It was to be nothing malevolent, just a routine examination of the circumstances surrounding her husband's death.

His first task would be to talk with the beneficiary, but that quickly proved to be no easy endeavor. Lynn Force would later estimate he made ten to fifteen calls to the Nickell residence, and though Stella returned many of them, no meeting time seemed convenient. He suggested a meeting at her home, but she said that would be out of the question.

Finally, ten days after he received the request for investigation, Stella Nickell agreed to talking on the job at SeaTac.

Stella Nickell answered questions about her husband's background and health and signed a medical release Lynn Force said was necessary.

Only after she signed it did she ask what he was going to do with it. He explained that he'd take it to appropriate medical facilities—Harborview, the family doctor in Auburn—in order to retrieve information for Northwestern.

Investigator Force had been with Equifax for a total of eight years, and had seen all kinds of reactions from beneficiaries. Oftentimes tears fell. Sometimes widows hauled out photographs of their husbands. Stella Nickell was not that way at all. Force explained that the medical release was only good for Northwestern. In an effort to spare her from additional contact, he asked a routine question.

"Are there any other policies?"

"No. He only had this one."

Between getting up and down, Stella Nickell lit cigarettes from the butt of another and asked about the policy at hand.

Lynn Force told her it had a $36,000 life amount, with $100,000 accidental.

"The $100,000 is only paid if he dies an accidental death?" Stella asked.

Lynn Force nodded. "The $36,000 will be paid. The insurance company is investigating now to determine whether he did die due to accidental means."

Stella Nickell answered the noise of the metal detector and got up again.

Armed with the release forms, Lynn Force moved on to interviews with Bruce Nickell's doctor and the staff at Harborview Medical Center. Information wasn't sitting quite right, and after discussing it with his supervisor, he made a call to the FBI.

He told them the amount of insurance he was investigating was about $136,000.

Ron Nichols didn't care about the amount. The amount Stella had mentioned, though smaller, was just as good, as motives go.

Others, however, started to turn around.

"She told us Nickell had only one small policy from the state, and it turns out to be $100,000-plus!"

It was the first week in August when Jack Cusack and Randy Scott headed to Lynn Force's Kent office for a meeting.

Stella Nickell now knew about the true value of the policy. Lynn Force had told her.

CHAPTER 37

When Stella and Bruce Nickell moved onto space #212 at the Auburn mobile home park in 1979 they were like most of the other folks there—Bruce was blue collar, a machinist for McDonald Industries, and his wife stayed home to take care of their place. Stella was always the first to admit she hated housework. She had to find other ways to occupy her time. As long as Bruce was in town, Walt's Inn and her other haunts were out.

Although she had always been distant or flat-out uninterested in women as friends, at White River Estates she didn't have much of a choice. She became friendly with Dee Rogers, A. J. Hague, and others because she did not have a car. Ceramics and Tri-Chem "liquid embroidery," the current crafts fads, could only kill so much time.

Days by the pool, or in each other's trailers passing the time by crafting, passed slowly. Sometimes baby-sitting was shared. A.J. and Dee had children, and they had heard that Stella Nickell baby-sat Vicki Bagby's little boy, and often watched her granddaugther.

Fourteen-year-old Jerry Kimble was Bruce and Stella Nickell's paperboy when they met. Problems with his father forced the boy to look elsewhere for a family. Jerry, whose CB handle was Lost Tiger, met the Nickells, Bruno and Squaw, over the radio.

Before too long he was calling the Nickells "Dad" and "Mom."

*　　　*　　　*

Jack Kimble, Jerry the paperboy's father, resented the Nickells' increasing influence over his son, though some of it was harmless. He could see Jerry emulate Bruce by copying his western-style attire. His boy's interest in CBs also escalated when he started going over to the Nickells' mobile home on space #212.

Then, when Stella Nickell cosigned for Jerry's first checking account, Jack Kimble blew up. He had told his boy that even though he had a paper route, he was not old enough to manage his own money. When Jack Kimble found Jerry's checkbook, he made another trip over to see the Nickells.

"I tried to explain to her we had our own family rules and this was the way I wanted it. She didn't seem to care. I realized they had kind of taken over," Jack Kimble recalled later.

Stella kicked off the New Year with a new interest—genealogy. She sent away for family birth certificates in January 1980, though she couldn't recall Ricky Slawson's first name when she wrote out the application for her daughter's.

Her children were on her mind.

She wrote again and again in the notebook in which she kept her papers: *"There are only two things we can pass on to our Children, 'Roots and Wings.' "*

On February 12, 1980, in support of her tenuous relationship with her youngest, Leah, Stella wrote a stinging letter to Pat Strong. Leah had passed along some of the stories that Pat had been reading.

"You may be Leah's stepmother by marriage, but you are not really any relation to her . . . You definitely will not be a grandmother by her . . . the main reason is she doesn't want you to be. You may claim to be her mother (Ha! Ha!) But you never will be as long as I'm alive . . . ,"

Stella could not let go of the past. Even though she had betrayed Bob Strong with "damn near every man in Orange County," she still held him responsible for leaving her after she did her jail time.

So what if Pat, her dear old friend and neighbor, had been there to pick up the pieces when she was locked up? She wanted the old girl to know someday it would be her turn:

"If a man will do it once, there is always the chance he will do it again. They are never too old," she wrote.

In the middle of June 1980, Pat Strong answered the phone to all-sweetness-and-light Stella Nickell, calling for Leah to come up to Washington after school let out for the summer.

"I really can't say," Pat answered. "It's up to Bob. He's her father."

"He'll say yes," Stella rejoined. "All you have to do is take him in the bedroom."

Leah could barely contain her joy when her dad and stepmother agreed to the trip. Though Leah felt Pat had tried to poison her with stories of her mother's past—"she was a biker . . . she was a bar lizard . . . a tramp . . . a crook!"—it had all been in vain. Stella was her mother. And that was enough for the seventh-grader. She took a Western Airlines flight after school let out.

A week after her arrival, Bruce and Stella took her youngest daughter on a cruise to Victoria, British Columbia, sponsored by a Seattle country radio station. Stella took photographs that she pasted later into a memory album. Leah wanted to stay for good. Stella was skeptical about having her daughter stay in Washington. The girl had been raised by what she considered to be a wishy-washy man and his man-stealing wife.

"We'll go through the summer. If things are starting to work out, then we'll consider going into the school year," Stella said. "But that's going to take you obeying the rules and regulations of this household, not the way your father has raised you."

By the end of July, Stella and Bruce gave in. Leah's return ticket to Orange County was canceled. They'd give parenthood a try.

Stella still wasn't "Mommy" material.

"She was more like a friend. We went shopping together, and I loved it. We'd go to the mall at Southcenter. She used to lay out in the sun. She wouldn't go bike riding with me. I could never get her to. She bought me a Radio Shack radio for my bike," Leah recalled several years later.

Stella *wanted* her to be a friend.

"I tried to do that with both of my daughters. To fit into their life instead of being above them, like a lot of parents are to kids," she once said.

Later that summer Bruce left for a job at Prudhoe Bay, Alaska. He hated to go, he hated leaving his wife, but at least Stella Maudine had her daughter, Leah Ruth, with her.

Bruce returned from Alaska in September, and Leah Strong enrolled at Olympia Junior High as an eighth-grader. She registered as Leah Nickell, because it made her feel that she was part of a family.

Yet, as the weeks passed, Leah began to wonder if, in fact, Bruce really wanted her around. She felt the man was jealous of her mother's attention. He was used to having supper on the table when he got home, and with a young girl in the house other things sometimes became more important.

As far as Leah could see, her mother *was* the dutiful wife. Not only did she take care of everything at home, she did the banking and paid the bills. Teenager Leah even got used to eating a big breakfast at the crack of dawn, because her mother always fixed one for Bruce.

In California, twenty-one-year-old Cindy's money woes continued. In November 1980, Bruce dispatched a money order for $100, presumably to help Stella's daughter and "husband" and their toddler get up to Washington for Thanksgiving. The little girl also needed to have her hips X-rayed for a minor hip problem she had at birth.

When Cindy came to Auburn, she and Stella went out drinking, fulfilling a mother's promise to her daughter when she came of age.

Later that night the two of them had a heart-to-heart talk: "After a few drinks," Cindy said, "the subject was brought up about my past because—That particular day was the closest that—and the most my mother and I had talked about in years and years and years."

The following month Cindy needed more money, and Bruce Nickell complied. Via Western Union, he wired $250 to Willits. Stella stored the receipts with some others, including gas charges from Willits to Tacoma, and a deposit for an apartment, totaling $600. Someday, Cynthia promised, she'd pay her mother back. Stella insisted on it.

The Nickells were in no position to give any money to anybody. Stella was answering the kind of ads found in the back of the *National Enquirer:* "Earn $$$ Stuffing Envelopes!"

She even tried to earn a few bucks composing a *Reader's Digest* "Life in these United States" article about one of her girls killing a spider. She just couldn't come up with a winner.

One night after Christmas 1980, Leah returned to the Nickells' trailer with a Polaroid she found while baby-sitting a neighbor kid. The photo showed a dining-room table piled high with marijuana.

Stella found out about it and sent Leah packing for California.

"This ain't going to happen! You're not going to do this when you live with me! You're going back to your father's! That's it!"

Leah cried, but she didn't beg to stay and she didn't ask her mother why the picture set her off.

"You don't ask questions. You don't ever ask no questions. When she says something, that's it. You don't ask why," Leah Strong said years later.

"I explained to her," Stella said later, "that this could cost all of us our lives. I said, 'These people don't play games. They get real serious.' And I said, 'Real serious means dead.' I said, 'No, you're going back to your father.'

"I looked at it as basically saving her life, because I told her, I said, 'I would be afraid for you to walk from this trailer to the mailbox and back,' I said, 'because you may never come back.' "

Leah never did come back to live with her mother.

In May 1981, the Nickells received new American Express cards, and they booked a flight to Hawaii. Stella even wore shorts, something she didn't often do because of the burn scars on her leg. She allowed herself panty hose, however, for a little cover.

The second marriage of Stella's favorite niece, Wilma Mae, lasted just 363 days. Her husband was twice her age, a manager at Rockwell International, and in many ways the best thing that ever happened to her. He taught her how to make a decision although that may have caused the end of the marriage.

"I treated him like dirt. I was starting to get my feet on the ground and didn't like to be told what to do. I learned I could tell him what to do. I was terrible," she later said.

One Tuesday afternoon, Wilma came home to find their place cleaned out. She could hardly blame her husband.

That same year, Wilma purchased a little house in Pasco, Washington. It was close enough for her to walk home from her drinking spot. Whenever she needed cheering up, she phoned Aunt Stella. A laugh or two, some words of encouragement, and she felt better.

"Hang in there, lady . . . it'll all work out, babe . . ."

If her aunt had some bitching to do about Cynthia Lea, Wilma didn't mind listening, either.

When she found a potential new beau, Wilma carted him off to her aunt and uncle's place in Auburn for the once-over. If Wilma Mae had a mother at all, it was Stella Maudine.

Stella Nickell and Dee Rogers—and occasionally friend and neighbor Vicki Bagby—spent the summer and fall of 1981 by White

River Estates' pool or in each other's mobile homes glazing greenware.

Stella Nickell won another first place for her artistic efforts, a coat of Bruce's she had painted using Tri-Chem liquid embroidery. Friends wondered if the poor guy was ever going to get to wear the damn thing, it had been entered in so many shows.

And Stella, on a roll, talked of opening her own business someday. Maybe a ceramics shop or a fish store. Bruce had already poohpoohed her plan of doing something with video rentals. She was convinced video would be the next big thing, but Bruce didn't think so.

CHAPTER 38

August 1986 was a month of new beginnings and endings for the principals mired in the Seattle tampering case. SA Ike Nakamoto returned the bags of powder taken from the Nickells' home in June. The lab determined the powder was for welding. SA Nakamoto asked if the widow felt up to the polygraph, and again she said she'd check with her doctor. She was still on medication for stress and anxiety.

Ron Nichols was no longer on the case, having been assigned to another.

Widower Paul Webking was making moves of his own. He met a flight attendant while at a reunion in Southern California.

A. J. Rider quit her job at the airport. She was needed full-time by her convalescing mother.

And Stella Maudine Nickell got a phone call from an old flame.

Nobody had it as bad for any woman as Harry Swanson had it for Stella Maudine. Though he was almost sixty, the man had mooned over Stella like a lovesick teenager doing hard time in a beach-party movie. Harry Swanson had known Stella since she first sauntered into a Kent tavern. He loved her back then and never forgot her, although she had decided it would be Nickell and not Swanson that would take the hottest woman in town as a bride.

But ten years had passed.

When a former barfly buddy came over to Harry's place in Chimacum on the Olympic Peninsula, he suggested he give Stella a call.

"What would a happily married lady like Stel want with a man like me?"

"Happily married? Don't you read the papers? Bruce is dead. Murdered by poison in his medicine. I saw Stella downtown and she asked about you. Harry, you really ought to call her. I think she needs help out there."

Harry wasted no time in calling. The two agreed to meet at the Starting Gate Restaurant in Auburn on August 18, 1986. After dinner, Stella suggested her old friend come up to see the property. Harry was thrilled. She let him stay the night.

The next morning, he followed her truck down to the valley.

"She was going to SeaTac and she blinked her lights at me and I went to the Starting Gate and had breakfast," he recalled later.

He bought a newspaper and wrote across the top of the nameplate: *Met Stel . . .* He pasted the clipping into a scrapbook.

Within a week Harry Swanson was a frequent guest on the Nickell property, parking his blue Lincoln or nearly antique Winnebago next to the mobile home.

"I thought, *Oh, a fire lit in me.* A big fire that went out . . . I guess it never did go out. I didn't forget Stel. I never seen her for five or six years. I never went to Auburn, because I figured I might run into her. He won. I lost."

Stella asked if he could help build a deck, a fence, work on the driveway.

"Stel, I'll be up in the week and we'll get the stuff done. Yes, in my mind, 'Oh, boy, I'll go to bed with her again.' But that's not really what was in my mind. Then it just came. It just fell in place. It was beautiful."

Stella made it clear she wasn't looking for a replacement for Bruce.

"You'll never fill Bruce's shoes," she told him.

Goddamn, I could never fill his shoes, Harry thought. *Never fill his shoes when you're second best.*

As autumn neared, the fence was completed so Stella's dog wouldn't run around.

As a thank-you, Stella set a card on the front seat of Harry's Lincoln.

"Just being friends with you is something I treasure. Affectionately and lovingly, for a very special person. Love, Stel."

If Stella half hoped the fence Harry built would keep the FBI out, she was wrong. They still came. One time an agent's car broke down and he couldn't get it going.

"They ended up leaving their car and calling a cab," Harry recalled.

By telling Harry how much she loved Bruce and that he couldn't possibly take her husband's place, Stella was able to keep Harry confined to his Winnebago when she wanted—or out in the yard to get some chores done.

The only complaint she made about Bruce was his insatiable taste for pornographic videos. One time Stella hauled out a stack of receipts to show Harry what she had been up against all those years.

Every night, Stella said, Bruce would camp out on the davenport with his afghan watching a blue video. She had no interest in it whatsoever, but she was his wife and had to put up with it.

Harry couldn't understand Bruce's fascination.

"God, he had at home what any man would want."

Stella started erasing the videos by taping a piece of a matchbook over the little square hole on the back of the cassette. She erased one each night, taping over them with films like *Conan the Barbarian* or *Red Sonja*.

When Harry was back at his cabin on the Peninsula, Stella would call with a progress report.

"I erased a couple more tapes and I got some really good movies for you and me to watch. We'll sit there and cuddle. This was a pornie tape; now it's a good movie."

Bruce also kept an impressive collection of Polaroids of his wife, and Stella had taken a couple nude shots of Bruce.

If some suspected Mrs. Nickell and her late husband's best friend Jim "Big Mac" McCarthy were having an affair, Harry Swanson was not among them.

Community college instructor McCarthy was at the property "all the time," consoling the new widow.

"One day he came over, and they kind of wanted to talk about what's going on, and I said, 'Well, Stella, I'll go over to Black Diamond and grab a beer or something. You guys go ahead and talk.' There was no worry with Jim around there."

The best news Stella Nickell had that month came on the last day when she received her widow's benefits—$6,162.98—from the

Automotive Machinists Pension Trust. She could have elected to receive $66.74 per month, for a total of $10,479.53, but given her circumstances, she said, the lump sum made more sense.

The cash, coupled with niece Wilma Mae's return from Houston, back to her ex-husband, Mel Stewart, in Pasco made things a bit easier.

Shortly after Harry and Stella reunited, Cindy took a break from life at Dee's apartment and spent a few days out in Auburn. Mother and daughter played Pac-Man.

Harry Swanson didn't like the young woman.

"She talked vulgar on the CB and on Bruce's ham set. 'Fuck this,' 'fuck that,' and all that bullshit.

"She was boy crazy, boy crazy, boy crazy!"

One night Stel and Harry pulled into the driveway to find the front yard was being used as a parking lot for an eighteen-wheeler.

"Who the hell is that?"

"Oh, that's one of Cindy's boyfriends."

The next day, it was a different guy, a different job, a phone call from wherever the hell Cindy was.

Things remained decidedly uneasy among Sue Snow's survivors. A week after Hayley returned from a California vacation with best friend Kammi Solberg there was a big blowout between Paul Webking and Sue's daughters.

Paul had heard through Kammi's mother, Kristi, that there had been a lot of talking behind his back.

Though she was hundreds of miles away, Sarah Webb was still a force in the dissension. She could not accept that Paul was not her twin's killer. FBI special agents had not done enough to let family members know that they were completely satisfied that SA Cusack's polygraph exonerated Paul Webking.

And so Sue's daughters and her husband were alone to do battle in the house on N Street. Paul, puffed up to superhuman size as only he could manage, was angry about the girls' lack of trust. Exa Snow did nothing to hide her feelings of hatred, and she snapped back and went toe-to-toe with her late mother's husband.

He said the girls were a disgrace. They were out having a good time, instead of thinking about their mother.

Hayley stood up to Paul. "That's not true," she said. "I grieve." It surprised her that she stood up to him.

He stormed away, slamming the bedroom door.

Hayley wrote on September 1, 1986:

> *I was just lying in bed thinking of Mommy. What did she ever do to deserve this? I think how sad it is for kids who have lost a parent and I look at myself and I'm one of those. I think "what did I ever do to deserve this?" What do I do now?*

CHAPTER 39

While her mother developed her skill at ceramics and Tri-Chem, in 1982 Cynthia Lea Slawson was just another beauty-school dropout who liked big, burly truck drivers. Cynthia met Dave McMurphy, a handsome thirty-year-old native Californian who met her criteria. And she met his, too. Like the red sauce truckers slather over everything, the girl was hot.

The newly single Cynthia Lea was also fun. When they weren't off in the truck together running wood chips, the couple partied at western bars, drinking, dancing, and sometimes using cocaine.

"Every chance she got, she'd get a line or two," Dave McMurphy later recalled.

Cynthia talked about getting back to beauty college, but Dave never felt she was serious.

They moved into a place between Willits and Ukiah and, in time, got to know each other.

Cynthia professed great love for her daughter, but didn't seem grown up enough to handle her. Beyond a few weekends and one two-week stretch, during the six months they lived together, she rarely kept her daughter with her. Instead, the baby's father's first wife cared for the little dark-eyed girl.

"It limited her running around. Her doing whatever she wanted to do whenever she wanted to do it. It tied her down," McMurphy said, explaining Cindy's reluctance to be with her child.

"I tried to get her to have her come live with us. She did for a while, but Cindy couldn't handle her, so she sent her back."

The relationship with her own mother had problems of its own. Cynthia's feelings were decidedly mixed.

"It was a love-hate situation. Just childhood beatings, abuse and everything else that she felt very bad about. She hated Stella, for things like this. At the same time, she loved her and valued her opinion on things. But I knew it was not a trust situation. No matter what her mother told you, it would be something else behind your back," Dave McMurphy later recalled.

Though the Nickells had always been on the edge of financial ruin, or because they were at the brink again, Stella had diamond earrings appraised at Federal Way Jeweler's. They came in at $1,967.

Cora Lee's problems were far worse. Heart trouble put her in the hospital in the late winter of 1982. Stella was the only daughter who knew about it—and her sisters were irate that their mother had trusted her with the information and she hadn't had the consideration to let them know.

Glen and Kathy Strand, known by their respective CB handles, Scotch 'N Water and Old Fashion, were among those who gathered for coffee or pizza at South King County restaurants for "CB breaks." It was at one of those breaks that they met the Nickells. Jim "Big Mac" McCarthy, Don "Salt Shaker" Webbly, and his wife Shirley "Sugar Shaker" Webbly were also part of the CB crowd.

Neither Bruce nor Stella wore matching vests festooned with CB rally buttons and awards ("Ratchet-Jaw!" "Bucket of the Month!" "Bitch Bitch Bitch!"), as others often did. Sometimes they wore matching western shirts and jeans, though Stella often dressed a notch above the other gals, wearing a skirt and blouse.

Most couples had a "queso" card, a kind of illustrated postcard with handles and channel numbers to give new friends. The Nickells were no exception. Before Bruce took the cure, their card featured a sketch of "Indian" wielding a tomahawk at "Bruno," who with stars in his eyes was running away, a bottle of moonshine and a radio mike in each hand.

When the Nickells pulled up to CB break, they were usually seen sitting very close to each other, like high schoolers on a date.

The Webblys found they and the Nickells had more than the radio in common. They also owned a Honda Goldwing Motorcycle.

Shirley, who was Stella's age, was a hard-bitten bottle blond whose golden hair truly matched her heart. She needed a friend as she struggled with a husband who drank as though booze were water. Stella Nickell, who had been through the same thing and come out a winner with a dry husband, would make the perfect confidante. But Stella was hard to get to know; she didn't seem to let too many inside.

"She puts on a facade of not caring, a very cold lady. When you get to know her, that's not the way she is. I think she had it pretty rough throughout her life, and she puts up a shield. She is a caring, loving person. It is hard for her to show it," Shirley said later.

Stella seemed to be the brains of the relationship, at least as far as technical know-how was concerned.

"Don't explain anything to me, explain it to Stella and she'll explain it to me," Bruce would tell people. When he got his new Kenwood CB, which was more complicated than his older radio, he had Stella read the book and tell him what to do.

"We used to tease him about that on the radio. And she teased him about it, but it was not done maliciously. It was not a real put-down. He'd dish it out too," Shirley Webbly recalled.

On the last Saturday in May 1982, Bruce and Stella, riding their motorcycle, were hit by a car in Wenatchee. The bike was wrecked, and Bruce and Stella both had some healing to do.

While Bruce convalesced from his accident, Stella battled the insurance companies and worked on throw pillows in her spare time:

> God can't be everywhere,
> so He created mothers

> Children need love
> especially when they
> don't deserve it

> Mothers are God's
> special people

On October 12, 1982, Cynthia Lea wrote her mother that Dave McMurphy had been laid off and was looking for work in Reno. She didn't know if she should follow her heart and go with him, or be more practical and return to beauty college.

"Sometimes I wish I was void of love and feeling so that I didn't have the need for a man in my life, but then if it weren't a man it would be something else."

Though Dave didn't know it, Cynthia was using Dave Mc-Murphy's last name when she wrote the letter. The young woman had once suggested marriage, but Dave McMurphy had his doubts.

Their relationship was on the verge of a breakup when Cynthia said her mother was sending her credit cards so he could get up to Washington to look for work.

"You can stay with her and it won't cost you anything."

Bruce was working in Alaska, and Stella would be free to take him around and help him find a job. When the Nickells' Texaco card came, the trucker headed north.

With pal Dee Rogers fixing to leave her husband, Stella's old man off in the frozen Arctic, and A. J.'s sugar daddy way over on the other side of the mountains, White River Estates became Party Time, USA.

Stella called A. J. one evening a couple of weeks before Halloween 1982.

"Get a baby-sitter over there! You're going out with us, lady."

"Going out where?"

"Out with us."

"I can't. I don't have any money."

"Don't worry about the money. Got it handled."

"But, Stella . . ."

"I don't want to hear no buts. You're going out with me and Dee."

Stella hung up, and A. J. rushed to change into clean pants and shirt.

Within a few minutes, there was a knock at the door. It was a baby-sitter, explaining that Stella had called her and told her to "get over to A. J.'s pronto."

"Stella's waiting outside," the girl said.

A. J. was dumbfounded. She told the girl she didn't know how she would pay her.

"Stella already paid me."

A. J. was stunned.

"She had paid her for a week's worth of baby-sitting. She had already informed Amy [the sitter] that anytime I went out, she was to be over there baby-sitting. She was going to live at the house for the next two weeks," A. J. later recalled.

The three women ended up at the Buzz Inn in Kent, playing pool and drinking wine spritzers and beer. The partying continued every night. The only hitch was that they had to leave after Bruce made his call from Alaska. Stella insisted. She'd be all fixed up and ready to go, and there she'd sit, waiting for Bruce to phone, usually before eight o'clock. The second he was off the line, away they went.

A. J. later winced at the way Stella prepared to go out. "Piled-on makeup, tight blouse, skirts up to here. She looked like a street-walker. Dee and I were not made up quite that good, I'm telling you."

For Halloween, other than the blond wig she wore, Stella's "hooker costume" was the same getup she always wore out to the bars. Dee borrowed her friend's silky black robe and went as a vampire. A. J., true to form, went western. The women even brought a coffin in for a prop for Dee. They rigged it with a rubber hose so Dee could sip from the crypt.

Stella seemed to enjoy her role as the hostess with the mostest, the belle of the ball, the Buzz Inn's Queen Bee, as she introduced A. J. and Dee to the wonders of the Kent bar scene.

Josephine Nelson's son, Tommy, was there too. Though he was quite a bit younger than the White River ladies, they tolerated him. When Dee and Stella suggested he return with them to White River Estates, he jumped at the chance.

He followed in his car. When Stella pulled over into a 7-Eleven parking lot, he approached the car and got the shock of his life.

"She had this .357 pointed out the window and loaded, cocked and everything. I thought I was dead," he later recalled.

"Oh, honey . . . it's you . . ." Stella Maudine said, returning the gun to her purse. "Don't tell nobody, not even your mother."

And Stella knew how to party. A. J. saw her take more than one trip to her truck canopy with a man; for sex, she figured. One man told A. J. that he and Stella had been having intercourse while she talked to Bruce on the telephone.

Another time, A. J. claimed Stella offered her Bruce's services.

"When Bruce comes home, do you want him?" she asked at the Buzz Inn one evening in the fall of 1982.

A. J. was surprised. "Excuse me?"

"When Bruce comes home, why don't you get him into bed?"

"Excuse me. No," A. J. answered.

"Why not? You've seen me with other guys, why not take Bruce?"

"Because I like Bruce as a friend, Stella. Just a friend."

When Stella Nickell suggested doing something, it became an order.

"We're going shopping," Stella announced one afternoon, and Dee Rogers knew that's what they were going to do. Now that she was on her own meeting men, Stella told Dee she needed to look her best. There was no arguing the point. They took the truck and drove up the hill to SeaTac Mall in Federal Way, where there was a Frederick's of Hollywood store.

"She said I had tiny tits and needed a push-up bra," Dee recalled. "Stella bought most of her lingerie there. She enjoyed the looks that she got—the boobs look big."

Dee appreciated Stella's advice, but the bras were just too expensive.

Bruce Nickell hated Alaska. The frigid weather, the confinement, the lack of anything to do ate at him. The X-rated movies offered as entertainment were the last things he needed to see. He spent his time in his room, reading, playing with Morse code and amateur radio books, and missing Stella Maudine.

Co-worker Dave Green knew Bruce Nickell was having problems with his renegade wife. Having gone through a divorce of his own, he knew how hard it was being up in Alaska with a wife way down in Washington.

"Bruce felt like he could talk to me because I had been through it. He told me that they were having problems, and he figured she was running around on him."

Although he had picked up a thing or two from relatives of his own living at White River Estates, Dave Green refused to add kerosene to the fire.

Bruce felt that if he could go home to Stella, he could fix the problems and save the marriage.

CHAPTER 40

John Sylvester, an SA from the Poulsbo resident office across Puget Sound, took the ferry every day only to put up with the hot August pet smells from one fin-and-fur store to the next. Armed with a photo lineup, he was on a search for the pet store that sold Algae Destroyer—the source of the green crystals—to the tamperer. He also had to endure kidding from Jack Cusack.

"Hey, Sylvester," SA Cusack cracked, "what's the price of gold-fish in Pierce County?"

The bright, young special agent took it in stride.

In August 1986, he pulled his car into a shabby Renton shopping center near I-405 and parked in front of the Fish Gallery and Pets.

He was looking for Thomas Wayne Noonan.

And Tom Noonan was inside, nervously waiting and wondering what it was that he'd done wrong enough to have the FBI looking for him.

By the time SA Sylvester came calling, twenty-four-year-old pet-store manager Tom Noonan was already acutely aware of the cyanide poisonings. Sue Snow had been his banker, the first to give him a car loan, when he was nineteen. Her death had been a shock. Sue was such a nice, approachable lady. Why her? he wondered.

SA Sylvester and Tom Noonan went outside, to a place near a rockery in front of the store. The FBI agent pulled some photographs from an oversize envelope.

"Do you recognize anyone?"

Tom Noonan studied the black-and-whites for several minutes. The photos were so pitiful, he almost asked who had taken them.

It wasn't instant recognition, but there was one that was familiar. He pointed to a woman with glasses and long dark hair.

"I don't remember her name," he said. "But she's been in our store. Did she do something wrong?"

SA Sylvester's eyes betrayed his reserved facade.

"His eyes got this big . . . he got really excited," Tom Noonan later said.

He had identified Stella Maudine Nickell.

Sylvester thanked him and left a bewildered Tom Noonan to figure out what it was about Stella Nickell that could possibly interest the FBI.

Things started to come back for Tom Noonan.

And so did the men from the FBI.

In 1979, Tom had started his career at the Renton location of the four-store Fish Gallery and Pets chain. But it was at the Kent East Hill store that he ran into Stella Nickell. He worked there for most of the calendar year 1985, before transferring in January 1986 back to Renton.

When SAs Cusack and Ron Nichols showed up to talk about Stella Nickell, Tom recalled other details. Later visits over the course of the late summer and fall would turn up additional and critical case information.

Stella Nickell was a frequent, sometimes weekly, patron of the Fish Gallery. The young man considered her a pleasant, if somewhat pesky, customer. Not overly sophisticated in her taste in fish, she was like a lot of other hobbyists. She wanted fish that looked pretty and didn't die. Stella once confided that she wanted to open her own store someday.

"I hated to talk to her because she would follow me around the store. I like to help customers, but at the same time I don't like to have them monopolize my time."

He remembered a cat bell Stella wore on her purse.

"She'd come in and wear that occasionally. If I was in the back catching fish or something and I heard that, I knew Stella was in the store. I'd talk to one of the guys working in the store: 'Is that Stella?' "

"She didn't wear a bell," SA Cusack said.

"Oh, yes she did."

Ron Nichols thought the guy was a kook. He'd never heard anything about the cat bell either.

Noonan told SA Cusack he thought Stella seemed lonely.

"I felt she would go home and there was no one to talk to there." The talk bothered him, though.

"Sometimes you would get the feeling that there was more to it than just idle conversation," he said, indicating he thought Stella might be hitting on him. "That got scary."

SA Cusack asked if Stella Nickell had purchased Algae Destroyer.

Tom Noonan thought long and hard about that one. He said he didn't normally carry it in the store; he preferred stocking liquids. Then he remembered telling Stella Nickell that he didn't care for the product when she said liquid Algaeon didn't really work for her and she wanted Algae Destroyer.

"Don't worry about it," he recalled her saying. "I'll just go next door and get it."

Not wanting to lose a customer, he put in an order for Mrs. Nickell.

"I'd get it, she'd buy some. Others did too. She was one of the primary people I obtained the product for. Twelve would last us maybe two or three weeks, depending on whether Stella was buying the stuff."

Noonan explained that moisture sometimes seeped into the blister-packed tablets, hardening them to the point where they became almost insoluble.

"As a matter of course, I would tell anybody that bought products packaged that way that the only way to get it to work is to crush it up. Add hot water to it."

SA Cusack asked again about the pulverizing procedure he recommended to Stella Nickell and other customers.

"I can't understand why are you so concerned about that crushing part."

"It's very important. Are you sure?"

"I told *everybody*."

Tom Noonan liked Jack Cusack. The FBI agent came across as a man who enjoyed his job and wished he could put more people in jail where they belong.

SAs Cusack and Nichols now knew how the green material had been mixed into the cyanide. It had been an accident. The tamperer had likely used a dirty bowl, one she had used to dissolve the crushed green Algae Destroyer tablets when she put the cyanide into the capsules.

Later, when Tom Noonan asked where the investigation was headed, it was Jack Cusack who told him it had stalled. Even though Tom Noonan had identified Stella as buying the product and recalled telling her to crush it and dissolve it in hot water before administering it to her fish tank, it wasn't enough for federal court.

From what the young man could pick up from the tight-lipped investigators who swarmed around the Fish Gallery, Cynthia Hamilton was a potential witness of some sort, but she was avoiding the feds at every turn.

"They were very upset that she didn't want to talk to them at all. A lot of them laid it down to emotional distress. Then—boom— she starts singing like a canary."

CHAPTER 41

If Californian Dave McMurphy felt uneasy about going up north to stay with Cynthia's mother in the late fall of 1982, it was only because he didn't know where he stood with his girlfriend. He hoped a short separation would bring them closer together. It didn't take long, however, to see that he was foolishly optimistic. By the time he arrived in Auburn, Cynthia Lea was in the sack with her baby's father again.

Stella Nickell consoled him. She also did her best to get him work by driving him to job appointments in Seattle and Kent. After two weeks of running around, however, it became clear Stella had other plans.

"What I took for casual at first, we'd go out and shoot pool, go into Kent to the bars, and run around . . . I didn't instigate anything and I really didn't expect something to happen, but it took me by surprise that she got sexually friendly," Dave later said.

The thirty-year-old trucker reveled in the attention. Stella took him out every evening to dinner to the Buzz Inn, then to her waterbed. She paid for everything. She treated him as if he was the only man in the world. She even paid for his truck driver's physical exam.

Stella complained that things weren't so great with Bruce. She was upset that his alcoholism made him a homebody. And though she griped about money, she spent it freely.

"She was happy to be able to go out with somebody she could have a good time with without worrying about if it was going to effect a problem or not," he said later.

The only intrusion on the cloudburst of attention occurred when Bruce would call from Alaska, and the call jolted Dave McMurphy back to reality. *He was sleeping with someone else's wife in their home.* He wasn't proud of it, but Stella was so good at it. He liked being with her. Afterward, he described her appeal.

"She had a sensuous way about her. She could make herself up to be attractive. But it was more she had a way about her that was hard to say no to. She knew how to play it."

On November 11, 1982, Bruce dispatched a final cassette recording:

"Hello, Babe:

"I wasn't really too happy with that little phone conversation we had the other day; that's been working on my mind. I don't know whether it's me in this place or what, but I just get kinda the feeling that something's not right at home ... on the phone the other night, I don't know, it just didn't seem like it was my wife that I was talking to. It felt like I was a stranger ... I don't know, I just ... in the middle of the night I'll wake up and toss and turn and can't get back to sleep. I dug your pictures out and looked through them and all that did was make my nuts ache."

Bruce went on to wonder what was going on at home. Obviously tired from work and lonely, he said he wanted more than anything else to have a long heart-to-heart with Stella when he came home to her.

"... I don't want you getting pissed or upset or ridiculous about anything, or going from one extreme to the other like we have in the past ... It seems like whenever we try to talk, one of us ends up getting mad and throwing a fit ... I don't want any accusations or none of that going on, I just wanna air out some things that's been bugging me and I want you to air out the things that's been bugging you, and if I ask you a question, dammit, I want an honest answer. I don't want any fence-walking or hanky-panky ..."

It was going to be hard for both of them, he admitted, and he felt poor communication was their toughest obstacle to overcome. Stella had had a large circle of family, whereas Bruce had been alone all of his childhood. "I never had anybody to get that close to."

"I get to looking at these pictures of yours and thinking about all the good things and it about drives me wild sometimes. . . . I wish to hell you knew how I missed ya. I wish you knew how much I miss the things we could've had but didn't have. Maybe we will have, I don't know."

On November 21, two days after Stella took Dave McMurphy in for a driver's exam physical, Bruce picked up his plane tickets at McDonald Industries offices at Prudhoe Bay. His flight home was scheduled for Monday of the following week.

"Things will be different now," Stella told Dave. Her husband was coming home and there wasn't room for three in the bed. Dave would be sleeping on the couch now, and eventually, when he got it together, he'd have to find another place to stay.

"Then it was just dropped right there. It was like two different people. She was one way when he was gone and she just totally did a flip-flop. It was like turning off a light switch. It was weird. It was like, 'You weren't even my friend.' "

Dave felt that even Bruce could sense something was wrong and that the young man sharing his trailer was troubled. Not that he was in love with Stella and felt dumped, it was just that when Bruce was back she flat-out ignored him.

The two men went out to chop some wood shortly after Bruce returned to White River Estates. Bruce didn't say anything, but as they worked he seemed uneasy and, McMurphy thought, suspicious.

"Whether it was anything she said or did when he came back, I don't think so. It must have been something he picked up on, 'cause he knew I was there."

Cynthia Lea Slawson, then twenty-three, surprised Dave McMurphy with a hand-delivered Dear John letter the first week in December. She and her little girl were back in Washington to start a new life—a life that didn't include him.

"I was in the trailer, asleep on the couch, and here come Cindy walking out of the bedroom. I was in total shock. She told me right then she didn't come up because of me. She come up to get away from Willits and away from everything down there—whatever that was—and her folks had brought her up," he said later.

Since it was no longer appropriate to stay at the Nickells', Dave McMurphy moved in with A. J. for a couple of weeks. He quickly learned that a couple of the ladies of White River Estates had a running competition.

"Stella told me that she and Dee were going to see who could get you to bed first," A. J. said.

Stella, of course, had won.

White River Estates continued as a kind of a low-rent Peyton Place, with Cynthia now going out with Dee's estranged husband, and Stella cheating on Bruce whenever she could. Dave McMurphy never claimed to be a saint, but it was too much for him.

He bought a '67 Chevy Belair for $350, loaded it up, and burned rubber for California. He couldn't make a getaway fast enough. The man who had been intimate with both mother and daughter figured the women were more alike than they were different. And that scared him.

"They both connive and work to get things the way they want in their favor. They both work that way. It's what they want, period. If I want this, I'm going to get this no matter how I have to do it. And they are both that way."

Stella Nickell's version of what did or didn't happen with Dave McMurphy, and who slept with whom, is markedly different than the California trucker's. Years later, she maintained there had been no fling with him—or any other man.

"Dave hadn't been there for three days, if I'm not mistaken, and Dee comes to me and wanted to know if she could stay with me, because she knew Bruce was gone for a month. And I let her stay with me. She said, 'I just left [my husband]!' And I said, 'Well, of course you can stay with me, you know that, if you need a place to stay.' Dee and I slept in my and Bruce's waterbed. Dave slept in the second bedroom. And Dave brought his dog with him and that cotton-pickin' dog chewed on my bookcase. I could've cut that dog's throat. But there was nothing between Dave and I and the reason that he came up . . . Cynthia wanted to know . . . if they could stay with us until he found some work. Bruce and I had talked about it, and we said yes. Well, the next thing I know, there's Dave without Cynthia.

"And her and Dave had a few things to discuss. She tried to get across to me, which I kind of grasped her meaning, that Dave and her were no longer together. When we had a chance to talk, I told her that I knew nothing of this. She didn't keep me informed of her life. As far as I knew, Dave had come up to get settled in, try to find a job, try to find a place for them before she come up. I said, 'When I'm left in the dark, what am I supposed to think?' "

                    *   *   *

If Bruce was furious about all the money his wife had spent while he was freezing his tail off in Alaska, no one could blame him. He hadn't worked so hard so she could run around and play pool and drink with a young man—her daughter's lover, no less. Soon after his return home, the Nickells were forced to temporarily ease their financial dilemma with a $1,500 loan from HFC. They listed current debts at $20,401.32.

Before Christmas 1982, Dee Rogers had left her kids with her soon-to-be ex and was on welfare and living in a $150-a-month apartment over the Buzz Inn. Trailer-park gossips insisted that the split had been Stella Nickell's doing. Dee Rogers wasn't really like the woman in space #212. She just hooked up with the wrong friend. Fortunately, Dee's troubles were short-lived. Within thirty days, she was hired by Safeco Insurance as a claims trainee.

Things might get better.

Stella, Bruce, and Cynthia Lea cut a pink and white frosted cake for Cynthia's little girl's "Strawberry Shortcake" fourth birthday party. Stella told friends she was glad the little girl was where she could keep an eye on her. She didn't really trust Cindy, not as a mother, anyway.

Stella Nickell frequently made her concern for her granddaughter a topic of conversation. She told pal Kathy Strand that Cindy treated the little girl as an afterthought.

One time while the men were puttering around with Bruce's electronics conglomeration in the living room, Stella and Kathy shared coffee in the kitchen.

Stella said she didn't want to be forced to take her granddaughter away from Cynthia Lea, but what alternatives did she have?

"Stella never knew where the granddaughter was or who was taking care of her," Kathy Strand said later.

Others had horror stories of their own. One time Cindy called the Churches to see if her mother was there; she needed her to come up and get her at the motel at Gee Gee's Truck Stop.

Laurie Church's blood boiled when she heard the rest: the little girl "was asleep in the room and spent the night in the room with Cindy and a truck driver."

By April of 1983, Stella and Cindy had had it out. It was time for the young woman to get her own place and live her own life. She obviously couldn't live by the Nickells' rules.

Others heard Bruce say he was concerned Cindy would bring

drugs into the house when she came to visit, and he didn't want the stuff around.

Jerry Kimble occasionally met Cindy up at Gee Gee's Truck Stop, where she was a regular. He also got a glimpse of her possible drug use.

"I'd be sitting around, and I'd hear certain things. 'Meet me out back,' or 'It's coming in . . .' Or she'd call somebody just to get her little trip for that night. You could see it when something's going on. I was pretty naive about what kind of drugs . . ." he said some years later.

Cindy packed up her daughter and lived with Dee Rogers for a while before getting her own place. The split with her parents was bitter at first, but when Cindy needed a sitter, Stella often got the job.

Stella had mixed, if not dangerous, feelings about her daughter.

"One minute she loved her," her friend A. J. recalled. "Next minute she couldn't care less about her. She was a bitch, she was a whore, she was a slut."

"Cindy's just like my mother," Stella once said.

That year, Stella's niece, Wilma Mae, married Mel Stewart for the first time. But by August 1983 she had decided she wasn't ready for marriage after all. By her own admission, she treated Stewart badly. She'd leave him at home to go drinking and dancing at the Red Lion in Pasco. It was wrong, and she was smart enough to realize it. She gave two weeks' notice and loaded everything she owned into a twenty-two-foot Jartran rental truck and arrived in Houston the day Hurricane Alicia hit. It was a fitting arrival.

She rented a beautiful redbrick apartment in Pasadena, Texas, and enrolled at the University of Houston with plans to become a mechanical engineer. At night, she worked at an upscale night-club as a cocktail waitress. *She was going to be somebody! It's my turn!* She divorced Mel through the mail and started dating a Houston police officer.

When she heard a lawyer was looking for a part-time secretary, she applied for the job.

"If you want somebody that's really good, you'll hire me. If you don't, you'll hire someone off the street," she told the attorney. She got the job on the spot.

About a year later, Wilma married the Houston cop, only to dump him a month after the wedding.

"I left him and sat in a little house for two weeks; no electricity, water. I became suicidal," she later said.

Me and men . . . a bad combination, she figured.

While Wilma Mae was rolling the marriage dice for the fourth time, Stella's daughter Leah Ruth Strong was going through typical teenage Stephenson angst. She worried she might be pregnant and wasn't sure if she'd be able to make it through high school. She was mad at her stepmother Pat for telling her what to do and calling her a whore.

Leah didn't have the money to buy a card, so in May 1983 she wrote a four-page Mother's Day letter: "You're the only mother I have, and love and respect." She signed the letter "Leah Nickell."

By the end of June, the Nickells did what they had to do to keep afloat. They hired Bill Donais, an Auburn attorney, and filed Chapter 13. A little breathing room was well in order. Casual talk of getting some property and sharing it with Cora Lee also became part of a seemingly brighter, optimistic future.

By late fall Bruce and Stella had picked out a beautiful spot, five acres off of Lake Moneysmith Road east of Auburn. There was even a spot for a duck pond.

Friends chuckled at how perfect it all seemed.

PART THREE

Cynthia Lea

CHAPTER 42

What an entrance the girl in the bathing suit had made! The man at the bar couldn't help but notice Stella's daughter when she sauntered into Gee Gee's Truck Stop one night in the summer of 1983. He was a trucker from New Jersey named Pepper Hamilton. He asked her if she'd like to come back later for a few drinks; she promised she would.

Years later, Pepper Hamilton summed up what he had been looking for at Gee Gee's.

"I was a truck driver. It was a truck driver's bar. I was free, single . . . wine 'em, dine 'em, and sixty-nine 'em. That's about what I was looking at."

And so it went. Over the next few months, whenever the six-four, 260-pound behemoth of a man returned to the Northwest, he'd call Cindy for a date. By the following spring, Hamilton decided to make a permanent move to the Seattle area. He took a job at a Tacoma trucking firm, and he, Cindy, and her little girl moved into a town house in Kent.

Even though Pepper Hamilton's CB handle was "Running Scared," it was his girlfriend who did most of the running.

Before daylight one morning, the trucker returned from a long haul earlier than scheduled to find the town house empty. He drove down to Gee Gee's and, without really even trying, found her car—but no Cindy.

He left a note: *"When you get back to your car, do you mind coming to pick me up?"*

When Cindy caught up to him, she had a ready excuse.

"It was an old friend, we went over to the islands . . ."

Pepper knew better.

"I'm not jealous," he said some years later. "I'm on the road and do what I want to do. Why should I tell someone else who I'm living with what in the hell they should do?"

Besides, he later said, the girl just couldn't help herself.

"She's got a fetish for truck drivers."

While stepdaughter Cindy was partying up at the truck stop, Bruce Nickell was laid off from McDonald Industries in the spring of 1984. When it became clear he was not going to be asked back, Bruce, devastated and depressed, filed for unemployment on April 2.

Stella took a job running a sewing machine piecing goose-down jackets, comforters, and slippers at the Eddie Bauer factory in Kent. Mother and daughter declared a truce and soon Cindy came to work there too.

Cindy told her mother that she and Pepper Hamilton were going to get married although he once had had a drug problem.

"If I ever found that he was back on the drugs again I would leave him," she said.

"How can you say that when you're on them yourself?"

"I'm talking about the hard stuff."

Stella knew her daughter was referring to heroin.

"She calls it 'hard stuff' when they start using a needle. Anything that you don't use a needle with, I guess she figures is not hard yet," Stella said later.

The mother of the bride doubted the marriage would work. Her daughter wasn't marriage material.

"Cynthia wants somebody to toe the line she lays down. But she doesn't want somebody she can run over the top of. And she wants everything her way; she wants somebody who makes good money so she can keep herself in style. Her temperament has a lot to do with a lot of things. If Cynthia thinks one little thing is unjustifiable, she goes off the deep end about it. And she can rant and rave for hours. If Cynthia thinks that she is not getting enough sex, then she feels he's getting it somewhere else."

*   *   *

Lake Holmes Road wound through leggy, sun-starved alders and the tight pyramids of Douglas fir and West Coast cedar just above the Green River like the wild loops of an amusement ride. Green was everywhere—the trees, the grass. At the top of the wild ride was a plateau of farmland and new subdivisions.

It was paradise, and despite continuing financial woes, Stella and Bruce Nickell moved onto their five acres at 17807 S.E. 346th in Auburn in May 1984. Jim McCarthy was on hand to move the trailer from White River Estates and set up the blocks on the Nickells' little slice of heaven.

It was a beautiful spot in the country, the kind of place where the frogs chirp so loudly at nightfall, windows are secured to hear the television. Stella made a checklist of things for Bruce to do and went into action herself. She talked about cattle, maybe a duck pond, and, of course, her own mother.

Cora Lee had made it all possible. Her life savings of $20,000 had been the money used for the property deal. When she arrived from Ukiah, she'd have her own trailer set on the property. Bruce and Stella would be there to help her in her old age. If the other Stephenson kids were jealous, that was too bad.

The Nickell property was a bona fide mud pie in late September, so Stella arranged to have Cindy's wedding at Stan and Laurie Church's place. She didn't want the wedding ruined by muddy shoes and short tempers. Stella did most of the work—from inviting guests to arranging the seating. All the bride and groom had to do was say "I do."

The words were easy enough to say, of course, but Pepper knew the marriage was an impending fiasco. Trucking kept him on the road twenty-four hours a day, seven days a week, and a woman like Cindy didn't seem to like to be alone. Even worse, he doubted she really loved him anyway. She was looking for support, mostly money.

Stella had had her own idea why Pepper Hamilton consented to marry her daughter.

"It's very possible that he done it to get her to shut her mouth," she said later.

The affair was simple, as homey as a parlor wedding in a big old house could be. The only contemporary touch was the wedding music. Cindy chose the song "Drive" by the Cars.

Karan Church pulled her mother aside when the cassette was played.

"Mom, listen to the words! Cindy's playing a one-night-stand song for her wedding!"

The bride wore a spray of tiny white flowers in her hair. Her wedding dress had white lace sleeves and a medieval lace-up bodice that gripped her so tightly, it did little to flatter her ample figure.

Stella Nickell looked trim and lovelier than her daughter on *her* wedding day. She wore a flashy dare-to-be-ignored red Oriental-inspired dress with twin slits to the thigh. Bruce Nickell dressed in his best brown leisure suit and a Qiana shirt, cuffs rolled back and collar wings stretched out like a condor.

Jerry Kimble, in his Air Force uniform, kept a quiet profile, talking mostly with Bruce and Stella and Jim McCarthy.

Dee Rogers was also at the wedding. Her recollections rivet not on the ceremony, but on something she later claimed Stella Nickell had told her.

It was about Jim McCarthy.

"Stella stood there and pointed Jim out to me. She flat told me that she was dinkin' Jim," she said some years later.

"Now, I'm not saying they carried on a continual affair," Dee later said. "She wanted to be free to be able to go with Jim. I think she felt that if she was free, then she could have Jim."

CHAPTER 43

In the second week of October 1984, Bruce Nickell finally got a job, albeit a temporary one, with the State Department of Transportation. Though things with her mother seemed to be going better since the end of her stepfather's long stretch of unemployment, it was not so with Cynthia Lea.

Just a little over two months after the wedding, Pepper Hamilton came home to an empty refrigerator and a letter from his wife.

"I can't handle this life, there's no money. I put your things in storage. Your dog is in the pound . . ."

In a way, Pepper felt relieved. Cindy was great at a lot of things, but being a wife wasn't one of them.

The date Cindy moved in with Dee and her children set the tone of the months to follow. It was New Year's Eve, and though Dee had trouble keeping up with her younger friend, it was party time again. Cindy was back looking for someone new at Gee Gee's.

Cindy had stayed with Dee off and on since she left the Nickells in April 1983. Originally it had been because Stella asked her old White River Estates neighbor if she'd help out. Stella told Dee that Bruce was worried that Cindy wasn't taking care of her little girl.

Dee had gone through another marriage by the time Cindy and her child came calling again the last day of 1984. Dee didn't mind the intrusion. The longer Cindy stayed with her, the more she became a part of the family.

She had a single rule: *"Never . . . nevah . . .* bring anyone home to sleep. If you want to sleaze, you call me and I'll take care of [Cindy's daughter]. Have your ass home by five A.M. I leave at five-ten."

Since Cindy Hamilton had difficulty holding down a job, the burden of the bills fell on Dee Rogers's shoulders. Cindy handled the household chores and often had dinner ready. For a time, it worked out.

Although out of necessity the two women shared the same bed, they were not lovers. In fact, Cindy occasionally called Dee "Mom."

Cindy Hamilton kept a date book in 1985. It was the kind with a soapy nude hunk on the cover, and endless notations of the dates with truckers she kept over the winter and spring months. When a man actually stayed the night with her, like a schoolgirl, she'd describe it in the date book. When she told a man she loved him, she also wrote it down.

She had her dates with the courts, too: her divorce, a speeding ticket, an unlawful-issuance-of-bank, or bad-check violation. A DWI and a night in jail in late April 1985 might have slowed her down a bit. But if it did, it wasn't for long. Cindy Hamilton kept right on doing whatever it was that was going to make her happy.

Katy Hurt, an attractive brunette with a track record much like the woman who would become her close friend and roommate, was working swing shift as a cashier at the 7-Eleven on R Street in Auburn when a woman came in and asked for some quarters. It was midspring 1985.

"We don't sell rolls of quarters, and if we did you can't have any!"

As the woman walked out of the store, she called, "What a scrawny little bitch!" She got into a lime-green Chevelle with a bumper sticker on the back that read: *B*eautiful *I*ntelligent *T. C. H.*

"The *H* stood for 'horny.' But I can't remember what the *T* and *C* stood for," Katy Hurt said some years later.

The next day, who should show up to be trained for the grave-yard shift? The same woman. Her name was Cindy Hamilton.

"You're the bitch who wouldn't give me any quarters," she said.

"Yeah."

"I couldn't believe it," Cindy said, laughing. "You were so little and had the guts to speak to me like that."

Katy immediately liked Cindy's confidence. She was so direct about saying what was on her mind.

Over the course of the next few weeks, the two talked at shift change. They found they had plenty in common. Both were the single mothers of daughters. Both were poor.

Cindy told Katy that she was behind on her rent and that she and her daughter were about to be evicted from their apartment. Even though she lived in low-income apartments and had a rent payment of only $120 a month, Katy was having financial problems of her own. She suggested Cindy and her daughter move in to share the expenses.

In the late spring of 1985, Cindy put her things in storage and she and her little girl moved into Katy's two-bedroom River Terrace apartment at 1415 31st in Auburn. When Cindy was home, she slept on the couch.

Katy Hurt liked to party as much as Cindy did. Whenever they had the chance, which was often, the two went drinking at the Eagles Nest in Auburn. Gee Gee's was still Cindy's favorite hang-out, but Katy didn't like the location up over the hill in Federal Way—she preferred to drink closer to home.

"She didn't bring a lot of guys around the apartment. I didn't see a lot of the guys she dated, I just heard about it. She pretty much kept it away from her house, away from her girl," Katy recalled later.

Shortly after moving in with Katy and her daughter, Cindy made the peculiar arrangements to move into the Auburn TraveLodge. She said she needed some time to get away.

At the motel, and later while living with a man in Sumner, Cindy entrusted her daughter's care to another person. Like so many things, it was a repeat of what Stella had done to her. Luckily for Cindy's little girl, Katy Hurt was an excellent surrogate parent. She thought the child was sweet, quiet, and a bit of a loner. She never asked for anything.

"She kind of reminded me of the perfect child. I don't ever remember Cindy getting angry with her. [The little girl] did what she was told."

Cindy had problems she needed to deal with, and compared to Katy's they were extreme. Her mother, her sister, her daughter—all seemed to be caught up in it.

She told Katy her mother said she had been a rape baby.

"Why did she tell Cindy that?" Katy wondered later. "Can you imagine the guilt that put Cindy through?"

There was also talk of abuse.

"I've come to the conclusion that Cindy realized she was an abused child," Katy said later. "She never acted like the poor little abused child. She acted like the confident woman who knew where she was going in life. The pitfalls of all her past kept dumping on her and dumping on her where she just couldn't be a real stable person."

Cindy said she was afraid she'd abuse her own child. Also to Katy she claimed she had worked the streets as a prostitute when she was a teen.

When Cindy moved into the TraveLodge and worked at an Auburn answering service, Katy never concluded that she was involved in prostitution, though it might have seemed like the perfect setup.

"I really don't think Cindy was doing that at that time. She never had any money," she said later.

Cindy seldom spoke of her little sister Leah, but when she did, it led Katy to later suggest, years later, that Stella Nickell had been more partial to her youngest daughter.

Then there was Stella herself.

"I recollect Cindy making the comment that she felt like she was in competition with her mother. And that's sad. Competition with your mother, come on!"

Competition or not, mother and daughter still seemed close. That same spring, Cindy stayed at her mother's trailer for a few days, even cleaning the place top to bottom. When Bruce needed a house-sitter while he and Stella attended his parents' sixty-fifth wedding anniversary, he called on Cindy. When Cindy wanted to record movies for her boyfriends, Bruce and Stella obliged.

Just after Cindy's daughter began summer vacation from school, Cora Lee finally moved onto the property in Auburn. Cindy was among the family members who helped her grandmother get settled in. The old woman brought up a bag of pinetree seeds to plant on the property. She just hated the fact that the area had only fir trees.

"Pines look a bunch prettier," she said.

CHAPTER 44

Casual fraternity among SeaTac Airport workers develops surprisingly fast. Rampers, baggage handlers, ticket agents, even food-service folks, pass through the security scanners, each with a hello for the lowest rung of the totem pole—PDSs, or Pre-Departure Screeners.

Even the Port of Seattle's janitorial staff made more money.

But when Stella Nickell went to work in 1985, she had no real skills other than a polite, buttoned-up, and respectful demeanor. That was enough to get her the screener job at Wells Fargo Security, the company holding a contract servicing Alaska, Horizon Air, Thai, and Continental.

Since turnover was an astonishing sixty to eighty percent, Stella Nickell had a chance to move up. She planned on it. When she set her mind on something, usually there was no stopping her.

The job, which paid about four dollars an hour, was hardly career material. The hours were long, and when no flights were leaving, it was humdrum. Employees later remembered Stella Nickell as aloof, with scarcely two words for anyone she didn't know. On her breaks, she often sat with a Dean Koontz or Stephen King paperback.

Becky Williams and her husband Bobby Bediones were already working at Wells Fargo when Stella hired on.

The new hire was a very controlled woman. She was seen as

the type of lady who bragged she carried a .38 in her purse, which in reality she did. Though Becky Williams couldn't really fault her technical grasp of her job, she just plain didn't like her. Stella's speech to airport passengers had a cool deliberateness about it. She ended each word with a decisive pause. Everything was a command.

"Please. Put. Your. Items. On. The. Tray."

Stella Nickell rarely spoke of "her old man," as she called Bruce. Her closest relationship seemed to be with her daughter, Cynthia Lea Hamilton.

From what Becky Williams ascertained, the relationship had only been recently forged.

"Evidently she hadn't had a relationship with her mother for quite some time, and this was a last attempt to work together and have some kind of relationship."

Cindy Hamilton returned to Katy Hurt's tiny apartment with a perplexed, bewildered look on her face. Katy noticed it right away. Cindy had just come from visiting her mother. She took a chair at the kitchen table, and Katy stood next to her.

"Cindy, what's the matter?"

"Nothing."

There was silence. Finally, Cindy spoke again.

"Katy, you aren't gonna believe what my mom asked me. She asked me how much cocaine it would take to kill a person."

"What did you say?"

"I told her it depended on the weight of the person."

Although Bruce Nickell's name was never mentioned in conjunction with the cocaine, the implication was that Stella had asked the question with regard to him. "Your mom wouldn't really do something like that," Katy said, "She's just asking about it, isn't she?"

"Yeah, I guess," Cindy answered, seemingly far away in thought.

Katy Hurt wondered about that conversation at her kitchen table.

"It was sort of like somebody cut me out of a cartoon magazine and put me in the real world. *This is only movie stuff.*"

The Wells Fargo employees operating the scanners at SeaTac were nearly without exception "have-nots" reveling in the power to tell the "haves" what to do.

"Move over here, ma'am."

"No, I said over here!"

"I want you to open your luggage."
"Sir, you'll have to take off your watch!"

Air travel was for businessmen and for those lucky few who could afford a vacation somewhere other than in an RV along some Western Washington river. Earning only $107 a week left no money for the luxury of an airplane ticket.

For the most part, they were either losers, down-and-outers, or people who liked the pseudopower of a uniform. Some were starting over.

Bonnie Anderson, a short, round woman who looked younger than her thirty-two years, was one of the down-and-outers, forced to take the job when nothing better could be found. The single mother had worked steadily for more than a decade for Washington Natural Gas. She had worked her way up from clerk to a good job in the utility's engineering division. She quit to become an insurance agent, a move she quickly found to be the biggest mistake of her life.

By the time she took a job at Wells Fargo in November 1985, she had moved in with her mother, run through her company stock and most of her pension. She was desperate. And desperation, for a woman such as she, was completely foreign.

Stella Nickell was standoffish toward new hires like Bonnie. But in time she found it comfortable to talk with Bonnie about her life, her marriage, and her daughters.

"Before he quit drinking," Stella said of her husband while the women were scanning luggage, "we used to go out and have a lot of fun, we used to go dancing, we used to go to bars. I'd get dressed up! Then he quit drinking and he never wants to go out anymore, we never do anything."

She said her husband couldn't fathom her need for a break from the stark boredom of sitting around the house night after night. The repetitiousness of the Nickells' lives was draining her—listening to him chatter on the CB while she retreated with a book. Sometimes Stella said she just had to do what she had to do.

Stella told Bonnie that one night she dressed in a tight, low-cut blouse and a miniskirt, and put on a blond wig to go out and party. She had a great time, but Bruce was furious when he found out what she had done. Stella said she just blew him off.

Bonnie could understand Stella's yearning to have fun, but a wig?

*　　*　　*

A. J., now married to Jim Rider, had been down on her luck more times than any of the White River gals, but she still had an optimistic "things will get better" attitude.

When she and her new husband were out of work in Yakima, it was Stella Nickell who said she probably could get them on at the airport. After all, she now wore the jacket of a supervisor. It was the answer to their prayers.

"But where do we stay?"

"There's no question about that, dammit," Bruce scolded her when he got on the line around Christmas of 1985. "You're staying with us. All of you," he said. He was in a good mood. Bruce Nickell told his friends he was about to be made a permanent hire with the Department of Transportation, a job he got after months of unemployment.

Neither Bruce nor Stella mentioned that financial troubles were rearing up again. A. J. was family. She and her husband, Jim, and son Donny and daughter Barbie were welcome anytime.

By early winter of 1986, Cindy Hamilton had joined her mother at the airport. If Stella Nickell seemed cool and indifferent, Bonnie Anderson found Cindy to be her mother's opposite. Cindy, an outrageous flirt, sucked in the attention. Bonnie, for one, was happy to be selected as a friend.

"Here I am this short little fat person, and you know, this gorgeous girl and she was so much fun to be with and she made me feel like she was having fun being with me. Like I was someone that she wanted to pal around with."

Bonnie used to marvel over Cindy's knack with makeup.

"I'd sit there and watch her putting eye makeup on before we'd go out or something. And she's putting on, like, fifteen different shades of eye makeup, and yet when she got done you couldn't tell."

There was something about Stella Nickell's daughter, and even years later Bonnie would fail at discerning exactly what it had been, but the young woman could—*should*—have been more than a luggage scanner at SeaTac.

"She had so much potential for making the world sit up and take notice of her."

The Wells Fargo employees had other things to talk about besides Stella and Cindy. One subject that became the buzz of the concourse was employees Jim and Jeanne Rice's plan to establish a private-bodyguard business "for rich people in Mexico."

Word was there was a lot of money in it. Others dismissed the plan as farfetched and ill-conceived.

Becky Williams, for one, thought Jim Rice had a pretty good head on his shoulders but his wife Jeanne was a space cadet, with zero credibility.

One time, Jeanne Rice said she had won a $10,000,000 sweepstakes but someone at home had thrown the ticket away. Another time, rumor had it that Jeanne was telling people Becky had been hired as a private detective by the boss to spy on Jeanne.

Supervisor Arlene Papkey later said that despite the Rices' shortcomings, Stella talked of joining them in their bodyguard venture.

"What about your husband?" Arlene Papkey asked.

"I'll just go. I'll just leave."

One morning, Arlene talked with Stella as she filled out paperwork. Stella said she was doing it to get her own credit and to get her own insurance card.

When Stella was well established in her job, she used her MasterCard to purchase $20,000 worth of All American Life insurance. Five days later she received a letter from the ITT School, stating she was in default of a student loan. Stella Nickell never even finished the class she started five years before. Still, she owed $1,019. Three days after that, she applied to the department of licensing for a vanity plate for the Nickells' '71 Chevy pickup. The plate: TP 4 2. It was a reference to the Indian heritage she held so dear.

The next month, she filled out a second group term insurance application, another $20,000 from all American Life.

Cindy Hamilton, who once again had returned to live with Dee Rogers and her children, told Katy Hurt of the bodyguard plan her mother and she had discussed at SeaTac. Stella had been pushing it as a way to make some real money. Cindy wasn't convinced.

"I don't think I could do a job like that—actually having to pull out your gun and shoot somebody. You think your mom or you could really do something like that?" Katy asked.

"I think my mom could. I think there's a possibility I could if somebody was shooting at me."

"Yeah, but sometimes they don't shoot at you, and you have to make the first move to shoot to protect your people's kids."

"Yeah . . . I don't know."

"Why would your mom want to do that?"

"She's bored with her life."

When Stella Nickell was promoted from the blue of a mere worker to the orange blazer of Concourse Security Supervisor, she accepted her responsibilities with great seriousness. She projected the kind of attitude employers appreciate and subordinates hate. She did things her way.

If there was a holdup in a line, Stella would let her employees know that they'd best get things moving along. She became angry at what she perceived was laziness or incompetence on the part of her crew.

"She'd get this look on her face, and those eyes. You know how they say if looks could kill, that's the kind of look she would give you. I'm not kidding. I just get the feeling that she'd just rather see you gone. Just that hard stare. It was scary," Bonnie Anderson recalled.

When a travel-crabby child fussed through the security gate, Arlene Papkey, also a supervisor, cringed when she heard Stella's solution.

"That kid really needs a good slap!"

On another occasion, Stella told Arlene that when Cindy was a defiant child she had to drag her by her hair, just to control her.

Arlene Papkey didn't say a word.

Wells Fargo employees could see Stella wanted more than she had. Out of her security uniform, she dressed like some country-singer wannabe, all fringe, boots, and a flamboyant attitude even a lariat couldn't hold down. Her clothes were younger than her age, her hair two or three shades too dark. It was the color of coal, soaked in crude and dipped in shoe-polish black.

Brown would have been more flattering, one co-worker thought.

When Stella spoke of Bruce, it seemed to be with a lack of affection. She seemed angry their life wasn't going anywhere. Her daughter, however, seemed to be running with the fast, fun crowd—the type Stella had hung out with when she was younger. As far as many could see, Stella thought she was young enough to run with her daughter.

CHAPTER 45

With the exception of his wife Kathleen and their teenage daughter, the females occupying Jack Cusack's mind more than any other were Stella Maudine Nickell and her daughter Cynthia Lea Hamilton. Around and around, the images of the women from Auburn circled in his head.

Other agents had met Stella and had firsthand impressions about her as a suspect or a person of interest, but by design, SA Cusack had kept his distance. This kept a kind of mystique, which was usually advantageous in an interview. And in the event that she'd consent to a polygraph, he'd be the one to do the job.

While Harry Swanson and Stella Nickell went off to Whistlin' Jack Lodge on White Pass on September 4, 1986, insurance advisers at the state offices in Olympia learned Equifax was investigating Stella Nickell's claim. The information wasn't of particular concern. Accidental deaths were always investigated. But there was other news: the FBI was also looking into the possibility that Stella Nickell was the tamperer.

Bruce Nickell's wife, however, continued to press the State Employees Insurance Board (SEIB) for more information on when she could expect her money.

On September 26, Stella Nickell phoned and left a message for Sandy Sorby, an insurance adviser whom she had met briefly in

July. She got a call back from Pam Stegenga, who was now handling the claim, the following Monday.

"The final report on the investigation is due in the first week in October," Pam Stegenga told the widow. "I'll have the information for you then."

Stella Nickell thanked her for her help. It had been three months since her husband's death.

The Olympia women, both in their mid-thirties, felt sorry for the widow.

"There's no way she did it," Sandy Sorby told her friend and co-worker when she first learned about the FBI investigation. "She seemed so lost, so sad. I don't believe it."

Yet it was information relayed by Sandy Sorby that added fuel to the FBI case. The state employee told federal agents that on July 7, Stella Nickell arrived at the SEIB offices on Evergreen Park Drive in Olympia to file a claim on her husband's life insurance. She had been expected. Dick Johnson, Bruce Nickell's boss, had phoned ahead on July 2 with the shocking news that Nickell had been a cyanide-poisoning victim.

The widow gave Sandy a copy of an amended death certificate, pointing out how her husband's original autopsy had been in error, and that he had been killed by cyanide.

From her briefcase, she spread out some newspaper clippings.

"Do you want to go through them and pick out what you need? Or do you want copies of each one?"

There were dozens. Maybe even a hundred.

"No. Just give me a couple of them." Sandy Sorby didn't look at them. It made her nervous standing there with the surviving spouse of the cyanide victim.

Stella Nickell had filed her claim after the amended death certificate was ready. She had waited until the papers were in order. The information was interesting, maybe even significant, to the FBI.

Jack Cusack and Ron Nichols both felt they knew why.

"Stella Nickell knew all along that cyanide was the cause of death, and she waited for the authorities to catch up with her, so she could claim that $100,000 accidental-death benefit," Cusack said.

With her briefcase full of clippings, she was just a lady out to take care of a little business, Cusack thought.

Later, SA Cusack and others on the case kept pressing Sandy

Sorby on whether the widow asked how much insurance she'd receive.

"I don't think she ever asked," Sandy said. "She never asked . . . and I never told her."

Even after talking with the FBI, Sandy Sorby still felt Stella Nickell would be dropped as a suspect. The sad-looking widow just didn't seem like a killer.

When Stella Maudine Nickell said she'd come in for an interview in mid-November 1986, Jack Cusack was finally going to get to talk to her, and, he hoped, "detonate" her.

Neither SA Cusack nor SA Nichols knew what the woman would say during the interview or if she'd finally consent to a polygraph. In case she did, they had to be ready.

Always one for an analogy, Jack Cusack liked to say the FBI had been gathering the checkers on the board before the game.

"Was Stella Nickell going to play or not?"

Jack Cusack and SA Ron Nichols planned to walk her through the chronology of the couple years prior to her husband's death. What did she have to say about Bruce? Her marriage? The insurance?

And what was she going to say about the bottles she claimed to have purchased at two different times, in two different places? The veteran agent figured enough time had passed that the woman would have seen the outrageousness in that scenario.

The questions, the approach, even the seating arrangement in the interview room were carefully planned. Both men knew that when interviewing a suspect, there seldom is a second chance for followup. No "Just one more question, ma'am" Columbo tactics.

Though he had stayed away from Stella Nickell, Jack Cusack continued to interview those close to her.

Jerry Kimble was one. He called the Nickells "mom and dad." If ever a person fit his CB handle, it was Lost Tiger. No one could sway his belief that Stella had been a victim of the whole thing. The warm-hearted woman who had befriended him when he was her paperboy could not have hurt anyone.

"Stella is the most intelligent woman I've met in my life," he told Jack Cusack. "I don't know if it's her Indian nature, her tarot cards, Ouija board, telepathy, or what. But when she wanted to talk to me . . . something would say to me *call Stella*. I'd call her and she'd say, 'As a matter of fact, I did want to talk to you.'"

Jerry Kimble said he had seen Stella and Cindy laying out tarot cards at White River Estates while he and Bruce watched television.

When he left the FBI office, he felt more confused than when he arrived. Jack Cusack wasn't like some of the other agents. The twenty-two-year-old felt that SA Cusack didn't believe Stella was guilty.

"The way he states it and the way he feels are two different things. The way he states it they got her cold turkey, that's how they are. I get the indication that they don't know a hundred percent for sure that she did it. But they tell me, 'All the evidence is there.' "

Maybe Jerry Kimble was just being hopeful.

CHAPTER 46

By default, Dee Rogers had become a mother figure to *both* Cindy Hamilton and her daughter. And, as it had been the times they had lived together previously, it seemed it was Cindy who needed the most care.

"She would have days when she was so depressed, then she'd be on such a high—giggling, laughing, wanting to go do this and that—then crash. Then she wouldn't get out of bed for two days. Hellacious ups and downs," Dee later recalled.

With her insurance career going full-tilt, Dee Rogers could barely find time for the "Witches and Bitches" dart team at the Buzz Inn. No more party hearty for her. It was time to leave that to a younger generation—Cindy's.

The woman was trying to grow up, Dee thought, but just didn't have a clue how to go about it. She certainly wasn't able to deal with a small child.

"I think she saw some of her mom in herself, and it scared the hell out of her," Dee Rogers later said.

When it looked as though Cindy's daughter was going to be Dee Rogers's sole responsibility, she laid down the law.

"Cindy, I cannot raise your daughter."

"It'll only be for a little while. I'm going to send her down to live with her dad."

She made good on her promise. By early spring 1986, the little girl had gone, she was out of sight, out of mind. All Cindy seemed to care about was Cindy. It infuriated Dee.

"What would it take for you to sit down and write your daughter a letter?"

Cindy Lea promised she would.

Stella's sister Berta flew from Michigan to Seattle to celebrate their mother's sixty-ninth birthday on March 17, and her own, on the twenty-fifth. Stella picked Berta up after her shift at the concourse.

On the way to Auburn, Stella radioed her husband on the CB to let him know—as she always did—that she was on her way.

"What's for dinner, babe?"

Stella said she hadn't given it any thought.

"I'm hungry. I want something with gravy on it."

"You know where the dog food is!" Stella joked.

Berta stayed with Cora Lee and saw the Nickells over the course of the week. She liked Bruce, whom she had never met before. Later, she would insist, Stella seemed happy too.

When she returned to Michigan, she told her husband about the great relationship Stella and Bruce shared. If there had been any financial or personal problems, Berta didn't see any.

"That's what marriage should be," she said.

On April 15, 1986, the Riders arrived from Yakima and moved in with the Nickells. By Jim Rider's birthday, a week later, he and A. J. were working for the security company. Things were looking up.

Initially Stella and A. J. shared the same work schedule, which made it especially easy for their commute to the airport. On the days Cindy went to work, they'd pick her up in TP 4 2. After a short time, A. J.'s schedule changed to Tuesdays, Wednesdays, Thursdays off. The days were ten hours long, three days off.

A. J.'s daughter, Barbie, a first-grader, went to Cora Lee's after school until her mother and Stella got home. Occasionally, Stella watched Barbie on her day off, but she made it clear she'd rather do other things.

When the Riders got home, off they'd go with Bruce on the motorcycles. Bruce seemed glad to have them there.

Wilma Mae Stewart did not like her first cousin Cynthia Lea. And though she was smarter and certainly more beautiful, in some ways she felt inferior. Cindy was her grandmother Cora Lee's favorite, and Wilma wanted to be.

There were plenty of reasons to disapprove of or even despise her aunt Stella's oldest daughter. Wilma did not like the way Cynthia Lea treated Aunt Stella, Uncle Bruce, and her own little girl.

"I did not like the fact that she used her mom for baby-sitting. She lied to them. They helped her with some schooling with promises of paying back, and that never happened," Wilma said later.

Cynthia talked about her cousin, too. And when she did, it was also with bitterness.

"Stella couldn't raise her own children, but she took Wilma in for a while. Stella and Wilma had a special relationship. There was jealousy with Cindy that Wilma got the respect and love Cindy wanted from her mother," Dee Rogers said.

Wilma Stewart had always dreamed of going to England, and in the middle of May 1986, she was on her way. She had saved her money from her job as an assistant in a Houston law office, run up her charge cards, and got her first passport. She was deep into her travel preparations when Aunt Stella called late one night.

"Uncle Bruce and I are having some problems. I'm thinking about leaving him."

Wilma suggested her favorite aunt should come to Texas.

"You can live with me and we can work and be two good friends."

"Well, I may," Stella answered.

Wilma liked the idea. She was lonely in Houston and her aunt had always been a lot of fun. She wanted to be "best buds" with Aunt Stella.

But there was a problem with the timing.

"Let me tell you this," Wilma said, "if you leave Uncle Bruce, you'll have to do it now or you'll have to do it after I come back from England. I'm not leaving that door unlocked and I'm not leaving the key under the mat!"

Stella understood.

"If you see my pickup coming, you'll see me; if you don't, you won't," she said.

Willie didn't question her aunt. She figured Stella would tell her all about it when she got down to Texas. The idea her aunt might have grown weary of catering to her uncle didn't surprise Wilma in the least.

"My aunt and I are very close," she said later. "We're very much alike. We have a tendency to wear the pants in the family, to call the shots. All the women in our family are very dominating. He goes to work, comes home, gives her the check. He expected the bills to be paid. My aunt Stella spoiled him. Uncle Bruce would say, 'Oh, I want . . . ' and Aunt Stella would find a way to get it for him."

By May 23, Aunt Stella's pickup still hadn't pulled into the driveway, and Wilma left for England, as planned.

CHAPTER 47

Dee Rogers was no Mother Teresa. Never pretended to be. Still, she couldn't keep up with Cindy's mood swings. The young woman's ups and downs became more pronounced. It was man after man, jag after jag, high after low. It didn't seem to improve, even with the responsibility of motherhood relinquished altogether to someone else.

Sense of humor wasn't enough. Dee couldn't laugh it off.

By October 1986, Cindy Hamilton was showing the stress of the FBI investigation. She was drinking harder than usual, and fooling around at Gee Gee's. She lashed out at Dee's children for no apparent reason, which bothered them. They loved their "Aunt Sin."

"What's your problem?" Dee asked after what had become another all-too-familiar row. "I don't even like you anymore!"

"You want to know why I'm doing this? You want to know why I'm so bitchy?"

"Why don't you just fucking tell me?"

"My mom killed my dad," she finally blurted out.

"What in the fuck are you talking about?"

And so, for the first time, Cindy told her story.

"She talked about how they had been working together, about the poisoning, things on the property . . . how Stella had talked about her father's death," Dee later recalled.

Dee recalled the time Stella phoned the apartment on Smith Street.

"She called me up and said, 'Is Cindy home?'

" 'No, she's out partying. She's just got her hair done, and she went down with a girlfriend. They're at the bar.'

" 'Can you get her right home? I have something very important to tell you two, and I want to see you together.'

"I said, 'Sure.'

"I called Cindy. 'You gotta come home. Something's up with your mom. She's on her way over, she's got something to tell you.'

"We had thought maybe one of Bruce's parents had died. Or maybe Cindy's grandmother had died. We never, ever thought that Bruce was dead."

Dee might not have thought it was Bruce, but Cindy told Bonnie Anderson she thought so on the way back from the Mexican restaurant.

At the time, it didn't strike Dee Rogers as odd that Stella Nickell had driven over to Wenatchee to tell her husband's parents face-to-face, though she knew Bruce had a cousin who could have told them.

She couldn't help but wonder later: "What did she do in the meantime? What calls were made? To whom? From Wenatchee? Who's to know?"

Cindy cried and rambled topic after topic:

"My mother was having an affair with Jim McCarthy . . ."

"My mother wanted to buy some heroin . . . I thought she wanted to be a drug dealer . . . then I knew otherwise . . ."

"My mother talked about putting drugs in his iced tea . . ."

"She said it would be easy to reenact the Tylenol murders. . . ."

Cindy told Dee she saw some white powder in a small Tupperware container in the locker she and her mother shared at the airport. It was just before Bruce died.

"I think it was cyanide," she said.

And as she sat, smoking, crying, and cursing, the color drained from her face.

"Oh, Jesus Christ," she wailed. "I took some of those! It could have been me who ended up dead!"

"What are you talking about?"

Cindy explained that after she and her mother returned from the funeral, she had had a *mega* headache. It had been such a long drive. When she got inside the trailer she went to the kitchen and took a couple of Extra Strength Excedrin capsules.

"You took some?"

"From the same bottle. It could have been me, too!"

"That bitch!" Dee Rogers was stunned. Cindy was now in high gear, spouting off more atrocities planned by her mother against her husband.

Dee knew what had to be done.

"Cindy, you have to tell the FBI."

"I can't . . ." Cindy cried. "What about Grandmother? What . . ."

"You have to. I know you, and you cannot live with it. You have to make it right. You *have* to."

"I can't."

"You *will*."

Cindy Hamilton had been building a ground swell of anger for weeks. She had been testy with everyone. Especially, or so it seemed, with her mother. She told Dee Rogers she "popped" her mom with her fist in front of Walt's Inn one night.

"Yeah, at least I didn't kill anybody!" Cindy cried.

Stella later told a different version of what happened between mother and daughter.

"There was no physical contact. The only time that Cynthia and I ever had an altercation in public is when Cynthia thought I was too drunk to drive home and she went out and took the coil wire off my truck.

"I would never hit Cynthia like that in public. I really don't think Cynthia would hit me. She knows she's bigger than I am, but she's not real sure whether she can whip me or not. And she knows being my daughter, if she were gonna hit me, she'd have to whip me. Because I'd bring her down a peg or two."

Dee Rogers made a phone call to the FBI from her office at Lincoln Mutual in Bellevue. Just exactly when she made that call is not entirely clear. Later, she would say she waited only a "day or two" before calling the Seattle field office. That would put it in October, the month Cindy told her.

"I called Randy Scott and had him meet me in Bellevue at my job. I said to him, 'I think Stella killed Bruce.' "

The agent wanted to know why she thought so.

"I told him that I had a conversation with Cindy and there was a lot of emotion and she wasn't ready to talk. I would talk to her some more and try to persuade her to talk to him."

"I remember I told him a little bit, maybe just enough to get his taste buds going . . . I remember distinctly telling Randy that Cindy should tell him . . . and if she wouldn't come to him, I would fill him in and he could take it to Cindy."

While Cindy was telling her story to Dee, Stella Nickell was methodically and politely doing her best to collect on her late husband's insurance policies. She was, she said, entitled to it.

She spoke with the SEIB's Pam Stegenga on October 10, but the insurance adviser told her she'd have to get back to her.

An SEIB supervisor called Northwestern Mutual on October 14 and learned the FBI was still investigating. The Equifax report was complete, but the FBI's was still pending. There would be no payout until Mrs. Nickell was released as a suspect. The report might be ready by the end of the month.

Pam Stegenga phoned Stella Nickell back the same day and relayed the essence of the news.

"Does it always take this long?" the widow asked.

Pam told her that sometimes it did.

Cindy Hamilton walked a thin and jagged line. She continued to see her mother, and by default, Harry Swanson, when his beatup old Winnebago was camped out at the property. But she had let a rabid, hungry cat out of the bag, and with the FBI involved, it was dinnertime.

When she returned from visiting with her mother, she told stories about the insurance and what Stella had promised they'd do when the money was released.

Dee thought that Stella was trying to buy her daughter's silence.

The two had even gone out looking for property for the site of their much-dreamed-of tropical-fish store.

"Cindy went along for the ride; she didn't want to tip her off as to what she was doing. It was kind of like making her sick to do it, but she was trying to play middle of the road."

And as Cindy Hamilton planned her betrayal of her mother, another Auburn daughter struggled with the loss of her mother.

On October 26, 1986, Hayley Snow crawled onto her bed in the room her mother had helped her decorate. She wrote in her diary:

> I miss Mommy so much. Everything I feel is beyond words;
> no one understands completely or has time to listen. It's tough
> but I'll pull through. Sometimes I swear I can feel her inside of
> me, my soul.

Paul Webking was going through adjustments of his own. But he didn't do it alone. He was already seeing a pretty flight attendant named Sheri.

The first Sunday in November, Paul and his girlfriend took in a concert. The fleeting picture of the couple off to have a good time only served to remind Hayley of the time her mother and Paul saw the Judds perform, shortly before her death. They had come home laughing, joking.

"Why can't she be here?" the girl asked herself.

In a few days, it would be five months since everything happened.

Sarah Webb wouldn't let her suspicions lapse. The polygraph results still meant nothing.

"He did it," she said. "He killed her . . . I don't know how, but he did." She pointed out how Paul had ditched Hawaiian shirts and shorts for a more professional look. He was spending money right and left. And now he had this girlfriend.

"Sue hasn't been dead a half a year!" she said.

Like Wilma Mae Stewart, Jerry Kimble didn't care much for Cynthia Lea Hamilton. What she told him shortly after he returned to Auburn after being discharged from the Air Force made his disdain even more abiding.

It was November when Cindy invited Jerry to go out drinking in Kent. They hit the usual spots, with Cindy leading the way as she always did. She knew everybody, and everybody knew her. Though Jerry had been away, it was evident his "sister" hadn't grown up much. The two of them and a bottle of tequila ended up alone at the Nickell place around 1 A.M. If Stella Nickell had been there, the conversation surely would have taken a different, more polite turn.

Cindy said her mother was the killer.

Jerry didn't believe her. *Couldn't* believe her. Was she drunk, or just spiteful? Maybe a combination of both? Whatever her problem, she was talking crazy.

"What makes you say that?"

Cindy told him her mother had confided plans of killing Bruce while they worked at the airport and talked of overdosing him with cocaine. She wanted information on drugs, but Cindy didn't know anything.

"Mom even read up on poisons."

Jerry thought it was crazy talk, and told Cindy so.

Cindy projected a "you can believe what you want to believe" stance as she made her case against her mother. The young man had no choice but to listen. Like mother, like daughter. He knew no one argues with Cindy Hamilton.

And around the time her mother was reading a book about poisons, Cindy claimed Stella gave her a small bag of "white powder to get rid of."

Though she never used the word "cyanide" when relating the incident, Jerry Kimble felt the implication was clear.

"She wanted me to believe a hundred percent that it was cyanide," he later recalled.

Jerry also recalled that Cindy also told a tale concerning tarot cards.

"Stella was into tarot cards and stuff like that. Them two set down at the house one night and were talking about poisons. How this one worked, how this drug worked, and what would this drug do and so and so. This is a conversation Cindy and Stella had. She had brought up all the stuff they had talked about, the different poisons, drugs, all that stuff. They were asking [the tarot cards] questions."

There was more proof, Stella's daughter insisted. She told Jerry that the authorities had found an algicide inadvertently mixed in with the cyanide used in the tamperings. Her mother used that very brand.

How could Cindy Hamilton have known that? Had Stella told her? Had the FBI leaked it to her in hopes the information would get her to come over to the government's side? Or could it have been learned through the Kent gossip mill? Dee Rogers had a pet-supply wholesaler friend who might have passed on information. FBI agents had been all over town, asking enough questions so that a reasonably bright person could fill in the blanks.

Cindy said the Excedrin capsules found in the bathroom also pointed to her mother's being the killer.

"Mom never kept any medicines in the bathroom, especially aspirin," she reminded Jerry.

Jerry Kimble had been drinking all night, but he wasn't drunk enough to believe a word of what he was hearing. He was angry, and it seemed clear to Cindy that he didn't buy into what she was saying. Cindy got mad at him, and told him off.

"Well, you can believe what you want to believe."

Later, Jerry checked out the algae killer Stella kept with her tropical-fish supplies. It was a *liquid*. He didn't know what that meant, if anything.

Thereafter, Jerry Kimble wondered about Cindy's motivation for telling him all this. Was Cindy setting him up to go against Stella?

The whole idea of Cindy's claiming ignorance of various drugs was a joke.

"Cindy knew very well what drugs are, but I didn't put two and two together then," he said.

And while Cindy Hamilton was stabbing her mother in the back, she also aimed a blade at her heart.

Or at least Harry Swanson's.

The man from Chimacum didn't want to move too fast with Stella, but he didn't want to wait too long and lose her again. Now he had a plan. He shelled out a thousand dollars for a diamond engagement ring.

Harry, Stella, and Cindy were eating at Ivar's, a fish-and-chips place on Seattle's waterfront, when he finally summoned the courage to put the ring on Stella's slender finger.

Stella became teary-eyed, but it was her daughter's response that Harry would later recount.

"I will never forget Cindy's reaction," Harry Swanson said some years later: " '*Well, big deal. How romantic!*' "

"The little bitch," he sneered.

"I know," said Stella Nickell when Jerry Kimble drove out to the property to tell her about all the "evidence" Cindy had insisted proved her guilt. Stella dismissed it. There had been no white powder, no discussions of drugs, no books on poisons.

When he told Stella government chemists had detected traces of an algicide mixed into the cyanide, Stella informed him that everybody used an algicide in their tanks. It was available at any pet store.

"I don't know why they're doing this to you," Jerry said. "I don't believe you did it."

Federal agents returned to White River Estates, where Jerry was once again living with his folks. One agent asked him about his conversation with Stella, though by the questions fired at him, Jerry felt the FBI already knew what had been discussed. He wondered if the Nickells' mobile home had been bugged. The agent's timing, knowledge of his visit, and conversation pointed to such a conclusion.

"It might be a good idea for you to stay away from the situation," the agent told the young man. Jerry took it as more of a threat than a suggestion.

The way Jerry Kimble saw it, the FBI had grown weary of losing cases like this. With the Auburn cyanide poisonings it finally had a chance to make a case against somebody on a product-tampering charge.

Jack Kimble, whose advice son Jerry seldom sought and resented when offered, had a few words for his son after the FBI's second visit to their mobile home.

"Don't lie. Those people will definitely know. They're not something to fool around with. If they told you don't go up there, don't go up there. I imagine the place is bugged . . . or they're watching."

For once, his old man was probably right, Jerry thought, but he didn't care. He continued to see Stella. He loved her too much. Besides, she was innocent.

CHAPTER 48

At about 10 A.M., November 18, 1986, Jack Cusack and Ron Nichols looked out a seventh-floor window of the Federal Building in time to see Stella Maudine Nickell walk across First and Madison. The suspect was flanked by two SAs who had "chauffeured" her from Auburn. While Stella cooled her heels in the waiting room, SA Cusack met with one of the agents and learned that during the drive in she had seemed confident and friendly, even chatting about her tropical-fish hobby.

"Did she say anything of interest?" Cusack asked.

In fact, she had.

"I have a question," Stella Nickell had said, somewhat timidly. "I wonder if you can answer it."

"We'll try, if we can."

"Do you think that Bruce's death is related in any way with that lady out in Maple Valley?"

"Darlene Seader?"

"Yes."

"No," the agent answered. "Darlene's death was a suicide."

The agent went on to explain that even though the deeply troubled Maple Valley woman had carefully planned her poisoning, she ingested far more cyanide than necessary to kill her.

"She took a lot more than her body weight called for," the agent said.

"I didn't think body weight had anything to do with it," Stella Nickell piped up. "I thought the stuff was so powerful, all you had to do was breathe it."

Later, Jack Cusack recalled interviews with friends who claimed Stella Nickell knew CPR. That had conflicted with Stella's statement. She said she didn't attempt to resuscitate Bruce. Had she been afraid to breathe into Bruce's mouth for fear she'd be exposed to cyanide?

The special agents greeted her and seated her with her back to the door at a huge conference table.

In this initial encounter, SA Cusack saw her as a woman who had decided she didn't have to give up the battle to age. She was a vision of extremes—her hair a startling inky black, her lips a deep red. Her second-skin jeans were tucked into cowboy boots, and as always, she wore the fringed buckskin jacket and when she moved her purse, the bell attached to it tinkled.

There was a bell after all. Tom Noonan had in fact identified the suspect with this oddest of details.

"I'm glad to be here," Stella said. "Just glad to do anything I can to help with the investigation."

Jack Cusack sat directly across from Stella, with Ron Nichols on his left. Both men tried to put her at ease without undermining the seriousness of the interview. SA Cusack asked her if she'd sign a document waiving her rights and indicating she was there of her own free will. With no hesitation, she complied.

For the next hour and a half, Bruce Nickell's widow talked and the agents listened.

She stuck to her original story that she had purchased the two bottles of tainted Excedrin at two different times, at two different stores. The SAs had fully expected she would have reconsidered the odds of that happening and changed her statement.

"I'm absolutely certain," she said, her direct gaze adding to her emphasis.

"Did you try to resuscitate Bruce with mouth-to-mouth while you were waiting for the aid car?"

"No. I do not know CPR. Besides, he was still breathing when they showed up."

Throughout the interview, she remained direct and responsive to the questions. She spoke with conviction.

When asked about insurance, Stella said her husband had the

one policy from his work. It was valued at around "$25,000 or $35,000."

"Any other policies?"

"No."

The agents ran through Bruce's life right up to his death at Harborview, with little, if any, deviation from the original story she had given to SA Ike Nakamoto in June. She did say, however, that she had suspected Bruce of seeing a prostitute in the weeks before his death. She even confronted him, but he had denied it.

Ron Nichols asked about her tropical-fish hobby, and the woman seemed to brighten. She and her husband both enjoyed fish. Bruce liked fancy guppies.

When he asked about any algae problems, however, the slight smile left her face.

"I've heard about that . . . I don't use that product."

"What product?"

She tightened up and said nothing more on the subject.

As the interview drew to a close, Jack Cusack leaned forward.

"Hey, Stella, we appreciate you coming down here today to help us cover some of these areas we've discussed. Are there any questions you'd like to ask us?"

She couldn't think of any.

"Would you be willing to help us some more?"

"Anything I can do," she said.

"Stella, we'd like you to take a polygraph this morning."

"What?" Her composure wavered. "What are you trying to do? I loved my husband. Are you trying to drag me through it all over again?" Tears fell. "I came here to help . . . and you're doing this to me?"

"A polygraph would help us put some of these questions behind us. It would help move the investigation forward."

She continued her sobs, insisting she couldn't go through such an ordeal.

"I can't believe you want to drag me through this again!"

"But it would be less traumatic than what you've already done here today. We've already talked about Bruce's death," SA Cusack said, trying to calm her. "I'd just like to ask you two questions. You'll know what those questions are beforehand. All I'll ask are two questions."

Stella dabbed her tears and said she just couldn't go through it without her doctor's permission.

"If your doctor says it's all right?"

"I'll do it."

Jack Cusack pressed it. "There's a phone right here. Why don't you call him?"

"Oh, no. I couldn't do that. I want to see him in person."

"If he says it's okay, and your attorney says it's okay, you will consent to the polygraph?"

She promised she would. At that moment, Jack Cusack figured Stella Nickell might have said just about anything to get the hell out of the FBI's office, but she couldn't really leave, she had to wait for her ride. An FBI agent was dispatched to retrieve the car from the garage down on First Avenue.

To Jack Cusack's way of thinking, Stella Nickell had been a woman on a mission that morning. She had wanted to see where the investigation was going, how much information the FBI actually had about her, and, if she could, throw them off the track.

If that had been her intention, she had failed.

"Well, Nichols," SA Cusack said. "I don't think Stella has any idea how she incriminated herself."

He agreed.

That afternoon, just hours after the suspect had left, SAC Mike Byrne called Cusack and Nichols into his office to go over a bit of news. Equifax insurance investigator Lynn Force had done it again. He had sent over a packet of information proving that Stella Nickell had sent correspondence to All American Life—concerning *two* policies.

Lynn Force had been shocked by the discovery. It had been only four months since he had talked to Stella at the airport, and at that time she had denied the existence of any other policies.

The insurance investigator considered Stella Nickell had "assumed that since these were two small polices of $20,000 each, there probably would be no investigation at all." The total coverage on her husband's life was now $175,000-plus.

"Here she was telling us this morning that she had only one policy on Bruce, after she had sent a letter a week ago?" SA Cusack asked.

The woman had such bad luck when it came to insurance.

First there had been Bruce Nickell's failure to take the physical for the $25,000 supplemental life for which he had applied. Then there was the "clerical error" that had cost her the MasterCard policy through All American, as she had told SA Ike Nakamoto back in June.

As SAs Cusack and Nichols both knew, Stella Nickell told the FBI that Bruce had been covered by a single "small policy from the state" during the November interview. Nothing else.

And now there was proof she had been lying. Stories were unraveling.

All American Life had received two separate letters from Stella, both written October 20, both accompanied by specification schedules and death certificates. It was clear she knew there were two policies totaling $40,000.

The first one referred to policy no. 200387, which had been applied for on September 5, 1985:

> *Dear Sir:*
> *I am writing in reference to a claim on the death of my husband, Bruce Nickell. I am not sure how to do this because I have never had to send a claim before. I called the 800 number and was told to send a certified copy of the death certificate, so I have enclosed one and a copy of the policy. Thank you.*
> *Very sincerely,*
> *Stella Nickell*

The second letter referred to policy no. 247301, for which she had applied October 14, 1985:

> *To whom it may concern:*
> *I am writing in reference to the claim on my insurance policy for my husband Bruce Nickell's death. Bruce died June 5th, 1986. I do not know how to go about this as I have never placed a claim before. I am enclosing a certified copy of the death certificate and a copy of the policy. This is what I was told I needed to send when I called. Thank you.*
> *Very sincerely,*
> *Stella Nickell*

There was also the claimant's statement filled out by her and witnessed by boyfriend Harry Swanson and her daughter, Cynthia Lea Hamilton. It was dated November 12, 1986—less than a week before the interview. It was further proof that Stella Nickell had sought the money from two more policies. She wrote: *"Both policies are the same."*

And while Stella Nickell's motives seemed clear, her daughter's feelings professed to Dee Rogers seemed at odds with her witnessing the signature. What was Cindy doing? Trying to go with the flow? Making a play for the best deal? If her mother could beat this, she'd get the money. If she didn't, there might be other payoffs.

On Thursday, November 20, two days after storming out of the FBI office, Stella Nickell phoned Pam Stegenga at SEIB in Olympia. Pam told her the investigation was still pending and Stella seemed surprised.

"I was downtown the day before yesterday talking with the FBI, and it's my understanding the investigation is over," she said.

She rattled off the names of three agents she had met with— "Ike Nakamoto, Larry [Montague], and Alex Suggs." She did not mention Cusack or Nichols.

Pam Stegenga promised to make some inquiries of the carrier and get back to the widow right away. She called Northwestern, who informed her the FBI told Equifax "they could not rule out the spouse as a suspect yet." Northwestern was reviewing the Nickell file, and after an upcoming meeting with the FBI, promised to send a letter to the widow.

"Assure Mrs. Nickell that the claim is being worked on," the benefits adviser was told. Passing on such assurance was something Pam Stegenga didn't quite feel up to.

The next day, an SEIB assistant manager called Stella Nickell and told her the state had no control over the investigation or the payment of the claim, and, in fact, she should cease from calling SEIB. Northwestern would deal with her directly.

Pam Stegenga felt relieved that she would not have to talk with the widow again. She dreaded Stella Nickell's asking point-blank: "What is going on? What do they think happened?"

Stella Nickell's shopping habits bore further scrutiny in the days after her FBI interview.

During the course of the interview, the suspected tamperer had denied shopping at Pay 'N Save North, where one of the tampered bottles had been recovered.

"I don't like the way that store is laid out."

She said the store located in south Auburn was more to her liking. Jack Cusack couldn't understand why she'd deny that, when it was so easily disproved. When her subpoenaed checks came back, seven written in 1986 were made out to Pay 'N Save North. None had been written to the south store.

CHAPTER 49

A lot had happened since Shirley Webbly had last seen CB pal Stella Nickell. Her husband Don had died of a massive heart attack and Stella's husband had been poisoned by cyanide. Both women were trying to put the pieces of their lives back together. Shirley had plans to enroll in a Kent business college to become a travel agent, while Stella was doing her best to put suspicion of murder behind her. When the two women ran into each other at the Auburn First Interstate bank, Stella suggested they go somewhere to talk. They picked up a pizza and some Pepsi and drove up to Shirley's house on Lee Hill.

With the kind of calmness reserved for more casual concerns, Stella confided that the authorities suspected she had killed Bruce. Stella wasn't worried, because she was innocent.

Shirley believed her.

"She's a very intelligent lady. But she is not a devious lady. And she's not that good an actress. If anything was wrong between Bruce and her, you would have seen it," Shirley later said.

It was all so ridiculous.

"Shirley, I already had his death certificate. If I had done it, why would I have called attention to it?"

"It just doesn't make good sense to me," Shirley offered. "Jesus, I hope they don't dig up Don and decide that maybe I put him away. Because I certainly didn't."

After four hours at the kitchen table, eating pizza, smoking cigarettes, and talking about Bruce and Don, Stella hugged Shirley
good-bye. She promised she wouldn't be such a stranger.

She wouldn't call from her house, however.

"My phone's being tapped."

Anyone who might have seen Cindy and Dee in taverns around
Kent in December of 1986 might have assumed they were the same
fun-loving, good-time gals that they had always been. They would
have been dead wrong.

All they could talk about was Stella Maudine and the FBI.

Both women knew Stella would eventually learn she had been
betrayed. How would she retaliate?

Neither considered her likely to make a frontal attack. Maybe
she'd go after the children? Dee grew so paranoid, she phoned her
first husband in New York and told him about the cyanide murders.
Would he take all three children if Stella got it in her mind Dee
had gone to the FBI? Even though only the two eldest were his, he
agreed.

At home, Cindy became frantic if the kids were ten minutes late,
Dee said.

"If she was home waiting for them and they were late, she'd
tear into them. 'You are given a time to be home, you are to be
home at that time!' "

Cindy even feared her mother would go after her daughter down
in California. Or maybe she'd try to kill them.

"If you die in an accident," Dee Rogers moaned, "what does she
have? She's got me on hearsay. She'll get off scot-free with all the
insurance money. And I'll be living in a podunk town somewhere
with a name like Mary Sue Buttercup. . . ."

As the holidays approached, Dee's sense of humor reemerged
and she joked that nobody was going to take any chances at their
place.

"If we get cookies from your mom for Christmas, they're going
down the toilet."

SA Cusack wrestled with his own problems, some small, some big.
It was the little things that sometimes crept up on him. While driving to the city, maybe in the shower or after a run on the island
where he lived.

What of the so-called third bottle, found under Stella Nickell's bathroom sink? It was the same lot number and count size as the one that led to Sue Snow's death. No safety seal, yet still full.

It was possible that Stella had forgotten about it. She had laced all the capsules needed to do the job she had in mind. Stella told the FBI she never bought that size, preferring the less expensive forty-count. *She was backpedaling.*

He also wondered about the insurance policies, now at the FBI in Washington. Did Bruce Nickell know about them?

CHAPTER 50

While SA Randy Scott was working with Pam Stegenga at the State Employees Insurance Board to gauge Stella Nickell's inquiries into her husband's life insurance, the suspected tamperer continued to flip-flop on her pledge to take a polygraph. There was always an excuse. Her doctor didn't think she was ready. Her lawyer didn't think it was a good idea. She reminded Jack Cusack of a little girl hiding behind the protection of two men. But by mid-December all of that changed.

Jack and Kathleen Cusack were at home having dinner when the FBI switchboard relayed the message that Mrs. Nickell was on the line and wanted to talk.

"Give me a second to get to my office and patch her over," he said, and went down the hall and shut the double doors to his office.

"Mr. Cusack?" Stella asked when he picked up the line. She seemed somewhat confused by the delay.

"Yes, Stella. This is Jack Cusack. What can I do for you?"

"I want to take that polygraph," she said. "This has dragged on . . . too long . . ." Jack Cusack told her it was a good idea.

Her speech was odd. She slurred her words slightly. At their interview in November, Stella's words had been clipped and deliberate.

"I'll even take that truth syrup if you want me to," she said. "I don't have nothing to hide."

"That won't be necessary," he said. They talked for a moment more, and she hung up.

The SA, now head of the case, leaned back in his chair, both excited and amused.

Truth syrup?

Harry Swanson could never forget the morning of December 15, 1986. The air was icy outside, but inside the mobile home everything was warm and wonderful. Stella woke up beaming.

"Babe," she said, "I'm ready to get this thing off of my back! I'm gonna do the polygraph today!"

Her mood was so positive, so upbeat, one would have thought that Stella Nickell was off to Olympia to pick up the first of twenty annual state lottery checks. She called Laurie Church to tell her she was on her way to be polygraphed. The news surprised Laurie since Stella had told her repeatedly she'd never take one because her attorney told her the tests were unreliable.

"The goddamn FBI keeps hounding me, and this is the only way out of it."

They got into Harry's Lincoln and drove to Dr. Smith's office. The doctor asked if she was sure she felt up to the polygraph. She said she was.

Harry made a stop at lawyer Bill Donais's office. He, too, questioned Stella to see if she was really up to it.

"It's the only way they'll leave me alone," she said. She wanted to take the lie-detector test to prove she hadn't killed anyone. Not her Bruce, not that Snow lady.

Bill Donais offered to drive her, and they made arrangements to meet Harry Swanson at Andy's Diner later.

At the FBI office, preparations had been made. Every detail had been readied. Evidence charts were organized in case she talked or argued. In the event Stella Nickell confessed, an Asst. U.S. Attorney from the Seattle office would be on hand to offer a deal: no death penalty if she talked. Ron Nichols was also there, but this was Jack Cusack's show.

"I feel like I'm walking into the lion's den," Stella said with a half-smile in the hallway on the way to the polygraph room. Her short skirt's hemline rose and fell like a Slinky as she walked. No jeans this time. Her lips were deep red, as they had been at the visit a month before.

Stella Nickell had two sides, and on this day both would reveal themselves. She tried to be what Cusack considered the charming, "win-you-over Stella," but she slipped toward the "you-aren't-going-to-make-me-do-anything-I-don't-want-to Stella."

She studied the examinee's chair. It was black and intimidating. Its arms were large rectangular padded platforms, support for the occupant's sensor-attached appendages. Though SAs Cusack and Nichols were there to greet her, the chair might have been all she saw. The white aggregate walls of the room were devoid of pictures, devoid of distractions. Window blinds were drawn.

As Stella took her seat, Jack Cusack explained the polygraph. Ignoring her "lion's den" remark, he was cordial yet professional. He told her he viewed all people as bilingual.

"There's what's audible, of course, and what comes from the heart. The polygraph measures what comes from the heart."

Stella took it all in, and though invited to ask questions, she had few.

He told her the sequence: they'd talk, then a pretest to show her that polygraphs really do work, and finally the exam itself.

First, the questions were qualified.

"When I ask about the cyanide," he said, "I'm talking about the potassium cyanide from this case. I'm talking about the cyanide that killed Bruce and Sue Snow. I'm not asking about cyanide from ten years ago. Do you understand?"

She nodded.

"When I ask about tampering with capsules, I'm talking about the capsules in this case. I want to make sure that you are comfortable with all the questions. We can't have any confusion here."

Again, she indicated she understood.

With components in place, Jack Cusack asked Stella Nickell to select a number, write it down on a slip of paper, and place it under her arm. She was told to answer "no" to each of his questions—even when he came to the number she wrote down.

"I'll be able to tell you what number you wrote," he told her.

And so he did. Charts indicated at which point Stella Nickell lied; it also showed how her heart had raced as Jack Cusack got closer to the number.

Then it was time for the real thing. The case agent asked a total of ten questions concerning aspects of the Seamurs case.

"Regarding the capsules, did you put any potassium cyanide in any of those capsules?"

"No."

"Did you cause the death of Sue Snow?"

"No."

If Stella Nickell had come to the FBI office to take the longshot chance that she'd somehow pass the test, she had failed. The serious look on Jack Cusack's face never indicated one way or another.

When he finished, Jack swung his chair around to the big black chair Stella occupied so silently. He spoke in a low, barely audible voice.

"Hey, Stella, it's over. I just want you to listen to me for a few minutes."

The woman hooked up to the black chair didn't speak or move.

"I know that if you could change things, Bruce would still be alive. But you can't. Stella, you're here today and we're going to work with you. You need help. Maybe we can arrange for the help you need," Cusack said, his voice still low. "First, you have to tell us in your own words why you killed Bruce and Sue Snow."

Stella's eyes were dark. Her lips tightened like a twisted rubber band.

"Are you accusing me of killing my husband?"

"Absolutely. I know you did it. And you know you did it. Let's work it out here."

Ron Nichols, who was standing by, stepped in to go over the evidence the FBI had gathered during Seamurs, all showing she was the killer. The bottles, the algicide, the insurance.

Stella Maudine Nickell sat and listened.

She's trying to see if we have enough to prove she's the guilty one, Cusack thought.

"This is going to be hard on your family, your mother. Do you really want to put them through this?"

Stella looked up. "I want to see my attorney."

Her vocal pattern was odd. Her words seemed choppy, as though she were speaking in a different dialect.

I. Want. To. See. My. Attorney.

Ken Parker, an Assistant U.S. Attorney, talked with Bill Donais briefly, but the Auburn lawyer didn't seem to know how to handle what was happening with his client.

"I'll get back with you next week," he said.

With that remark, Stella Nickell would be able to buy time. The FBI polygrapher with the silver hair and the dark eyebrows knew that getting a confession out of her was not going to happen.

Ron Nichols was a little disappointed when the suspect and her attorney left the office. So convinced was he of Stella's guilt, if she had passed the polygraph he would have accused SA Cusack of being lousy at his job.

"I'd like to have seen more fight from her," Ron Nichols said.

Later, Jack Cusack described Stella Nickell during the closing moments of the polygraph and interview:

"She looked like a female bank teller sitting there watching a video replay of her stealing money out of the till when she has been emphatically denying it for weeks. She looked like a broken-spirited young girl in a forty-two-year-old's body."

Stella Nickell was totally dejected and deflated when she and Bill Donais arrived at Andy's Diner.

"Boy, they came in with sad faces. She passed three tests and they rigged it and she failed the last one. They heard the papers being crumbled and thrown in the wastebasket or something. Her lawyer said, 'I can see where this is going, come on, Stella, we're leaving,' " Harry Swanson recalled.

Stella was never quite the same after that trip to the Federal Building. She kept saying she wasn't a killer and she was being set up.

"It's me they are gonna nail," she told Harry. "They have to have somebody, and I fit right in."

That same evening, an upset Stella and Harry showed up at the Churches'.

"I have never been so disgusted with people my whole life," Stella said, explaining that Jack Cusack had "failed" her on the polygraph. She suspected some kind of "hanky-panky" had gone on.

"I did a test, and another test, and Mr. Donais was in the outside office and he wanted to see the test and they lost it. From one office to another with a connecting door, they lost it.

"They kept saying, 'You might as well tell us the truth—you're guilty. Come on, Mrs. Nickell.' "

"She was shaking and crying, they got her so darn frazzled. And Stella don't get frazzled," Laurie Church said some years later.

Cindy Hamilton was waiting for Dee Rogers when she came home after working another ten-hour day.

"She failed the fucking polygraph!" Cindy said, barely waiting for Dee to get into the apartment.

"She fucking failed it!"

Cindy said her mother had called her with the news at the gas/minimart where she worked.

CHAPTER 51

The holiday season following the passing of a loved one is usually the most difficult time for survivors. Hayley Snow's thoughts were on her mother and the kind of Christmas they would have had, they always had. Sue Snow had liked to decorate a great big tree in a single color, all pink or rose, her favorite shades.

But the house on N Street had no pink decorations. No tree. No stockings. Christmas presents sat in a forlorn heap on the living-room floor.

Paul Webking had made plans to marry Sheri, the flight attendant, and in doing so, caused Hayley increasing confusion and bouts of depression. Her mother was dead, her sister was gone at school, her aunt . . . everyone was out of touch. She was in the house that had been her home, but it didn't feel like it anymore. And while it was true that Connie Snow, her real father, was only a few miles away and she could have moved in with him, she had elected to stay. Leaving Paul would mean leaving her mother's memory. Her mother's house. *Her* house.

Sarah Webb continued her "Paul is the killer" drumbeat, but Hayley didn't really believe it. At least, not always. The fact that Paul was marrying Sheri so soon after her mother's death troubled her.

Had he known her before Mommy died?
She wrote in her diary:

> Paul and Sheri are probably going to get married around the
> New Year. Then she'll move in around February or March . . .
> It won't bother me having her around until she tries to be too
> much of a mom to me . . . She'll be my friend, not my mom.

Stella Maudine Nickell looked like ten miles of washed-out road
when she pulled TP 4 2 into neighbor Sandy Scott's rutted driveway
on December 22, 1986. She was pale, and befuddled about something, even agitated. Stella Nickell was not the kind of woman to
be unhinged about anything.

"They said I lied," she said, informing Sandy of the polygraph.

"Lied? About what?"

"About taking the pills out of the same bottle as Bruce."

"What do you mean?" What did her taking capsules out the the
same bottle as Bruce have to do with how Bruce died?

"They asked me if I took pills out of the same bottle that Bruce
had, and I said no. They said I lied."

Her story didn't make sense. "Stella, you *did* say you took some
of those."

"I did?" The woman looked blank.

"Yeah, when we were sitting there with that FBI agent you said
you had taken some out of the same bottle. When I came home, I
said to Scotty, 'My God, can you believe Stella took capsules that
could have had cyanide in them? Can you believe the luck of the
draw that she would take capsules out of that bottle and not die?' "

Sandy reminded Stella that she had told her the night before the
FBI came that she had a backache from all the driving after the
funeral. She had said she took some Excedrin.

"I did?" Stella repeated. Then, oddly, she shook it off and
seemed to accept that she had made an error on the polygraph answer she gave.

"They tried to make me confess. Of course, I'm not going to
confess to something I didn't do. I'm telling you, Sandy, I was set
up. I don't know how, but I was. That polygraph was a fake!"

Sandy was surprised by the conversation. Stella had told her that
she wasn't going to take the polygraph. Why had she changed her
mind?

It was just before Christmas when Stella Nickell and her daughter
Cindy came face-to-face, or toe-to-toe, for the last time.

Stella Nickell later told her version of what happened.

"She was kinda standoffish and she flipped out when I told her I was thinking of going down and seeing [Cindy's daughter] over Christmas."

Stella wanted to tell her that Bruce had died. Curiously, Cindy didn't want her to know, even though it had happened more than six months earlier.

"I think she has a right to know about her grandpa."

"You stay away from my daughter."

"She's also my granddaughter."

"I will tell her when I think the time is right. I'll tell her myself."

"Well, I was just trying to help, because you haven't had any experience in this. If you tell her the wrong way, it's gonna scar her the rest of her life."

"You haven't had any experience in this, either."

"No, but I'm a little bit older. I basically know how to break it to [the girl] so it doesn't scar her for life."

"I'll tell her myself. If I don't do it right, we'll just have to get over it."

"That's not the way to do it. You have to be careful with her; you can't tell her over the phone, you've got to be there face-to-face with her."

Cindy took a dress she had left at the trailer and never came back.

Stella later said she wondered how the little girl was getting on with such a mother.

"She does not like Cynthia very much. She loves her because that's her mother; she's supposed to love her, and that's the way kids feel. But the way [the little girl] acts around Cynthia you can tell that she does not like her mother. She hasn't since she was a baby because Cynthia is constantly abandoning her."

For Christmas, Stella and Harry drove to Wilma's place in Pasco. Dee and Cindy went to celebrate with friends north of Seattle.

There was no turning back for mother or daughter.

Though the stress must have been unbearable, Stella was never without a sense of humor. She had a quick retort when Sandy Scott asked her if she knew how to handle a mole problem. The little rodents were playing excavation all through the Scotts' yard.

"Use cyanide," she said with a short laugh. "At least, that's what I've always heard."

And if Cindy Hamilton truly had severed her ties with her

mother before Christmas, as she would later tell the FBI, how was it that Harry Swanson would later recall overhearing a phone call her mother received from the Washington coast in January 1987?

"I met an old boyfriend."

"But, Cindy, what about your job?"

"I'm not worried about it. . . ."

CHAPTER 52

The rural neighborhood off Lake Moneysmith Road was the kind of place where FBI surveillance would have been embarrassingly conspicuous. Even the most resourceful agent would have been hard-pressed to find a place to park a car that could go unnoticed. As the investigation progressed, neighbors caught on when the Feds had been by. Radios—or some electronic device—triggered one couple's garage doors to open.

"Gee, I wonder who's been out today," they joked at the mailboxes.

Jack Cusack needed an extra pair of eyes, and it was Sandy Scott's name that surfaced on an FD 302 report as the neighbor who had been at the Nickells' when the FBI came out. The woman's husband, Harold "Scotty" Scott, was a police officer. It was likely his wife would be on the government's side.

But then again, Jack Cusack couldn't be sure. Who was to say how deep their relationship ran? If she was Stella's confidante would she tell her that the FBI had sought her help in making the case?

Jack Cusack worried needlessly.

Sandy Scott felt relief when the FBI knocked on the door of her mobile home. Stella Nickell's visit after the polygraph had rattled her. She didn't want to believe Stella was guilty, but she could not ignore what Stella had told her after her polygraph. She had lied about taking the capsules *after* Bruce's death.

If Jack Cusack hadn't come calling, Sandy Scott would have called the FBI anyway. As if to soften the real objective of the meeting, Sandy Scott set out a plate of her butter-loaded chocolate-chip cookies. Jack Cusack wasn't shy about eating them or asking questions.

Over the next few hours, Stella's neighbor free-associated recollections of the Nickells and the comings and goings from their place down the road.

Sandy remembered the phone call Stella made after returning from Eastern Washington.

"She called me fairly early in the evening and asked me to call the neighbors and let them know Bruce had died. Normally, it's done before the funeral. But this was *after*."

"After the funeral?"

"That's what she said."

"What did she do after she got back from the hospital after Bruce died?" SA Cusack asked. "Did she have someone come over?"

Sandy didn't know.

"But I did see her take a walk where she and Bruce used to go . . . down the trail behind their mobile."

She told the agent Stella was concerned about Cindy's whereabouts.

"Where is she?"

"Let's just say we know exactly where she is," SA Cusack said. *Why don't you just say you have her in protective custody?* Sandy thought.

The FBI agent asked if the name Jim McCarthy meant anything to Sandy.

She said it did. In fact, she had wondered if there had been some kind of affair going on between Mac and Stella. He had been a regular visitor on the property, often arriving when Bruce was away at work.

"Stella said Mac's wife suspected them of having an affair. Stella said Mac's wife was a 'very uptight person.' That's why she didn't want his wife finding out about it."

Sandy never saw his car there overnight, but she wasn't looking for it, either.

"When the FBI left after the interview in June, Mac showed up and he gave her a gun. I thought it was ridiculous," Sandy said, "because she already had an arsenal in there.

"If she was having an affair . . . Harry looks like one step up from skid row, which made Mac look great. Maybe she had Harry out there because she was interested in Mac but wanted to remove suspicion from them? I've wondered about that a couple of times."

The agent inquired about family relationships and Sandy responded as best she could.

"Cora Lee was mad at Bruce because he wasn't able to chop her wood for the winter—she used wood heat—and he had his new job."

As far as she knew, or at least from what Stella had told her, there had been problems over Cindy's wanting money.

"Bruce would not give her money one time, because Stella said she had to sneak it to her. I don't know what for, probably drugs."

Cora Lee had also told her once that "Bruce had kicked Cindy out a couple of times, but she didn't say what for.

"And there was something about Stella and Bruce splitting up over Cindy."

Jack Cusack asked Sandy Scott, former flight attendant, a bright woman stuck out in the hills of Auburn, if she'd play spy for the FBI.

"Just keep tabs on her. Listen very carefully to what she is saying and write it down," he told her.

Sandy said she would do it, but she wanted them to know why.

"I'll do it to prove she's innocent, or else to prove she is guilty. If she's guilty, I don't want her in the neighborhood. I hope she's innocent."

Once Sandy had made up her mind that she'd help the FBI out, she felt free to record her recollections in a log she kept. The Seamurs case agent encouraged her to call with any information or questions, and she did so. She made the first of ten pages of entries in her homemade FBI log on January 7, 1987:

> She said she called because she heard Sue Snow's husband talking about the symptoms of her death and that they matched Bruce's. I don't remember them talking about symptoms . . . She said Bruce said he felt funny and then said he thought he was going to faint. Then she tried to get him to the couch and he couldn't make it . . .

A few days later, Sandy called SA Cusack about a conversation during which Stella had told her that she was taking financial management and investment courses out at Green River Community College.

Cora Lee had also huffed and puffed about some polygraph expert from back east who had come to look at her daughter's test results, but the FBI had kept him from the charts.

"Just thought you'd want to know."

Jack Cusack thanked her. Sandy Scott had definitely been the right one to seek out for help. She seemed to be working the case as hard as an FBI first-office agent. Cusack didn't tell Sandy Scott that Stella Nickell's story about the polygraph man was partially true. An expert had come to help the suspect, and he had been turned away without getting a look at the paperwork.

It had been an unintentional screwup. Nothing more.

No two people write in exactly the same manner. Each person's writing contains singular distinctions, which develop as an individual matures. The investigators had asserted that Stella Nickell's motives had been greed. She murdered for insurance money. If, in fact, that truly was the case, then the insurance applications were of critical evidentiary interest.

If Stella had forged her husband's name, the answer would be right there, undisguised by the blue ink of her Bic pen.

It was Lee Waggoner, a ten-year-veteran document examiner in the FBI's forensic lab in Washington, D.C., who provided SAs Cusack, Nichols, and the rest with the information that they had been seeking. And it wasn't easy.

Lee Waggoner would have needed a paperweight the size of Mount St. Helens to hold down all the documents he had analyzed for signs of outright tracing or the telltale signs of hesitant strokes of a person attempting a casual simulation of someone's penmanship.

It was known that for many of the Nickells' business needs— everything from credit applications to employment questionnaires— Stella filled out the documents. Often Bruce would provide his signature. Sometimes, however, he did not.

The document that lent the most sinister aspect was Bruce Nickell's September 5, 1985, All American Life application.

Though the agent, whose only tools are good lighting, document magnification, and years of study, couldn't establish exactly who had written the "Bruce" portion of the signature, he was certain it had not been Bruce Nickell, but Waggoner was unable to discern if Stella had been the one wielding the pen.

Lee Waggoner had no doubt about the endorsement on the All American Life application from October of 1985. What purported to be Bruce Nickell's signature had unquestionably been forged by Stella Maudine.

The "Nickell" portion was freely written with a majority of characteristics consistent with Stella's handwriting. Three slight variations mimicked the samples known to have been written by Bruce Nickell. "Nickell" was written by Stella.

A Firemen's Life Insurance application, another bit of potential evidence uncovered during the FBI probe, was a poor microfiche copy, useless for analysis. The cancellation document of the same policy, dated June 10, 1985, indicated, however, that Stella had likely forged that one as well.

As the pace of investigation stepped up, Stella Nickell began to show signs that she thought she might be arrested. Harry Swanson returned to the property one afternoon to find her hovering over the smoking caldron of a burn barrel behind the mobile home.

Stella dropped scores of nude Polaroids into the flames. One by one. Harry recognized many of them from an X-rated album he had seen stored in a bedroom drawer. Most were of Stella in her younger days, though some were of Bruce in various states of sexual excitement. Stella Maudine allowed herself to keep two of Bruce, and later stored them in her green plastic jewelry box.

Harry also got a keepsake: a photograph showing a somewhat demure Stella Nickell standing next to a kitchen counter. Her black robe opened to show her breasts. Later, the lovestruck man trimmed the photo to wallet size and carried it with him.

Stella cried as she dropped her remembrances into the fire.

"I'm gonna be the fall guy . . . who else can they get but me?"

"Oh, honey," Harry offered, "it's kind of rough burning all your memories of Bruce."

Stella had no choice. She didn't want anyone, especially Wilma, seeing the photographs.

In January 1986, Wilma Stewart received the kind of letter that breaks a mother's heart. It had been forwarded to her Pasco home by the Washington State Department of Social and Health Services, through which she paid monthly child support to her three sons she had left with their father in 1978. Richard, her youngest, had leukemia.

She was unemployed, her aunt was the suspected product tamperer, she was five months pregnant, and she was in a second-time-around rocky marriage to a husband who didn't seem to give a damn. But none of that seemed important.

Not with Richard dying.

Wilma called her son's father in Tonasket, a northern Washington State village, and started the process of getting to know her sons again. Somehow there had to be an answer to what was going on. Some hope, somewhere.

Whenever she spoke with Stella—or remembered anything that she considered potentially helpful—Sandy Scott phoned Jack Cusack. He'd make notes and request additional information as needed.

He asked Sandy to try to get Stella talking about her algicide. He wanted to avoid having to get another search warrant to find out what she used in her aquarium. Sandy recalled that Stella had confided earlier that an algicide had been the trace element.

One Sunday, January 18, Sandy left her son with her husband and hiked on down to the Nickells' mobile home for coffee and any incriminating information.

When she had the chance, she brought up the algicide.

"What kind do you use?"

Stella said she didn't use any, but she had bought a liquid called Algaegon.

"I'll show you," she said as she pulled a small bottle from her aquarium supplies.

Stella explained that she had purchased the product before she got her algae-eating bottom fish. The bottle, she claimed, had never been opened.

"I don't like to use chemicals in my tank."

Sandy opened the full bottle and hesitantly held it to her nose and sniffed.

"It doesn't smell like almonds! It doesn't smell like anything."

While the two women laughed, Sandy studied the bottle, trying to memorize its batch code—0400500—in case the FBI wanted the number.

During Sandy's visit, Stella spoke of fights she and Bruce had had about money, though they were nothing any other couple didn't go through.

Bruce had been worried about his job and would often come home agitated. Stella wondered if stress was causing the headaches he had just before his death. Yet, Stella also said, Bruce's co-workers all agreed that he liked his job and was doing well.

Sandy wondered later if Stella was hinting that Bruce might have taken his own life. He was so stressed out and depressed.

The minute she got home, Sandy took her place on the sofa and pulled her FBI log from an end-table drawer. She had a lot to write down.

"Could it cause headaches?" she wrote of the bottle of algicide in a note for her next conversation with Cusack. *"Could Stella have given her husband some of that liquid? Is that why he was so strange the last time I saw him?"*

Later, Sandy Scott recalled the last time she had seen Bruce Nickell alive. She thought it had been on the evening before he died. She was down at the Nickells' picking up paperwork for the neighborhood road committee.

"Bruce was sitting in the family room; he didn't even acknowledge me when I walked into the room. He stared straight at the TV. He did not move a muscle. My thought was they had had a fight. Stella was acting like it was the normal way he acted."

Sandy wondered if he had already been poisoned somehow.

"It was almost like his eyes never blinked. His hands were on the arms of the chair. He didn't move a muscle."

CHAPTER 53

Even with the insurance policies, the forgeries, the failed polygraph, the apparent lies, the FBI still didn't have a case—not one that would indict Stella Maudine Nickell as the nation's first product tamperer under a federal law passed after Chicago's poisonings. Joanne Maida, the Assistant U.S. Attorney who would prosecute the case, kept calling for more evidence—evidence that plainly didn't exist. Cusack, Nichols, and the others at the FBI needed a stroke of luck.

Their break came in the form of Dee Rogers's call.

"Cindy knows her mom killed her dad . . ."

Exactly when the call was made remains in dispute—before or after the polygraph? What had been the motivator? Joanne Maida put great significance on the premise that Cindy came forward after her mother told her she failed the polygraph. Dee Rogers, however, would later insist the polygraph came after the phone call to the FBI.

"It just confirmed that what we were doing was right," Dee said later.

Whatever the timing, the phone call was a breakthrough.

Jack Cusack and Randy Scott stopped at a Burger King off the Kent-Kangley Road for Cokes, and, more important, to strategize before going on to see Cindy Hamilton and Dee Rogers. It was already dark when they got to the restaurant. Jack Cusack, who had spent the better part of his career orchestrating interviews, needed to make sure he and SA Scott were on the same wavelength. Though neither knew what to expect, both knew one possible scenario was that Stella's daughter would freeze up and say nothing at all.

The two agents and two women gathered around a dining table in the alcove off the kitchen. Over the course of the next couple hours, a story unfolded that seemed bizarre enough to be true. Stella Nickell's daughter told them her mother killed Bruce because she was bored with him and wanted more excitement in her life. She killed him because she didn't want to lose "half of everything she had worked so hard to get" in a divorce.

Stella also planned to open a ceramics or fish store. Cindy said the plan called for her to handle the care of the fish and breeding, about which she said she was quite knowledgeable. Her mother would manage the in-store operation. The idea of killing one's husband for a ceramics or fish store didn't cause an inward wince for Jack Cusack. Over the years he had heard people say they killed for far less.

Of course, the FBI wanted to know how it was that Cindy knew Stella was going to kill Bruce.

She said her mother had told her she had been having an affair for more than a year with Bruce's buddy Jim McCarthy.

"He has Indian blood, and that's a big deal for my mom. She said she was in love with him. She wanted to marry him, but he wouldn't leave his wife. He was over at the house on my mom's days off from work—when my dad was gone."

Cindy said her mother also complained about Bruce's sex drive.

"She couldn't stand being with him," she said.

Neither of the women seated at the dinette table could prove it, but they felt Jim McCarthy was one of the underlying reasons for the whole plot. They pointed out that he had a darkroom setup, which they knew sometimes contained cyanide.

"My mother told me cyanide is used in photography."

"How did she know that?"

"She researched it at the library."

"Which one?"

"I don't know . . . she went to all sorts of libraries, bookstores. That's the kind of woman she is."

Stella's daughter said that she and Bonnie Anderson were drink-

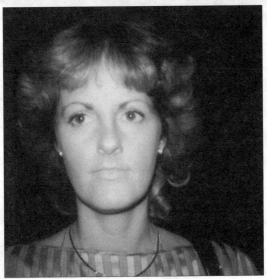

Stella Nickell wanted out of her marriage to Bruce Nickell (TOP)—Sue Snow was an innocent casualty of a stranger's murderous plans (BOTTOM). (Hayley Snow)

Early in their marriage, Stella and Bruce loved to camp and ride motorcycles. (Bruce Nickell)

Stella and favorite niece Wilma Mae Stewart. Wilma stood by her aunt even after she made a startling discovery after the trial. (Bruce Nickell)

Just four months before her arrest, Stella holds Wilma's baby, Missy—telling those closest to her that her daughter had turned her in for reward money. (Wilma Stewart)

Stella with Bob Strong, Cynthia, and Leah. Bob Strong thought Stella and Cynthia were headed for big trouble long before the murders. (Orange Coast Photography)

Sarah Webb, Hayley and Cindy Snow, and Paul Webking—Sue's survivors were at odds after she died. (Duane Hamamura)

Sarah Webb (LEFT) and Sue Snow (RIGHT) were as close as any twin sisters could be. (Hayley Snow)

Sue was so proud that even at 15, her daughter Hayley still called her "Mommy". This was taken a couple of years before Hayley found her mother collapsed in the shower. (Hayley Snow)

Despite the efforts of a private detective to prove Stella Nickell had been framed, Hayley Snow is more secure now that the right person is behind bars for the death of her mother. (Gregg Olsen)

FBI Special Agent Jack Cusack doggedly pursued Stella Nickell as one of the leaders of the case the FBI dubbed "SEAMURS," for Seattle Murders. (Gregg Olsen)

Stella Nickell's love for tropical fish proved her undoing. A product used to keep algae from growing in her fish tanks was found mixed in with the cyanide that killed her husband and Sue Snow. (Courtesy FBI)

The familiar red capsules of the Excedrin product, shown in this lab photograph (Courtesy FBI).

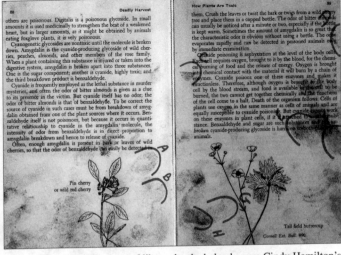

others are poisonous. Digitalis is a poisonous glycoside. In small amounts it is used medicinally to strengthen the beat of a weakened heart, but in larger amounts, as it might be obtained by animals eating foxglove plants, it is very poisonous.

Cyanogenetic glycosides are nontoxic until the molecule is broken down. Amygdalin is the cyanide-producing glycoside of wild cherries, peaches, almonds, and other members of the rose family. When a plant containing this substance is injured or taken into the digestive system, amygdalin is broken apart into three substances. One is the sugar component; another is cyanide, highly toxic; and the third breakdown product is benzaldehyde.

Cyanide is frequently employed as the lethal substance in murder mysteries, and often the odor of bitter almonds is given as a clue to its presence in the victim. But cyanide itself has no odor; the odor of bitter almonds is that of benzaldehyde. To be correct the source of cyanide in such cases must be from breakdown of amygdalin obtained from one of the plant sources where it occurs. Benzaldehyde itself is not poisonous, but because it occurs in quantitative relationship to cyanide in the amygdalin molecule, the intensity of odor from benzaldehyde is in direct proportion to amygdalin breakdown and hence to release of cyanide.

Often, enough amygdalin is present in bark or leaves of wild cherries, so that the odor of benzaldehyde can easily be detected in

Pin cherry
or wild red cherry

them. Crush the leaves or twist the bark or twigs from a wild cherry tree and place them in a capped bottle. The odor of bitter almonds can usually be noticed after a minute or two, especially if the bottle is kept warm. Sometimes the amount of amygdalin is so great that the characteristic odor is obvious without using a bottle. The odor evaporates rapidly and can be detected in poisoned animals only by immediate examination.

Cyanide poisoning is asphyxiation at the level of the body cells. Each cell requires oxygen, brought to it by the blood, for the chemical burning of food and the release of energy. Oxygen is brought into chemical contact with the material it will burn by a chain of enzymes. Cyanide poisons one of these enzymes and makes it functionless. Therefore, although oxygen is brought to the body cell by the blood stream, and food is available to the cell to be burned, the two cannot get together chemically and the functions of the cell come to a halt. Death of the organism follows. Cells of plants use oxygen in the same manner as cells of animals and are equally susceptible to cyanide poisoning. But cyanide exists only on these enzymes in plant cells, if it is attached to another substance. Benzaldehyde and sugar are such substances and the broken cyanide-producing glycoside is harmless to both plants and animals.

Tall field buttercup
Cornell Ext. Bull. 990

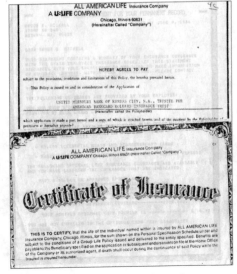

Fingerprints found on pages of library books helped prove Cindy Hamilton's story that her mother had been planning different ways to kill Bruce for several years. (Courtesy FBI)

Insurance money was the motive.

Stella Nickell had bigger dreams than this Auburn, Washington trailer. (Dale Wittner)

Her new home now is a cell at a Federal Women's Prison near Pleasanton, California. In 2002, she still maintains her innocence. (Gregg Olsen)

ing at a bar on June 5 when Dee called to say her mother was on
her way over with some news.

She told the FBI agents her mother sat at the table, her voice
cracking. " 'Your dad died last night at six o'clock,' and I just
looked at her, and I just felt—I just felt sick to my stomach, and
she looked at me and she said, 'I know what you're thinking, and
it's no.' "

Cindy felt her mother was trying to set aside any thoughts her
daughter might have had about her being responsible for Bruce's
death.

But the young woman said she knew otherwise.

Her mother said she had ordered an autopsy, even seemed preoccupied with it. After all, she said, Bruce's physical only a few
months earlier showed him to be in good health. Within a day or
two of her stepfather's death, Cindy said she and her mother went
to the family doctor to collect Bruce Nickell's medical records.

Shortly after the funeral, Cindy claimed, her mother was "whoring around" Kent, dropping her Levi's, hiking her skirts for anyone.
Her hangouts were Walt's Inn and the Eagles Nest in Kent.

Cindy said she was embarrassed by her mother's sleazy behavior.

"You don't know my mother," she said. "To her sex is a con-
quest, and she uses it on men to get what she wants and so she
won't be forgotten."

The story got wilder, yet throughout her recounting of it, Cindy
Hamilton maintained full composure. No matter how traumatic the
events she described, she did not cry. Dee served coffee to the
agents, spiking the ladies' cups with a shot of Irish cream.

As she had told her roommate, Cindy claimed her mother saved
empty capsules and kept them near her fish tanks.

She also used capsules or tablets to kill algae—until Cindy suggested she switch to a liquid algicide.

Cindy said the conversations, which came and went, heated up
again around Christmas 1985 and the New Year, while they worked
at SeaTac. Her mother kept telling her, "We could have so much
fun with Bruce out of the way. With his insurance, we'd have the
money to open a fish or ceramics store."

"Did you really think your mother was going to kill Bruce?" SA
Cusack asked.

"I knew she was going to do it because she was so calm and
intense about it."

Though the talk had gone on for years, it escalated into action around the start of 1986 when Cindy hired on at SeaTac. Her mother said she filled capsules with some poisonous seeds and fed them to Bruce. They only made him sluggish.

"Why would he take them?" Cusack asked.

"My mom always gave my dad capsules," she said, going on to explain that Bruce suffered from bruxism—nighttime teeth-grinding. "My mom gave him stress vitamins to relieve it so she could sleep at night."

Another time, Cindy said, her mother also talked about hiring a professional hit man who could shoot Bruce through his truck window.

"She said how nice it would be if dad had an accident. A hit man . . . a hit-and-run . . . someone to mess with his brakes on his truck."

But her mother didn't have the money, and a lack of cash was the pressure that was pushing all the scenarios.

Over the years there were other aborted plans. Heroin or cocaine in Bruce's iced tea was considered. Cindy claimed her mother brought up the Chicago cyanide case during a ride to the airport one morning.

"She talked about how easy it would be to reenact the case. How people would be looking for someone to take something from a store, not to put it back."

A couple of months before her stepfather's death Cindy said she noticed a Tupperware container filled with white powder in the airport locker she and her mother shared. There were also some capsule medications.

"It surprised me, because Mom never used sugar or salt at lunch."

After Bruce died, the packages and container disappeared.

"I thought it might have been cyanide," she said.

Stella discussed the possibility of driving to niece Wilma's place in Texas and leaving Bruce, and while she was gone she'd have a hit man come kill him. Cynthia confided that she had seen a diary at her mother's trailer one day. In it her mother had made entries reflecting a kidnapping plan.

"I saw the diary on the table and read it," she said.

When Dee's teenage daughter came home the interview ended. SA Cusack suggested reconvening Saturday at the Seattle office. It would be quiet on the weekend. The women agreed.

The federal agents knew that if Cindy Hamilton's story could be substantiated enough to hold up in court, Stella Nickell's time might be running out.

"Cindy might be leading us on," Cusack said in the car on the way back. "Here's a woman sitting there at SeaTac having these daily exchanges with her mother, and she says she didn't know for sure her mother was talking about her father?"

Randy Scott agreed as Jack Cusack went on, his mind racing with the information—the incredible, outlandish information—provided by Stella Nickell's own daughter.

"We need to get that girl polygraphed. Maybe she's just trying to save herself."

Two days later, on a characteristically blowy and rainy Seattle Saturday, Cindy and Dee arrived at the FBI office. SA Cusack was relieved. He worried whether the day in between would cause them to change their minds—or stories.

Settling into the big black polygraph armchair, Dee made jokes about its being an electric chair. The women seemed even more relaxed than they had been at their own apartment.

Randy Scott took a statement from Dee, which basically echoed what they had heard two days before.

Both agents knew the only way anything could really come of Cindy Hamilton's allegations would be complete substantiation. Dee had little firsthand knowledge of anything, so it was all up to Cindy.

It was clear the women preferred Jack Cusack and his easier-going nature over Randy Scott's. True to form, Cindy had no problems making her feelings known.

SA Scott mentioned the $300,000 reward offered by the drug companies and Cindy blew up.

"Randy is the one who said to Cindy and me, 'You girls, there's a large reward,' and this was *after* we already came forward. We looked at him, like, 'get out of our fuckin' face, if you really think we're in this for the fuckin' money, you've got another thing coming,' " Dee later recalled.

"Cindy," Jack Cusack said at last, "a lot of people who hear your statement will think you're in on it. How is it that you know so much yet are not a part of the crime?"

Cindy Hamilton fixed her smudged raccoon eyes on the FBI agent.

"You and I both know that if I would have called the police, nothing would have happened. I loved my mother. I didn't want to believe her. All my life I've been bounced around . . . now I had a family. My mother was almost like a sister. . . . I love her. I had the mother I always wanted.

"How many wives have said, 'I'm going to kill him'? 'I'm going to wrap my hands around his throat and I'm going to choke the very life out of him'? They're not going to do anything about it, and if I would have went to my dad and told him, I really honestly don't think he would have believed me. He would have thought I was losing my marbles."

It was a reason that on the surface seemed easily discounted, but SA Cusack felt Cindy Hamilton was, at least partially, telling the truth.

Now that Cusack had her daughter's statement, it seemed that Stella Nickell hadn't just killed for the insurance money. She didn't want to split up the goddamn trailer, and she wanted to have a business of her own. She also was sick and tired of babysitting her no-fun, homebody husband.

And while it was true Cindy knew plenty, there was always the concern she knew too much. And if Cindy's story had disturbing lapses, it wasn't because she was lying, her friend Dee Rogers later insisted.

"She was watching her mouth. She didn't want to say 'fuck' too many times to the FBI. Not until she got to know them, anyway."

CHAPTER 54

Hayley Snow was doing her best to hang on to her mother's memory as her world continued to wither. Diary entries dwindled somewhat because she found herself repeating the same thoughts. She wrote on January 29, 1987:

> Paul got married . . . two weeks before he even planned. It doesn't bother me too bad. I can tell it bugs the shit out of Exa. She hates Paul's guts. I try to please everyone . . . I miss Mommy so much.

Many felt Paul Webking had slapped Sue Snow's daughter in the face when he married the flight attendant Sheri only six months after Sue died at Harborview.

An FBI agent who talked to Sarah Webb when she called for an update on her sister's case couldn't believe it either: "He did fucking what? You've got to be kidding!"

It was a different Stella Nickell who paid a visit to her CB girlfriend Shirley Webbly in early February. Stella was very concerned, very upset, and for the first time seemed even scared.

She was afraid of her daughter.

"Why are you worried about Cindy?"

"Because she'll turn me in for the money."

"No, she wouldn't," Shirley said, echoing what Stella had been told by others. "A daughter wouldn't do that kind of a thing."

As they talked, Stella suggested that Cindy's motives might have gone beyond the reward money being offered.

"Stella told me that she thought Cindy had always wanted Bruce . . . as a lover," Shirley said later. The idea didn't surprise her. She had seen Cindy in action before with other men, including Jim McCarthy.

It was possible she wanted Bruce Nickell. And if that was the case, there certainly was opportunity.

"Anytime Cynthia was off work and I was working," Stella said, "she would go keep 'Dad' company. She was usually at the house when I got home from work. Sometimes she would leave before I came home."

Stella also told Shirley she hadn't been the best mother in the world when Cindy was growing up.

"God, Stel, we do the best we can with what we have at the time."

Stella nodded, but worry showed on her face.

"I think I'm going to be arrested."

"If you haven't done anything, how can you?"

"Cynthia won't stop at anything."

Stella also told her friend she had failed the polygraph.

Shirley couldn't believe it, but when she thought about it figured she might have failed one also.

"I would have been a stark-raving idiot. I don't know what I'd say," she said later.

Stella insisted she had answered truthfully, but the way the questions were worded didn't lead to an easy yes or no.

"Sometimes people ask questions and they—like a voter's pamphlet—do I say yes or no? When you say 'yes,' you're voting against it," she said.

On February 10, 1987, Sandy Scott bumped into Stella Nickell and casually asked if she'd heard anything more from the FBI. Stella said things had been quiet on her end but Mac had been out to the property to tell her the FBI had interviewed him three times recently.

"She seemed mad at him," Sandy wrote in her FBI log.

Cora Lee had a few questions of her own. She wondered out loud to Sandy Scott what Stella was living on: "She always has money. And she's always going off without telling anyone!"

One of those places Stella went off to was Walter and Ruth Nickell's Wenatchee apartment. She rode over with Harry Swanson, but left him and her diamond ring in the Winnebago parked down the road from the Nickells' apartment.

"It's too close to Bruce's death," she told Harry.

She told Bruce's parents that some friends had dropped her off.

That night while she chatted away, Stella told the Nickells about the polygraph.

"I flunked it."

Later, at ninety-nine years of age, Walter Nickell remembered more.

"She said they had it set up on an old rickety table, they could make that thing do anything they want it to."

When Harry showed up at the apartment the next day, Walter asked Stella where the man's wife was.

"She's out shopping somewhere," she said.

Walter didn't believe her.

"When she got up in the morning, she dolled up and all. She looked real pretty. She did it for that guy. There wasn't a wife at all!"

Even Harry Swanson felt foolish about the ruse. "Where else would I go? I was in love with the goddamn woman," he later said.

After the visit from her daughter-in-law and boyfriend, Ruth Nickell, nearly blind, could almost see some things clearly. She finally began to accept that Stella killed Bruce.

"It's a wonder that she hasn't killed us," she told her husband.

The Nickells' will hadn't been changed, but plans were being made to delete Stella Maudine Nickell's name. The sooner, Walter figured, the better.

Cindy Hamilton was agitated and flighty during the early weeks following her FBI statement. A trip to the coast, out of the house, away from Dee's children, became her pattern. She seemed to feel constant movement would keep her mind off the tampering case. When she did sit to talk, however, it was almost always about her mother.

"What's your problem?" Dee asked after a prolonged period of ups and downs.

"What if she didn't do it? What if I'm wrong?"

"Cindy, do you believe she did it?"

"Yeah."

"She did it. She'll never admit it. She'll take it to her grave."

Cindy nodded and bucked up. By now she knew she was critical to the federal case. She told Dee she had passed a polygraph and she'd soon go before the grand jury.

"Jesus, Cindy, you're going to get through this. You'll see."

Dee saw Cindy's taking a stand against her mother as an act of courage, one that would free her from the torments of the past.

When had the wheels been set in motion for mother and daughter to start down the long path leading to the Seattle courtroom? Georgia Mae Stephenson saw problems from the beginning.

When Stella's oldest sister briefly lived in Orange County during the early sixties, she took care of Cynthia Lea while Stella Maudine was off running around. Cora Lee was welding circuit boards on an assembly line at Hughes Aircraft and didn't always have the time.

Cora Lee's sister, Lucille, also lived in Southern California, and she too became a convenient, and perilous, caregiver for little Cindy.

Yet Aunt Lucille—who had wanted to adopt Stella when she was first born—had a problem.

She beat babies, Georgia later said.

"First time I got her," she remembered, "my mom brought her up. She was bruised . . . like a wide belt, a bruise on that baby."

Stella might have ignored her daughter, even neglected her, but Georgia Mae never thought her sister beat Cynthia Lea. It had been Cora Lee's youngest sister, Lucille, and there was no doubt about that.

The little girl showed other disturbing signs of abuse from visits at Aunt Lucille's.

When Georgia scolded the little girl, Cindy would run off to the bathroom and stick her head into the waters of the toilet bowl.

"Whatever had happened to that child when Lucille had her?" Georgia Mae asked later. "Her punishment was to put her head in the toilet bowl."

During that time, Wilma Mae and Stella's little girl shared a bedroom. Wilma had been told to watch out for her little cousin. She made sure the toilet lid was down and the bowl flushed. No one wanted to be the cause of Cynthia's drowning in a toilet.

"If I ever get my hands on that woman, I'll do to her what she done to that baby," Georgia told her mother one day when they talked about Lucille's beating of Cynthia Lea.

Georgia Mae recalled that Stella Maudine had lived with Aunt Lucille too. What had she learned from her? Had the cycle of abuse been started during those six months the Stephenson children spent in Colorado while their mother was getting a divorce from their father?

Ron Nichols was back and forth on the Seamurs case so often, it got to be joke among Seattle special agents. Jack Cusack kidded other agents when they asked if SA Nichols was working the tampering case.

"When it's going great, he is. When it's going nowhere, Nichols flips it right back and says, 'What do I care? I'm not the case agent!' "

After Cindy and Dee ran to the FBI, things were going much better. Still, Jack Cusack knew he could use more help with the case, so he stopped by Mike Byrne's office early one morning.

"Mike, I need another full-time, aggressive-type guy to complete the threesome nucleus."

"Anyone in mind?"

"Yeah, Marshall Stone."

The choice surprised Mike Byrne.

"He's a first-office agent. Why'd you choose him?"

"Stone's upbeat and positive, detail-oriented." Then, with a smile, Cusack added, "He held his own in that shoot-out with that Ballard bank robber. He's a ballsy son of a bitch, and that's the kind of guy we could use."

Mike Byrne agreed. No one could forget how thirty-two-year-old Stone had single-handedly caught a bank robber. In February, the agent who dressed better than anyone in the Seattle office, and with the accent that told the world he was from Boston, joined the Seamurs team.

CHAPTER 55

From what Cindy Hamilton and Dee Rogers had confided to Jack Cusack, Jim McCarthy was now a key player in the case.

"He's either a potential witness or an accomplice," he told Ron Nichols on the way out for one of the first of what would be many meetings.

Community college instructor McCarthy told the FBI agents he had been at the Nickells' home around 7 P.M. the night before Bruce collapsed. Such visits were not uncommon, he said, since he lived only a mile or two away. Nothing, he said, was amiss.

"I was over visiting and he was sitting on the couch. He's got his shirt off and he was eating crab salad. They were talking that there was enough left and did I want any and I had already eaten. So she said, 'All right, I'll take it tomorrow for lunch.'"

He stayed approximately an hour and a half.

"What was Stella up to that night?" SA Cusack asked.

"She was working in the kitchen all the time I was there. Doing her little wifely chores."

"Did you know that she did not go to work that day?"

He didn't.

"I never questioned her work times. When she was home, she was home. I was never privy to a schedule as such."

Jim McCarthy, a big man with lots of thick dark hair and sparkling brown eyes, poured on the sincerity. He was just as shocked

as anyone when Stella showed up at his home around noon on June
6. Tears had filled her eyes when she told him Bruce had died the
night before.

"She sat on the couch very rigid, on the edge, and said, 'Bruce
is dead.' "

Jim McCarthy claimed he was so unprepared that he asked,
"Which Bruce? Our Bruce?"

Stella was a wreck. But as he would have expected, she held
her own.

"She was ragged out. Like she was really stressed out, and stiff.
What I would assume somebody that's under a heavy burden of
sorrow or whatever would be like. Trying to put up a strong facade;
but very very sad inside. It wasn't Stella as I knew her, because it
was obviously traumatic," he later recalled.

"Jim, you're a nice-looking guy. Stella's a good-looking
woman," SA Cusack said. "Why don't you make it easy on yourself
and tell us what your relationship really was?"

The dancing dark eyes stopped sparkling.

"I was Bruce's best friend. Stella was his wife. End of story."

Jack Cusack asked the man about his photography hobby.
"Could we have a look around? Maybe take some lab samples of
your processing chemicals?"

"Listen, if you think I had anything to do with this you're wast-
ing your time. But, yeah, I've got nothing to hide. You can take
whatever you want."

It didn't take long for word to get around that, as Stan Church
would later term it, "there was a skunk in the well." While the FBI
stayed away from Stella and Bruce's best couple of friends, Cindy
and Stella did not. At least, not at first.

When the Churches heard Cindy might have turned her mother
in, they might have shrugged it off as a bad joke if it weren't so
serious. It simply didn't make sense. None of the family could
forget that when Cindy came over to the house after Bruce died,
she was steamed at the FBI. She said the FBI seemed to have a
vendetta against her mother.

" 'My mom would never do this. My mother is innocent.' She
said it point-blank to us," Karan Church recalled.

"And then, boom! All of a sudden Bristol-Myers pops up with
the reward money and Cindy says, 'My mom did this. *My mom
talked about doing this!*' "

And then Cindy changed her tune and disappeared. No one knew where she was.

One night at a Kent tavern, Karan Church did a double take. It really was Cindy Hamilton pouring beer behind the bar. Karan, out barhopping with friends, didn't know whether to speak to her or leave. The word had been that Cindy had called the FBI on her own mother.

Cindy was not her usual brassy self. She looked nervous, frightened.

"Karan, please don't tell my mother where I am."

"Are you working here?"

"Yeah."

"How long?"

"None of your business," Cindy snapped. With that, she turned her back and Karan went back to her beer.

The next day, Karan told Stella where Cindy was working. Stella seemed to appreciate the call. She knew Cindy was in the area but didn't know her exact whereabouts.

"How did she look?"

"The same, I guess," Karan answered. "You know, she told me she didn't want me to tell you where she was at."

"Oh."

Karan felt Stella wasn't surprised by her daughter's request, but she could tell she was hurt by it.

She went back the next night to see Cindy again, but she was gone. An employee said she had quit at the end of her shift.

Karan Church never saw her again.

Paul Webking told Sue Snow's daughters he had lost their mother's jewelry—jewelry the girls had counted on, not for its monetary value, but because it had been their mother's.

Hayley and Exa Snow refused to believe him.

"Lost it? What did it do, hop out of a drawer and walk away?"

Sarah Webb, who was supposed to keep it for the girls, felt it was a lie. Had he forgotten what Sue had meant to the family? To him?

Hayley tossed and turned on Valentine's Day night. Memories haunted her. She and her mother would have exchanged little notes, gifts, and cards. At three o'clock she gave up the battle and hauled out her diary:

Paul asked me about my hostility. He says he senses it to him from me. It's a "hard way for him to live." . . . Doesn't he realize why I have some hostility towards him? . . . It's been 8 months & 4 days . . .

Outside the courtroom, friends considered tiny Joanne Maida a bit introverted, even shy. Some described her Japanese-American features as delicate. Within the walls of a courtroom the Assistant U.S. Attorney was driven to win. When toughness was needed, it was not a problem.

As one admirer put it, "Soft is not Joanne."

Folks around the King County Courthouse remembered her well. Joanne Maida served as a deputy prosecutor, successfully obtaining convictions in a number of notorious cases, including the Wah Mee Massacre, one of the worst mass killings in American history.

Behind her back they called her "Ice."

An only child, Maida was raised in Hawaii and attended private schools. She had "privilege" stamped on everything she did. With Joanne Maida, it was always her way.

On February 19, the Fish Gallery's Tom Noonan was questioned by Joanne Maida as he took his turn before the grand jury. Yes, he told the jurors, Stella Nickell had purchased Algae Destroyer. And yes, he had told her to crush the tablets into a powder and "dissolve it in hot water prior to administering it to the tank."

It was too bad no one thought, or was able, to tell Hayley or Exa Snow, or Paul Webking and Sarah Webb, how the government's case was coming along. There was another suspect, and finally, the grand jury was hearing the kind of testimony that could lead to an indictment.

Maybe Cindy Hamilton didn't want to leave it to chance, or maybe she needed to plant a seed, or maybe she was just being helpful. She had promised Jack Cusack that she'd come up with the names of some people who could back up her claims.

No longer at the airport checking passengers' luggage, Bonnie Anderson was employed as a King County 911 operator when Stella's daughter called to tell her the FBI would be contacting her soon.

"I'm not going to say anything else, except tell them everything you know," Cindy said.

Bonnie didn't know what she was talking about. She didn't think she knew anything.

"Don't worry about it, just tell them everything you know. Remember when she came over after Dad died . . ."

CHAPTER 56

Over the weeks of the drizzly winter, Stella Nickell's daughter recalled bits and pieces investigators thought sounded promising, though they seldom said so. Cindy Hamilton had told Jack Cusack that her mother had checked out library books to read up on poisonous plants she could use to kill Bruce Nickell. She said her mother had learned that plants native to the Auburn property had toxic seeds.

"They were very small seeds, and I don't recall from what plant, and she placed them—she stuffed two or three capsules full of these seeds, some extra capsules that she had had in the house, and she gave them to him," she said.

Extra capsules? That was interesting.

SA Cusack wondered how Stella would be able to account for her husband's dying from eating a weed.

True to form, Cindy Hamilton had an answer.

"She mentioned that it would possibly be easy to explain because my dad was always one for reaching down and yanking up a hunk of something, like grass or whatever, and chewing on it. My dad was raised in the country, and he chewed on grass stems and whatever. You know, it was just part of your being countrified, I guess."

Stella told her daughter the seeds made Bruce "lethargic for a couple days" and nothing more. She was disappointed. She had expected him to die.

Cindy said she didn't know exactly where her mother had gone to do the research, but it seemed that she went to the Seattle library quite a bit.

"She also went to University Bookstore quite often and to a little occult bookstore that's just down the road a few blocks from University Bookstore."

It was SA Marshall Stone who was given the assignment to find out where Stella did her research.

Unlike Cindy, Dee Rogers didn't know anything, really. But when it came time to see if she could worm some information out of the suspected tamperer under the guise of a tavern get-together, the tough little New Yorker was game. The plan was to have her call Stella and ask her down for a friendly little chat. Easy enough, but was it safe?

The FBI promised an agent undercover in the Virginia Inn.

"That's nice, in case she wants to shoot me. Is your agent going to know when I'm scared? I'll have my own people watch me, you worry about you," she half joked.

When Dee saw the agent dispatched as her protector, she knew her initial instincts had been correct. The agent stuck out like a sore thumb.

"A bearded guy, with a baseball cap and vest on, nobody had ever seen before in a neighborhood tavern where everybody knows everybody? Here's a stranger drinking a Pepsi!" she said later, laughing.

That night, Dee asked the bartender to keep the corner of the bar vacant so there'd be a clear line of vision—in case Stella tried something. Dee sat at a back table, drank a beer, and waited for Stella and her boyfriend Harry Swanson to arrive. Right on time, they did.

Harry took a seat at the bar, and Stella sat down with Dee.

"Look, I gotta tell you something," Dee said from across the table. "I really don't know what's going on, and at this point I really don't care, but I tell you I can't sleep at night. I feel uneasy about Bruce's death. Stella, did you poison Bruce?"

"No, Dee, I didn't," she said, looking her old bar buddy right in the eye.

"I don't think I can believe that."

Stella remained blasé. "You'll have to believe what you have to believe," she shot back coolly. Her voice was monotone, deliberate.

Dee thought Stella's response was strange. If the tables had been turned and she had been asked the question, she would have slapped Stella and left. But Stella was cold stone.

Dee took a last look at Stella, clinging clothes, black hair swept back, lips cherry-red. Stella Maudine Nickell might have thought she was hot stuff. But Dee Rogers thought otherwise.

Though she had received the pension money only a few months before, and had Harry Swanson's wallet to fall back on if need be, Stella Nickell was running out of money. She bounced a nineteen-dollar check at 7-Eleven at the end of February 1987.

She needed a job.

She was hired by Burns International, a private security firm on Interurban in Tukwila, an industrial park of a town between Kent and Seattle. The job paid over $600 a month.

If the new hire was worse for wear because of the stress of the investigation, it wasn't apparent to her boss, Ron E. Miller, Burns's forty-five-year-old district manager. In fact, within a few short days of her hire date, Stella distinguished herself as an extremely conscientious employee. One of her first assignments had her stationed in a parking lot to provide extra security at a strike site at Southcenter Mall.

"Even the client singled her out as an excellent employee," Ron Miller said later.

Cindy and Dee apparently felt comfortable enough to dream and talk about the reward money. Others connected to the Kent tavern scene also knew of their interest in it.

If they got the $300,000, they'd split it right down the middle.

"Put money in the trust for each of the kids . . . buy ourselves a house somewhere . . . and we had both decided at the time that we wouldn't hook up with anybody, that we were going to stay 'Cindy and I,' " Dee Rogers recalled.

The way Tommy Nelson saw it, Cindy had her sights on more than just the reward.

"The way Cindy talked, she was *going* to get the insurance money. She was telling a lot of people at the Virginia . . . she was going to get the property . . . the insurance money *and* the reward," recalled the young man who had chauffeured Stella and a boyfriend from motel to motel in the seventies.

CHAPTER 57

Mary Margaret Stanton, forty-two, had been only a couple of years on the job as the director of the Auburn Public Library when Marshall Stone came calling the first week in March 1987. She told him beforehand, that the FBI would need a subpoena for a patron's library card. The issue was a patron's right to privacy.

When SA Stone arrived with the paperwork in hand, the librarian readily complied. The subpoena sought only Stella Nickell's library card—Cynthia's name was not included; neither were the names of other obvious choices: Cora Lee Rice, Jim McCarthy, and A. J. Rider.

The young agent camped out with the Dewey decimal system and scanned titles for books on poisons, chemistry, drugs, poisonous plants, anything that might reference cyanide. He pored over dozens of books and subject catalogs, and nearly two hours into it, he finally found one stamped with Stella Nickell's number. *Deadly Harvest*—what a title!

After more searching, the librarian helped him turn up the record of an overdue notice on another book checked out by Stella Nickell but never returned. The title was *Human Poisoning from Native and Cultivated Plants*.

Wait 'til Cusack hears about this.

The poster on the wall was right: libraries *do* open up a whole new world. One just might help make a case for the FBI.

SA Stone had other libraries to cover in Seattle and Renton, but Auburn was the only place he found anything of value.

The book and the overdue slip were sealed in evidence bags bound for FBI labs in Washington, D.C.

Paul Webking tried to get his stepdaughter Hayley to see where he was coming from, and as the first anniversary of Sue Snow's death neared, he almost succeeded. But when he tried to reach out to her, he often missed.

"It would have been so much better for everyone if I had been the one to take those pills instead of your mother," he said during the spring of 1987.

Hayley didn't jump up to tell him, but she did wish he had been the one.

Still in college in New Mexico, Exa Snow and her little sister kept in contact over the phone. Most of the time their conversations berated Paul, mourned the loss of their mother.

"We have to face it," Sue's oldest daughter said, "we will never, ever see her again and there is nothing we can do about it."

Ron and Penny Mauel lived catty-corner to the Nickell property. Just across the road from their own five acres was what Stella Nickell called "the lower part" of her land. From the Mauels' driveway, the shipping container Bruce and Stella used for storage could be seen through the young alders.

Penny never knew Bruce Nickell. She and her husband and young son and daughter signed the papers on their place a few days after Nickell died.

Penny chatted occasionally with Stella, even sold her some eggs from her henhouse. She considered her a friendly, "washed-up, honky-tonk girl."

She spent more time visiting over coffee with Cora Lee at her trailer. The tough old woman sang a convincing song of her daughter's innocence. Cora Lee was angry that all this was happening to Stella.

In the early spring of 1987, the Mauels' son, David, found a molehill-sized pile of empty gelatin capsules he called "pill shells" down by the Nickells' shipping container. The discovery worried the nine-year-old's mother, so she went down to look for herself. She told her children to stay away from the red-orange casings.

"I figured the FBI had already seen them," she said later. If they had, she wondered, why hadn't they cleaned them up? There were kids in the neighborhood, for godsake.

The discovery was interesting. Paul Webking once told a friend that the FBI had said some tainted capsules were different-sized. Jim McCarthy believed the same thing. Cindy Hamilton said her mother kept some empty capsules around the house. She said she had seen them herself.

In time, the casings melted into a gelled goo and disappeared in the waterlogged soil.

Why would anyone keep empty capsules?

In mid-March, Cusack caught up with A. J. Rider at her home in Las Vegas. The first contact was over the telephone. By then, A. J. and her husband Jim were turning their backs on their old friend Stella and were more than willing to talk.

Looking to buttress the government's star witness, the FBI was searching for things to back up Cindy Hamilton.

When SA Cusack said Cindy had come forward with information on her mother's plans to kill Bruce for insurance money, A. J. thought it was a joke.

"She's trying to get back at Stella," she said quickly. "She's just jumping on the bandwagon, trying to get some green here."

The FBI agent shared some minor details, but A. J. still didn't think Cindy's story rang true.

"I have a hard time believing that Stel would ever tell Cindy anything like that, of any of her plans. Stella didn't like Cindy to start off with. Why would she tell her? One minute they were friendly, and the next Stella could kill her."

When SA Cusack asked for a rundown on Stella's daughter, he got more than he bargained for.

"Cindy was horny all the time. If you drive an eighteen-wheeler and you got a hard-on, just call Cindy."

"Excuse me?"

"I like Cindy," she continued, softening somewhat. "Away from everything, I like Cindy. But put her with her truckers and her bullshit, I cannot stand her."

A. J. claimed Cindy had used Bruce Nickell's CB at White River Estates to pick up truckers.

"The best place in the world for Cindy to have sex was in your truck. If you drove an eighteen-wheeler, by God, she'd climb in. She was hung up with eighteen-wheelers. Cindy never stopped.

Want a blowjob driving down the road? No problem! The reason Cindy and I got along so good was I drove an eighteen-wheeler and Cindy knew that."

After the phone interview, Cusack and Marshall Stone booked flights for Las Vegas. A. J. Rider would be worth a trip.

It was springtime in the Northwest when Fred Phelps met Stella Maudine Nickell. At first the thirty-eight-year-old reddish-haired Burns Security field supervisor didn't think the Auburn woman was anything special. Sure, the lady was nice enough, sitting out in her truck watching the inside of a fence at a Kent strike site. But there were no sparks. She signed his security log and he left.

The second night, he met an alluring Stella Maudine. She had changed her hair somehow, though later he was unsure exactly what was different, and applied some makeup. She looked good. Her uniform looked even better. He wondered if she got dolled up just for him. She gave him her phone number.

A week or so later, he phoned her.

"We made a date for me to come down, go out to dinner. In my mind, I thought, nice-lookin' woman, go down, say hello, have a few drinks, have dinner, do a little dancin', go home and zap into bed and that would be it. Have a good time. What the hell?"

While leaving an Auburn restaurant after dinner and drinks, Stella tripped on a step and fell onto a concrete parking strip.

Stella just got up, blood flowing from her head, and brushed off her knees. Fred thought the injury would have knocked him cold, but not this woman.

"We've got to get you to the hospital!"

Stella just shook it off. "I'll be all right. I'll put a cold rag on it," she said.

"No, we're going."

As his date's head was being stitched in the emergency room, Fred Phelps figured his plans for the evening had been kiboshed. To his surprise, they weren't. He and Stella went back to her place and went to bed.

Days later, Stella Nickell made an offer too good to pass up.

"Why don't you come on up and stay with me for a week?" By then the security supervisor knew about the FBI investigation through the company rumor mill, but he hadn't asked the lady about the case.

"Stay for a week?"

"You stay for a week and you'll move in. I guarantee it."

She was right. In April 1987, Fred Phelps, a curly-headed, supertanker-sized man who made Harry Swanson look like a pipsqueak, started packing up his West Seattle basement apartment. As soon as Harry was gone, he was moving in.

Cora Lee told Stella she didn't like Fred. She suspected he was a federal undercover agent sent to Auburn to entrap her daughter. Stella told her she didn't think so, and besides, her relationship with any man was none of her mother's business.

Most of the new couple's time was spent riding the waves of Stella Maudine's waterbed.

"Once in a while we'd go out to dinner, come back, make love. Go to bed, make love, get up in the morning, make love. A lot of times on the couch, on the floor, in the bathroom. Always made love in the morning, always. She was A-plus. She was hot all the time," he said later.

Georgia Mae was the first to admit she drank more beer than she should. She battled the urge. And when she dried out, memories flooded back with such wincing pain that they forced her return to a six-pack. If Cindy hated her mother enough to set her up, it was Georgia Mae who had the best story to back it up. There was more than the childhood beating.

Georgia Mae said her niece told the horrifying yet unproven story shortly after her baby girl was born. It was November of 1980 when the young mother brought her little one up to Washington to see an orthopedic surgeon in Seattle. The conversation took place during a visit at Georgia's home south of Tacoma. Cindy wasn't emotional, just matter-of-fact.

"You know, Aunt George, you know why I don't respect my mom, it was because . . ."

Cindy told her aunt that her mother had sold her for sex when they lived in California.

Georgia Mae had no way of knowing if it was true, but she didn't think Cindy would lie to her.

"If I had had Stella in the same room, we'd have come to an understanding," she said later, rage coloring each word.

"I think that Cindy and Stella—they were related, but there was nothing there. There was no tie there."

"Have you ever met anyone that has no feelings about anything one way or another? Even wild animals have feelings."

CHAPTER 58

On Wednesday, March 18, Cynthia Hamilton stepped into the grand jury room under the protective wing of Asst. U.S. Attorney Joanne Maida and stood behind the podium. There would be no turning back. She needed to be believed.

At times, Cindy's delivery didn't help her cause. She repeatedly stopped and restarted her story, as though searching for the right words.

Maida asked for some personal background, and Cindy told of growing up in Santa Ana Heights, the forgery charges, and her mother's divorce from Bob Strong before moving to the Seattle area.

"After we moved up here, I became rather rebellious. I didn't like the lifestyle she was leading and I wanted to go back to my stepfather in Southern California, and I was constantly just packing up my bags and going. So I was moved around to a lot of different schools between foster homes and just running away from home and my mother's moving around, also."

She told the jurors about the beating charges that put her mother in jail. And despite all of it, Cindy said she "adored" her mother.

"I really did. When they questioned me the time that she was caught and they pulled me into the principal's office and they asked me about it, it took quite some time to get it out of me because I didn't want my mother in trouble. I lied. Well, I fell down, my dog knocked me down, you know, different excuses until they finally had me in tears and I had finally told, because they kept asking me and asking me and asking me, and I did finally tell them what happened, and still even after that I basically always loved my mother.

"As I got older, like I said, I went through a real rebellious period when we moved up here because my mother—she was drinking a lot, she was running around a lot, and just really wasn't the mom that I thought I had. I was a little bit sour against the fact that she was dating several men and going out and drinking and I didn't get much time of her myself."

Cindy told the jurors Bob Strong retained custody of her sister Leah "because the courts found my mother was unfit to have her." Eventually Cindy moved in with her grandmother, and she and her mother "didn't talk for several years."

She said she was "miffed" that her mother sent her a wedding invitation a month after she married Bruce Nickell. She was, after all, her daughter.

She said she had done some "reading and investigating" into child abuse, and learned it was common for a child to adore "and basically worship a parent that abuses them, and it was kind of uncanny that they almost had all of my feelings and my thoughts in what I was reading."

The reading helped her understand her mother.

"It helped me understand why she did it, because I looked back, and I would look back and think, well, I really didn't do anything to deserve to be hit quite that badly, but in reading and investigating into it, I could understand. I mean, I couldn't condone it, but I understood it, and basically forgave her for doing it."

The witness testified that she didn't care much for Bruce until after he gave up the booze. She liked his sense of humor; he was intelligent.

"He was just an obnoxious boor when he was drunk, I thought, and our relationship started changing at that point that he was getting along. He was my stepfather, my mother was married to him, there wasn't a whole lot I could do about it."

After he stopped drinking, their relationship improved considerably.

Maida asked how she felt about his death.

"That's a feeling I don't know if anybody can explain. I think about the closest thing you can really—the closest thing you can really come to is if somebody comes up to you with a bucket of ice water and just slowly pours it over the top of your head."

Cindy proceeded to recount the events of the evening of June 6, 1986. She and Bonnie Anderson were out when Dee Rogers phoned. They returned to the apartment, Cindy was "99.9 percent sure" her stepfather was dead.

"My mother walked in the door—she looked like she'd been crying; in fact, she looked very, very tired and she looked very old at the time."

Cindy's mother told her Bruce was dead and said, "I know what you're thinking, and it's no."

For four years, Cindy Hamilton testified, her mother had planned a killing, although, she said, she didn't know it was Bruce Nickell that her mother was talking about. It started when Stella was baby-sitting at White River Estates.

"She baby-sat all the little kids in the trailer park. She got much better with children as she got older, believe me, and she asked me if I knew where she could acquire some heroin. 'Heroin? No.' You know, I don't like heroin in the fact that it's a very harsh and it's a very nasty drug, period."

"Why did she ask you this? Does she know something about your background?"

"Yes, she does. She knows that when I lived in California, I did a lot of crank, which is speed. . . . Anyway, she knew that I did a lot of speed, and in working two jobs and trying to be a mommy and everything else, you know, it helped a lot, and I told her no, that I had no idea where she could get ahold of any heroin. I said, you know, 'I have drug connections as far as crank goes and speed and cocaine et cetera, but not heroin. I don't like it.' "

Stella Nickell hadn't said why she wanted the drug. Cindy assumed her mother had gotten herself into a financial hole and contemplated being a drug dealer to make some quick money.

"I was concerned, and I didn't want my mother pushing heroin to small children, or anybody for that matter."

If the proceedings hadn't been so serious, Cindy Hamilton's statement might have brought laughter.

The witness also told the jurors that her mother had asked about drugs, cocaine, crank, and heroin among them, and the dosage needed for overdosing.

"I told her with heroin it doesn't take a whole heck of a lot to OD a person."

Her questions, Cindy told the jurors, addressed neither why she was asking nor if anyone was a target. She didn't ask to satisfy her own curiosity, because "you don't ask my mother questions."

Maida asked why that was so.

"Because from the time I was born I was taught—and this still overrides into my adult life; I guess maybe you could say it was beat into me—that you don't question. There's just a certain attitude that she gets that says your answer—'I'm going to ask you this and you answer this. Don't question me,' and it's just an attitude she's had. It's very authoritative, it's very intimidating, and that's just the way it is, so it's really—I probably could have questioned her, but my mind wouldn't let me."

Yet, as Cindy claimed, Stella hadn't said it was Bruce she wanted out of the way. Time and several conversations passed before she knew.

"There was one time in particular before that I knew that it was my dad that she asked me about a hit man. That's when I knew somebody was in trouble."

Later, she learned the target was Bruce.

"Once it was brought to my knowledge that it was my dad, there was a lot of it that was discussed in depth, and I shouldn't really say 'discussed.' She would do most of the talking, and I in turn would either answer or listen, one of the two."

Cindy came up short when asked to put the discussions into an exact chronological context. They spread over almost three years.

"The next conversation concerning hit men came after I was aware that she was contemplating killing my dad, killing Bruce, and she had thought about getting a hit man, but she didn't have the funds, the money to hire one. She wasn't sure how to go about finding one, but she did discuss the possibilities that he could be— like, if she could hire a hit man, and he could be out on the highway when my dad was coming home from work, and possibly run head-on into another vehicle, like a—"

"This was your mother suggesting this could happen?" Joanne Maida interrupted.

"Yes, this was what my mother suggested could be done. That he could possibly be shot during rush hour in the middle of traffic, just be shot through the car window or the pickup window; that he could be caused to have a very, very severe accident."

The hit men were followed with the cyanide plan.

Cindy said her mother brought up the idea of reenacting the

Tylenol murders. It would be easy, her mother said, to put something back on the shelf.

"And that was the start of talking about cyanide. I knew absolutely nothing about it. I told her I believe that cyanide was found in peach pits or something like that. That was probably the extent of what I knew about it, and she had informed me that she knew that you could acquire it through a photography store."

"Why do you remember this?"

"Because it—I didn't know at the time. I gather little bits of information, and I didn't know that cyanide was part of photography processing, but it was just—it was just an interesting piece of information."

She said besides cyanide, her mother researched toxic plants.

Cindy said she remembered her mother talking about hemlock. She also recalled little black seeds that her stepfather could eat in some capsules her mother had. When he died, she could say he ingested them accidentally.

The jurors also learned of Stella's use of the various public libraries.

"Did you ever go with her so that you knew that she went to the Seattle library, or did she tell you that?"

"No, she told me this. I don't like to come to Seattle."

The last statement was interesting, as though accompanying her mother to the library to research a murder wasn't enough. Cindy Hamilton rushed in with further support of her lack of involvement.

In contrast to what she told the FBI back in June 1986, Cindy Hamilton painted a vastly different portrait of the Nickell marriage. When Bruce was an active alcoholic, he and her mother partied from evening to daybreak. "After he was treated and he was no longer active in alcoholism, this tapered off to almost nil," Cindy said. "He was the stereotypical couch potato. He didn't want to go do things anymore. He was no fun. He wasn't social really very much with other people. He wanted to sit at home and watch TV or play with his CB radio or take naps."

Joanne Maida, just as SA Cusack had done, made a statement that asked a big question: "Generally people don't talk to other people about such things unless they perceive the other person as being receptive."

"As I stated before, if my mother chooses to talk about something, I didn't argue the fact with her. I guess you could say that I—I'm still intimidated by my mother basically. It's something you

don't just outgrow overnight, and my mother still intimidates me
to the point of—I mean she doesn't scare me, but it's just old
childhood habits that if Mom wants to talk, you shut up, you listen
. . . it gets real nasty if you argue with her or try and tell her that
she's wrong . . . My mother and I developed a very close relationship when I moved up here four years ago, and I always did want
to be very close to . . . even though everything that we had been
through when I was younger. I still loved my mother dearly. . . . I
tried walking like her and talking like her. I still find that I have
gestures that are almost identical to hers. . . .

"My mother talked to me about everything, and I talked to her
about everything, and when she started talking about killing my
dad, I was torn between not really wanting to talk about it and the
possibility that it would blow over and it would just end up getting
a normal stereotyped divorce, and I would still have the relationship
with my mom, whereas should I say, 'No, I don't want to talk about
this,' well, she would cop an attitude and then there would be nothing . . . and if nothing ever came of it, then there we were back at
square one trying to start another relationship again between the
two of us."

"That's different from being intimidated, isn't it, where you
wouldn't want to squelch whatever your mother was saying? You're
making a deliberate decision then to hear her out, to blow off this
steam."

"Yes."

"You don't strike me as the kind of person from your demeanor
to be easily intimidated by other people."

"No. Intimidation being—I guess basically I didn't want to go
through the big hassle of saying, 'Look, I don't want to talk about
it,' and having my mother cork off and, like I say, basically destroy
a portion of the relationship that we had developed, and it's still
very hard for me to question my mother, you know . . . because you
just don't tell your mom what to do."

Next, Asst. U. S. Attorney Maida moved on to finances. Didn't
it make more sense to let Bruce live so her mother would have a
decent source of income?

Cindy said her mother wanted to collect on her stepfather's "substantial" life insurance.

"My mother spoke of this around the same time that she was
talking about cyanide poisoning, reenacting the Tylenol incident,
and also about the cocaine. That I remember because I told her that

for—She asked me about it; I said, 'Well, you can't just OD all at once because cocaine stays in tissues in the system,' I said, 'and they're going to know that it was a one-time thing if they do an autopsy,' and I tried to feed her a lot of negative aspects.

"And she says, 'Well, if I were to, like, maybe put it in his iced tea.' They drank iced tea a lot, gallons and gallons and gallons of it, and they had two separate containers, because my dad drank his with sugar, and my mother, she drinks hers straight. So there were two different containers of iced tea in the refrigerator and she could, like, put some in his iced tea and get it into his system to distribute itself throughout his system, and I told her I had no idea what the difference between ingesting it and inhaling it, whether it diffused through the system differently or not, and she said she couldn't do that before his physical examination in January because he had to pass the physicals to be accepted on a permanent basis for the state and get his life insurance."

The witness's statements were troubling, and since grand jury proceedings are secret and the jurors anonymous, it is not known how they felt about them. It seemed Cindy's so-called discussions with her mother involved more than mere listening. She told her mother cocaine would be discovered.

"Why would she want his life insurance money?" Joanne Maida asked.

"Why wouldn't she want it?"

The question was repeated.

"Because the life insurance—she indicated that the life insurance policy would pay off the property, the trailer, and she would still have enough left over to live comfortably."

Mother and daughter would share the money.

"She said to the effect of that we could get our dreamed-of fish store. We started talking about that years ago, about going into business together and opening up a pet shop dealing strictly with tropical fish."

She did nothing to dissuade her mother from the idea that she wanted to be in the fish-store plan.

"No, I didn't discourage her in the fact, like I said, that—I mean, at least she was on another subject. She wasn't talking—even though she was talking about this would be the effect of after he was dead, but she wasn't talking about the actual enactment of it, and I didn't discourage her about talking about it, other than when she was talking about actually trying to kill him, I tried to give her a lot of negative feedback on that."

Why hadn't Cindy warned Bruce Nickell?

Cindy said she agonized over it but she didn't know exactly what to do, whom to tell. No one would believe her. It would ruin her relationship with her mother if the police followed up on it.

"Possibly even if they wanted to go talk to my dad, my dad would think that I was out of my mind or wouldn't know what to do. Eventually, possibly—I even thought, well, maybe it would cause enough of a rift that they would just get the divorce and, you know, everything would be fine and I could try and work on getting back together with my mother, and that doesn't settle well because I figured, knowing my mother as well as I did, she would be able to talk her way out of it one way or another."

She told the grand jury her version of why she had come forward. At first, she didn't believe her mother had murdered Bruce, though "basically" she knew. She tried to convince herself it was a coincidence Bruce had died. She "latched" on to the idea of the emphysema autopsy ruling.

"And when I found out that my dad had died of cyanide poisoning was after I had read about Sue Snow in the paper, and I didn't even connect the two then.

"Then my mother calls me on the telephone one night and told me that my dad had died of cyanide poisoning, and that was another bucket of cold ice water because I knew, but I still kept denying it, and then we had the FBI out to the house. I stayed with my mother for about two or three days after I found out about that. And we had the FBI out there to the house, and internally I panicked when they wanted to talk to me in private. I knew what they were going to question me about because they were out there just tearing the house apart. I mean, they were looking in every little nook and cranny they could find looking for other bottles of Excedrin, looking for anything, you know, that they could find. And I—with the information that I knew, she'd already told me . . . I was still denying that she could have actually done it. I was still going, 'This is my mother, this is the flesh and blood I was born of,' you know.

"So when they questioned me, I denied knowing anything. I guess you could basically say I lied, because I did. . . . And I was just being protective, and I didn't know for sure. And I thought afterwards when I was done giving my interview and I went back home—I had nightmares. I still do. I'm twenty-seven years old and

I've never had a nightmare in my life until this, never."

Cindy said she had hoped the investigation would die down. But the FBI kept on.

". . . they'll leave me alone, they'll leave my family alone, it will just die down, and I'll figure out a way to live with myself."

It was Sue Snow, her husband, and daughters that really hit her.

"I mean, it upset me tremendously, of course, that my mother would kill my dad, but it really, really bothered me that somebody we didn't know, had never seen before in our lives, had no effect on our—our lifestyle, our family, or anything, was dead because of something that I was almost sure my mother did. And their whole family was basically destroyed because of it."

By the time SAs Cusack and Scott showed up, she still wasn't certain she'd say anything.

"Until they sat down at my kitchen table and sat across from me and said, 'We want to talk to you about this,' up until that point when I opened my mouth, I still wasn't sure . . . and it just clicked that I had—I had to say it, I had to get it out. I had to say something to somebody, and I had already—I had already discussed it with my roommate, and I had told her—about three months after my dad died I told her . . . I told her that I knew that my mom had killed him, and she asked me how I knew, and I told her about the conversations that my mother and I had had, and she was very concerned because I hadn't said anything prior. She knew that it was quite a load to carry around, and Denise [Dee] and I are very, very close, also, and we talked about whether we should say anything or not. And for a few months after that I didn't say anything, because it's going to have a real effect on a lot of people."

She said she was worried about her grandmother Cora Lee, who she said was on the verge of a stroke, Walter and Ruth Nickell, and her own daughter, who still didn't know.

"I don't know how to tell her. . . . What am I going to tell her when they take her gramma to court? When they try and prosecute her for murder, what am I going to tell her?"

When asked by a juror, Cindy Hamilton said her stepfather never made any passes at her when she lived with the Nickells.

"Do you think Stella felt that he had made any approaches to you?"

"I don't know—I don't think she felt that he made approaches to me, but my mom has been jealous of me in the past," she said, telling the jurors about the time her mother struck her over her boyfriend's fondling her back in Southern California.

A juror asked if the witness's mother was living the kind of life she wanted since Bruce died. And if she was, how soon after Bruce's death?

"Within two weeks after we buried my dad, my mother was out getting drunk and sleeping with other men and taking them home to the same bed that her and my dad shared together."

Cindy said she saw it firsthand when she stayed at the property after Bruce was buried.

"I spent a lot of time baby-sitting my mother. That's one of the reasons I lost my job at the airport . . . I have a reputation myself to uphold in the town of Kent . . . I have a lot of friends that go into the taverns, and it makes one feel very uncomfortable when you've got your mother going downtown where she hasn't been for eight years, you know, and starts running around and whoring around within two weeks after your dad dies and people are, you know, 'That's your mother?' "

A juror asked if Harry Swanson might have been an accomplice.

Cindy didn't think so. Harry hadn't been in contact with her mother until after Bruce died. She had someone else in mind.

"My mother was intimately and emotionally involved with my dad's best friend, Jim McCarthy, prior to my dad's death."

Characterizing the witness as tough and cool about even the most sensitive subjects, Joanne Maida asked if her assessment of her demeanor was fair.

Cindy, who said she was in "shutdown mode," rambled an answer. Though outwardly calm, she was on the verge of "hysteria."

"Not really hysteria," she corrected herself, "I shouldn't say that. . . . Once I made up my mind that this has to be done, I'm going to have to do it, I'm doing it. To go through it and not break out into a blubbering emotional mass of Jell-O, it's like—it's like I'm disassociating myself from my mother."

She said she was trying to block out the emotional bond. She still loved her, but her mother needed help. Later, she said, she'd probably break down.

"I just kind of have to shut off all emotion and feeling and just kind of say what I know . . . just say what the facts are and just have it done and be over with and don't even associate it emotionally until later. I can't."

She learned all of this from her mother, she said.

"So I just fall back on my rearing of 'you just don't show emotion.' . . . I can't remember my mother ever having an emotional outburst . . . downright raw, jagged feelings. I guess maybe I'm thankful for part of it, because if I didn't have that I don't know if I could do this, and I'm still having my problems with it . . . so it's not as hard and crass as it looks."

CHAPTER 59

With Cindy Hamilton singing to the grand jury, Jack Cusack plowed ahead with the investigation. Corroboration remained critical. Not only had Cindy Lea suggested Bonnie Anderson as a witness, she had phoned her in advance to remind her about the encounter with her mother at the apartment. It was mid-March when Cusack and another agent interviewed 911 operator Bonnie at the dimly lit King County offices where she worked.

The details, the preciseness of her recollections, were welcome after the sometimes hit-and-miss information Cindy had offered as she tried to get her story across to the grand jury.

On key points, Bonnie's story was an exact match of Cindy's. She recalled how they'd been out drinking when Dee summoned them.

"On the way back to the apartment, Cindy said, 'It is either Bruce's parents or Bruce . . .' " Anderson recalled.

Stella arrived later.

"She looked horrible. She looked wiped out. She had a bandanna over her hair. She just really looked washed out. Really worn out. And really hyper . . . that's the impression I got," she said.

Most crucially, Bonnie remembered word for word: *"I know what you're thinking . . . and the answer is no."*

"Cindy knew nothing about this. She came apart. She didn't even know her dad was in the hospital . . . She just couldn't believe

it. Her reaction was the same reaction I had when my dad died . . .
This man was very close to her."

Bonnie summed up her friend's personality and the reason why
she turned her mother in: "Cindy's not perfect. She did her things
her own way. But she looked on that man as her father. I think it
finally got to the point that the more she and her mom talked . . .
she became convinced that Stella had done it. Regardless of the fact
that Stella was her mother, nobody was going to get away with it."

SA Cusack asked if Stella would confide in her daughter.

"If anyone knew what was going on with Stella, it was Cindy.
I think Stella told her just about everything."

It was raining when Jack Cusack and Marshall Stone checked into
rooms on the seventeenth floor of the Showboat in Las Vegas to
meet A. J. Rider and her husband Jim for a breakfast interview the
next day.

For the Riders, the FBI certainly wasn't old hat, but by then
they had talked with agents in Yakima, local agents from the Las
Vegas field office, and SA Cusack on the phone. By the time they
settled down to talk at the Showboat, they were more comfortable
with the feds than they could have imagined.

The Riders both wore jeans to the interview. A. J. wore little, if
any, makeup. Where Stella Nickell would put on the dog to make
an impression, A. J. was simply herself. She had light-brown hair
she wore in a layered cut. Her husband's hair was darker and longer,
but that wasn't the only contrast. Where Vietnam vet Jim Rider was
quiet to the point of nearly blending into his surroundings, A. J.
made her presence known. She talked nonstop.

The Riders told the FBI men they were still "pissed off" that
they had learned of Bruce's death through their foster son's chance
meeting with Cora Lee.

"She had went to Wenatchee. Now, in my realization, I mean
I'm a country hick, I'm a bitch, I'm everything, but in my realization, if somebody dies—especially my husband—I sure the hell
don't go running over to Wenatchee to talk to his folks, least of all
alone. We had only moved out three days before! How hard would
it have been for her to tell us?"

SA Cusack asked if either of the Riders ever had any inkling
that Stella might leave Bruce.

Drawing on a cigarette, A. J. nodded. "One of the days we were going to pick up Cindy at Dee's, she said she was thinking of taking off to see Wilma."

"With Bruce?"

"Definitely without Bruce," A. J. recalled, adding that Stella dropped the subject.

Did Stella Nickell have a lover? Cindy claimed she did. Dee said she did. Both insisted Big Mac was the man, but Jim McCarthy denied it. If anyone might have had a glimpse of what was going on, it was A. J. She worked with Stella while living at their place.

"Our schedules got switched, and she had Fridays off. She didn't have anything going on those days, but she was never home the whole damn day. And she wouldn't get home until after Bruce on that day."

A. J. wondered if Stella had "gone off to some motel." She doubted she was shopping, as Stella had claimed. She never came home with any packages.

"I also knew she had played around before, so why not now? Maybe she was tired of being the straight-laced little girl who couldn't drink and all this shit because of her husband."

It was Big Mac who seemed the most likely candidate.

"He was there in the daytime when she was home and Bruce was at work. He'd be there and I'd be off on my runs. Most of the time she had someone there, I'd be off on my bike. She'd get pretty hushed when somebody's around. You didn't know whether they were talking business or whatever."

On May 25, 1986, the Sunday before the Riders moved to their foster son's place in Renton, A. J. said she went shopping with Stella.

"She bought two bottles of Excedrin."

"Two?"

"She was the typical woman. When you go to the store, do you buy one or two? You buy two. I was with her when she bought the Excedrin. She bought two."

SA Cusack lowered his voice and leaned forward. "Do you think anyone could have been in on this with Stella?"

"If anyone, it's Dee," she said.

"You really think so?"

"I think Dee knew what was happening before anyone else. I've always thought Dee was in on it. I always thought Dee knew."

                    *   *   *

If Stella Maudine Nickell had worried about losing everything she had fought so hard to get, as her daughter avowed, she was well on her way in the months before Bruce Nickell died. Money was more than tight. It just plain didn't exist.

From the files of North Pacific Bank, the lienholder on the Nickell residence, FBI agents came up with more damaging information on the Nickells' deteriorating finances. Late with payments, as records showed, was typical of the Nickells—the file indicated thirty-nine times when payments were received ten or more days late. But things had worsened in the fall of 1985.

> If you just have patience, I will eventually catch up—just don't push. I would also like the insurance explained that you put on my home without my okay. . . . Your letter said $33 per month for the next nine months would be added onto my payments. I cannot believe insurance of $100 per month. Please explain.
>
> Sincerely, Stella Nickell

It was a problem that wasn't going away. A Final Notice of Delinquency written and sent on April 9, 1986, indicated total payment of $1,892.01 was due by April 25, 1986. By that time, the Nickells hadn't made a payment since September.

A letter from Stella Nickell was sent back on the deadline date.

> Dear Sirs:
> I know that I am tremendously overdue with my payments. There is a good reason for it. I am having marital problems. They are about solved, and I would like to ask if you will have faith in me, personally. Bruce is no longer involved and I would like a chance for me myself to prove my worth to you. . . .
>
> Sincerely,
> Stella Nickell.

She closed the letter with a promise to pay $500 a month and enclosed an $800 check.

Her marital problems were about to be "solved" . . . Her husband is "no longer involved." She never mentioned "we."

Stella Nickell sent another letter, this one on stationery showing a smiling girl picnicking atop a checked blanket. "Good feelings make every day sunny." It had been dated June 1, 1986. In it Stella enclosed a double payment and wrote:

> *My payments will now stay current.*
>   *Very sincerely, Stella Nickell*

Bruce Nickell would be dead four days after his wife sent the letter. Cusack wondered where Stella got the money to make the double payment. A friend, a boyfriend? He didn't know Bruce Nickell had been out to see his father in Wenatchee and had returned with $1,000.

SA Cusack felt he knew, however, how Stella was planning to stay current. It certainly wasn't through her job at SeaTac. She was looking for her insurance windfall.

The financial picture supported Cindy Hamilton's contentions. All of the troubles were coming to a head when Mrs. Nickell started talking about cyanide and the murder of her husband. The clock was ticking and she had to do something, or she'd lose everything.

CHAPTER 60

Sandy Scott received an angry phone call on Saturday morning, March 21, the day after she was served to appear before the grand jury. The woman barking on the other end of the telephone line was Cora Lee.

"Cindy, what in the hell do you think you're doing talking to the FBI about your mother?"

"Cora Lee, this is *Sandy*, not *Cindy*," she quickly said, defusing the misdirected onslaught.

Stella's mother apologized for her outburst and muttered something about having misdialed. She was so angry, she said, she could hardly see straight. The FBI had been out to see her two days before, and Stella's mother said things were starting to fall into place. Rarely the chatty type, Cora Lee was in the mood to talk.

"Jerry told me Cynthia and Dee had gone to the FBI against Stella," she said. "Jerry said he and Cindy had been out drinking one night when Cindy told him Stella had given her a bag of white powder to keep for her."

The insinuation was that it was cyanide. Whether Cora Lee didn't believe it or didn't want to, would be hard to say. She was exasperated at her granddaughter for going to the FBI with a pack of lies.

"We don't even know where she is now," she said.

Cora Lee also missed her great-granddaughter. Stella had been barred from seeing the girl, but why should she?

"I didn't have anything to do with this, and I'm stuck out in the cold and can't see her either," she said.

Sandy wondered when Stella had given the sinister "white powder" to her daughter. It must have been before the murders. Why would she have given it to her after Bruce's death? Wouldn't it make more sense for Stella to destroy any leftover poison? What in the world did Cindy have to do with all of this?

A day or so later, Jack Cusack called Sandy to see if she knew of any toxic plants in the vicinity of the Nickell property.

"Nightshade and foxglove are about all I can recall," she said.

He asked her to go down to the Nickells' to see what she could dig up on plants.

"Get Cora Lee talking and see what she says."

So Sandy traipsed down the hill, armed with a story for the nice old lady in the trailer behind Stella Nickell's.

"I'm worried about my boy eating some of those pretty little berries," she told Cora Lee.

"Oh, I know just what you mean," Cora Lee said, puttering around her trailer, offering coffee or a can of beer. "Before Bruce died we cleaned out that front ditch so [Cynthia's daughter] wouldn't get into any of it." She also said Stella had once pointed out some nightshade.

Cora Lee said that years ago she and her children supported themselves gathering cascara bark in the woods of Oregon. Another time, they had harvested flax for its fiber, and even collected foxglove leaves that were needed by drug manufacturers to make digitalis.

Cora Lee gave her neighbor lady a book on Indian herbs. Sandy thanked her and hurried home, eager to see if it held any clues for the FBI.

Jack Cusack and others considered Cora Lee might possibly be involved in the crime. She had a lot to lose. It was her property and trailer home that teetered on a wire as the Nickells' considerable financial troubles escalated in 1986. When fingerprint analysis was done, hers were on the list for comparison. Might mother and daughter have schemed together. Cora and Stella? Or Stella and Cindy?

Some sources suggested Cora Lee was mad at Bruce Nickell. Cora Lee had put up the $20,000 for the land, with promises no doubt from Bruce and Stella. But Bruce was a couch potato and didn't get the chores done as fast as the old lady had wanted.

The fact remained that if Cora Lee was involved, Cindy wasn't implicating her.

Stella Nickell told friends her mother stood by her. She said it was more than a mother hoping her daughter was not involved.

"I know for a fact that you did not do this," Cora Lee said time and time again. "If she gets you convicted," she said, "I'll kill her."

"Mother," Stella said, "you're angry, it's something you're saying."

"No, I'm serious. If Cynthia puts you in prison, I'll kill her."

Years later, A. J. Rider's most vivid memories of testifying before the grand jury were the questions they asked her.

She was asked point-blank if she thought Stella had killed Bruce.

"Yes," she answered.

"Why?"

"It's not one specific thing. It's all the comments, actions, innuendos . . . that didn't mean anything, but you put them all together and the big picture says she's guilty."

She told the jurors about shopping a few days before Bruce's death and how Stella bought two bottles of Excedrin.

Jim McCarthy, laughing eyes no more, also stood before the grand jury. But whatever his testimony was would remain secret. Jim later said he stated firmly that he and the suspect had not been lovers.

Nervous and exhausted from working twenty-four hours straight as a rent-a-cop, Jerry Kimble didn't fare too well at the grand jury either. Joanne Maida asked so many questions, so quickly, he couldn't keep up with her.

"She started firing questions right off. 'Ma'am, slow down. Stop throwing 'em out like a damn baseball.' "

When she did, he told the grand jury what he knew: Stella loved Bruce. They had a good marriage.

Strangely, no one mentioned the white powder Cindy claimed to have kept for her mother.

Jerry left downtown Seattle unsure whether he had helped or harmed the case. He felt he was only a drop in the brew they were mixing in that courtroom.

In late March, Marshall Stone interviewed Stella Nickell supporter Vicki Bagby Moen, now remarried, at a Tukwila, Washington, restaurant.

"When she told me that Bruce had died, tears were in her eyes. He was gone a week. I didn't know. I just couldn't believe he was gone."

Stella had told her that pathologists believed her husband had died of emphysema but she had trouble accepting it.

"Stella said she called the police because she found the bottles and wanted to have it checked."

"I said, 'Oh you don't believe . . .' "

" 'I don't know.' "

She didn't think her friend did it.

"If she did do it, she deserves what she gets, but if she didn't do it . . . I don't believe she did it," she told SA Stone.

Vicki took a turn accusing Cindy Hamilton, but with little to go on.

"I think she did it, period. I just think she was that devious to do something like that. I really do. I think that she loved Bruce and she didn't like her mother being married to him. She liked him like crazy. She just couldn't stand it—the thought that her mother was married to him and she just couldn't have Bruce. I think Cynthia was very jealous of her mother."

Vicki was another who would never believe Stella Maudine Nickell was sneaky and diabolical enough to kill her husband with a drug tampering.

"If she was going to kill Bruce, she wouldn't have killed him with cyanide. No way. She'd take a gun and shoot him."

A few days after her cousin had done her best before the grand jury to send her mother up the river, Wilma Stewart sat at home with her water-puffy feet up. Her marriage was on the rocks, her baby was due the following month, son Richard was battling leukemia, and her favorite aunt was a suspected murderer.

Her office called with word a man in a suit had been by asking for her. Since he might be a big-time real estate client, Wilma told the office manager to send him over to her duplex if he came back.

When she opened the door, SA Dave Hill from the Seattle field office stood before her. Though he usually worked foreign counter-intelligence, Hill was the ideal special agent for the job of inter-viewing Stella's niece. One of his responsibilities around the Seattle office was the coordination of the Employee Assistance Program, an assignment that demanded equal doses of patience and compassion.

That was exactly what interviewing Wilma Mae required.

"I'd like to talk with you," he said, after identifying himself and handing her a grand jury subpoena. SA Hill had been told she was fiercely loyal and would be hostile. And though she chose her words guardedly, she had some things to get off her chest.

Wilma told SA Hill about Cynthia Lea's peculiar behavior at the funeral and how "Cynthia hated her mother—hated her for years." She told the FBI how close Stella and Bruce had been. Her aunt had helped him quit drinking. She told about the anguished calls after Bruce died.

Still, he asked the question.

"Do you think your aunt killed your uncle?"

"That's impossible," she said. "She wasn't going to kill him, she was going to leave him and come live in Houston with me." She tried to protect her aunt and defuse what Cynthia Lea had told them. Wilma told the truth.

Dave Hill asked if Cynthia Lea and Uncle Bruce had a sexual relationship. She laughed it off. He also asked if Stella might have been having an affair.

"No, my aunt would never do that," Wilma bristled. "Once we're married, we're married."

Wilma Stewart was infuriated by the stories Cynthia Lea had told the FBI.

Dave Hill returned to Eastern Washington several times to meet with Wilma Stewart for coffee, maybe a meal, and information. Sometimes he gave as much as he got. Wilma didn't know it, but her statement that her aunt planned to leave her uncle Bruce was met with great interest in Seattle. Stella had denied any marital discord, yet she was going to leave Bruce.

It was another nail in her aunt's coffin.

On another visit, SA Hill recounted Stella's call to 911.

The dispatcher: "Is he conscious?"

Stella Nickell: "I don't think so, his breathing has slowed down . . . I can't see him . . . I couldn't get to the phone . . . I'm not in the same room he's in. He's in the den."

The seasoned special agent tried to plant the seed of doubt: Why would Stella drag Bruce to the couch and go into another room to make the call, when there was a telephone in the very room in which her husband had collapsed? Logically, she'd go to the nearest phone in an emergency.

"I don't think so . . . I can't see him."

SA Hill said Stella was "calm, cool, and collected."

Wilma still didn't buy any of it. She stood firmly on Aunt Stella's side. The FBI or someone was out to frame her.

When he asked what she knew about Stella's beating her daughter so severely that the little girl was hospitalized, Wilma exploded.

"That's a damn out-and-out lie!"

SA Hill mentioned the reward money. There was no guarantee she'd get any, but cooperation could put Wilma in line for some of it.

"You take your money and jam it," she snapped.

Dave Hill laughed. "It could set you up a little better."

"I don't want to be set up. I don't want any money."

The FBI knew about the calls Stella had made to Houston, so Wilma figured they must have subpoenaed her aunt's phone records. They also had her Visa and MasterCard account information.

None of it would change Wilma's mind. When she heard stories that federal agents had tried to link Aunt Stella to the Tylenol murders in Chicago, Wilma knew for sure they were barking up the wrong tree.

"Ridiculous! These guys don't give up, do they?"

CHAPTER 61

Cindy Hamilton needed irrefutable backup. It was possible Stella's daughter conceived the story to get back at her mother or to collect the reward money. Maybe even to save herself. Whatever the case, it was almost certain if Cindy's charges against her mother were devoid of substantiation, it would end up as a spitting match between mother and daughter. Neither could expect to hold up under even the poorest cross-examination—if the case even got to court.

Case Agent Jack Cusack and Asst. U.S. Attorney Joanne Maida both knew that.

Early one morning, SSA Mike Byrne called Cusack into his office and handed him a "greenie," or teletype, from the FBI lab.

"Look at this," he said, a big smile on his face. "The bureau has made Stella's latent prints on the library book."

The library books gathered by SA Stone, the Excedrin, and the Anacin-3 bottles, and capsules had been forwarded to SA Carl Collins' Jr.'s, Washington, D.C., laboratory for processing. It was there, under the eerie glow of lasers and meticulous examination, that the FBI had truly hit pay dirt.

The bottles, however, were a bust. Oddly, only the Sue Snow bottle held a print. It belonged to Sarah Webb.

Even more surprising, none of the bottles recovered from Stella Nickell's home had any fingerprints of evidentiary value.

Not even Stella Nickell's. Not Sandy Scott's, who claimed she touched the mysterious third bottle.

Likewise, SA Collins was unable to record any prints on the capsules themselves. Perhaps the tamperer had used gloves; perhaps his or her hands were devoid of oil or perspiration.

The books from Auburn Public Library, however, were another story.

SA Collins saturated book pages with ninhydrin, a chemical agent sensitive to amino acids found in perspiration. The resulting chemical reaction leaves a blue-violet-colored indicator disclosing latent prints.

The copy of *Deadly Harvest* became so mottled with prints, it looked as if it had been pelted with overripe blueberries. In time, SA Collins found more than eighty finger and palmprints matching the ink-print cards of the suspect.

Though some forty-six book pages, and the checkout-card holder page, had fingerprints belonging to Nickell, some pages had more than others. Pages 88–89, with passages on cyanide, showed the greatest number of prints found on any two facing pages—eight. It also featured the print with the greatest number of points for comparison, an exceptionally clear print with forty-seven characteristics matching Stella Nickell's.

That was an astounding forty more points for comparison than SA Collins required before testifying in court with utter conviction.

One print was severed in half, indicating the reader had held a piece of paper or a tool with a straight edge to the page to aid reading or note-taking.

Facing pages 66 and 67 showed the second-highest number of prints, seven. Those pages, dealt with hemlock and toxic seeds.

A fingerprint belonging to the suspect was also recovered from the membership enrollment card for Bruce Nickell's All American Life Insurance policy.

The FBI expert also found two latent prints on Bruce Nickell's January 8, 1986, Long-term Disability Enrollment Change form from the SEIB. Again, the fingerprints were not Bruce Nickell's, but those of his wife, Stella Maudine.

Now the Stella Nickell product-tampering case was moving along after a drought of information.

Through the library books—books with her fingerprints all over them—it was clear Stella Nickell had read that a gassy derivative of potassium cyanide gave off the odor of bitter almonds.

Holed up in his office after dinner, SA Jack Cusack could only imagine Stella Nickell's surprise—and likely outrage—when the Harborview pathologists hadn't detected the telltale smell. Without an official accidental cause of death, she would lose everything she wanted. She wouldn't have her fish or ceramics store.

God knows the woman had tried. Stella Nickell called Harborview on June 7 to inquire about the autopsy findings. They weren't available. She made another call on June 13, pressing for answers. Still nothing. *She even called about the goddamn crocheted afghan!*

Someone had to die. As Jack Cusack saw it, Stella Nickell needed an excuse to focus attention on her husband's true cause of death. Sue Snow was the excuse. When she heard about the news report she was ready with her story, and the Albertson's receipt to show where she bought the laced bottle.

The bottle of Anacin-3 was interesting. When had she mixed that one? Mike Dunbar of the Auburn Police told the FBI he thought she had put it on the shelf after Sue Snow's death had been in the news and after the FBI had been out to see her.

"It was getting a little hot for her. She knew she made a mistake with the two bottles of Excedrin, and needed a diversion," Detective Dunbar had said.

SA Jack Cusack wasn't so sure. After all, the green crystals were present, pointing to the same mixing as the Excedrin.

He also disagreed with Joanne Maida's theory that the additional bottles were placed on shelves after Bruce Nickell's funeral. Jack Cusack believed it was all done at once.

CHAPTER 62

It was time for hapless Harry Swanson to leave Auburn. Stella Nickell had her reasons. Could have been boredom. Could have been waiting-in-the-wings Fred Phelps. Maybe she had used him for all he could do around her place? It was even possible she had Harry leave for the reason she gave: she loved him.

"I'm going to be the scapegoat," she told him one morning. "They don't have anybody else; it's going to be me."

She said it would be best for him to leave town.

"Honey, you better get your motor home off the property. They'll confiscate it. I don't want that."

When Harry didn't move fast enough, Stella became derisive and more direct. She told him to get the hell off her property; she even cleaned out his motor home to send him off in a hurry.

"It hurt like hell for her to tell me those dirty things," Harry Swanson recalled years later. "She wanted to come out and say 'get the fuck out of here! They're gonna eventually pin this on me, and it will give you some time.' I seen it when she cried. And Indians don't cry."

Weeks before he pulled his Winnebago off the property for the last time, Harry knew Stella had met someone else, a man named Fred Phelps.

"I knew that's who she was working with out in Renton," Harry said of Phelps. "This was when she'd start treating me real bad."

Harry never believed Stella was in love with Fred. And she was only getting rid of Harry to save him hurt later.

"When she turned her head, she'd cry. Every dirty word she said to me, she cried."

Jack Cusack advised Sandy Scott that the FBI was concerned that Stella might flee. Since the grand jury had talked to just about everyone who had anything to do with her, word was likely getting back.

Sandy went undercover—under the cover of brambles and bushes—to keep a watch on the Nickell place. Of particular interest was Harry Swanson's RV. If Stella was going off somewhere in that rusty little Winnebago, Sandy Scott was instructed to notify Cusack lickety-split.

Cloaked by alder seedlings, sword ferns, and other waist-high spring foliage, Sandy crouched across the road and watched as Stella told Harry sayonara.

Stella's phone rang, but no one moved to answer it. Sandy strained to hear the conversation.

"Call . . . Cynthia . . . something's going on . . ."

Though she heard only a few utterances, Sandy Scott took Stella to mean she had expected the call she ignored to be from her daughter.

"*. . . something's going on . . .*"

If Stella only knew, Sandy thought as she crept back through the thicket to make her report for Cusack.

The second week in April, Wilma Stewart had a baby girl, a beautiful little blue-eyed blonde. A month later, mother and her new baby visited Stella at her Auburn trailer. Aunt Stella was clearly not herself; she was preoccupied with the investigation and the insurance money. Her niece could certainly understand that. It *had* been getting rougher.

Even Harry Swanson was a problem. He called the house bawling.

"Let me talk to your aunt," he sobbed into the phone.

"She's not here," Wilma lied for her aunt.

"I know damn good and well that she's there."

Wilma stuck with the charade. When her aunt said she was finished with someone, that was it. There was never a "let's try again." When a Stephenson girl said it was over, she meant it.

Dave Hill let up on his repeated interrogations of Wilma and made the hop over the Cascades to Wenatchee to meet with Dick Nickell, Bruce's cousin. The retired Chelan County Sheriff had sputtered on for months about Stella's killing Bruce. He offered SA Hill a litany of anecdotes about her, mostly having to do with character. Stella had stolen from Walter and Ruth, Stella had a boyfriend just after Bruce died, Stella had acted inappropriately at the funeral.

As Dave Hill sat in the comfort of Dick and Pat Nickell's western-decorated home, he could tell that all of it had weighed heavily on the man's mind. He couldn't be sure if it was because he cared for Bruce or that he just wanted to solve a case as law-enforcement man.

Dick Nickell said Stella was aware of a $100,000 policy on Bruce's life. But she was unsure if it was any good, because of the problem with the physical. He also related the story of a $2,500 check Ruth Nickell had wanted to cash at a Cashmere bank, but when she couldn't get there for a while, the check disappeared and later was cashed by someone else.

"We learned it was a woman with long, dark hair," Dick Nickell said. "It must have been Stella."

Jack Cusack could count on daily calls from Cindy. "Goddamn it, Cusack! Why in the fuck didn't you tell me there was a fucking reward being offered!" Cindy screamed one time into the phone.

SA Cusack didn't know what her game was. Cindy Hamilton *knew* there was a reward. Maybe it was a strange attempt to get him to believe she didn't know a thing about it, therefore couldn't have made up a story to get a piece of it. He had never thought she'd come forward because of the money in the first place.

Dee Rogers put in a call to the FBI with something of her own to contribute to the investigation. And it was bizarre enough to be true. She told Jack that she and Stella shared an interest in the supernatural. Dee, raised Catholic, said she had some frightening experiences associated with the occult when she lived in New York. Both women had their own Ouija boards and decks of tarot cards while living at White River Estates.

Dee now remembered how Stella Nickell, shaken and distraught, had come to her Kent apartment the fall before her husband died. Though Cindy was living with Dee at the time, she was not home.

"She had a steno book with a spiral binding. In this book, she had all these different things and says she wants me to do Ouija."

Dee refused. She was afraid. Yet Stella was frantic. She said she was reading the tarot cards and they indicated Bruce was going to die. She said she tried to pinpoint it but couldn't.

"Dee, it's real important to me. I've got to know what's going on; what is going to happen."

Dee told SA Cusack she looked at the steno pad and saw notes Stella had written indicating Bruce was going to die in a car or truck accident. She was looking for a date.

"Stella, you cannot change this. It is destiny. You cannot change it, and if you do you'll pay. If this is how Bruce chose to die, you have no right to change his destiny."

"She begged me to do it," Dee said later, adding that she finally gave in.

"If you really want me to," she said. "If it is really that important to you, I'll do it. But I don't own a Ouija."

"I'll get you one," Stella said quickly.

She never heard from Stella again on the subject of the Ouija.

SA Cusack told Marshall Stone about this latest from the Rogers/Hamilton camp.

"It would give us some traction if we could get that damn notebook out of Stella's house."

"Yeah, if it exists," Stone answered.

The steno book was interesting because it clearly was different from the diary Cindy had seen in the trailer setting up the kidnapping plot.

Cusack didn't doubt the story. Others might have thought Dee was painting in the colors to fill in the gaps because she wanted the reward. He didn't think so. He believed her.

During a subsequent interview, Dee told Jack Cusack about the camping trip she and Stella had taken to Eastern Washington after Bruce died.

The Seamurs case agent figured Stella had asked Dee to come along because she wanted to use her as a sounding board.

"Dee was New York tough, and Stella needed to run her story by someone, just to test the waters," he said.

Whatever Cora Lee knew or didn't know about the crime, she wasn't going to say much to Sandy Scott. She stopped by the Scotts' place and chatted for a while the morning of April 13, 1987.

They talked about insurance. Sandy was still bothered by a rec-

ollection of three policies Stella had fanned out at the kitchen table
in front of SA Ike Nakamoto.

Cora Lee said that as far as she knew her daughter had only a
single policy—for $20,000—on top of the one from Bruce's job.

Cora Lee thought highly of Big Mac, but she took the opportunity to disparage Dee Rogers again.

Stella's mother complained that Dee hadn't been out to the property to see the Nickells since Cora Lee moved there in June of
1985. But the minute Bruce died, the pushy New Yorker was there.

"She came out here and took over," Cora Lee said, still bitter
over the camping trip she and Stella took after Bruce died. "She
said she was 'going to take Stella away from all of this.' "

Cora Lee said she knew why: Dee Rogers smelled money, and
that was the reason she reentered their lives.

Sandy asked if Stella's wayward daughter had turned up yet.

"Stella knows where Cindy is, but she won't tell me."

Sandy thought that was strange. Why didn't Stella want her
mother to know where her daughter was staying?

Cora Lee was also afraid she and Stella would lose their mobile
homes and the five acres.

"Stella is so far behind on her bills!" she told Sandy Scott.

That same week, Cora Lee called her daughter Berta in Michigan. "I might say the wrong thing," a frightened and tense Cora
Lee told her daughter about her upcoming appearance before the
grand jury. "They might take anything the wrong way!"

As the two talked, Berta picked up information suggesting her
little sister had been framed. The third bottle was among the tidbits
Cora Lee shared.

"Medicines were kept in the kitchen, not in the bathroom. If
there was one in the bathroom, it was a plant," Berta said later.

In mid-April, another pack of Stella Nickell's friends and others
gathered to testify before the grand jury. As they sat in the hallway,
waiting to go into the jury room, the SEIB's Sandy Sorby and Pam
Stegenga listened to an old woman, who identified herself as the
suspect's mother.

Though they had been instructed not to talk with one another,
Cora Lee was not following any orders.

Cora Lee asked Sandy Sorby if she was a friend of her daughter's, and the Olympia woman explained that she had met her only one time.

"I know they are thinking Stella did it," Cora Lee said, "but there is no way she would have done it. I don't know why they are doing this."

Cora Lee talked quite a bit about cyanide, saying that her daughter did, in fact, have some of the deadly poison.

"She uses it in her aquarium . . . we also used it to kill coyotes."

Sandy and Pam could see the pain Stella's mother was enduring. All the old woman wanted to do was protect her daughter.

Harry Swanson, still standing by his woman, as he had since she dumped him for Bruce in the mid-seventies, also went before the grand jury in April. He stayed overnight at Stella's place and kept the government's per diem for hotel. He felt as though he was really showing that damn FBI.

Stella Nickell might have convinced her closest friends that she and Jim McCarthy had never been intimate. Harry Swanson, for one, believed her. Fred Phelps, however, refused to buy it.

Early in his affair with his co-worker, he came into her mobile home and saw her engaged in a "passionate embrace" with the man she introduced as Jim McCarthy, or "Mac."

"There's nothing to this," Stella said.

The remark spoke volumes.

Fred said he didn't care either way. Who was he to care?

One morning Stella got up to answer the telephone when Fred was still in bed. It was Jim McCarthy, and the call left Stella fuming.

"That was the kiss-off," Fred later speculated.

He wondered if Mac had been involved with Stella before Bruce Nickell's death. But it was none of his business, so he put it out of his mind.

Stella Nickell, looking the worse for wear, stopped by for coffee at Sandy Scott's. She was grim, angry, something was burning her up.

"What is it?" Sandy asked.

"I think Cindy turned me in." Her tone was resentful and sad at the same time.

"Oh, Stella, don't be silly."

The look on Stella's face was without a hint of doubt.

"Why in the world would Cindy do that?"

"For the money. She's doing it for the money."

Sandy tried to console her neighbor, but it wouldn't work. "She's your daughter, she wouldn't do that."

"You don't know my daughter. She'd do it for the money."

CHAPTER 63

Living with Paul Webking and his son, Damon, was like living with roommates. Hayley Snow's nighttime curfew utterly disappeared. She could do whatever she wanted. Some teenagers would jump for joy at such freedom. At sixteen, Sue Snow's daughter felt abandoned, with no reason to come home.

Money pulled them even further apart.

"He told us when he got the insurance money he was going to pay off the house bills and put the rest into CDs for us. We trusted him," she said later.

But in the spring the year after Sue died, money became inexplicably tight. Paul told Hayley she'd have to dip into her Social Security to help keep things going on N Street.

When Paul was out of the house, Hayley went to his desk to see what she could find out about her mother's missing jewelry, the family finances. But it was locked.

She vented her frustration in her diary on May 4, 1987.

> Paul—Oh God he's a dick! Now he tells me we're broke. I suppose he's spent all of Mommy's insurance, too. $20,000 worth . . . I may as well move out. I live on my own anyhow.

Every chance she got, Wilma Stewart and her baby made the trip over the mountains to see Richard at the Fred Hutchinson Cancer Research Center in Seattle. She almost always stayed overnight with her aunt in Auburn.

It was during one of these trips that she saw her mother for the first time in years.

Wilma was in the bathroom blow-drying her hair when Stella told her Georgia Mae was on her way over from Cora Lee's trailer. It was more of a warning than an announcement. Their estrangement had been so long, Wilma decided it was time to face her mother.

Holding her six-week-old, Wilma stuck out the olive branch, not knowing if her mother would take it or bite it off.

"How are you?"

"Fine," Georgia answered. Her voice had not warmed over the years.

"I miss you."

"You should."

"I need you. You know Richard is dying."

"Well, you deserve it, the way you lived your life."

That was enough. Wilma didn't want to listen anymore. As she turned away, the last words Wilma heard were: "I hope that bitch you're holding . . ."

Wilma put the baby into Stella's outstretched arms and started down the hallway after her mother. Georgia made a run for the front of the mobile home.

"Nobody is going to say that about my daughter!" Wilma yelled, taking a swing at Georgia. Cora Lee stopped her from hitting her.

"Grandma, get out of my way!"

"All the anger was like bile in my stomach was rising. I wanted . . . forget the fact that I'm a Christian . . . 'Let me get ahold of her!' " Wilma Stewart recalled years later.

It had not been a happy reunion. Stella's favorite niece was angry and hurt, and there was no one to help. No one, except SA Hill.

"Dave Hill was the kind of person I could scream at, then I could go to Seattle to see Richard and call him up and say, 'Dave, I just need someone to talk to.' "

Sometimes both would agree the conversation was "off the record" and personal.

Stella Maudine hoisted herself out of bed one morning and told Fred Phelps she had to meet with her lawyer. It was an excuse she often used. In fact, she had heard the indictment could come any time, and she needed an attorney. The Nickells' lawyer, Bill Donais, was in far over his head, and he and Stella both knew it.

On May 14, 1987, Stella did what she had to do: she filed a financial affidavit for a government attorney. She listed her salary as $621, and monthly payments on her property, two Visa cards, and a MasterCard totaling more than $650.

The next day, a thirty-nine-year-old federal public defender with a faint country twang named Tom Hillier was appointed to represent her.

Tom Hillier's most famous case was one he lost. It involved his defense of a Puget Sound man named Steve Titus who was wrongly convicted of a rape—because of police shenanigans and a polygraph that made him out to be a liar. He knew firsthand that polygraphs were not an exact science.

Stella Nickell found great comfort in that. At least that was one area she wouldn't have to argue.

Defense Investigator Sal Ramos considered Tom Hillier "pathetically committed" to his client.

"If you're in trouble, you would hope you had him. He was more emotional than Stella, he'd be hurt more by things that would happen than she would," Ramos said later.

When Stella Nickell walked into the Federal Public Defender's office in Seattle, it was with purpose and style. The purpose, clearly, was to save her neck, the style, decidedly western. She wore her fringed buckskin jacket, western shirt, even a scarf. She also carried a briefcase, a kind of 1970s vinyl relic, that contained the start of her war chest.

"Just takin' care of business," was the way Sal Ramos described the client's attitude. If he had been suspected of such a crime, the thirty-nine-year-old investigator knew he would have been a wreck.

Stella Nickell was cool. Guilty or innocent, she carried off the whole matter as if it were some kind of major inconvenience. When she spoke, she often seemed remote. She used a short laugh to punctuate her conversation. She posed for muglike photos, and then, with a click of her cowboy boots, she was on her way.

Katy Hurt's life had improved substantially since she and Cindy Hamilton had been roommates at the low-income housing of Auburn's River Terrace in 1985. She was married and had a second baby, another beautiful daughter. She had given up drugs and alcohol and had happily settled into a calm new life. Katy and her new baby and Cindy were driving through Kent one afternoon when Cindy told her that the FBI might be contacting her.

"I didn't even think I knew anything that would make a difference," she said later.

"I gave them your name," Cindy said at the time, "and I told them about that incident that I told you about where I came back from my mom's."

Katy didn't hesitate.

"I'll go for you. I don't have a problem with that."

Cindy told her friend that there was a $300,000 reward being offered and some were saying she was after the money.

"I wasn't even supposed to know about it, but some FBI agent told me," she said, adding that he was taken off the case for telling her.

"I really don't care if I get it," Cindy told Katy.

"If anyone deserves reward money, you do. Nobody else does. You're the one stepping forward, and it is your mother. You're the one who should be compensated. It's never gonna make everything all right."

And while Cynthia Lea was shoring up her story, Sue Snow's survivors finally learned that someone else, in fact, was being investigated for Sue's murder—and it wasn't Paul Webking.

Sarah Webb got the news about Stella Nickell from an attorney working on the suit against Bristol-Myers. It was hard to swallow.

She told a friend visiting in Artesia:

"I still think Paul's the killer . . . we just can't prove it. . . ."

Hayley and Exa Snow just wanted to know who had done it. They were focused on the lawsuit, which was dealt a blow when a federal judge dismissed the negligence portion against the drug manufacturer.

But, as Hayley Beth Snow learned, no matter what—you go on.

The bartender at Kent's Virginia Inn baby-sat Cindy Hamilton and Dee Rogers as the investigation pushed on. She let them get as sloppy drunk as they wanted, and looked the other way when they danced on the bar. When they were too drunk to drive, they happily surrendered their car keys to the woman.

There wasn't a soul in the taverns around Kent who didn't know Cindy had gone against her mother, mostly because the star witness did little to keep it secret.

"Hey, I've been with the FBI all day!"

Cindy needed to say little more, and a bottle would be set before her.

During this time, it seemed to hit Cindy that her mother had a big price to pay. They even talked about capital punishment, but Cindy had learned that no federal crimes carry the highest penalty. Murder, of course, was different.

"I don't think I could kill my mother. What if the federal case falls through and the state brings murder charges?"

Before Dee could respond, Cindy answered her own question.

"I will not testify."

Cindy also said she was worried about what the trial would do to the family; she was especially worried about her grandmother.

Dee told her she had to go on, not think about that.

"You have to do what's right."

Sometimes they talked about Wilma Stewart.

Dee Rogers had her own take on why Cindy and Wilma were on opposite sides when it came to Stella Maudine. Stella had taken Wilma in when she was growing up, yet she didn't seem to want her own flesh and blood.

"There was jealousy with Cindy when Wilma got the respect and love Cindy wanted from her mother."

As Dee and Cindy talked about it, and as the FBI probed deeper to learn the loyalties of the clan, the roommates were clear where Wilma Stewart stood. And it made them furious.

"She wasn't here," Cindy said. "She didn't see what we saw! She doesn't know what we know!"

All Wilma Stewart knew was that she loved Aunt Stella.

Jack Cusack made enough appearances down at Olympic Security to give Stella's old boss Gerry McIntyre cause to believe his former employee was the tamperer.

Company president Mark Vinson thought so too.

"They're gonna nail her," he said.

The FBI agent had searched in vain for traces of cyanide in the locker Stella used. He dug up employment records and time cards showing Stella had been off the days before Bruce's death.

But so had Cindy.

The fact that Cindy Hamilton had waited before coming forward with her story didn't surprise Gerry McIntyre. She was biding her time for a reason, the reward.

"Knowing what I know of Cynthia Hamilton and knowing the majority of people on the face of the earth, if there's a way to make a buck, they're gonna do it. Somebody saw some money. Cindy was no fool. And she wouldn't be anybody's fool. She'd whip your butt in about thirty seconds, and she was big enough to do it," he said.

At the end of May 1987, doctors told Wilma Mae Stewart her ten-year-old son was terminal. Radiation treatments at Fred Hutchinson had proved ineffective—the leukemia had returned. Richard had four—maybe six—weeks left. Stella Nickell's niece turned to Dave Hill for support. He took her for a walk along the pathways of the University of Washington's gorgeous arboretum. SA Hill postponed Wilma's grand jury appearance for the second time.

CHAPTER 64

Stella Nickell came into Ron Miller's office at Burns International one June morning with an offer to resign. A front-page article in *The Seattle Times* was the impetus. Though it did not mention her name, the headline read:

**TAMPERING PROBE CENTERS ON 1 SUSPECT
NO CHARGES YET IN YEAR-OLD CASE**

She told her boss it was she who was under suspicion for the tampering murders. She was concerned the media would find her at her job.

"I know that adverse publicity can affect you."

Once over the shock of his employee's true confession, Ron Miller felt he owed her some measure of loyalty. She hadn't been charged with the crime, and she was a good worker. Ron listened with great sympathy—and mentally scratched her name off the promotion's list.

"Ron, I didn't do it. I want you to know that I didn't do any of the things they are saying."

Then she talked about Cynthia Lea. Stella said her daughter and another person had cooked up the story to try to get the reward.

"She was not real complimentary," Miller recalled later. "She said she was a 'money-grubber' and she was strictly after the money—a large amount of cash."

"Cynthia is an extremely greedy person," she said. "No matter who she hurt or how, she was going to get some money."

Ron Miller couldn't bring himself to believe Stella was shrewd enough, conniving enough, even smart enough to have done the crime.

"I just didn't think that it was possible that she could concoct the whole thing and carry it out," he said later.

As the weeks passed, Wilma Stewart began to believe Richard was going to survive his heroic battle with leukemia. Ongoing prayers had been answered. When her on-again, off-again husband, Mel Stewart, suggested a drive to Lincoln City, Oregon, over the Fourth of July holiday, she agreed.

After a couple of nights near the Pacific shore, the Stewarts returned to the Tri-Cities, stopping only to buy a sheepskin, with hope that the soft fur would offer Richard some relief. The boy had been suffering bleeding ulcers.

When she heard the phone ringing, Wilma, without answering, knew what it was about.

Mel hung up the phone and went to his wife. "Richard died this morning . . . at 2:55. His last words were 'Mommy . . . Mommy . . . Mommy.' "

After her son's funeral in the northern part of Washington State, Wilma and Mel took their baby and went to see Richard one last time. "My first impulse was to get on the ground and start digging him up out of that dark place. The other part was saying, 'You've got to maintain. You have a baby,' " she recalled later.

In mid-July, newspapers across the state carried an AP story about the cyanide case. The Wenatchee *World* headlined it:

PILL VICTIM WIDOW NOW CHIEF SUSPECT

That same day, Marshall Stone arrived at Stan and Laurie Church's place, now an apartment in Pacific, a tiny town south of Auburn. In what continued to surprise both the Churches and Stella Nickell, it was the first time an FBI agent had contacted the Nickells' closest friends. Daughter Karan was also at home.

SA Stone set his briefcase on the kitchen table and they all sat

down on the yellow dinette chairs. Stan Church explained that he
was on the way out the door for the shipyards, but he told the young
FBI agent that while their friend might have been smart enough to
do such a crime, she flat out didn't do it. He told the agent his wife
would tell him the same thing.

Laurie Church appreciated the vote of confidence. She needed
it. She was so anguished about the whole thing, she could barely
look Marshall Stone in the eye. She wanted to help her best friend.

*Maybe if they found someone who believed in her they would
find out they were making a mistake?* she wondered.

SA Stone worked from a prepared list of questions pulled from
his briefcase, marking them off as he asked. He wanted to know
how Stella had acted when she came over to tell them Bruce had
died.

"She cried. Any woman who lost her husband would," Laurie
said.

"Did you know the Nickells were filing for divorce?"

"No."

"Why not?"

"Because it's not true. If she was, she would have told me about
it."

Karan Church would have decked the guy if he hadn't been FBI.

"I got so angry with that man. When he came over to the house,
it wasn't like asking questions: 'Did you ever see them fight?' It
was more like: 'They did this!' And get a reaction from my parents," she said later. "I thought, rah rah, team."

"Did you know Bruce donated his eyes to the Lion's Eye Bank,
and that's how we were able to test for cyanide?" Stone asked.

"Bullshit!" Karan Church sputtered.

"What do you mean, 'bullshit'?"

"Stella turned in the lot numbers from the Excedrin bottles . . .
that's how they found out he died of cyanide."

*Can't you see? How could she be guilty if she had been the one
to call about the poisoning in the first place?* Karan thought.

When the Churches met with federal public defender Tom Hillier and investigator Sal Ramos, however, they felt they were with
allies. These men were going to do something to help their friend.

Tom Hillier asked if Laurie thought Stella could have done the
crime.

"No. Stella is the type of person who would take out a gun and
blow somebody's brains out, then call the sheriff and say she did

it. Poisoning someone is a sneaky way of doing things, and Stella is not a sneak. She is straightforward and direct. If she wanted to get rid of Bruce, she'd have blown his brains out. That's the way she is."

They talked about Stella's daughter. Cindy's name came up so frequently that later the Churches would insist Hillier must have considered the young woman the more viable suspect. In that light, the Churches told federal defender Hillier about Cindy's strange appearance at Kim Church's wedding.

"She acted as if there was no problem. You could not tell that her family member had passed away two days before. You could not tell there was something wrong."

Cindy was no angel, had no credibility. The drugs, the neglect of her little girl, whatever mud they had to sling was slung.

Tom Hillier seemed to take it all in.

By the time Stella's attorney left, Stan and Laurie had agreed to testify if needed, and even Karan was left with the impression she might be called to testify about Cindy.

Because of the rules of discovery, the defense, of course, didn't have anything in the way of real information on the government's case. All they had was Stella.

When the defense learned that A. J. Rider was considered a key government witness, Sal Ramos asked Stella why.

Stella didn't know.

"What could she tell them?"

Again, a blank.

"Well, where is she? Think, babe, think."

Babe. Hon. Ramos found himself using the same words as those used by the circle of friends kept by the suspect.

"Las Vegas, I think. It's been a while."

It wasn't much of a lead, but after a couple of days meandering around in a place he considered "ugly" and "desperate," Sal Ramos knocked on A. J. and Jim Rider's door. It was midmorning.

While her son and daughter played in the pool, A. J. jump-started her lungs with a cigarette and downed some microwave-heated coffee. She did not mince words. A. J. told Ramos the story of going with Stella to buy several bottles of Excedrin just days before Bruce Nickell collapsed.

Stella's former friend was adamant, foulmouthed; another of the hard-core, hard-living persons who ran in Stella Maudine's throng of friends.

He asked if she thought Stella killed Bruce.

"You're goddamn right the bitch killed him."

That was all he needed to know. He thanked her and left.

Hayley Snow spent July in Denver with her aunt Sarah, and though she had a happy time, she was surprised to find herself missing Paul. But even though his new wife had now moved out of the Auburn house, Sue Snow's teenage daughter had made up her mind that she would live with her aunt.

It seemed more like a home, more like a family.

With Paul, I feel I make him mad he won't love me
... NOT A GOOD FEELING

SA Jack Cusack ran the same time line through his mind chronologically, and much of it seemed to back up the bizarre story given by the suspect's daughter.

Work records from Bruce Nickell's job showed several instances when he had complained of stomach troubles that might have resulted from little black seeds his wife gave him.

The final weeks of desperation seemed to support Cindy's story as well. In late April, Stella Nickell had written the lien-holder that her problems were about to be solved and her husband was no longer involved.

By May, Stella Nickell had declared she was sick of fighting with her husband and called Wilma Mae Stewart to see if she could live with her. Yet she never showed up. Then, on May 27, a foreclosure notice was sent to the Nickells. That very same day, she shopped at Johnny's and Pay 'N Save North. A. J. Rider said she saw Stella buy more than one bottle of Excedrin.

On June 1, Stella had written to North Pacific Bank and said her payments would stay current. She still didn't have any money—how could she have told them that? Two days later, she shopped at Albertson's and Johnny's—two places where tainted capsules were later found. On June 5, Bruce Nickell was dead.

CHAPTER 65

Smoke from twin cigarettes corkscrewed the heavy air of her aunt's trailer as Wilma Stewart sucked on a menthol-eucalyptus cough drop and suffered the battle the FBI and her aunt had waged for her allegiance. She smoked and said little as she listened to her troubled aunt Stella drone on.

"Those goddamn FBI! Every time I turn around they're here, poking their noses in someone else's business."

Stella Nickell rarely raised her voice in anger. She was not the kind of woman who hammered her fist to a table. Even so, her wrath was never in doubt.

The woman in the tiger-striped vest, silver bangles, and tight Levi's was, as always, in total control.

"Killed Bruce for insurance money! Give me a break! They're trying to hang that on me as some kind of a motive . . . kill my husband for $200,000! I didn't even know about the Visa policies! No money could replace your uncle Bruce!"

It went on and on . . .

Two hundred thousand dollars! Wilma was sick of hearing the figure. She heard it from Aunt Stella and Dave Hill every time she sat down with either one of them. It was as though the two of them had sucked in their stomachs and jutted their jaws, face-to-face, in some bizarre shouting match.

Winner takes Wilma Mae.

Aunt Stella had no reason to kill her husband, not when the man was worth more alive than dead. He had a good job. He was back on his feet. No cause at all. She said so herself.

"Now, if the man had beat me into the floor every day and beaten me to a pulp, I might have possibly had a reason. But Bruce was not that type of person."

After hours of listening, with barely an instance when she could offer anything beyond an occasional nod, Wilma grew weary of the tirade.

She wanted to talk about what was going on in her own life, her troubled marriage, her son, her baby. Aunt Stella had so many problems, she couldn't be the person anymore.

Thank God I have Dave Hill, she thought.

The night before she was to testify before the grand jury, the government put Wilma Stewart and her four-month-old baby in a Seattle hotel overlooking I-5. It was exactly one month after she buried her little boy. Only one month. She adamantly maintained that her aunt was innocent, and that was the way she was going to approach the jurors.

Aunt Stella did not kill anyone. She just wouldn't.

When she looked at her aunt, she saw a mother figure, a friend. Stella Maudine Nickell was a woman who had overcome great hardship, and though she did not always make the best choices in life, she had survived.

"I did not agree with the way she lived her life. I did not condemn her for it, because mine was very similar," Wilma said later, holding back tears.

Stella was not a mommy type, and Wilma, at least before she had her daughter, had considered herself of a similar mold.

Stella hated Georgia, and so did Wilma.

"I could say to her, 'My mother is a bitch . . .' "

"She'd say, 'Well now, Wilma, things are going to get better. You don't need her. You have me.' "

When she looked at her aunt, she saw the single family member she could love and trust.

Aunt Stella is innocent, and the FBI and all their arguments about money could go straight to hell.

While the FBI watched her baby, Wilma testified about her aunt's phone call to Houston. Stella had asked her not to say anything to Bruce about her plans to leave him.

Joanne Maida asked if insurance money as a subject of conver-

sation came up, and the witness said it had—"all the time." Both
aunt and niece broached the subject.

The total was "close to two hundred grand."

All of the talk of insurance was irritating, she testified. She had
a new baby, and wanted to talk about her. But all conversations
seemed to focus on money.

"I mean, my uncle had died and he was a really neat person,
and I was getting sick and tired of hearing about what she was
going to get."

Wilma Mae Stewart tried to skirt the Houston issue.

"I was in deep shit," she said, looking back, "and didn't know
how to get out of it."

And yet, she still trusted Dave Hill and the FBI.

"They were being very nice to me. *Very, very* nice to me."

After the grand jury, Wilma Stewart drove to Auburn and stayed
the night at the property with Stella and Fred. Her aunt entertained
her baby daughter with a musical teddy bear, and Wilma was filled
with hope that things would work out after all. A miracle hadn't
spared Richard, but maybe something would save her aunt. Maybe
Cynthia Lea would come to her senses?

There had to be a way out.

Some time later she asked her aunt to consider changing her
stance. From what she was hearing from Dave Hill, it didn't look
like Stella would walk away from this without going to prison.

"Has it ever dawned on you to confess to this and throw yourself
at the mercy of the court?"

"I'm not doing that," Stella Maudine said, her face frozen in
that look of utter determination she seemed to wear like a mask.

One evening the first week of September 1987, while Bob and Pat
Strong were eating pizza, Cindy Hamilton knocked on the door of
their Ranchero Way home in Garden Grove and reentered their
lives. She acted as though she'd never been away, though it had
been at least seven, maybe eight years since they'd seen her last.
She just showed up. She and her trucker boyfriend needed a place
to stay. Her daughter wasn't with her. The little girl had been living
with her father's ex-wife since Cindy sent her there just before
Bruce Nickell died.

The next day, Cindy started talking.

"I guess you heard about Mom," she said.

They had.

"Well, I'm going to be testifying against her."

The information surprised them. The Strongs couldn't understand why.

"I can't discuss any of it until after the trial," she said.

Cindy was there to hide out and wait for her mother's trial. She told them that only Jack Cusack of the FBI knew her whereabouts. On September 2, she made the first of many calls to the Seattle FBI office, to check in.

"I don't want the family to know where I am," she said. "And I don't want the press to know either."

The Strongs knew Stella was in big trouble, but they hadn't known Cindy was going to testify. Both Pat and Bob felt it was somewhat believable that Stella might discuss Bruce's murder with Cindy. The two were extremely close.

As though she needed to bolster her story that she could have been a victim, and therefore could not have been involved in the tamperings, Cindy changed her story on "almost taking the capsules" after Bruce's funeral.

She now claimed she had the bottle in her hand and was about to take some capsules, when she remembered they had Advil in the house.

She put the capsules back in the bottle and took some Advil, because "Advil is stronger."

"It could have been me too," Cindy said, shaking her head. She might have died by her mother's hand.

Bob Strong felt as if he wasn't getting the whole story.

"When I seen my daughter down here . . . she was secretive, like. . . . I realize that everybody's private life is their own, but it just seemed like it was more than that with Cindy. It seemed like she was always trying to hide something," Bob Strong said years later.

Cindy said she had nothing to hide. She told the Strongs she had even been polygraphed by the FBI and passed with flying colors. Bob didn't give a hoot about any polygraph.

"It don't mean a thing," he said later.

Cindy didn't say much about Bruce and Stella, but occasionally something slipped.

She told Bob that she would get up in the morning and cook breakfast for Bruce.

"Mom would come out and be really upset and jealous at us being out there."

Bob could easily believe that. Stella was jealous of anything that wore a skirt.

Over the next few weeks, Stella's eldest daughter eventually got a job "temping" and working for an answering service in Costa Mesa, and she seemed to slip into old habits. Sometimes she disappeared at night.

Stella Nickell's bottle-to-the-mouth drinking and mental depression had worn her down. She seemed lost. She was still working at Burns, though boss Ron Miller had moved her to a much less visible position as a scheduler in the office.

"I'm the guilty one in the government's eyes, but I didn't do it," Stella told Laurie Church over coffee at Andy's in Auburn.

"Why don't you just leave?" Laurie suggested.

Stella said she couldn't leave her mother, or the property.

"Besides, if I ran," she added, "they'd be right after me. We're talking federal government: 'She ran, she's guilty. That proved it.' I'm going to stay right here and show them I'm not."

Laurie wasn't so sure about her friend's strategy. If she were Stella, she'd have been in South America like a shot.

"I know they're going to get me," Stella said. "Every time I turn around I'm looking at an FBI agent. They seem to be standing outside my house. I know they are going to arrest me. I don't know when, I just know they are."

Hayley Snow kept the secret from Paul Webking for three days. She had finally decided she was going to accept the invitation to move to Egypt with Aunt Sarah and Uncle Rodney on his new job assignment.

Paul seemed stunned.

"Are you sure? Are you sure you're not running away? I'm concerned about how you're handling your mother's death, that's all."

Hayley understood, but she was going anyway.

"I *want* to go." She had to get away from Auburn.

On September 16, 1987, she wrote in her diary:

I'm beginning to understand his side. Now, it's hard. I'm yanked from Paul to my family. They'll never like him . . . Aunt Sarah and I argued. She says Paul is trying to make me feel guilty for going.

As if the whole story at once was too painful, or too difficult to recall, Cindy Hamilton dropped information in erratic snatches. At one point, she told SA Cusack she recalled something about her mother's using library encyclopedias to research cyanide. As she had been before, she seemed a bit unsure, a bit vague.

She did not know where, but a good bet was the Auburn library. Marshall Stone returned to Auburn, and again added another win to his successful library search for evidence.

SA Stone packed up several "C" volumes from the Auburn Public Library, and again, more pay dirt from Carl Collins and the FBI lab.

Sections on cyanide in the various encyclopedias also turned up prints. *McGraw-Hill's Encyclopedia of Science and Technology* turned up nine of Stella Nickell's latent fingerprints and one latent palm print.

Two more of Stella's fingerprints appeared in the *New Caxton Encyclopedia*.

Finally, five additional fingerprints and another palm were detected in the cyanide section of the *Merit Student's Encyclopedia*.

CHAPTER 66

Contact became infrequent between Stella Nickell and Sandy Scott after the grand jury. When defense investigator Sal Ramos contacted Sandy for an interview, she called Jack Cusack. He told her she could decline if she wished. She did. Sandy Scott wondered if that had been the reason for her neighbor's distance.

In October 1987, however, the women crossed paths on the gravel road in between their properties.

"Any news on the case?"

Stella shook her head. There wasn't much to report. Things had slowed considerably since the grand jury convened in March and April.

"If the grand jury can't or won't reach a decision, then the case will be allowed to just fade away," she said.

"Heard from Cindy at all?"

"No, I haven't," she replied. "But I have an idea where she is."

Two days later, Cora Lee walked up the hill to get some tomatoes Sandy had promised. The visit was pleasant, but it was the last the two would share. A week and a half later, another neighbor returned some books Cora Lee had borrowed.

"Stella's mother doesn't want to talk with you anymore."

Tom Hillier dispatched Sal Ramos to interview after interview with friends and those considered adversaries. The one they could never pin down, and who flat out refused to talk with them, was the government's leading witness, Cynthia Lea Hamilton.

Sal Ramos was certainly a competent investigator with an impressive résumé. He had been a research specialist for migrant workers for HEW, and had a contract with the Bureau of Prisons concerning opening halfway houses for rehabilitation.

In October he made his first visit out to Stella's "desperate little trailer" in Auburn. While his client chatted and scuttled about the kitchen fixing glasses of iced tea, Sal couldn't help but notice how Stella, though still all business, had relaxed somewhat over the months. She even showed a sense of humor when she served iced tea.

As she set the glasses on the table, there was a slight waver.

"Why don't you take this one?" she said with a sly smile. "Come on, I'll take yours."

Her short laugh punctuated the moment.

"Am I still going to have the wrong one?" he joked back.

Dave Hill continued to work Wilma Stewart, and Stella's niece continued to see the man as a friend. She needed one.

Her daughter came down with spinal meningitis in late September, and by the first week in October her teeter-tottering marriage to Mel Stewart was over. This time he moved out for good.

There was no doubt Dave Hill believed Aunt Stella had been the killer. He said so many times. Yet somehow, and though she was never able to put her finger on it, Wilma believed that in the FBI man's kindness he didn't really want her to believe her aunt had tampered with the capsules.

"It was almost like my whole life had been so rough up to this point that I don't want to ruin this panacea of the only person you can hold on to in this family."

For Wilma, it was as if SA Hill was saying: *"I don't want you to know that she's the same kind of person your mother is."*

Of course, he never said any such thing.

At times, however, he'd tell Wilma things about the reward. He said he hoped there was some way of getting some money to Cora Lee, who would surely lose her place without the cash.

He said the FBI believed Stella didn't want to feel guilty about taking any other lives, so she called 911 as soon as she heard of Sue Snow's death. She might have moved the Anacin-3 bottle at the store, just to save some lives.

"Her conscience was getting to her," he said.

Stella's niece refused to fall into the trap of acceptance. "Why should her conscience get to her? She did not do it. And that's a fact!"

From the Webbs' rented flat in Cairo, Hayley summed up her life on October 29, 1987:

> Sometimes I forget all that's happened to me and I pretend I'm Hayley Snow with a perfectly normal life. Look what's happened . . . We leave Daddy when I'm 5 years old, Move to N.M. There almost a year, come back. We introduce Mommy and Paul. We move into Auburn. Sister leaves. Paul moves in next door. Then moves in with us. We get our own house. Grandpa comes, passes away in Sister's room while Kristin is staying over. Paul cheats on Mommy. They finally get married. Everything gets normal, Mommy dies of cyanide, something the whole world knows about. Paul & I try to stay together. Something doesn't hang right there. Here I am now, sitting in Egypt with my Aunt, Uncle and Cousin.

Stella Nickell's days of freedom were slipping by. On November 4, Joanne Maida filled out an "Indictment Status Sheet." Arrest was imminent, though a few loose ends needed tending.

It was Joanne Maida's nearly obsessive need to cover loose ends that caused some frustration down the hill at the FBI office. No one doubted the woman's capability. But for some, the grand jury process had dragged on far too long. Jack Cusack, for one, wanted Stella Nickell picked up right away. Cindy Hamilton had told the Seamurs case agent her mother might commit suicide if faced with prison, and Jack Cusack didn't want Stella Maudine to take the back way out.

It was now clear the government's case was going to hinge on the insurance money and the proceeds from a civil lawsuit Nickell filed against Bristol-Myers the month after Bruce died as the motives. The alleged affair with Jim McCarthy, although it might have been the impetus, would not be stressed because it would only serve to cloud the issue and confuse the jury.

As the indictment neared, federal grand jurors continued to meet on the case. Cusack had lunch with documents expert Lee Waggoner at the Metropolitan Grill across the street from the Federal Building.

Both men were frustrated with Joanne Maida. In her zealousness to tie up the case, she had pressed Lee Waggoner on the subject of the Nickell signatures he was still unsure about.

"You can't tell me that Stella Nickell signed for this insurance?"

"No. She may have, but I can't say with certainty."

While Stella waited for the FBI to come calling with an arrest warrant, she passed her free time and days off drinking Wild Turkey and reading the Bible. Fred Phelps also watched her send money to television preachers Oral Roberts, Robert Schuller, even Jimmy Swaggart.

"What are you watching that for?" Fred Phelps asked, not waiting for an answer. "If you want that, go to church instead of watching these fools."

"It makes me feel better," she said.

He didn't argue. He had learned soon after he moved in that no one argues with this lady.

Even when the money was scarce, she still donated whatever she could scrounge from her purse or bank account. Stella Maudine always had money for the preacher.

Later, Stella would say that she didn't watch that kind of broadcast religion.

"I do not like religion in that way. If I want religion, I go to church. I don't like television preachers. With mother sitting with me, I had watched one or two."

She did not study the scriptures, either.

"I had read through the New Testament three or four different times. Every so often I would sit down and read it, because you pick up something new every time. I believe in God, yes. I believe in a higher divine power."

CHAPTER 67

Stella Nickell had made a fine scheduler for Burns, but it wasn't to be a career.

"I've got the word they are going to arrest me at work," she said with the matter-of-fact calmness that continued to amaze Ron Miller.

He put Stella on a leave of absence and told her they'd play it by ear. If she wasn't arrested soon, she'd be reinstated as an active employee.

"Fred was a lot more nervous about the whole thing than Stella appeared to be. Fred can be very jittery, visibly nervous. She didn't show anything," Ron Miller later said.

Stuck at home and unemployed, Stella seemed to grow more depressed. All she was doing was drinking and waiting, waiting for Jack Cusack to come and pick her up. Fred joined her and her bottle when he got home from Burns. Since she didn't want to go out anymore, she usually planted herself on the davenport cuddled up with an afghan, drinking Wild Turkey and coffee.

One night in early December while the couple was watching a video, some old *Conan*-type thing, Stella reportedly let her guard down for the first, and only, time.

She rested her head on Fred's shoulder and started to cry.

"I'd looked at her and she had tears coming down her face," he said later.

It's not like Stel.

"I did it," she said.

"What are you talking about?"

"I did it," she repeated.

"I know," he said.

Stella Maudine cried some more, and Fred held her.

"We never talked about it again. I didn't give a shit one way or another. It didn't bother me," he said later.

Fred Phelps never told anyone about what Stella had said. Nobody ever asked.

Tom Hillier told Stella her arrest was looming; in fact, he had arranged through the U.S. Attorney's office to have her surrender when the indictment was handed down. She was no danger to society, he said, and had had ample time to run over the past year and a half.

SA Cusack thought the very idea was not only ridiculous, but insulting.

"Send a goddamn letter! Here's a woman who killed two people, one she didn't even know, and the government was going to send her a note or make a phone call so she could waltz into jail?"

Around that time, doing one of his "double-back" interviews, Jack Cusack took the scenic drive over to the Olympic Peninsula to meet Harry Swanson at Nancy's Café one last time.

"I only have one question to ask you today, Harry. Does Stella pack a gun in her purse?"

"Jack, you've known that for eighteen months. You know where the gun is in the back door, the front door, the rifle rack in the den, the bed stand."

Harry Swanson babbled on. "She's a woman. Name a woman who don't pack a gun or Mace in her purse."

SA Cusack knew Stella Nickell didn't carry a gun at Burns. She didn't have a permit. So what did the love of Harry's life do with her gun when she was on duty?

"It's under the seat in the pickup. You're gonna arrest her, aren't you?"

"No, no," he lied.

Jack Cusack returned to Seattle, reported the gun information, and phoned Sandy Scott to ask her to take a jog through the brush to see if Stella and Fred's vehicles were still there.

"Don't let her know you're watching her," he said, though he needn't have. Sandy Scott had taken her mission as an FBI spy to heart; she was getting good at sneaking around the saplings. She wrote in her log that she did a check at 2:45 P.M. on December 7. She followed that with two more entries the next day, one at 8:55 A.M. and the other at 3:40 P.M.

December 9, 1987, eighteen months after the case began with Hayley Snow's call to 911, Jack Cusack took the stand before the grand jury. His testimony concerned fingerprints on library books.

He told Ron Nichols to get a car from the garage ready to go before he went to testify. If a True Bill indictment was sent down, both wanted to be able to make the trip to Auburn in time to be the ones arresting Stella Maudine Nickell. Auburn police detective Mike Dunbar and SA Marshall Stone were already there, watching the Nickell place from the gravel road.

After the Assistant U.S. Attorney asked her last question, the silver-haired special agent asked if he'd be recalled. She said no, he was finished, and Cusack and Nichols set out for Auburn.

At around 11 A.M., they arrived on the dirt road cutting between the Nickells' and Scotts' property. Just as they neared the knoll above Stella's mobile home, the call came in that the five-count—one for each bottle—indictment had been handed down.

Cusack knocked on the trailer door, and Fred Phelps answered.

"We're here for Stella. You must be Fred," he said as Stella's boyfriend was frisked and secured.

"Stel doesn't feel good, she's laying down. We knew you were coming . . . just didn't think it'd be so soon," Fred said.

"Are there any guns in the house?"

"Yeah, a .357 pistol in the bedroom, a .22 automatic in the bedroom, there's a rifle out here, a shotgun out here, they're all loaded."

While the agents gathered the weapons, Stella came from the bedroom, still in her bathrobe. She looked pale. She didn't even have her Kool-Aid-red lipstick on.

"Stella, you are under arrest. Consider yourself in our custody. Don't move."

She was shown the warrant and advised of her rights.

"I understand," she said softly. She seemed resigned, nearly emotionless.

Agents checked out the bedroom and cleared it of firearms, before allowing the prisoner to dress for the ride downtown to the King County Jail.

She put on slacks, cowboy boots, a plain shirt, and pulled her black hair back in a barrette. She allowed herself one ring, a Casale watch, and a lion's-head pin as her only adornment. The jacket she chose would provoke the most comment later. It was a blue windbreaker embroidered with her late husband's name.

On the way in, little was said. Stella Nickell listened to Christmas carols on the radio.

Jack Cusack hummed right along. Finally, it was done. Finally, she was on her way to jail.

That afternoon the winds picked up, eventually gusting to fifty mph. It was fitting weather for arrest. More than an inch of rain had fallen since the day before. Trees crashed in the Green River valley.

Cora Lee, bundled up in the driving rain, told the lone reporter seeking a comment from her that her daughter was innocent.

"If she is not found innocent, I tell you I will take it to a higher court."

Cynthia Hamilton found out her mother had been arrested when it came on the news. She called Cusack and complained vociferously.

"Goddamn it! Doesn't anybody do their job and keep me informed?"

Over the next few days, the prisoner made two appearances in court. First a detention hearing was held and the U.S. Magistrate denied bail, citing that the government's evidence—which was sealed—indicated their case was strong. In a five-minute appearance that Friday, Stella Maudine Nickell was arraigned and pleaded not guilty to each of the five counts before a federal judge. She managed a smile for Fred Phelps. Trial date was set for February 16, 1988.

CHAPTER 68

If she had looked like a heap destined for a King County landfill just before her arrest, Fred Phelps saw a different Stella Nickell when he went to visit her at the jail. It was as if a switch had been flicked and she now had the unmistakable air of confidence. She even looked younger, somehow. Refreshed. The waiting and Wild Turkey could no longer drag Stella down. Her winter-white skin glowed against her licorice-twist hair.

"I know one of the reasons Cynthia Lea is doing this," she finally said, seated in the visiting room. "She owed us money."

Stella said she and Bruce had bailed Cindy out financially more than a time or two. They were glad to do it, but they had always expected they'd be reimbursed. Cindy found a way to get out from under her commitment.

By killing Bruce and setting up Stella to take the rap.

"I have it all written down somewhere," she said, but she needed Fred's help. In her briefcase, which was in TP 4 2, he'd find three ledgers. In the back of one were some entries outlining Cynthia's debts.

"Get them and go through them and look for the entries," she said. "She owes me twenty-three, twenty-four hundred dollars."

He'd also find a "board" in the back of the truck.

"I want you to burn it. Will you do that for me?"

Fred wanted to know what kind of board.

"You'll know it when you see it," she said. "It's in a thin box."

That afternoon, Fred Phelps poured himself a drink and sat at her kitchen table. The stack before him included the ledgers and a Ouija board he pulled from the truck.

He figured he had the "board" Stella had told him to destroy.

Why burn this? he thought. *Who believes in this shit anyway? What's the big deal?*

The first two ledgers showed no entries for anything concerning Cynthia Lea and any money she owed her mother. The third volume, a red-cornered and green-colored leatherlike bookkeeper's ledger, gave him pause. Three quarters into it, Stella's affable and rotund beau found some questions and statements—relating, he believed, to the Ouija board.

"I remember reading it," he said several years later. "They were up in the woods and stuff like that. She wanted to know basically when Bruce was going to die. If he would die by Christmas . . . Fourth of July. And would her boyfriend—the Indian guy—if he would leave his wife by then and when Bruce would die and come to her and shit like that.

"She was asking different questions—all about Bruce and Big Mac, all about Bruce's demise. Will he be dead by such and such? By this date?"

By Halloween?

By Thanksgiving?

Will Mac leave his wife for me if Bruce dies by . . .

There were about a dozen such handwritten pages; every third or fourth question related to Mac. And from what Fred Phelps read, he believed Stella's friend Dee Rogers was involved in some way. It was possible that she had been camping with Stella when the questions and answers were written.

The ledger made it all so clear. Fred had thought from day one that Stella and Mac had been seeing each other. He remembered the encounter with the two of them out at the property.

"They were in a passionate embrace, and that really surprised me. She said when you come over, just come in, she didn't expect me that night. I could just tell by the looks that came on both their faces," he said later.

Now with the Ouija board and ledger, it seemed Stella and Mac had been involved before Bruce's murder, but to what extent?

"With Bruce gone, she got the money, they would get together. But things started going tits-up," Fred later suggested.

When Stella called Fred the next day, he told her he couldn't find anything about Cindy's owing money.

Stella was impatient. "Well, I know damn well it's there."

"I looked at every page . . . but what is this shit I found in the back?"

"I don't know what you're talking about."

He read a line from the ledger.

"I want you to burn that book for me," she said.

Years later, Stella Nickell and Fred Phelps parted company because of what he had found in the truck—and what she had asked him to find. Stella's attorney, Tom Hillier, had told her to find proof that Cynthia owed the Nickells money.

"Tom wanted a page where I wrote down that Cynthia had owed me money, Dave [McMurphy] had owed Bruce and me money. I asked Fred to look for that page, it was in a red notebook . . . and it had two rings and something like a ledger. And I described it to Fred and told him to look for it and look to see if that page was in the back of it, because Bruce wanted me to keep track of everything Cynthia owed us so when she got on her feet she could pay it back."

Stella emphatically dismissed the very idea that she had kept a ledger or used a Ouija board to predict her husband's death.

"For one thing, if my husband's ever going to die, even if he had had emphysema and I knew for a fact that he was gonna die, I wouldn't wanna know *when*. So why would I question cards or whatever on this and then write it down? Because I believe in living the days right up to the last and letting come as a surprise whatever may be in store."

Fred Phelps later claimed he broke the Ouija board into pieces, doused it along with the ledger with gasoline and burned both in the barrel behind the Nickells' mobile home.

"Right after I did it, I was sorry I did it. As I was watching it burn, I thought I should have kept this. I don't know why."

Later, when Fred told Wilma about the journal and the Ouija board, she didn't believe him.

It sounded like some kind of a joke.

It was SAs Cusack and Nichols who climbed the grade from the Federal building to the King County Jail to hear what a little gal named Daphne Cole had to say.

The inmate told the FBI that Stella Nickell had admitted to her during the time they had been in jail together that she had killed her husband for the insurance money.

It would take all the agents' strength to stop from standing up and leaving, the information was so likely a fabrication. But what she said next kept them riveted to their chairs.

"She told me she got the cyanide out at Sundstrand."

Sundstrand.

There had been a fairly well-known case concerning a woman who had committed suicide by ingesting cyanide on Sundstrand property in Redmond.

Sundstrand.

They had cyanide in their labs out there.

And there was more. . . . Stella Nickell had worked for Eddie Bauer, whose corporate office was just a business park away from the Sundstrand operation.

No promises could be made to Cole; in fact, both investigators repeated several times that she would get nothing for the information, not money, not a reduced sentence. The only thing they'd do was move her to a Tacoma jail, and that was for protection. Jail ladies eat snitches with gravy for lunch.

Daphne Cole, questionable witness that she was, was added to the government's list.

Later, Stella Nickell refuted inmate Cole's tale. She had twisted all the information. Stella said she had been out on a job at Sundstrand on a tour with an employee to learn security responsibilities—*after* Bruce Nickell's death.

"There was a lab there. The kid explained that a woman had committed suicide with cyanide from the lab. She did it on the grounds at Sundstrand. I told my boss, 'No way can I work out there. I don't want access to any keys. Nothing. I'm being investigated by the FBI for killing my husband with cyanide. I can't work there. It's too close to home. That is how my husband died.' "

Even with Stella arrested and awaiting trial, Jim McCarthy, the man who Cindy Hamilton swore up and down was her mother's Indian lover, wasn't going to budge.

Jack Cusack met with him again.

"What would it take to convince you?" he asked over coffee.

"The source of the cyanide. Where she got it. The motive. Things like that that are concrete, not circumstantial."

The FBI agents didn't know the source of the cyanide but were still working on it. The motive, SA Cusack said, was insurance money.

McCarthy refuted the idea.

"I don't think the paltry insurance was reason enough for murder. He had just gotten on permanent with the state. He got $30,000 a year and the place would have been paid off."

SA Cusack asked if Stella had access to Mac's photographic supplies and darkroom equipment.

"No, I don't think so, but even if she did, I don't think I have anything in there that qualifies as cyanide. So it's a moot point."

They knew that. He had given them chemical samples from his darkroom, and none had contained cyanide.

"Did you know she has an interest in herbs and plants?"

"Yeah, she liked plants. Like every woman does.

"Did she buy fertilizer that had cyanide in it?"

"How the hell should I know? I don't have a green thumb in the first place. How many people read the ingredients on a package of fertilizer?"

Here you are accusing her, but you keep asking me for the clues. You're not convincing me, Jack, he thought.

"How do you explain all of the bottles in this area, and Stella having two of the five found?"

"Jack, come on, goddammit, you know as well as I do. Of course, I've been in the transportation business all my life; as things come down the belt to be packaged, they go into bottles, bottles go into a case, the case goes onto a conveyor, a pallet board is stacked, then destined to an area. Where would the pills be, Jack?" Jim McCarthy had heard the tainted capsules were different brands, even different sized capsules.

"Jack," he said, "doesn't that seem rather strange to you? It seems to me that if they were a different batch number of the capsules themselves, that it would come from the conveyor belt at the manufacturer's. Somebody walked by and took a handful of the cyanide-coated pills, they then would go into one box, because they are going down the conveyor belt.

"Why would Stella take a cap from a different brand, or different batch, and put it in the bottle? Wouldn't it make more sense that she would take one apart and put it back in? They would be the same batch, wouldn't they?"

Cusack just listened.

Jim McCarthy told Cusack he thought the government would do

just about anything to solve one of these cases. Even fabricate evidence.

"I bet you're under pressure. I know goddamn well you're under pressure. You gotta tie a ribbon on this sucker, and I don't blame you. I hate to think you'd do that."

"No, we wouldn't."

"There are just too many things in this case that don't smell right. Been out in the sun too long."

Why wasn't anybody helping her aunt Stella? Why would the feds believe someone like Cynthia Lea? If only Wilma had a way to come up with money to hire an attorney who could see that her favorite aunt was being railroaded by a band of federal agents.

In the way that only she could, Stella Nickell asked her niece to change her story.

"You made an awful mistake, babe, telling the FBI that I was coming to Houston to live."

"But you were."

Stella took her "let's clear up the little matter" posture. It was very familiar. Wilma had seen it since she was a child.

Everyone else is wrong. I am right. Listen to me. Good girl!

"Say I was coming to Houston to *visit*. Not to live. You made a mistake, you didn't hear me right." Her tone was insistent.

Wilma didn't say anything. How could she? Her aunt was in jail, and she didn't want to lie to the federal government and end up joining her. She couldn't alter her testimony. Besides, her words had been offered to protect, not indict.

"Aunt Stella wasn't going to kill Uncle Bruce . . . she was going to leave him!"

"I didn't realize they were using it against me," she said later, embarrassed by her naïveté.

PART FOUR

Wilma Mae

CHAPTER 69

The United States Courthouse for the Western District of Washington sits solidly on Fifth and Madison in Seattle. In the right light, it is a seemingly rose-hued ten-story box punctured with vertical slits of tiny windows like air holes a child would cut for a boxed lizard or snake. For the defendant, it would be home for the weeks of her trial.

Trees shade the grassy approach from the street, providing cool cover for office workers picnicking the lunch hour, and shelter for a small band of homeless curled up with blankets and shopping bags at the base of the 1939 building. The imposing architecture underscores its "federal" purpose. Judge Bill Dwyer's courtroom was adjacent to his chambers on the fifth floor. Gold letters proclaimed the number: 506.

It took only two days to impanel the Nickell jury, surprisingly fast, given the extensive publicity of the case. The defendant sat quietly, even smiling faintly as Tom Hillier and Joanne Maida narrowed the jurors from a field of 97 to 36 to 12—five men and seven women, plus two alternates.

Among those on the jury were a dental technician, a secretary, a real estate agent, an automotive painter, and a seafood consultant. All would be considered average, hardworking, but none had lived a life like Stella Nickell's.

*   *   *

The Stephenson girls, tougher than mobsters, as first husband Bob
Strong suggested, gathered around little sister Stella Maudine to
show support and to see what was going to happen. Cora Lee had
brought them all together: Mary from Redmond, Berta from Michigan, Wilma from Pasco. Even Georgia said she'd be coming,
though no one knew when.

Cora Lee, now seventy-one but looking a decade older, still
wanted to find Cynthia Lea to "tell her a thing or two," but the feds
still kept her whereabouts secret. No one knew if Cora Lee would
hug the girl or wring her neck. Her true feelings were mixed. Inside
her purse was a wallet photo of a curly-topped baby, Cynthia Lea.

"She looks just like Shirley Temple," Cora Lea would say
proudly, before her words trailed off to questions of why and how
Stella's daughter could do this to the family.

During noon recess on Tuesday, April 19, 1988, the Stephenson
women made their way to the 6th Avenue exit of the courthouse
to dodge the reporters and get a cup of coffee. No one was hungry.
Cora Lee remarked how Stella Maudine had looked heavy as she
sat next to lawyer Tom Hillier. Cora Lee ranted about Fred Phelps,
whom she considered to be taking advantage of her daughter's jail-
ing. She was angry that Georgia Mae hadn't yet buried the hatchet
with Wilma and shown up for the trial.

The women left the courthouse and walked across the steep
grade near the corner of 6th and Madison—one of those Seattle
streets that plummet from hilltop to the Sound. As she started to
step, Cora Lee fell backward on the pavement, hitting her head. Her
glasses flew off, her hearing aid popped from her ear. A bystander
rushed over and put his sweater over her trembling body.

"Mary, in an emergency, bounces off the walls. And of course,
not having had that type of emergency, the first thing she wanted
to do was grab mother and pick her up. It was no 'leave her lay.'
I rolled up my sweater and put it under her head. She was completely out," daughter Berta said recalling the frightening incident.

Their mother was rushed to Harborview, where she was listed
in critical condition.

While Cora Lee lay in the hospital, Berta returned to her
mother's trailer to look for medical and insurance documents.
Among the considerable stash of papers, she found a letter Cindy
had written to Stella during the time the girl lived with Cora Lee
in Ukiah. It had never been mailed.

"She was sorry, please take her back, she couldn't stand it with her grandma anymore. Her grandma was all sorts of things, words I cannot even speak. She wrote she couldn't go anywhere, she couldn't do nothing, how she hated Mother," Berta said later, recalling the contents of the letter that made her sick to her stomach.

"I already knew what Cindy had grown up to be—A child I would not want as my child, a child I would put under my thumb, a child needing to follow rules. She was wild, she didn't show any feelings for anyone but herself," she said.

"When Cindy took [her little girl] for her first shots, it was Cindy who cried. This portrays a loving mother. Then something happened. Should we call it getting involved in drugs? Then nothing mattered."

Cora Lee had saved the letter for a reason. Berta thought it was her mother's intention to show it to Stella Maudine.

Later, going through more of her mother's papers, Berta found a copy of a "will" Stella Maudine had written in her own handwriting:

> Cora Lee Rice has invested $23,000 into 5 acres I have purchased. Her portion is one-half . . . to leave in her will to my 3 sisters and 1 brother . . .

> Stella reserved the right to buy out her siblings.

> *If anything happens to me the property goes to my daughter, Cynthia Lea Slawson Hamilton. But all will be held in trust for her by Cora Lee Rice, my mother, until such time as Cora Lee Rice dies.*
>
> Signed, Stella Nickell.

Oddly, the will made no mention of two people: Bruce and Leah. Leah and Stella had not been estranged, except for the brief time after she made her daughter leave White River Estates when she found the photo of the marijuana. Why leave her youngest out? And why omit Bruce? Was it simply Stella's take-charge way of writing, as she had to North Pacific Bank? Or was Bruce already dead? The paper was not dated, but since Stella used the name Hamilton, it clearly was written after her daughter's late-1984 marriage to the trucker, Pepper.

Was the document an agreement, a promise, or an inducement? Over the days of the trial, an unconscious Cora Lee would be scanned for a blood clot. When she woke, she called her daughters by her sisters' names.

"I'm not Lucille. Mother, I'm Bert."

Her daughters knew the tough old bird would never be the same.

For friends who hadn't seen Stella Maudine Nickell since she started the big slide before her arrest, their first glimpse in the courtroom on the morning of April 20 must have been a shock. Stella, who once had a lovely figure and thick black tresses, was now puffy and dull. Twenty pounds heavier, she wore her old skinny clothes. Her face was so puffy and her lipstick so red, it looked almost as if someone had struck her full in the face.

In a way, someone had.

As she moved to her seat, she still managed a kind of confidence and swivel in her walk. It wasn't quite The Walk, but it was as close as the circumstances would allow. She wasn't going to let anyone get the best of her.

Projecting her buttoned-up, cool version of confidence, the defendant sat rod-straight in a black leather, brass-riveted chair. Before her, a pencil on a legal pad. Throughout the morning and the days to follow, she wrote note after note for Tom Hillier. At times when the attorneys discussed matters among themselves, she gazed out the window on her left. Through the slashes of windows, she could see the Smith Tower, Seattle's oldest skyscraper. A wind sock fluttered from the pencil-point roofline.

Of Stella Nickell's boys and men, only Fred Phelps took a spot on one of the walnut benches provided for spectators. Harry Swanson claimed he had been told by the feds to stay away. Jim McCarthy also made himself scarce. He had wanted to be a witness on Stella's behalf, but that had been nixed by the defense lawyer. He told people that if he was going to be there at all, it wasn't going to be to watch.

Jerry Kimble was one of many who just couldn't bear it.

The other players were there. SA Ron Nichols sat at the U.S. Attorney's table. Joanne Maida had called on him to carry the exhibits on a little cart to court.

"Is that Mr. Maida?" a spectator joked as he pushed by with his cart.

SA Nichols kept a good sense of humor about the gibe. At times, it *did* seem as though he was just an usher.

Jack Cusack sat on a chair next to the double doors leading to the courtroom. His job was to make sure the witnesses were ready.

Judge Bill Dwyer directed his instructions to the jury, imploring each to listen to the evidence, and solely the evidence presented in the courtroom. The judge reminded each not to discuss the case with anyone, even another juror. Such an instruction was a formality, a necessity.

With that, the trial began.

Assistant U.S. Attorney Joanne Maida spoke with an impressive deliberateness, a preciseness that jurors would grow to accept as her trademark delivery. Her salt-and-pepper hair was pulled back from her forehead tightly, then released down into a short mane in back. She opened with a detailed recounting of the case against Stella Nickell, a woman who wanted more from life than her marriage could provide. She developed a chilling scenario involving tampering with consumer products and an insurance payoff that depended on discovering the tampering. When Stella Nickell's husband died, Maida suggested, the defendant had expected the pathologists to rule death by acute cyanide poisoning. But that didn't happen. Instead, pathologists ruled emphysema—a natural cause.

Sue Snow had died to give Stella Nickell a reason to call attention to the circumstances of her husband's death.

There was plenty of evidence to incriminate the defendant, the prosecutor said. Insurance policies, inconsistent statements and out-and-out lies. And the defendant's own daughter had come forward with information in January 1987, after a conversation with the defendant.

"You will hear a lot of talk about money in this trial. You will hear about money to be collected from insurance proceeds, about monetary damages requested by the defendant, who had sued Bristol-Myers, the manufacturer of Excedrin, one month after her husband's death. You will also hear about a $300,000 reward that was put up by a pharmaceutical association for the arrest and conviction of any person brought to justice for this cyanide poison case, this one among several in the nation.

"You will be asked to make decisions about people you will hear testify during the course of this trial. Some of these people may be questioned about that financial motivation, what financial motivation, if any, exists for their cooperation with the United States.

"I represent the United States. They have been promised nothing by the United States in return for their testimony in court. The reward is offered through a private organization, which will make an independent determination regarding any payout terms."

The jury was told that Cindy Hamilton revealed to the FBI that for several years preceding her stepfather's death, Stella Nickell had talked of killing her husband and that six months before Bruce Nickell died, the talk had become more concrete.

"You will learn the specifics of these discussions between mother and daughter at this trial. You will also learn that mother and daughter have certainly had their share of disagreements, but they are still mother and daughter and they relate as mother would to daughter. You will see that Cindy Hamilton and Stella Nickell resemble each other physically, so much so that in the past they have been mistaken as sisters."

Joanne Maida warned the jury that Cindy Hamilton might appear to be flat and unemotional.

"Lessons learned from childhood die hard, and her mother taught her that a display of emotion was a sign of weakness."

Joanne Maida touched on the fingerprints found in the books on poisons the defendant had read. . . . The green crystals were also a clue. . . .

As the Assistant U.S. Attorney ended with a plea for justice, no one had a doubt—even before hearing Tom Hillier give his opening statement—that this was both a whodunit *and* a case of betrayed loyalties.

Tom Hillier stood next to Stella Nickell and Sal Ramos as he began his opening argument. His style was warmer. He was the kind of guy jurors liked. Folksy and friendly, that was Tom Hillier.

The case against his client was circumstantial, but he could easily reconcile all of it with Stella Nickell's plea of innocence.

If spectators, friends, family members, the media, had thought the trial might be a daughter up against a mother, Stella's lawyer gave the notion greater foundation.

"We invite you now and encourage you now to give your closest attention to the testimony of Cindy Hamilton. As outlined by the prosecutor, her testimony and its credibility is central to the prosecution's case. Ms. Hamilton's testimony will be contradicted in all essential details by Mrs. Nickell, who will testify on her own behalf and tell you about the events that led to and after Mr. Nickell's death."

Yes, Stella Nickell and her husband had life insurance.

Yes, she was the one who filled out the paperwork. An FBI

handwriting expert was not needed to verify that. She was not forging his name, just signing it as she had done on all such papers during their marriage.

"The evidence will show that when Bruce died, that question of his taking a physical to obtain the coverage he had applied for was unresolved. He hadn't taken a physical yet, and Mrs. Nickell was unaware when Bruce Nickell died just how much insurance he really had coming, if any, from the State of Washington."

Yes, there had been books. Tom Hillier boasted his client was a voracious reader. But the subject of poison plants was a concern related to her baby-sitting responsibilities, first at White River Estates, and later on the Nickells' wooded Auburn property. Stella was concerned about her granddaughter.

The jurors were told to pay careful attention to when the books were handled by his client.

"Significant will be the dates concerning the checkout time of these books, the dates of the checkouts in mid-1984. May of 1984 and September of 1984. Dates absolutely consistent with the time frame that the Nickells moved onto their property in Auburn, Washington. That was in May of 1984."

Yes, she read encyclopedias.

"Again, there is no controversy concerning the fact that Mrs. Nickell read in the encyclopedias about cyanide. Mrs. Nickell will testify and tell you why, and I invite you and encourage you to listen closely to her and her explanation. She will say that she did do some general reading about cyanide after she found out about the tragic circumstances concerning her husband's death.

"Who wouldn't?"

Yes, Bruce and Stella Nickell had struggled financially. At the time of Bruce Nickell's death, both were working full-time and still unable to make ends meet.

That was not in dispute, he said.

Why had Cindy Hamilton changed her story? Tom Hillier implored the jury to pay close attention to the defendant's daughter.

He repeated the word "anticipate" in reference to what testimony Cindy Hamilton would give. Anticipate . . . on heroin . . . her mom being a drug dealer . . . anticipate testimony on hit men . . . poison him with plants found on the property . . . running off to Mexico, leaving a note behind suggesting that she had been kidnapped.

"We anticipate that she will say she decided to let it play its course, even though she knew in her heart, as people say, that she

thought this was going to actually happen. We anticipate this because we don't know what Cindy Hamilton will say, because the
evidence will show since January of '87 when she went to the FBI,
she has fastidiously avoided contact with her mother and cleverly
avoided each and every contact attempt by Sal Ramos and myself
to interview her, in stark contrast to the cooperation and availability
of Stella Nickell."

Joanne Maida objected. Hillier's statement was an "improper
characterization of Ms. Nickell's availability to the government and
of Cindy Hamilton's nonavailability to the defense."

Judge Dwyer agreed that the claim defense had made was ar-
guable, but let counsel proceed.

Finally Tom Hillier mentioned the reward.

"The prosecution disavows any governmental interest in that
$300,000. That doesn't matter. What matters is, it was out there.

"Your considerable task will be to weigh against the testimony
of Mrs. Nickell the story of Cindy Hamilton, because resolution of
that conflict will necessarily control your verdict."

He wrapped up, and thanked the jury for their attention.

CHAPTER 70

After morning recess on April 20, King County volunteer fire fighter Bob Jewett sat in the gleaming witness box between the judge's bench and the jury box. The slightly nervous young man had always believed his brother-in-law, Eric Oehler, should have been the one called to testify. It was Eric who had talked with the defendant about the shredded cigarette. But here he was, and oddly, no one was asking about the cigarette.

He told the court the squad had arrived at 5:13, June 5, 1986, just eleven minutes after the defendant's 911 call, uncertain about whether they were at the correct address. Stella Nickell stared from the doorway.

From behind the wooden podium that made her look even smaller than she was, Joanne Maida asked if the fireman knew if it was the right place.

He did not, but after thirty seconds or so, Mrs. Nickell finally started to wave him over.

". . . It looked like someone was just watching us."

Bob Jewett testified that Bruce Nickell was inside, lying on his back as they set out to stabilize him. He showed signs of agonal breathing. His eyes were fixed, his blood pressure rapidly falling. Stella Nickell told the witness that her husband had taken a physical for state employment and had passed with no problems. She also emphasized that Bruce had been having problems with headaches.

Though her hands shook, she "seemed pretty calm."

Tom Hillier stepped to the microphone with great assurance for a brief cross-examination of the witness.

"Do you see the full range of physical response from people who have made the call?"

"As far as their reaction to the situation?"

"Right."

"Yeah."

"So you see people who seem calm outwardly and you see people, as you say, so hysterical that they can hardly talk?"

"Oh, well, I'm not saying that all people I see are that way, no."

Barry Rickert, fire fighter for the city of Auburn, was up next. He had been among the first to arrive at the Snow house on June 11, 1986.

He testified that Hayley Snow directed the emergency squad to the bathroom, where her mother was on the floor. And, like Bruce Nickell, Sue Snow was just barely breathing. They tried everything they knew to rouse her, with no success.

"Then what happened to her physical condition? Did it improve or did it get worse?" Joanne Maida asked.

"She was deteriorating."

Tom Hillier had no questions.

Sue Snow's husband was the government's third witness. Paul Webking looked lost in the witness box, his pain obvious. He testified about their life together, the phone calls from the road. Webking described his wife's morning ritual of taking two Excedrin capsules for caffeine, instead of coffee.

The widower continued with his story of his June 8 comment to his wife to buy more Excedrin as he left on a long haul to Chico, California. In fact, Sue had already written Excedrin on her shopping list.

Phone records indicating their conversations the days before Sue Snow died were received into evidence. They were followed by more documents identified and admitted without objection—Sue Snow's Albertson's and Safeway checks from June 8.

"Mr. Webking, what was Sue Snow doing the last time you saw her alive?"

"She was sleeping."

The last question was a nice touch, the kind prosecutors often use to elicit sympathy for a victim. *Sleeping.* Unaware of impending doom.

Federal defender Hillier had no questions.

* * *

Other testimony that first morning came from King County Medical Examiner Corrine Fligner, who explained autopsy procedures and how her assistant had picked up the smell of bitter almonds, the first clue Sue Snow had died of cyanide poisoning. She told the court that the ability to smell cyanide is genetic, that anywhere from twenty to ninety percent of the population is unable to smell it.

Dr. Fligner told the court that the toxicity report indicating cyanide was received on the morning of June 16, 1986. Two days later, Bruce Nickell was suspected to be a possible victim; testing later that day also showed cyanide.

Tom Hillier's cross-examination went nowhere in particular. He restated some of Dr. Fligner's testimony regarding under whose jurisdiction Bruce Nickell's death came. Suspicious deaths were autopsied by the M.E., and the physicians at Harborview hadn't felt Mr. Nickell's death fell under such guidelines.

But it still didn't change his cause of death.

As far as the autopsy went, the Medical Examiner testified, the hospital doctors had requested the autopsy, then sought permission from the widow.

"And the reason for that normally would be to try to confirm the cause of death if there was some question?"

"Yes. I think the physician's desire to know the cause of death."

"Did you have any personal contact with my client, Mrs. Nickell, during the course of your investigation of this case?"

"Yes, I did."

"When was that?"

"I have to get the dates right. I spoke to Mrs. Nickell twice, to my recollection. One time was to inform her that her husband had died of acute cyanide poisoning, and that was, I believe, on Wednesday, the eighteenth of June, after the testing had been performed and the cyanide tests were positive."

"Did you make both of these calls, Doctor? Did you initiate the calls?"

Dr. Fligner said the calls had in fact originated from her office.

Johnny's Food Center's Dale Reid took the stand while Ron Nichols set up a chart on an easel for the jurors. His brief testimony concerned the tainted bottle of Excedrin recovered from Johnny's on June 16.

The store manager stood before the photo chart of the bottles and identified the fluorescent orange sticker as one from Associated Grocers. It was the bottle from Pay 'N Save.

Hillier, again, had little to question. The bottles in evidence were not in dispute.

Ed Sexton, still with the King County Sheriff's Office, though now based in the Federal Way precinct, was sworn in. He told the court that on June 17, 1986, he answered a radio request for help at the Nickell home. When he arrived, Stella Nickell gave him two bottles of Excedrin—both with lot numbers matching Sue Snow's.

"Did you see how many were left in this particular bottle of capsules?"

"Yes, I believe there were seven."

The witness went on to tell the court that the defendant said Bruce had been taking the capsules from the bottle because he "had been having severe headaches and the only pills that he likes to take were the Excedrin . . . he would take three to four pills a day."

Stella Nickell had told him her husband had been suffering from headaches for "two or three weeks."

Asst. U.S. Attorney Maida told him to look at his report, but he didn't have it with him. She produced a copy from the defense table.

He reviewed the document, and amended his response to "about eight days" before his death.

When the prosecutor tried to determine the number of times Stella Nickell contacted medical authorities concerning her husband's autopsy, she again met with a vague response.

After considerable review of his notes, the best he could offer was "more than once."

"Did she tell you what had been reported to her about what the cause of death was in her husband's case?"

"Yes. She said it was—they determined natural causes."

"Did she use the words 'natural causes'?"

"Yes."

When asked about the second of the two bottles given to him by the defendant, the police officer said Stella Nickell had retrieved it from the upper kitchen cabinet. Unlike the first, it was in a box. He noticed it didn't have a safety neck band.

Ed Sexton said the defendant told him she had purchased one bottle at Johnny's in Kent, the other bottle from either Johnny's or the North Auburn Albertson's store.

When Joanne Maida sought details, Officer Sexton reviewed his report.

The one she bought at Johnny's was the one in the box. She had purchased it two weeks after the first one, he said.

Tom Hillier had a good chance with the diminutive King County officer and he knew it. He started with the suggestion that the old recollection was not as fresh today as it had been two years before. The witness agreed.

"All right. You testified on direct that Stella Nickell said that she—that her husband had been taking Excedrin for eight days prior to his death. Is that what you testified to?"

The witness said that was correct.

"Could you find in your report where it says that Stella Nickell indicated her husband had been taking Excedrin for eight days before?"

Ed Sexton futilely searched the document. His face reddened.

"I talked to Mrs. Nickell about—Let's go back up. Okay. Doesn't say that she said it. I asked Mrs. Nickell how many pills Bruce was taking. Mrs. Nickell mentioned he took four at a time. Being that there was only seven capsules in a forty-capsule bottle, that meant Bruce had been taking the Excedrin eight days."

"So that's arithmetic that you accomplished, isn't it?" Tom Hillier prodded.

"Yes, but she also mentioned that he had been taking them eight days."

"Look at your report again."

Ed Sexton admitted it wasn't there, and the defense lawyer had him read a line from his report: *"Mrs. Nickell told me that Bruce had been feeling ill several days before his death and that he had been taking the Excedrin for his headaches."*

"So that's what Mrs. Nickell told you, isn't it?"

"I remember her saying seven to eight days."

Both men repeated the number of days. Tom Hillier to reinforce the inaccuracy, Ed Sexton just to make it real.

"So at first, on direct examination, it was two to three weeks, or two weeks prior, then eight days, now seven to eight days."

"I misunderstood the prosecutor's question at that time."

Hillier did the same with the officer's recollection of the number of calls Stella Nickell had made to Harborview. It had not been in his report either.

*   *   *

After the afternoon recess, FBI Special Agent Ike Nakamoto took the stand. Nakamoto was in court to testify about the interview he and the FDA's Kim Rice conducted with the defendant on June 19, 1986. After establishing the basics surrounding the interview, Joanne Maida launched into her direct examination.

Ike Nakamoto's retelling of Stella Nickell's story of her husband's death, matched, without exception, the defendant's account. Bruce came home a little after 4:00 P.M., took a shower, watched television, had a headache, took four Excedrin capsules . . . collapsed . . . airlifted to Harborview.

Agent Nakamoto reviewed his notes concerning the number of calls the defendant made to medical authorities regarding her husband's autopsy. He reported three calls: June 7, 13, and one after she heard of Sue Snow's death on television.

On the subject of where she shopped for the two bottles she turned over to Officer Sexton, SA Nakamoto said that the defendant said she shopped at Albertson's North, Pay 'N Save South, and at the Johnny's Market in Kent.

"What did she tell you about where she purchased, she thought, each bottle?"

"The open bottle was purchased probably two weeks prior to Bruce's death, probably at either the Albertson's North End or the Johnny's Market."

"And the new bottle, the one that was in the box?"

"The unopened bottle was purchased probably two days prior to Bruce's death at Johnny's Market."

SA Nakamoto also referred to his notes when he testified that the defendant had told him her husband had taken a physical as a requirement to gain full-time employment with the Department of Transportation.

Direct continued on the subject of Bruce Nickell's "depressed mood," just before his death. Stella Nickell had told the FBI agent her husband was unhappy about missing a physical necessary for an additional $100,000 in life insurance.

"Do you have any question in your mind that she was talking about an amount of $100,000 being contingent on the taking of a physical examination, as opposed to any greater or lesser amount?"

"No doubt."

Next, the prosecution produced the June 16, 1986, letter—written three days before SA Nakamoto's interview with the defendant.

The letter carried the initials of Wally Strong, Senior Special Underwriter, Group Division. It was read into the record.

"Dear Mr. Nickell:

"We have received your letter in which you are requesting additional information as to why we incompleted your application for the requested $25,000 of life coverage offered through the State of Washington.

"According to the underwriting guidelines which we must follow for this group, anyone age 51 and applying for over $20,000 of life coverage must complete a medical examination. Our first request for you to take a medical exam was sent out on March 11, 1986. We closed out your file as incomplete on June 2, 1986.

"We would be happy to reopen your file if the completed medical examination would be sent in to us . . ."

"Mr. Nakamoto, the letter references requested $25,000 of life coverage. At any time did Stella Nickell in this interview that you had with her ever revise the $100,000 figure she gave you, that according to her was contingent on taking the medical exam, and say she was mistaken; that it was $25,000?"

"No."

Joanne Maida pulled the statement of insurance again, and with the FBI agent's help, deciphered the state's coverages for Bruce Nickell. They totaled $135,000.

Further, according to SA Nakamoto, Stella Nickell stated she and her husband each had applied for an additional $20,000 through Bank Cardholders of America, but a clerical error had left her husband without insurance. Only she was covered.

The membership enrollment form dated October 14, 1985, was identified by the agent. The cardholder was Stella Nickell; spouse, Bruce Nickell. The document showed the defendant had checked off that she and her husband were both beneficiaries *and* insured.

The Asst. U.S. Attorney asked how the defendant explained the clerical error that left her, and not her husband, insured. SA Nakamoto recalled Stella Nickell's showing a small card indicating she was the insured. She said she had called the insurance company's 800 number and discovered "a clerical error had been made and that her policy was issued but Bruce's was never issued."

Under further direct, the FBI agent said that the third Excedrin bottle had been recovered from the cabinet under the bathroom sink and was turned over to FDA investigator Kim Rice.

On cross-examination, Tom Hillier prevailed with his prepared questions, promising to wade through them and get on to some new ones based on the Assistant U.S. Attorney's direct examination. Hillier recalled that the unopened bottle had been said to have been purchased at Johnny's "a couple of days before" her husband's death . . . around June 3.

When the defense lawyer asked about the Albertson's receipt from June 3, the agent didn't recall seeing it.

Tom Hillier had the witness confirm that Stella Nickell retrieved some papers to provide information on insurance, that it had not been something she said off the top of her head.

"She told you that—she expressed some question about what insurance coverage they actually had in view of some correspondence concerning a physical, didn't she?"

"Yes."

And yes, the witness also agreed, Stella Nickell didn't think her husband had $100,000 coverage. And yes, there had been a delay in receiving notice from the insurance company regarding the insurance. No, she didn't know the exact amount from the state policy.

Tom Hillier recalled the June 16 letter Nakamoto had read into evidence.

Bruce Nickell had not been alive when the letter was written.

"And this letter, was it given to you on that day?"

"This is the first time I've seen it."

"All right. So you don't know if Stella Nickell had seen it on June 19 when you were interviewing her, do you?"

"No."

Tom Hillier had the witness take a look at the document addressed to Bruce Nickell by Northwestern National.

"And is there—are there two dates on there, one of which is scratched out and one of which is stamped on?"

"The scratched-out one looks like March 11, 1986, and the stamped one is April 17, 1986."

Hillier asked the witness to read the message into the record.

"We are pleased to receive the request for insurance coverage which was recently submitted . . .

"Please contact the physician or paramedical examining firm of your choice for an appointment . . ."

Next, Hillier had SA Nakamoto read the letter to Northwestern from Bruce Nickell, dated May 27, 1986. It had been stamp-dated June 2, 1986.

> *"I received a letter from your company today informing me I have to take a physical. This letter is dated in final notice and my application had been delayed. . . . I was not aware I had to take a physical. I would appreciate more information . . . as I am in the dark on this matter."*

Under further questioning, Ike Nakamoto conceded that the defendant had said her husband was depressed that she was the one covered and not he. It was also true that Stella Nickell had given the FBI agent information on the All American policy, stating that a clerical error left her insured and Bruce uncovered.

Tom Hillier concluded his cross with questions regarding the third Nickell bottle, the one found under the bathroom sink. He asked SA Nakamoto to relay the defendant's response when shown the bottle.

"I believe she was surprised that the bottle was there."

"She indicated she didn't know where it came from, or that was the impression that you had?"

"Yeah, that was the impression I had."

FDA investigator Kim Rice followed SA Nakamoto with testimony about the third bottle, the one from under Stella's bathroom sink. The witness testified that the defendant told him she didn't know of its existence.

The Asst. U.S. Attorney had the clerk hand the sixty-count Excedrin bottle, still in an evidence bag, to the FDA investigator. He identified it and the bottle was received into evidence.

The Albertson's receipt from June 3, 1986, was next.

Joanne Maida asked if Rice had asked Stella Nickell where she purchased the tainted bottles. He had. When searching for the source of the bottles, the defendant produced some receipts. The one from Albertson's was among them.

"There was really not much that she did say about this receipt," he said. "She had no recollection concerning what the items might have been on here that were purchased."

Tom Hillier took the podium and drew from Kim Rice support for his opening statement that Stella Nickell had been cooperative:

She had recovered the Albertson's receipt, along with others, at the request of the FDA and FBI. Kim Rice told the court that, in fact, the Albertson's receipt had a price—$3.39—that matched a price sticker on the intact forty-count bottle of cyanide-laced Excedrin.

Investigator Rice agreed that Stella Nickell had told him that, to the best of her recollection, Johnny's was where she bought the unopened bottle.

"And she indicated that she thought she bought that a couple of days before Bruce's death?"

She had.

"Which, of course, would be June 3 or thereabouts?"

"Yes."

"Did you ask Mrs. Nickell why that conflict?"

"I did not."

James Nordness, the store manager for the Pay 'N Save on Auburn Way North, took the stand and in brief testimony confirmed he had found the box of Anacin-3 and on it saw a red "As Advertised" tag from his store and a generic, non—Pay 'N Save regular price tag, but his particular Pay 'N Save did not carry the fifty-count size.

On cross-examination, Tom Hillier, who didn't have much to dispute, asked how a consumer could purchase a product the store didn't even carry.

"They simply could have picked it up as I did and taken it to the front cashier and purchased it, based upon the sale price on the tag."

Equifax insurance investigator Lynn Force was called to fill in the last bit of the day. His voice was so soft that Judge Dwyer asked him to speak up. Force told the National court he was investigating on behalf of Northwestern National, and its $100,000 accidental-death and a $36,000 life insurance policy, when he met Stella Nickell at the airport to have her sign a release so he could obtain the autopsy report to complete his investigation. She accommodated his request. He had asked her if there were any other policies, and she said no.

Joanne Maida asked if anything suggested that the defendant didn't understand what the investigator asked of her. Lynn Force said there had been numerous interruptions at the concourse security area.

Under further direct and subsequent cross-examination, the insurance investigator told the court that although he hadn't written the $136,000 total on any paperwork, he recalled telling the defendant the amount.

With Cora Lee's condition the day after her fall of prime concern, Berta's visit with her sister in jail was brief. Berta told Stella she had to get to the hospital. Mother needed her.

Though concerned about her mother, Stella Maudine had other things to worry about. She told her favorite sister she had braced herself for Cynthia Lea's testimony.

"You watch and you're going to see one of the greatest performances you've ever seen. Cynthia is a good actress. She could make you believe anything."

Berta left trying to make sense of what was happening. She wondered if Cindy had been given her freedom as "a payoff for testifying."

Stella Maudine later said she knew her daughter would never back down.

"She sticks to what she says even if it is all lies. Because she will never admit when she is wrong, and never has in all her life, unless it is to her advantage. She always follows through no matter who gets hurt in the process. She wants people to believe she is not capable of lying, that she only tells the truth no matter what the outcome."

CHAPTER 71

Jack Cusack brought his wife Kathleen along to SeaTac to pick up the government's star witness before her day in court. With the FBI agent's wife in the car, Cindy did her best to act poised and lady-like. Jack Cusack couldn't help but be touched by her effort. The girl was really trying her damnedest, he thought. He had endured a great deal from Cynthia Lea since she had betrayed Stella Maudine. In the last weeks, the young woman's dramatics had escalated enough to cause concern. Case Agent Cusack, whose goal was to make sure the defendant's daughter didn't completely back out of testifying, tried to calm her. If she did freeze up, Jack Cusack would need to take the stand to testify about what she had told him—that, of course, would be an extremely weak presentation compared with the dramatic value of daughter against mother.

Words of assurance did little good, however. Cindy kept saying she was worried that if her mother were acquitted she would seek revenge.

"She'll come after me . . . she'll kill me."

"Cindy, it won't happen. Stella's going down."

"You don't know my mother!"

Cindy told the FBI agent that she didn't want to check in to a Seattle hotel, which would have certainly been more convenient for the trial.

"I don't want the media to find me and hassle me," she said. "I can't handle it."

Of course, there was nothing Cindy Hamilton couldn't or wouldn't handle, but that was the beside the point. Just like her mother and her grandmother, she was tough as leather and strong as the bull it came from.

The Cusacks drove Cindy to the Bellevue Holiday Inn, just ten minutes east of Seattle. Cindy, professing great concern lest the media locate her, told the front-desk clerk, "I'm a witness in a very important federal trial. I don't want anyone to know I'm here."

It was Cindy goes Hollywood. She was lapping up the attention.

"All my life my mother has had the upper hand," she told the Cusacks. "Now I'm going to court and I'm the one calling the shots. I don't know how I'm going to react."

That kind of talk was daunting. Without Cindy, Stella might walk from the courtroom a free woman.

"You'll be fine," Jack told her. "It's your turn to stand up to her."

SA Cusack, who later said he saw "a woman in agony," was one of many worried about Cindy Hamilton.

"She was a pivotal piece of the prosecutor's case. None of us knew what she might say. If she got real cantankerous or if she got real upset on the stand, she could blow the case."

Back at the Seattle offices of the FBI and U.S. Attorney, clocks were watched in anxious anticipation of Hamilton's testimony.

Cusack later recalled that the mood was "like a Ted Bundy countdown."

Dee Rogers saw the trial as the end of her friend's dangerous family cycle of abuse, neglect, and jealousy. By testifying against her mother, Cindy was breaking free from all of it.

SA Cusack had told Cindy that she couldn't see or talk to Dee before the trial, but she called her from the Holiday Inn anyway.

"She didn't give a shit what they said," Dee Rogers said.

Paul Webking also understood that the defendant's daughter was the key witness. He wondered how it was that she could know so much and yet not be involved in the crime.

"At the very least," he said later "she could have come forward after Bruce died . . . she could have saved Sue."

Paul Webking wanted the whole ordeal over, though he knew it never would be. Even if Stella Nickell was convicted, there would still be those whispering behind his back that he had been the killer.

*   *   *

The defense finally got its hands on Cynthia Hamilton's grand jury testimony, only hours before she was to take the stand.

Tom Hillier asked Stella to go through the sixty-nine pages of testimony page by page. He told her to make note of anything that could help her case.

And so she did. When Cindy whined about moving around from school to school, Stella bristled and wrote: *"She went to one school 'til 6th grade. I changed her school because of behavior problems."*

Cindy said she was rebellious when they moved to Washington because she "didn't like the lifestyle" her mother was leading.

Stella wrote: *"She was all of 14 and she didn't want me to marry Bruce."*

When Joanne Maida inquired about the beating and other corporal punishment, Stella scrawled: *"The only other corporal punishments she had was Room Restriction or no T.V."*

Cindy testified to her fear about being a child abuser herself, and how she read up on the subject.

"She had no worry about that except in her own mind. So she would know what to say to convince people she was an abused child . . . she also told everybody at one time she was adopted."

Joanne Maida asked if the relationship with her mother had remained constant.

Stella wrote: *"Yes it has remained constant—she doesn't like me."*

On the beating: *"She never got hit. She got a spanking when called for and that wasn't often. From the way she turned out, not often enough."*

Every time Cindy mentioned her first husband in California, Stella Nickell scratched it out and wrote "man." She amended marriage to "living with."

When Cindy told the grand jurors her mother was intimidating, Stella Maudine scribbled: *"Where she got that, I don't know."*

Cindy testified that when Bruce was drinking, he was an "obnoxious boor," but there "wasn't a whole lot" she could do about the relationship.

"You can hear the anger in her words."

On the page showing Cindy's statement that "she was 99.9 percent sure" it was her stepfather her mother was going to say had died, Stella wrote: *"Why was she so sure it was Bruce? Why wouldn't it have been her own grandmother?? She knew Mother was not in the best of health."*

Stella also wrote that she, not Cindy, was at Dee's apartment first. She made numerous notes refuting the whole story.

She claimed the "I know what you're thinking" statement came later.

"I was trying to relieve her guilt feelings about sending [her daughter] to Cal. away from her Grandpa. Bruce was very upset about that. I was trying to tell her that Bruce didn't die still being mad at her . . ."

Stella wrote more: *"We were in financial problems to where I was supposedly 'thinking of dealing drugs'? Now we are talking 'Hit man'? As far as I had ever heard that is Big Money on the spot. Where did I have the money??"*

"If I was unfamiliar with her life, how is it that she is so well versed in mine?"

With respect to conversations at the airport when her mother could talk in half-sentences and Cindy said she'd know what she meant, Stella wrote:

"If I was talking half sentences, then she filled in the rest from her own imagination, thoughts, wishes, desires, etc. Is that the way it went???"

On the subject of Jeanne Rice's bodyguard business, Stella wrote that it was just talk . . . Jeanne wanted friends and *"nobody liked her."*

"At age 42 I am going to get beat to a pulp and get shot at??"

Concerning her daughter's tale about the hit man forcing Bruce's truck into a head-on, Stella snapped: *"And the alleged hit man is going to risk his life in the process?? She never worked that lie completely out."*

When Joanne Maida got to the subject of Stella asking her daughter about cyanide, Stella wrote: *"Why would I ask her about something I was sure she had no knowledge about??"*

Stella Nickell corrected her daughter's testimony concerning the idea of the cyanide tampering coming from a discussion of the Chicago Tylenol killings.

"If she is referring to the only time we talked about anything of the sort, it was about the news article about the guy in Texas that put Rat Poison in Caps. The Tylenol was mentioned in that article."

The defendant also wanted to know *"where did I get the extra caps to do this"* with?" when Cindy informed the grand jurors that her mother had filled some extra capsules with toxic seeds.

Cindy testified that although she hoped her mother was just

blowing off steam, deep down she knew she was "capable of it, but . . ."

"Her own feelings are speaking. She has never seen me be vicious or mean to anybody in her life. Nor has she ever heard me talk about killing anybody, much less my husband."

About Cindy loving her mother to the point of mimicry, Stella wrote: *"She didn't try to act like me because she Hated to be told she looked and acted like her mother."*

On why Cindy said she didn't tell Bruce about the murder plots, Stella wrote: *"She knew he wouldn't have believed her. Bruce knew beyond a shadow that I loved him and still do."*

Cindy "panicked" when the FBI first questioned her at the trailer.

"Why would she panic?? (a guilty conscience? Maybe)"

"And I thought more and more about Sue Snow and her family, and it bothered me . . ."

Stella wrote: *"It should have!!"*

Cindy used half a page of testimony to tell why she hadn't told her daughter Bruce had died. She didn't know how to.

"Tell her the truth, that you set grandma up and sent her to prison."

Cindy said she sent her daughter to California because she was "moving around a lot," and Stella wrote: *"from one bed to another and [the child] was in the way."*

When Cindy's testimony indicated that her mother was "intimately and emotionally" involved with Jim McCarthy before Bruce's death, Stella wrote: *"She believes that because she couldn't get into Jim's bed, from what she told me. All he talked about was how great her mom and Bruce were."*

Cindy closed her grand jury testimony stating that although she might project a hard exterior, inside she was still having problems, nightmares even, as a result of the ordeal.

Stella Maudine wrote: *"As well she should have."*

Tom Hillier made a number of notes of his own, mostly pointing out how rife the testimony was with time conflicts and mismatched stories.

In the margin next to Cindy Hamilton's testimony about her mother's plan to mix Bruce Nickell's iced tea with drugs, he wrote the words: *"Accomplice to plots."*

CHAPTER 72

Ron Nichols moved from his place at the prosecution's table to the witness box on the second day of testimony. The blue in his suit brought out the red of his hair, though now it showed more gray than it had when the case began. After establishing his role in the Nickell investigation, Joanne Maida turned the court's attention to the interview he and SA Cusack conducted with the defendant in November 1986.

The witness identified the stores the defendant had said were places she shopped, and probably where she purchased the tainted bottles. SA Nichols named the same stores as SA Nakamoto had the day before.

Concerning life insurance, SA Nichols testified the defendant "stated that she had a life insurance policy that paid approximately $25,000, and that she was supposed to have a life insurance policy that paid $100,000, but Bruce did not take a physical."

Joanne Maida presented the June 16 letter that had been discussed the day before, addressing the $25,000 coverage incomplete due to failure to take the medical exam.

"Did Mrs. Nickell at any time during this interview correct any of her statements to you by calling to your attention the existence of such a letter?"

"No, she did not."

And though she had many months in which to do so, the witness said the defendant never recontacted the FBI to correct her statement about the $100,000 coverage. Further, the defendant said she did not have any other insurance policies.

"Did Mrs. Nickell indicate whether she had any interest in any money benefiting from her husband's death?"

"Yes, she did indicate."

"What did she say?"

"She said that she was not interested in benefiting from her husband's death in any way."

Asst. U.S. Attorney Maida asked the clerk to give the witness the next exhibit, Stella Nickell's lawsuit against Bristol-Myers. SA Nichols read the date it had been signed: "July 30, 1986."

Throughout all of Ron Nichols's testimony, Stella Nickell continued to write on her legal pad, occasionally looking up to brush a loose strand of hair from her face. She never once betrayed her feelings. If Sal Ramos had been right, this, too, was just another major inconvenience.

"Moving on, Mr. Nichols, at the conclusion of this interview with the defendant, did you tell her anything to indicate that your investigation of her was over?"

"No, I did not."

Tom Hillier began his cross-examination by asking if it would be fair to say that when Stella said she didn't want to benefit from her husband's death, what she really meant was she'd prefer he was alive.

SA Nichols said he didn't take it that way.

"So what you've testified to today is your impression?"

"Yes, sir."

It was true, the witness also said, he didn't know whose idea it was to file a lawsuit against Bristol-Myers.

Tom Hillier turned his attention to the June 16 letter.

"Is there anything in that letter which suggests or states that a $100,000 policy is intact?"

"No."

"Does it even mention the number 100,000?"

"No, it doesn't."

"Does it give specifics concerning what insurance is covered or isn't covered?"

"No, it doesn't."

Yes, SA Nichols said, the November interview repeated questions from June's. Yes, her responses concerning where she shopped, purchased the Excedrin, were consistent with what she had said back that spring.

While the court clerk pulled Excedrin bottles, Gary Lande, vice-president, logistics, for Bristol-Myers Products Division of Bristol-Myers Corporation, took the stand and identified the Excedrin bottles as a product made by the company.

He testified that upon learning of Sue Snow's death, Bristol-Myers recalled Excedrin nationwide. A day later, the company discontinued the manufacture of the product altogether.

The witness demonstrated the packaging safeguards of the Excedrin bottles available in 1986. A cellophane overwrap on one box and the plastic neck bands were shown to the court.

On cross, Tom Hillier asked about the reward, but Gary Lande said he knew nothing about it.

It was time to talk insurance, the motive of the government's case against Stella Nickell. Up first was Sandy Sorby, of the State Employees Insurance Board. She took the stand wishing she was anywhere but the federal courthouse and testified that Bruce Nickell's death benefits through Northwestern National totaled $136,000.

The Asst. U.S. Attorney asked her to step down to review the chart of insurance policies. She asked the witness to explain the numbers on the right-hand side of the chart, under the label: "Northwestern, January 6, 1986 Application."

The witness said that $100,000 was accidental death and dismemberment, and another $5,000 AD&D was provided by the State. A figure of $26,000 was optional life, taken by the employees at their own expense. That figure increases as salaries rise. Another $5,000 basic life is provided by the state to all employees.

Joanne Maida asked about a bracketed figure of $25,000.

"The employee had applied for an additional $25,000 that was incompleted. That means that he did not get that amount of insurance because he was requested to take a physical exam by the insurance company and that was never done."

Next, Sandy Sorby identified a life insurance enrollment form used by state employees and reviewed by her office.

It had been signed by Bruce Nickell on January 8, 1986, and indicated the following amounts purportedly requested by Bruce Nickell: optional life for $25,000; supplemental life for $25,000—the one that had been incompleted; optional life or optional accidental death and dismemberment for $100,000.

"The sum that you have originally testified to of total coverage on the insured Bruce Nickell came to $136,000. What is the $1,000 amount that appears on its surface to be a discrepancy, the extra $1,000?"

The witness said optional life automatically increases with the employee's salary. Records showed Bruce Nickell had received a raise.

The insurance enrollment form was admitted in evidence.

Sorby also told the court about her July 7, 1986, meeting with Stella Nickell when she came to file the claim. Stella Nickell told her she had waited for an amended death certificate, since her husband's cause of death had been changed. She also testified about a hundred-plus news clippings she saw in the widow's briefcase.

Tom Hillier stepped forward to drill the nice lady from Olympia on the news clippings.

She told the court she had not counted them. And yes, they were originals, not photocopies.

"So you're saying that there were a hundred original newspaper clippings in there?"

"I'm not saying a hundred. It was a full briefcase and—"

"You saw—"

"—a hundred is the largest amount I could imagine in a briefcase."

"So you're imagining that's a possibility?"

"Yes."

Under further cross, she told the court the clippings were brought appropriately, necessary for the processing of an accidental-death claim.

She said Bruce Nickell's supervisor, Dick Johnson, contacted SEIB on behalf of the defendant on July 2. When the defendant showed up five days later, it had been a month since her husband's death. The time frame was not unusual.

It was fitting that Sandy Sorby's friend and work colleague, Pam Stegenga, was next. She stepped up into the witness box and said her contacts with the defendant had only been over the phone.

Stella Nickell called three times in late 1986, each time wanting to know when the insurance claim would be paid.

During the call on November 20, Stella Nickell said the FBI agents had met with her two days before.

"And what, if anything, did she say about the status of the investigation?" Joanne Maida asked.

"She said that she thought the investigation was completed."

Under cross, Tom Hillier tried to pin down who had made the late-September call—the witness or the defendant. There was much give-and-take over who had called whom. Finally, after cross and re-direct, the jury learned that Stella Nickell had placed the last call and the witness returned it.

Robert Chesterfield, Jr., mortgage banker for Pacific Coast Investment Company in Seattle, followed Pam Stegenga. His company held the deed of trust on the Nickell property, after the original owner took out a loan and assigned the deed of trust on the acreage as security. Pacific Coast Investment had held it since January 24, 1986. The Nickells, he said, owed $30,328.68. By May 14, the Nickells were $1,471 delinquent and in collection. They were to pay within a week or face legal action. Reviewing an exhibit proffered by Joanne Maida, Chesterfield testified that it was a notice of default addressed to the Nickells. It was dated May 27.

Tom Hillier had no questions and the witness was excused.

Joanne Maida commenced direct examination of Auburn Public Library director Mary Margaret Stanton by asking about checkout procedures for library patrons. At the time in question, it was a simple system of stamp-dated book cards, imprinted with due dates and patron numbers.

Stanton identified Stella's registration card and a checkout card for *Deadly Harvest*. It had been stamped with Stella Nickell's number, with due dates of June 16, 1983, and May 22, 1984.

The librarian also identified a book card for *Human Poisoning by Native and Cultivated Plants*. It had been due on September 19, 1984.

But the book, Mary Margaret Stanton testified, had never been returned. An overdue notice was sent to Stella Nickell on September 26, 1984.

After the lunchbreak, librarian Stanton identified books belonging to the Auburn Public Library: *Deadly Harvest*, volumes of *McGraw-Hill Encyclopedia of Science and Technology*, *New Caxton Encyclopedia*, and *Merit Student's Encyclopedia*.

All were admitted into evidence.

Tom Hillier, of course, had no cause to pick on a librarian. He asked if she had looked at *Deadly Harvest* before it went to the FBI labs. She said she hadn't.

*   *   *

SA Marshall Stone was Joanne Maida's next witness. First, she focused on the agent's search in March 1987 among the stacks at the Auburn library. He testified he reviewed the checkout cards of all books relating to cyanide and toxic plants and chemicals. He said he was acting on information from Cindy Hamilton.

At the library, he found the copy of *Deadly Harvest* and the overdue notice for *Human Poisonings from Native and Cultivated Plants*.

Later, he said, he returned to the library, again the result of information from Stella's daughter. This time, he told the court, he was looking for the "C" volumes of encyclopedias—sections on cyanide. Three volumes were found, and submitted to FBI laboratories for fingerprint examination.

Over Hillier's objections, Maida had the witness read an encyclopedia passage.

"Cyanide is frequently employed as the lethal substance in murder mysteries and often the odor of the bitter almonds is given as a clue to its presence in the victim, but cyanide itself has no odor. The odor of bitter almonds is that of benzaldehyde...."

Tom Hillier stepped up for cross-examination of the young FBI agent. He had the witness tell the court that the information concerning the libraries came in to the Bureau in waves—from late February to November of 1987—based upon information that was provided by the defendant's daughter.

Tom Hillier moved on to the encyclopedias.

"Do you recall reading anything in any of the texts relating to cyanide that the detection of the odor which accompanies a cyanide poisoning can't be detected by anywhere from twenty to ninety percent of the population? Twenty to ninety per cent."

"I don't recall reading anything like that," Stone answered.

Emerald City Chemicals supervisory salesman Paul Lindgren testified about the relative ease of purchasing cyanide prior to June 1986. He told the court that for $13.50, a customer could walk out of his store with a pound of cyanide. No identification or signatures were required.

On cross, Tom Hillier tried to support the defense contention that Stella Nickell had never purchased cyanide—Lindgren told the court that it was true the FBI had shown him photos but he was never able to identify Stella Nickell.

*   *   *

Valerie Williams, a compliance officer, whose responsibilities also included managing bank records for North Pacific Bank, took the stand. North Pacific was the lienholder on the Nickells' mobile home. The witness identified various documents, including the Final Notice of Delinquency dated April 9, 1986. The letter indicated that total payment of $1,892.01 was due by April 25, 1986.

Next, the witness identified the letter written by the defendant on April 25, 1986.

"I know that I am tremendously overdue . . . I am having marital problems. They are about solved, and I would like to ask if you will have faith in me, personally. Bruce is no longer involved . . ."

Williams identified a second letter, dated June 1, 1986, in which the defendant promised to stay current, after making another double payment.

"Dear Sirs:

"I am trying to work around to where I can get my payment in by the 12th of the month and not be behind. . . ."

The next letter, also from Stella Nickell, was undated. Joanne Maida had the witness read the letter for the record.

"If you just have patience, I will eventually catch up—just don't push. . . ."

Joanne Maida had the witness point out that in none of her letters concerning payments due did the defendant use the words "we" or "our."

After discussing payoff of the loan, the Asst. U.S. Attorney had nothing further.

Tom Hillier pointed out that the letters' chronology was suspect—the March 5 letter from the bank to the Nickells did not reference a $100-per-month insurance increase.

Further, Tom Hillier had the witness consider that the letter in question might be only a portion of a larger one.

Somewhat reluctantly, the witness agreed it was a possibility.

If there was a chance for trouble in the government's case, Tom Noonan of Fish Gallery and Pets was it. Not that he wasn't truthful, but sometimes his story changed slightly, and that left room for the defense to discredit the witness. The young man's courtroom attire brought smiles to some observers. He wore a sweater, pressed

slacks . . . and tennis shoes. He didn't like to stuff his feet into uncomfortable dress shoes.

When his eyes met Sal Ramos's he gave his best shot at a glare.
He couldn't forget how he felt duped into talking to the defense
before trial.

He identified Stella Nickell as a regular customer and told the
court that although he recommended the liquid Algaegon, Stella
Nickell preferred Algae Destroyer. At her request, he said, he even
ordered her a supply.

He told the court that the blister-packed product sometimes ad-
mits moisture, causing the tablets to become insoluble. "On the
average, I told people when they bought a product like this or a
manufacturer's product similar to these, that to make them easier
to use they could crush them up and dissolve them in warm water
before administering them to the tank."

"Do you have any specific recollection of having discussed that
with Mrs. Nickell?"

"I can't really say if I did, but my general—"

Tom Hillier bolted up. "Your Honor, I think he's answered the
question."

Judge Dwyer agreed. "The question has been answered."

Unflappable Joanne Maida went into damage control. In order
to make the record "understandable," she asked if Tom Noonan
made a general practice of advising purchasers of the algicide how
best to use the product.

He said he told them to crush and dissolve it in warm water.

The court recessed for fifteen minutes, and Tom Noonan, feeling
the stress of the witness stand, was grateful for every second.

Joanne Maida asked the question again: had he given Stella
Nickell the same advice as his other customers?

He said he had. In fact, he remembered "to try to get her to
purchase a product we already had, I told her the drawbacks of the
product she wanted to purchase, that you had to crush it up to make
it effective."

Tom Hillier stood to ask Tom Noonan how he was doing.

"I've been better," the young man deadpanned.

The response drew laughter, though no one knew why Tom
Noonan might have felt that way. He continued to kick himself for
talking to Tom Hillier before trial.

After brief testimony concerning the defendant's interest in
opening a fish store—with her husband as partner—the defense

attorney brought up the subject Tom Noonan had dreaded: the meeting he and the defense team had earlier in the month.

"And you had talked to Mr. Ramos before, hadn't you?"

Tom Noonan shot another glare, and finally answered, "Yes."

"All right. And do you recall telling us that you had no specific recollection of telling Mrs. Nickell about crushing algicide tablets but that you did as a general course?"

The witness tried to get out of it. "He came to me—"

"Just answer. That's a yes or no. Do you recall saying that during our conversation?"

"Not with him, no."

"During the conversation that I was present at, do you recall saying that?"

"That it was just general practice?"

"Right."

"Yes."

"Do you remember indicating that you couldn't recall having said or instructing Mrs. Nickell in that respect?"

"What was the question again?"

"Do you recall having told me while Mr. Ramos was there—We had a conversation, the three of us, didn't we?"

"Yes, we did."

"—that you had no specific recollection of telling Mrs. Nickell that she should crush those tablets!"

"At that time of the morning, I didn't, no."

Tom Hillier asked what had prompted Tom Noonan's recollections. He said it had been the review of his grand jury testimony just before court.

"Do you recall, then, Ms. Maida asking you with reference to this crushing, and this is something that is quite conceivable that you would have told her, referring to Mrs. Nickell, because she purchased this product all the time."

Tom Noonan fumbled with his papers.

"Quite conceivable. Is that what you told her?"

It was.

Now he recalled a specific conversation with the defendant, and Tom Hillier wanted to know when it occurred. He had the witness tell the jury he started working at the Kent store in December 1984 and left for the Renton store in January 1986.

"One year, through 1985," Hillier stated. "Did the conversation take place in '85?"

The witness said it did, in the wintertime.

"What month?"

"Probably October, to the best of my recollection."

"So this would have been the first time she would have talked to you about algicides?"

"That particular product, yes."

"So she didn't buy that particular product before October of '85?"

"Not from me, no."

"Let me ask you this: Is it possible that you didn't tell Mrs. Nickell that you should crush and dissolve in warm water these tablets?"

"No."

Joanne Maida stood for re-direct. The Asst. U.S. Attorney had the court clerk hand the witness his grand jury testimony.

Yes, he said, his memory was better in February 1987 than it was at that moment.

She directed him to the passage just before the question Hillier had read during cross. Yes, he said, reading it, he did suggest she dissolve the tablets by "pounding on them into a powder" or warm water.

"Q: And this is something that it is quite conceivable that you would have told her because she purchased this product all the time?

"A: Right."

Having worked out some problems with the defense, Joanne Maida made a run at having Stella Nickell's checks and bank records admitted into evidence. Marshall Stone was recalled to go over his summary chart, which itemized the defendant's checks from Albertson's North and South, Johnny's Market, Pay 'N Save North, Fish Gallery and Pets, Auburn Market & Garden, and Carousel Pets in Auburn.

The SA testified that six checks had been written at Pay 'N Save North between February 23, 1986, and May 27, 1986.

The witness also testified about the defendant's work schedule on the days before Bruce Nickell died. Stella Nickell had not worked May 27, or June 3 through 5.

Next, Joanne Maida took the opportunity to offer a number of exhibits, by prior stipulation. Documents from Western Savings Visa, balance of $2,723.80, Stella Nickell's application for Social

Security lump-sum death benefit, dated June 24, 1986, and three documents—an application dated Aug. 22, 1986, and a couple of letters—pertaining to the Automotive Machinists Pension Trust Fund widow's benefit of $6,162.98, the Chapter 13 petition and dismissal documents, the Nickells' tax returns for 1984, deceased's long-term-disability enrollment change form, and medical/dental enrollment change forms dated January 8, 1986.

Other employment records were also admitted: Bruce Nickell's application with the state, dated September 4, 1984; and a document called Temporary Employment Understanding, signed by Bruce Nickell and dated October 15, 1984; and a document showing Bruce passed a physical on January 3, 1986. Her last documents were Bruce Nickell's sick-leave work records from January 22, 1985, through May 27, 1986.

All were admitted.

A slimmed-down and pretty-eyed Bonnie Anderson took the stand, telling the court she had met Stella Nickell in November 1985 when she started working at Wells Fargo at SeaTac. She said she met the defendant's daughter four months later.

She told the court Stella Nickell could be intimidating.

"She had a way of staring you right in the eye, and you got the impression that either you did it her way or you didn't do it."

"During the course of this professional relationship with her, did you ever have occasion to challenge her or to question her judgment?"

"You didn't do that with Stella."

Tom Hillier asked that the answer be stricken as not responsive, and Judge Dwyer told the jury to disregard it.

The witness said the defendant would occasionally talk about her marriage while on the concourse. Stella Nickell said when she got home she'd read a book while her husband watched TV or talked on his CB.

"Did she tell you whether she was happy or unhappy with this state of affairs between herself and Bruce Nickell?"

"I can't say that I remember that she actually said 'I am unhappy with this situation.' "

"Then how did she describe it to you?"

"She said that she liked being on the late shift because that way she didn't have to see so much of Bruce."

"Did Mrs. Nickell ever discuss with you leaving Bruce?"

"Yes."

"Would you tell us what she said about that?"

"Well, we were talking about this plan that some of the employees there had of opening a security system in Mexico, and evidently Stella had been asked to go, and I asked her what Bruce thought about it and she says, 'Well, I haven't told him.' I asked her if she was going to, and she said, 'No. I don't care. I'm just leaving.' "

To the best of Bonnie's recollection, the conversation occurred "sometime between January and March."

Joanne Maida directed the witness to the day Stella Nickell made her announcement that Bruce died. Bonnie told the court that she and Cindy left a Kent bar when Dee Rogers called. At the apartment, Stella arrived and told Cindy, " 'Your dad is gone.' "

"Did she say anything else?"

"She looked Cindy straight in the eye and she said, 'I know what you're thinking and the answer is no.' "

The witness said mother and daughter stared at each other for "maybe ten seconds" before taking seats and pouring drinks in the kitchen. At that point, Cindy "got very upset and almost hysterical."

"And how did her mother, Stella Nickell, respond?"

"Stella was pale, but quite composed."

The Asst. U.S. Attorney had nothing further, and because of the lateness of the hour, Tom Hillier deferred his cross-examination until Monday.

CHAPTER 73

Wilma Mae Stewart brought her baby to Seattle for her day in court, Monday, April 25. She knew she wouldn't be able to take the baby into court with her, but SA Dave Hill had promised that a woman from the FBI office would look after her. That kind of assurance was typical of SA Hill.

Wilma Mae had struggled for months with the conflict of liking and trusting Dave Hill when he was after Aunt Stella. She even put in her mind that Dave Hill didn't really want her to think the worst of her aunt. Wilma didn't doubt that he felt Stella was guilty, but that didn't mean she had to think so.

Stella had warned her beautiful niece more than once: "Be careful, babe. He may seem nice, but he's FBI!"

"I know," Wilma would answer. "But this guy's different. He's not your typical cop."

Fifteen minutes before she was due in court, Wilma Stewart put her one-year-old on the hotel bed to diaper her. The baby rolled over and onto the floor and hit her head. Any mother would have been in a panic, but none more so than Wilma Stewart. God had taken her son Richard, but nothing was going to happen to this one. In a frenzy, she called the hotel's emergency number. *She needed help! Her baby was hurt!*

A moment later, someone was at the door.

"About the same time I got a knock on the door, I got my

[daughter] in my arms and obviously I'm shook up, went to the door, and it was Dave. I told him that I couldn't testify, I had to make sure [she] was okay. That's when he grabbed my arm and said: 'You *are* going to go testify.' He was pretty adamant. [The baby] was fine, there wasn't anything wrong with her! Let's get my stuff out of here," she recalled later.

It was a turning point. Dave Hill was not really a friend. All he cared about, Wilma thought, was the conviction. Wilma felt she had been used.

"He had been very helpful, very understanding of what I had been going through and sort of leading me down the yellow brick road," she said later.

The phone calls, the concern, the walks through the University of Washington's gorgeous arboretum . . . all of it now seemed bogus.

"It was Dave Hill who was there when my ex-husband and I learned my son was terminal. It was Dave Hill who was calling me and asking me how I was getting through the day. It was Dave Hill I called right after the funeral when I needed someone to talk to. It was Dave Hill who said, 'I'm your friend.' In fact, he really wasn't."

Wilma Stewart kept thinking she should have listened to Aunt Stella. She should have seen it coming. She felt angry and embarrassed that she had been taken in.

A Seattle reporter approached Wilma and her aunts Berta and Mary and other relatives outside the courthouse.

"Any comment on the trial from the family?"

Stella's sisters looked at the ground and said nothing.

Where's all the power, the strength you had while I was growing up? Willie thought as the women shifted from side to side.

"We have no comment!" Wilma finally said to end the discomfort of the moment.

"We'd like to know . . ." The reporter pushed forward.

"You don't understand," Stella's niece said, her words growing harsher with each syllable. "We have *NO* comment."

The Stephenson sisters sighed with relief as the reporter backed off.

At that moment, Wilma Stewart's world had turned.

"I could no longer look up to anyone in my family," she said later.

*   *   *

After a weekend of rest—if rest was possible in jail—friends had hoped Stella would put on a better appearance than she had the week before. Her old cut-to-the-thigh-to-catch-his-eye skirts strained at the seams. Boyfriend Fred Phelps, for one, thought his babe should have dressed up. She was a good-looking woman, but you couldn't tell by what he saw in the courtroom.

A reporter for a local TV station sat in front of Fred every day of the trial. Fred Phelps, following the lead of the Stephenson girls, refused to talk to the media. He figured the TV hack was hoping for some little crumb to come his way.

That morning, Fred was talking to Berta when Stella Maudine entered the courtroom.

"There's my girl!" he exclaimed. He noticed the TV reporter scribbling.

"That son of a bitch wrote that down," he said later. "Give me a break!"

Stella Nickell later said Tom Hillier and Sal Ramos were trying to make her dress, but she didn't want to go along with all of it. They suggested she wear glasses instead of the contact lenses she had now preferred.

At half past nine, Bonnie Anderson resumed the stand as court was called into session for Tom Hillier's cross-examination. The witness testified that when Jeanne and Jim Rice left the airport that spring, the bodyguard business left with them. Stella Nickell's plan for going to Mexico had been dashed.

The witness admitted that Stella "never came out and said" she wasn't happy in her marriage. Then Joanne Maida, on redirect, questioned Anderson's take on the Nickell marriage. Stella Nickell never came out and said she was unhappy, but "bits and pieces" of information indicated she was.

"What did she say, if anything, about why she worked certain shift hours as it related to Bruce Nickell?"

"She said that she didn't mind working the late shift because that meant that much less time she had to spend with Bruce."

Shaking from the ordeal with her baby daughter and SA Hill back in the hotel room, Wilma Mae Stewart, dressed in a striking dark-blue suit and looking every bit the beauty of the Stephenson clan, took the stand as a government witness. She was glad Dave Hill left the courtroom.

She testified that she and her aunt were so close she considered her "my mother." Her aunt and uncle's marriage was normal; occasionally Stella got a little irritated at Bruce.

"She, you know, he would come home from work sometimes and sit in front of the TV and she might need to have something done, and like all of us women, she would rather they do something more than watch TV, so she'd get a little irritated with him."

The two women kept in contact at least once a month, up until just before Bruce died. She was in Houston preparing for a trip when her aunt made a phone call out of the blue.

"She just wanted to know if she could come to Texas and stay with me."

"Was that a matter of surprise to you, or had you expected that?" Joanne Maida asked.

"No, I had not expected it. It was a surprise because, you know, she's always working things out and it just came as a shock that she would not want to stay there."

"What did she tell you had happened between her and her husband Bruce?"

"She didn't say anything had *happened*."

Even though she was a prosecution witness, her tone made it clear whose side she was on.

"How did she characterize, then, her relationship as the reason why she was coming down?"

"I don't understand what you're getting at."

"Was she happy with Bruce or was she unhappy with Bruce?"

"Well, I don't know how she was with Uncle Bruce, but you know, she wasn't happy when she called."

"What did she say about that?"

"She was just upset. She was just mad all over."

And so it went. Wilma Stewart trying to defend her aunt, but her words falling short. Yes, she thought her aunt was serious, but she wanted her to move to Houston. Stella Nickell didn't fly off the handle. She didn't get mad often.

"Did she make the statement to you that she was sick and tired of fighting with Bruce all the time?"

"She may have made that comment."

"Did she tell you whether this would be kept from Bruce if she decided to come down to stay with you at Houston?"

"Well, it seems like we talked about that, but I don't recall that part of the conversation."

Wilma Stewart sank in her chair as Joanne Maida had the clerk give the witness her grand jury testimony. She hadn't counted on that at all. After looking at it, she finally answered.

"Well, I don't know that she wouldn't tell him. It was more me keeping my mouth shut and me not to say anything to him."

"She asked you not to say anything to him?"

"Yeah."

Wilma Stewart testified she returned to Washington around Labor Day 1986, and contact with her aunt increased. Often the two talked about the case.

"And how did your aunt, if she did, make it clear to you she wanted to talk about the investigation?"

"Well, it wasn't a matter of being clear. It was a matter of we'd sit down and she would talk awhile about what went on in her life, and then as soon as I could pleasantly do so, I would interrupt and tell her what was going on in my life."

Maida asked if insurance money came up and the witness said it had—"all the time."

"Did she give you a ballpark figure, so to speak, about how much insurance money?"

"She talked about the insurance money that was involved, but not in the terms that she expected to get it."

"When did she talk about this?"

"Well, from the time that it dawned on her that that's what the government was after."

Joanne Maida asked what, if anything, Stella Nickell had told Wilma "about how much your uncle Bruce was covered for."

"Well, she talked about his—The policy that he worked at was about $25,000."

"I'm talking about the total amount at this time."

"Oh, total amount? A couple hundred grand."

"As best as you can recall, in her words, how did she say that, as to the amount?"

"As to her words, she never gave a total. I mean, as best I can remember, she didn't give a total total amount. Now, she did talk about the different policies or—"

The Asst. U.S. Attorney cut her off. "When you testified before the grand jury, do you recall saying that it was 'close to two hundred grand,' according to your aunt?"

"Okay."

"Do you recall that?"

"Yeah. I recall saying it at the grand jury."

"You indicated earlier in your testimony that there came a point in time where you didn't want to talk about insurance monies. Is that correct?"

It was. Wilma Stewart told the court it was irritating. "It got irritating because I just don't think it's—It was just irritating. . . . Well, I just don't think it's true."

"I'm just asking you about the discussion about the monetary amounts. Did you have any kind of resentment about these discussions?"

"Oh, well, yeah. I . . . yeah, I did."

"And in fact, did you tell the grand jury that you were resentful because it was about your uncle's death and he had been a really neat person and you were getting sick and tired of hearing about what she was going to get?"

"Not . . . I was sick and tired of hearing about the insurance money versus my uncle passing away."

"Is it your recollection today that she didn't talk of the close to two hundred grand amount in terms of money she was going to get; they were just monies that Bruce was covered for? Is that what your recollection is today?"

"That's right. My aunt never talked about what she was going to get."

"Was your recollection when you testified before the grand jury on August 5, 1987, better than it is today with respect to that particular question?"

"Sure it was."

Joanne Maida read from the witness's grand jury testimony:

"You indicated that she brought this up in about ten or so of these discussions. Did that become a source of some irritation to you, that it kept coming up? How did you handle that?"

She asked Wilma to read the answer.

"Well, it did me for a couple of reasons. One is I had just had a new baby and I wanted to talk about the baby, how she smiled or burped, or whatever, and the second source of irritation was that based on my interview with Dave Hill from the FBI, I kind of was resentful that there was even money involved. I mean, my uncle had died and he was a really neat person, and I was getting sick and

*tired of hearing about what she was going to get rather than the
fact that my uncle was gone."*

Before his cross, Tom Hillier gave the devastated witness a moment
to compose herself.

He asked for clarification and explanation of her last answer on
direct. She said it was the FBI that irritated her with talk of insurance money.

"Were you irritated with Stella Nickell?"

"No."

It was the FBI who told her what the insurance proceeds were,
not her aunt. Any conversations with her aunt indicated that the
insurance coverage was $25,000, plus the two credit-card payoff
policies.

"And she had no expectation of $200,000?"

"No, she never did."

Regarding her aunt's phone call to Houston just before the trip
to England, Tom Hillier elicited testimony suggesting the defendant
was blowing off steam. By the end of the call, her aunt was no
longer angry, typical of her aunt's way of doing things.

Wilma Stewart further testified that her aunt and uncle had a
good marriage. She described them as "together people." There was
nothing that would lead her to believe her aunt would kill her uncle.

For re-direct, Joanne Maida hauled out the witness's grand jury
testimony again.

*"A: I mean my uncle had died and he was a really neat person,
and I was getting sick and tired of hearing about what she was
going to get rather than the fact that my uncle had died.*

"That's your statement. And when Mr. Hillier asked you a few
questions, did I understand you correctly, you agreed with Mr. Hillier that what that really meant is that you were sick and tired of
hearing from the FBI about what your aunt was going to get, or
were you sick and tired of hearing from your aunt about what she
was going to get?"

"No. What I was sick and tired of hearing was about the insurance money from the—You know, I heard it from the FBI and
everybody talking about my aunt Stella did it for the money. I was
sick of hearing it because I knew it wasn't true."

"My question to you is when you said that you were sick and

tired of hearing what she was going to get on this particular passage, were you talking about being sick and tired of the FBI telling you that or your aunt telling you that?"

"The FBI."

"Now, I heard you testify, and correct me if I'm wrong, that you only talked to the FBI a couple of times about the insurance amounts, and I thought you also said it wasn't very often you talked with them about the insurance amounts. Is that true?"

"That's true."

"And on the other hand, you did talk to your aunt about the insurance amounts a great deal, did you not?"

"Yes, I did."

"Were you not sick and tired of hearing from her as well about that?"

"No. You're not understanding. I'm not being very clear about what I'm saying. When my aunt Stella and I talked, it was basically that the FBI or the United States government was saying that she did this terrible thing because of money, insurance money. It's not true."

Again, that damned grand jury was brought up.

"Did you make the statement that your aunt was expecting close to two hundred grand?"

"I may have said that in the grand jury."

Joanne Maida read from the testimony.

"Q: How did she describe this grand total to you?

"A: She told me pretty near—not pretty near; that's my word—almost 200,000. Close to two hundred grand.

" 'Close to two hundred grand.' Is that correct? I'm asking you at this point. The way it's phrased, it's in quotes, the words 'close to two hundred grand'?"

"Are those supposed to be my quotes?"

"Let me see if I understand you correctly. The words 'close to two hundred grand' was your aunt's description of how much she was expecting. Is that not correct?"

"No. No. You keep using the word 'expecting.' "

Joanne Maida moved on to another question.

"Q: That she would be expecting if she were not indicted or if she were acquitted if she were indicted.

"Answer?"

"Right."

Tom Hillier had a single question for re-cross.

"Mrs. Stewart, is it your testimony today before this jury that your aunt Stella was expecting $200,000?"

"No, it is not."

Dave Hill returned to escort Wilma out of the courtroom. As they turned toward the elevators, a woman stepped out with FBI Special Agent Jack Cusack. Wilma didn't recognize her cousin at first. She was made up, perfect hair, perfect eyebrows . . . It was her, but it wasn't.

Wilma felt herself lunge forward. She wanted to smack the girl. Hard. Decisively. She had taken Aunt Stella away.

But Dave Hill was there. Or maybe it was the realization of the futility of an attack at the Federal Courthouse, and it didn't happen.

It was the last time she would see Cynthia Lea.

Robert Lesniewski, vice-president of underwriting of Amex Life Insurance Company, formerly Firemen's Fund, took the stand to identify Bruce Nickell's application for $50,000-life insurance, dated January 20, 1984. The beneficiary was the defendant. The policy was canceled as a result of a letter written by the defendant on May 14, 1985, protesting an increase in premium payment rate from $27 to $45.65.

The premium had been raised in March of 1985 because of Mr. Nickell's age following the first anniversary of the policy.

The witness identified a form letter sent by customer service.

"Apparently we got a telephone call from Stella Nickell and we couldn't locate that in our alpha index, so we sent this inquiry out to try and find out what policy they were referring to."

The letter, entitled "Insufficient Information," was sent to Stella Nickell on June 3, 1985.

The form was returned, completed by Stella Nickell. It indicated that the insured was Bruce Nickell; the policy in question was Life and Accidental Death, $50,000.

It was admitted into evidence.

Next was a letter from Stella Nickell canceling the policy, though only the applicant-owner, Bruce Nickell, could make such a request. Another letter was sent out by the insurance company, and it was returned signed by Bruce Nickell on June 10, 1985.

Judge Dwyer warned the jurors that morning recess might run a bit longer than usual. Legal matters needed attending.

Tom Hillier was concerned about the witness, and what she

might say. The government's trial brief had referred to the poly-
graph, and he wanted firm directions given regarding the subject.
He cited three pages of Cindy Hamilton's grand jury testimony.
None of it indicated the polygraph as the reason she came forward.

The Asst. U.S. Attorney said the witness had been instructed not
to mention the polygraph. Joanne Maida said she had, in fact, told
Cindy Hamilton not to mention the polygraph to the grand jury
because she did not want to have the grand jurors "tainted" by the
information. But trial was a different animal. The Asst. U.S. Attorney said she didn't seek to offer the polygraph for its truth, but for
its relevance in Cindy Hamilton's coming forward, "especially if
Mr. Hillier gets up on cross-examination and says her motivation
was the reward money."

Tom Hillier said he did not intend to cross-examine Cindy Hamilton on the reward, that he wanted to probe the witness's prior
inconsistent statement—six months before she came forward.

"I don't intend to open any doors and I have been careful with
the way I've prepared my cross-examination, because I don't want
this polygraph stuff to come in because it's so confusing, so prejudicial, and so unreliable," he said. "I think I can testify firsthand
as to the unreliability of the polygraph testimony better than most
lawyers can in view of my experience with them," he added, referring to the Steve Titus case.

Both parties had agreed to stipulate that the reward money was
available. As far as Tom Hillier could see, it was as relevant as the
insurance money the government said had been Stella Nickell's
motive.

Judge Dwyer needed more time for his ruling. If the cross-
examination attacked the witness's motivation, he tended to lean
toward admitting the phone call Stella purportedly made to her
daughter with a limiting instruction to the jury.

That phone conversation wouldn't go away. Both mother and
daughter were adamant in their positions about the call. Cindy said
it was the reason she went to the FBI. Stella said the call never
took place, that it was one more of her daughter's lies.

While it is possible both mother and daughter were lying about
the phone call, if there was any truth to the story, only one was
telling it.

Cindy told people she was "irked" when her mother called her
at work at a Kent 7-Eleven the day after she took the polygraph.

"She told me that she had gone in to take the polygraph, and I didn't say anything."

" 'Well, the man that gave it to me said that I failed it.' "

Cindy said she didn't, *just couldn't*, respond. She told people she had reached the point where she "couldn't play the games with her mother anymore . . . the protective 'Gee, Mom, you couldn't have done it.' "

Stella Nickell tightened up just thinking about her daughter's phone-call story and the pressure it was putting on her defense. Opening the door to the phone call could pave the way to disclosing the polygraph.

Stella Nickell stuck with her story; she told her attorney that she would never have called her daughter at work unless it was an emergency. She wasn't even sure where Cindy was working at the time, anyway. The defendant blamed Dee Rogers for passing on the information to her daughter.

"Dee had called me later that day. You see, I also found out that Dee was working very closely hand in hand with the FBI, she was recording all of my moves, all of my conversations with her and everything else to the FBI."

Stella later said she didn't worry what she said to her old friend Dee Rogers. She had nothing to hide. When Dee Rogers called on the day of the polygraph, Stella Nickell later insisted, her Tri-Chem crony already knew she had failed it.

Some of Stella Maudine's story made sense. Dee Rogers had, in fact, pushed Cynthia Lea to tell her story to the FBI—but it had been in the early fall, long before the lie-detector exam. SA Cusack gave the defendant the polygraph exam at the Seattle field-office in mid-December.

Dee Rogers later brushed off any duplicity. Her version had Cynthia coming home from work with the news. And it had been *after* they had gone to the FBI.

That afternoon, while Stella's sisters shifted on the uncomfortable spectators seats, Lynn Selby was sworn in and seated in the witness box. She was another corporate records keeper, the vice-president of a division of Direct Mail Insurance Company, underwriters of the All American Life policies.

She identified two applications for $20,000 group term life insurance bearing the dates of October 14, 1985, and September 5, 1985. Both Bruce and Stella Nickell were to be beneficiaries in the event of the other's death. Both had been billed to the Nickells' MasterCard.

"Are these policies—do these policies pay out or are they limited in any respect to how much the credit-card bills are of these people?" Joanne Maida asked.

"No. The credit card is only used for paying."

The witness next identified the certificate of insurance sent to the Nickells after the insurance had been approved. In bold black letters it clearly indicated "Life insurance benefits for insured."

And as far as the corporate records indicated, there had been no clerical error in the issuing of the October 14, 1985, policy.

Stella Nickell's two letters from October 20, 1986, seeking information on making a claim, were identified and admitted. The letters referenced the two different policies and had death certificates attached, as well as two different personal specification schedules. Further, Lynn Selby identified the claimant's statement, an original and photocopy, again referring to both policies by policy numbers G666-BL-200387 and G666-BL-247301.

Tom Hillier tried to prove his client's assertion that she believed the policies paid off credit cards. He had the witness read the words hidden under the policy-number sticker on the membership enrollment card.

"Two thousand dollar credit-card payoff at no cost as long as you remain a member, I think," Lynn Selby answered.

"All right. That's what it says with respect to credit-card payoff on the application?"

"Yes, but that has nothing to do with the $20,000 group term life."

Next, Tom Hillier also tried to lay the groundwork for Stella Nickell's contention that she didn't understand that they were two different policies.

Lynn Selby stated both had the same group policy number, both were solicited through MasterCard account, premium costs were the same, and the letters, the applications, the claimant statements were all sent to the same place: All American Life.

Through cross, Tom Hillier had the witness confirm that the policy numbers both appeared on the letter, circled, with the handwritten notation: *"Both policies are the same."*

"Assuming that it says as it states, 'Both the same policy,' and assuming that the writer is saying that these are both the same policy, relating to those two numbers, I gathered from your testimony this morning that the writer is wrong. Correct?"

"Maybe; maybe not. Both policies are the same as far as benefits are concerned."

FBI document examiner Lee Waggoner was sworn in, and under Joanne Maida's direct, testified to eleven years' experience in the FBI lab in Washington. No one would doubt what he had to say, and as Tom Hillier had stated in his opening remarks, Stella Nickell would not dispute she signed her husband's paperwork.

He identified the two All American policies as documents he had examined for handwriting analysis.

Joanne Maida asked who signed the blank titled "Spouse Signature"—the purported signature of Bruce Nickell on the September 5 document.

Waggoner said he was unable to determine who had written "Bruce"; however, it was his opinion Stella Nickell had written the surname.

Charts with enlargements of the signatures in question, and showing "known" handwriting samples of the defendant and her late spouse, were admitted into evidence for illustrative purposes.

The Asst. U.S. Attorney Maida had the clerk pull the illustrative chart for the October 14, 1985, application.

The FBI expert said it had not been signed by Bruce Nickell, but some variations in the letter strokes prohibited him from positively concluding that Stella Nickell had signed it.

The Firemen's application signature was next. SA Waggoner testified that the copy quality was too poor to determine who had signed it at all.

The cancellation letter to Firemen's Fund dated June 5, 1985, however, was not signed by Bruce Nickell.

"The Nickell portion I couldn't be sure. I think Stella probably wrote it. The Bruce portion of the signature, I couldn't tell whether or not Stella wrote it."

Tom Hillier asked the witness if he had reached any conclusions about who signed the change-of-insurance form that was introduced into evidence earlier in the trial.

"In my opinion, the document was filled out and signed by Bruce Nickell."

Cindy Hamilton was next . . . and nobody wanted to miss her. For once the recess was not wanted.

* * *

Out of the presence of the jury, the inadmissible polygraph and the phone call once again became the greatest point of dissension between the prosecution and the defense. With Cindy Hamilton about to testify, it was necessary for another go-around with Judge Dwyer.

To explain why it was that Cindy Hamilton went to the FBI, the government wanted to ask the witness if she had received a phone call from her mother during the time period. She was not going to ask about the content of the call.

Tom Hillier suggested it would be safer if the Asst. U.S. Attorney simply said that the witness went to the FBI. If the call was mentioned, the jury might speculate on what was said. A confession, perhaps?

Judge Dwyer wanted to avoid entirely questioning her communications with the FBI.

If a deal between the feds and Cindy Hamilton had been made, as Stella's supporters speculated, it was Joanne Maida who might have given the greatest clue.

The phone call, she said, "is part of the reason that she came forward, and to explain the circumstances of the interview that was arranged through the FBI, that that was not of her own making. It was as a result of the telephone call. . . . I don't intend to get into, obviously, the subject matter of the polygraph, but because of that phone call she will say that she considered very seriously what she should do, and she found out that the FBI had arranged an interview of her. She consented to that, but her consent was based on the telephone conversation she had with her mother. So the timing on that, to put it into perspective for the jury, does become important."

Not of her own making.

She found out the FBI had arranged an interview.

She consented to that.

Was Stella Nickell correct when she told friends she thought her phone lines were tapped? If a conversation indeed took place, had the government used it to push Cindy into going against her mother?

Mother and daughter both had compelling reasons to deny such an episode.

And so it went. Finally, it was left that the question asked of Cindy would be something like: "Did you hear something about the case that you hadn't heard before?"

Tom Hillier objected; the jury would still speculate on what had been said between mother and daughter.

CHAPTER 74

Cynthia Hamilton, looking every inch her mother's daughter, took the stand the afternoon of April 25. She wore a yellow outfit, skirt and jacket. Her hair was a bright orange-red. She was a bit thinner than the last time her mother had seen her.

Everyone hushed as Jack Cusack handed her off to Ron Nichols to be sworn in. Many, including the defendant, were curious. Spectators stared at mother and daughter again and again, tracing the lines of resemblance in their faces. The defendant's feelings were in check, more so than the witness's. She seemed nervous. Even frightened.

Stella Nickell seemed to stare a hole through her daughter's chest. She thought Cindy looked terrible. Awful, she said later. The government had tried to make her look weak and distraught. Stella Maudine knew better.

In what was clearly an attempt to show the difficulties the daughter had to endure during her childhood, Joanne Maida established family relationships, including a mention of Leah.

"What did you strive to be, based on your mother's upbringing of you?"

"I tried very hard to be everything that I thought my mother wanted me to be, to always have control of myself, to present myself in a fashion that would please my mother at all times."

When not looking at the witness with a hard stare, Stella scribbled notes on a legal pad. If her movement was any indication, everything the witness said could be refuted. The defendant's arms and hands worked overtime as Cindy told the jury that she and her mother did not have a close relationship prior to her move up to Washington in late 1982. They grew close, she said, after "we discussed a lot of different things in my childhood and were able to overcome problems that she and I had had with each other during my growing up."

This was a contradiction Tom Hillier must have missed. She had told the grand jury that the only time they ever discussed her childhood was after her twenty-first-birthday celebration, around Thanksgiving 1980.

Cindy told the court that she and her mother became close when they lived together from December 1982 to April 1983. Whatever problems they had were gone. They became more like best friends than mother and daughter.

"What prompted the move out of the house in April of 1983 after living there for four months?" Joanne Maida asked.

"My mother and I were having some disagreements as to my lifestyle and the upbringing of my daughter."

Stella Nickell wrote angrily: *"Because she would be gone for 2 & 3 days at a time and no phone calls to let me know how she was nor to ask about her daughter."*

The witness said she didn't like Bruce Nickell when she first met him, because he was an alcoholic. By the time she moved back to Washington in 1982, however, he had stopped drinking.

"He was a lot less obnoxious. He was a very intelligent man. He was very funny and he was very witty when he wanted to be. He at times could very easily endear himself to you when he wasn't drinking."

Cynthia Hamilton testified that after Bruce dried out, he became a homebody. The days of running around and partying were gone. And her mother wasn't happy about it.

"Well, she was very pleased and very grateful that he had stopped drinking, and she made sure that he knew that, but she was discontented with the fact that they didn't do anything anymore. Oh, they would go camping or they would go and visit Grandma and Grandpa east of the mountains, his mother and father."

"Based on what your mother told you, how did their social life change after Bruce became a reformed alcoholic?"

"Their social life changed in the effect that most of their friends and acquaintances he chose not to associate with anymore because most everyone that he knew and they knew together drank."

"How did your mother feel about that in the relationship that she had with Bruce?"

"She made friends of her own, but she was discontented with not being able to go out partying anymore."

As her testimony continued, Cindy told the court she and her mother sewed for Eddie Bauer. Later, she and her mother worked at SeaTac. She said she started in February 1986, and left a couple of months after Bruce died.

Next, Joanne Maida focused on the shift hours, the fact that mother and daughter often rode to the airport together. They were alone for much of the time, and passed the time talking.

"Most of the time we were able to talk was in the morning on the way to work, on the shuttle bus, on the concourse. When we would take the shuttle bus in, there were a lot of times we were there just shortly after four-thirty."

"Were you able to talk about a lot of personal things during these times?"

She said they were.

Asst. U.S. Attorney Maida asked the witness to tell the court how she learned of Bruce Nickell's death.

Cindy Hamilton said she and Bonnie Anderson were out drinking when Dee Rogers called from their apartment and told her to come home right away. Within a few minutes, Stella Nickell arrived.

"She came in. She sat down at the kitchen table and she told me that my dad had died."

"Did she say anything else?"

"Yes."

"What else did she say?"

The witness started to cry. "Just a minute . . ."

Judge Dwyer called for a recess so the witness could calm herself.

Ron Nichols noticed that one of the women jurors was crying too. *That was a good sign*, he thought.

When the questioning was resumed, Maida asked, "Did she say anything else?"

"She looked at me and she said, 'I know what you're thinking, and the answer is no.' "

"Based on your past relationship with your mother, your past conversations with her, did you feel you knew what she was talking about?"

"Yes, I knew exactly what she was talking about."

"In the days following this announcement made by your mother about your dad's death, did you ever confront her about his death?"

"Not after that, no."

"Did you ever ask her point-blank, did she cause his death?"

"No."

Even with a microphone, Cindy Hamilton's voice was so soft that Tom Hillier strained to hear.

She said she stayed with her mother for a short time after Bruce's death. She even went with her mother to the family doctors' to find out why Bruce died.

"Based on what your mother told you, what did you think to be the reason he died?"

"Based on what my mother had told me prior to my dad's death, I believed that she did it. I basically knew that she did it, and—"

Tom Hillier objected to the witness's rambling, but the question had been answered.

Joanne Maida asked for Stella Nickell's reason concerning her husband's death. On the verge of tears, Cindy further stated that she didn't press her mother for information, in light of the emphysema ruling.

"Why not?"

"I didn't want to ask her."

"Why not?"

"Because I didn't want her to tell me the truth and I didn't want her to lie to me."

Under further direct, Cindy Hamilton told the court that her mother called her and told her the FBI would be coming out to the property for an interview. Cindy made arrangements to be there too.

"Why did you plan to be there?"

"I was scared for her, and I guess to protect her: I've always been very protective of my mother. I was afraid they were going to find something there that was going to be proof of what I basically knew she had done."

Stella Nickell's daughter testified that FBI agents asked her the "obvious" questions about the Nickell marriage, if her "dad" had any enemies, if her mother could have done it. She told them their marriage was relatively happy, and no, she didn't think her mother did it.

"Was that the truth?"

"No."

"Why did you lie?"

"To protect my mother."

Or herself?

While her mother looked on, shaking her head slightly, Cynthia proceeded to tell the jury that the truth was her mother's marriage had soured by the time Bruce Nickell died.

"There was a lot of dissatisfaction on my mother's part."

"And how did you know that?"

"She told me."

The discussions occurred over a period of several years.

Joanne Maida had the witness discuss her version of the Nickell finances. The young woman was aware of the bankruptcy petition, the layoff from McDonald Industries.

"What, if anything, did your mother tell you about this period of time, the six months or so that your dad had been laid off?"

"She—At first everything was fine. He was making out applications and sending out résumés, and then towards the end of that time period he wasn't really making a great effort at finding another job. He had already sent out his résumés and he wasn't really following up on them, and she told me she felt that he was not making a great effort to get out and get a job, and she was very upset about it."

"According to your mother, what was the relationship between her and her husband?"

"Their relationship progressively worsened."

Cindy told the court her mother had even discussed divorce within a year before Bruce Nickell's death.

"Did your mother stay with that option or did she change?"

"She changed."

The defense attorney objected. The question assumed facts that weren't in evidence.

Joanne Maida tried again. "According to your mother how, if at all, did this option of divorce remain?"

Cindy said her mother considered divorce for a "short time," but decided against it because "she was not going to lose half of everything that she had fought so hard to get."

"What options other than divorce, then, did she discuss with you, if she did?" the Asst. U.S. Attorney asked.

"She discussed killing him."

"Did she, over a period of time, discuss how she would accomplish this?"

Her mother had, but Cindy did not know it was Bruce when her mother started talking about it. The first conversations were about "two years prior, at least."

Maida tried to get Stella's daughter to nail down the time frames.

"At least two years prior to Bruce's death, and a maximum of four to five."

"And why do you put it at four to five?"

"Because I can remember certain questions that were asked of me shortly after my moving here on a permanent basis."

"What kinds of questions did she ask you in and around December of 1982?"

"The first question that I can definitely recall had to do with heroin, and she asked me if I knew where I could acquire any." But the witness said she had no idea where to get any. Her mother also asked her about cocaine and speed.

"What did she ask you about cocaine, particularly?"

"What it would take to overdose a person."

Cindy's recollection of the date was interesting. Katy Parker had told the FBI that Cindy talked with her about Stella's interest in cocaine overdoses in the fall of 1985. How could that have been one of the first conversations?

The witness said the questions about speed and cocaine were general, with no names attached.

Cindy explained that, yes, she had used drugs, primarily speed. It was a habit that her mother had known about; hence the questions about it.

"What about cocaine? Did you ever use that?"

"I have indulged in cocaine but very, very, very few times. It's—it wasn't of use to me for the same reasons that I was using speed."

She went on to testify that she was a single mother at the time, holding down two jobs, coupled with an active social life. ". . . There just wasn't enough time in the day to do all that and sleep, too."

"Did you have a reaction to your mother when she asked you

questions about heroin and speed and cocaine, where she could get them?"

Cindy stammered.

"I was—I didn't have any real severe reaction, no. I was curious as to why she was curious, but it didn't strike me as odd, no."

She said she had no information on heroin—"a very harsh, hard drug."

"I do know that it doesn't take a lot to overdose a person, through what I've heard and seen on documentaries."

Concerning cocaine, Cindy claimed that she told her mother she was unsure what quantity would cause an overdose. She also told her mother that the drug stays in the system even after the user ceases taking it.

"What did you say to her about speed?"

"About speed? It depended. It's a lot harder to overdose a person on speed. It also stays in your system, and I don't know how the body treats it in distributing it, whether you ingest it or whether you inhale it, the different methods of using it, and I really didn't know how much it would take to overdose a person."

"With respect to which drugs was she asking about overdosing?" Joanne Maida asked.

"Over different periods of time, at different times she was asking about overdosing on all of them."

As direct continued, Cindy Hamilton said her mother also did some research on drugs.

The next question was important. The Asst. U.S. Attorney asked if Cindy knew which books her mother had read when she told the FBI about library research. It was important because of the possible charge that daughter and mother had been coconspirators. Cynthia Lea Hamilton could know too much, and that would be damaging.

The witness said she did not.

"Did there come a point in time that your mother began specifying names of people in these conversations about death?"

"Eventually, yes. Names were brought into it."

"Whose name?"

"My dad, Bruce Nickell."

Court adjourned until the next morning.

CHAPTER 75

Before eager spectators and the jury were seated for Cindy's second day of testimony, the intention of the government to bring up the polygraph and phone call were argued again before Judge Bill Dwyer.

Judge Dwyer addressed the dilemma. He acknowledged that the government had not sought to probe the *content* of the phone call, only to establish that a call had been the catalyst in Cindy's coming forward. Since such testimony would lead to much speculation as to what had been said, Dwyer had suggested the question be: "Did you hear something about the case you had not heard before and then decide to go talk to the FBI?"

But in light of the preceding day's testimony, that wouldn't work either. Cindy Hamilton told the jury she knew all along her mother was the killer. The phone call would invite speculation about a confession or the reward being discussed. A curative instruction admonishing jurors not to speculate on the conversation wasn't worth the risk.

After considerable discussion it was agreed that whether the phone call would be mentioned would depend on the defense's case and rebuttal later. Dwyer told the attorneys that if the reward came into play, and if Cindy's testimony reflected no motivation related to that, then she should be allowed to testify to the call.

* * *

Cindy Hamilton returned to the witness box as Joanne Maida renewed the testimony that the young woman had heard her father's name connected with her mother's interest in drug overdoses sometime after the discussions began.

Cindy said her mother told her that her stepfather had been treated for alcoholism at Schick Shadel, and through subsequent experience with counselors and tapes, Stella had learned that "it was not uncommon for an alcoholic to turn to other substance abuse."

"What did your mother say when she became more specific to the point where she mentioned your dad's name in conversations about drugs?"

"I can't remember exactly the first time, but in some references of bringing up his name and in overdosing him, specifically with cocaine, that it could be placed in his iced tea."

"And according to your mother, why would she put cocaine in your dad's iced tea?"

"It basically couldn't be tasted in the iced tea, therefore being able to be distributed throughout his system, and then eventually to just overdose him on it."

Cindy Hamilton said her mother told her that when Bruce was autopsied, the cocaine could be explained as an accidental overdose. She said the conversations occurred in late 1985 and early 1986.

Asst. U.S. Attorney Maida asked how Cindy could pinpoint the date.

"Because my dad had to pass a physical in January to become a permanent employee of the state, and the idea was shoved around that she could not do that prior to the physical because there would be—it would be found in the physical."

She said her mother was concerned that if doctors found cocaine in his system, Bruce would lose his job, and she'd lose his life insurance. The plan was dropped.

Under more direct examination, Cindy Hamilton said she didn't think "terribly much" of her mother's questions about overdoses of cocaine. She didn't know it was Bruce Nickell she had in mind.

"She is a very intelligent woman and she does a lot of information-gathering. So it's in a lot of different areas. Trivia, nothing real specific. It struck me more as woolgathering. Just questions. Picking my brain, so to speak."

Joanne Maida asked what went through the witness's mind when her mother asked where she could acquire heroin.

Again, as she had before the grand jury, she stammered in her response.

"I answered her questions and afterwards, after we had—well, her presence, I thought about them, and it briefly ran through my mind that she may have been possibly asking me about acquiring it to supplement her income to—"

The prosecutor interrupted: "To go out and sell it?"

Cindy nodded. "To go out and sell it, or she maybe knew someone that wanted it and would sell it to them. As I said, the thought that crossed my mind was that it was an income supplement."

Describing how she felt when she learned of her mother's intent to kill Bruce, Cindy said she "was hoping she was just talking out of frustration and dissatisfaction, and then on the other hand, the actual thought and fright that she was going to do it."

Her words trailed off and she started to break down.

"There was a lot of conflict in what I thought."

"Would you tell us why, if you can, why there was a lot of conflict in how you reacted and what you thought?"

"I know my mother very well, and basically I knew she was capable of it, but I was hoping she wouldn't."

Joanne Maida asked if Cindy had confided her mother's plans to anyone.

She said she had.

"It kind of threw me off tilt. It was such a crazy idea and it seemed so feasible. I needed some feedback from somebody on it."

The conversations about murder increased in detail. In mid-1985 her mother even discussed hiring someone else to kill Bruce Nickell.

"Actually it was somewhere around the time of April of '85 that the discussion and the questioning of hit men came into being, and more intensely to the end of the year, after I knew for sure when it was my dad.

"By late '85 I knew for sure. I could not tell you really exactly when I knew for positive—when the first time was that I knew for sure."

When the hit-man idea was discussed, Cindy said again, she passed it off as more information-gathering on the part of her mother. Her mother wanted to know if she had any connections, or knew the cost. Cindy said she didn't have any answers.

"When you heard these questions from your mother, did you

take them seriously or did you just dismiss them as being outlandish?"

"No, I didn't dismiss them. . . . Once getting to the subject of hit men, I knew someone was in some trouble."

Maida returned her questions to SeaTac, to establish when the discussions occurred. The witness said they started February 1986, and as she said the day before, she and her mother talked during the drive to the concourse.

Before working together, she said, they talked about cocaine and hit men when out shopping. She said it was late '85 or early '86 when Bruce Nickell's name was mentioned as the target of the hit man.

"It was towards the time after I started, because she had plans to become a bodyguard. And then she spoke of the hit man prior and also afterwards, because when the thing, the position with the bodyguard operation fell through, then she couldn't just up and disappear."

Cindy Hamilton said co-worker Jeanne Rice had been behind the Mexican bodyguard-company idea.

"She told me she was just going to get in—just leave the airport one day and not come back.

"She told me the way she was going to arrange that was she was going to keep a diary, and in that diary she was going to make entries of a strange person watching her at the airport, just a slight mention in her diary, because she found it strange that this person was there every day watching her. And these entries in some way were going to be made into this diary so that when she just disappeared, it would look as if she was kidnapped or abducted and she would never be heard from again.

"There was talk of the possibility that while she was away, that a hit man could be employed to kill my dad and she would not be anywhere around to be found responsible for that.

"She also entertained the same thought in going to Texas, to go to Texas to visit my cousin Wilma Mae, and that while she was on her way down for vacation or a visit, that a hit man could kill my dad in some way and then she would be all the way in Texas and pretend not to know anything about it."

Joanne Maida asked if Stella Nickell was to fake an abduction and disappear, how she would collect life insurance.

"There was never any discussion of her coming back from being a bodyguard."

Was the Texas plan the same as the Mexican plan—a complete disappearance?

Cindy said it was not. Her mother was going to Texas to live. She had even invited her daughter to come too.

The hit-man idea frightened her.

"I just had a—I was scared. I was afraid she was going to do that."

"Did you see the idea as being realistic?"

"Oh, yes. Very much so."

"How so?"

"Because of the modes of death that she talked about; things that the hit man could do."

Cindy explained: "He could be shot in traffic going to or from work; he could be run head-on into by a truck, or just plainly run off the road with a truck. Different other methods in just a very violent way and seeming more as a random killing."

To the witness, it all seemed plausible. Accidents happen on the freeway all the time. But her mother didn't have the money to hire anyone.

The diary had been mentioned so often, and so many had claimed to have seen it or something like it, one might have thought it would be entered into evidence. But it wasn't among Joanne Maida's vast arsenal of paperwork.

SA Cusack had heard Cindy talk about the diary. Girlfriends heard her say she had actually *read* it, and that was how she knew of the kidnapping plot.

"I was over at my mom's trailer and I saw it on the table and read it . . ."

But in court she didn't say that. She distanced herself from the book by saying that her mother had *told* her about it. Reading it would have been a bit too close to home.

Fred Phelps and Cora Lee Rice later joined Dee Rogers on the list of people with claims to having read the Ouija ledger with questions pinpointing the date of Bruce Nickell's demise. Had Fred burned it? Or was he holding out for some movie deal or something, as one of Stella's relatives suggested?

No one could say.

Stella Nickell said none of the documents existed. "Another of Cindy's lies," she explained.

*   *   *

Berta and her sister Mary left for the hallway outside the courtroom aghast and disgusted by Cindy's testimony; but in the hallway they overheard one woman say with a sigh, "Oh, that poor girl. She lost her daddy."

Berta couldn't hold her tongue.

"That was not her daddy, that was her stepfather. She never called him that until court."

"Oh, really?" The woman looked puzzled. "Why would she do that?"

Stella's sister went on. "What would you do for a lot of money?"

Berta considered the encounter "a little of our own input" to help Stella Maudine. The things that needed to come out in court hadn't come out yet.

"Of course," she said later, "we couldn't get to the jury."

After recess, Joanne Maida asked her star witness if the disappearance of her mother to Texas or Mexico would mean she would lose all of her property.

"My mother told me that in going to Mexico to be a bodyguard that she would acquire a substantial amount of money in salary for doing this and would basically have no need for the property or anything having to do with my dad or the property or the trailer or anything; that the substantial amount of money she would receive as a bodyguard was what she was after."

The Texas plan differed.

Stella's daughter said her mother's plan was to come back for "the property, the trailer, because of course with my dad dead, it would all be hers."

Cindy Hamilton said she was "very relieved" that her mother had considered just disappearing.

"Because if she just packed up and left and went to Texas to be employed as a bodyguard, then she would drop the whole idea of trying to kill my dad."

Joanne Maida moved on to testimony about discussions mother and daughter might have had concerning toxic plants. Cindy's mother had said she could put a toxic plant into her husband's food, and the resulting poisoning "could be explained as an accidental ingestion due to the fact that my dad was one for picking something, a piece of grass or a twig, something, and sticking it in his mouth and chewing on it."

"Did your mother tell you about any opportunity she had to feed him a toxic plant?"

"Yes."

"What did she say?"

Tom Hillier asked for a time frame for the discussions.

Cindy Hamilton said they occurred during the six-month period before his death, again while she and her mother were working at SeaTac.

"She told me specifically on one occasion that she had indeed fed him . . . it was either two or three capsules full of small black seeds. I cannot tell you for sure exactly what plant. I'm sure she told me at the time. I cannot remember exactly. I know that the plant was lethal, or supposed to be."

The Asst. U.S. Attorney asked if Cindy knew what plant her mother said she had used.

"The name 'hemlock' stays in my mind, and foxglove, and foxglove seems to stick out more."

"Why?"

"Foxglove, to the best of my knowledge, is a very common plant, and she also had in turn discussed foxglove at one time."

Joanne Maida had pointed out with other witnesses that memory deteriorates and grand jury testimony is a great aid to recall. Yet Cynthia Hamilton could recall things now that she never could before. Foxglove had not been mentioned in her grand jury appearance.

Cindy said her mother told her she was doing some research on toxic seeds, though she couldn't recall any besides hemlock and foxglove.

"What did she say about the capsules containing the seeds?"

"She just said that she had given them to him and that they really had no real adverse effect."

Cindy said her mother told her of the seeds in the capsule six months before her stepfather died. Her mother indicated she had done it within two weeks of telling her daughter.

Joanne Maida again asked how the witness could establish the time frame.

"Because it came after her telling me of her research into the toxic-plant area, and it came before some other discussions that we had."

Under direct, the government's star witness said her mother told

her she had researched cyanide at the library within three months
of Bruce Nickell's death.

"The discussions came up having to do with the Tylenol tamperings back east; that it would be very easy to reenact those tamperings."

"Why?"

"The actual act itself of putting something tainted or tampered
with back on the shelf, in her own words, would have been easy
because they were looking for people to be shoplifting and taking
things from the store, not looking for somebody to put something
back."

Cindy also claimed her mother told her cyanide could be purchased at photography stores and Stella Nickell planned to call on
different stores to see if identification was required.

"Was any of this discussion, according to your mother, related
to your dad?"

"Yes. She—these plans per se were being made. The foundation
was being laid to kill my dad in a way that she would not get
caught in doing so."

"Was there any discussion in particular among all these different
methods that concerned you the most?"

"The hit man and the cyanide were the two that actually panicked me the most."

The witness said her mother abandoned the hit as too costly,
and she focused on the cyanide.

While her mother discussed the insurance money during the time
of the cyanide discussions, the witness said, she did not mention
specific amounts, though it would be enough to pay off the property, the trailer, "and the possibility that she would have enough to
live on comfortably, and the possibility that we could entertain the
idea of starting a fish store."

The witness also was greatly interested in fish, and boasted that
her expertise went "far beyond" her mother's.

As Joanne Maida moved the testimony along, Cynthia told the
court that she offered her mother advice concerning algae growth
a year before Bruce Nickell's death. She knew this because after
her parents moved to the property, the tank was near a door, which
was open in the summer, causing algae growth.

"We were talking about the trouble she has with her tank, and
algae can be a real major problem and how to keep it down or get
rid of it, and she was using algicide in a tablet form."

"Did you have your own opinion, based on your own knowledge about fish, about a product that you personally preferred to use to kill algae?" Maida asked.

She said she preferred Aquatronics liquid and told her mother about the product, and eventually she convinced her mother to switch.

Could this young woman with the tear-streaked eyes, yet oh-so-tough demeanor—the kind that prompted one courtroom observer to say she "has a lot of miles on her too"—really have thought her mother would carry out her murder plans?

"My innermost thoughts and my own personal innermost knowledge of my mother, yes, I basically knew she would."

"Did you have any reservations about that?"

"I was going through a lot of conflict. I knew she would, and I thought she would, and I hoped she wouldn't, and then I didn't think she could but I knew she could. . . ."

"Why did you feel this conflict?" Joanne Maida asked.

"I knew she was capable of it, but when it's your own mother, you don't want to believe—you don't want to believe that she could."

The witness said she didn't warn Bruce because she didn't think he'd believe her.

"What proof did I have?" she asked, tears falling again. "I had nothing that I could take to him and present him with the truth. How do you make your stepfather who has only been close to you, real close to you for four years, believe that his wife of almost twelve years who is supposed to love him is going to kill him? How do you approach somebody with that?"

"Did there come a point in time, after that, that you came forward with information to the FBI, basically what you've testified to in court today, that information?"

"Yes."

"The second time that you talked with the FBI, was that in January of 1987?"

"Yes, it was."

"That's about a six-month lapse between interviews. Is that correct?"

"Yes."

"Did you do a lot of serious thinking in those six months?"

"Yes, I did."

"Just answer yes or no to this question. By January 1987, had you thought it over? Had you decided to tell the FBI what you knew?"

"Yes, I did."

"Ms. Hamilton, you came forward to the FBI, as you've indicated, in January of 1987 and then to the grand jury in March of 1987, and now to this jury. As a general principle, why have you been willing three times to come forward with your knowledge about your mother's involvement with your father's death?"

"It was the right thing for me to do. It was a decision that I made and I knew it was the right thing to do, and that's what I done."

Joanne Maida asked when the witness had last talked with her mother.

"The last contact that I had with her was when I went to go get my dog from her property, where I was keeping her, and that was the last time I seen or spoke with my mother."

"Was this in the same year that your dad died?"

"It was—no, it was after my first two statements to the FBI."

Again, Cindy Hamilton's testimony suggested going to the FBI before January 1987.

Only mother and daughter know for certain when it took place and what their last meeting truly was all about, but both agree that it was out in Auburn at the Nickell mobile home.

Cindy had told the grand jury she went to get her Doberman a month and a half before her grand jury appearance and that she stayed only twenty minutes.

"She asked me if I had been spoken to by the FBI. I told her no, that they hadn't contacted me. She said, well, they had contacted so and so, and so on, some friends of hers, and went on to tell me about the plans with her lawyers and et cetera, and I really didn't have much to say. I just listened a little bit, and said, 'Well, we got to go,' took my dog, and left."

Her mother's version of the encounter, which Stella maintained took place just before Christmas, is markedly different.

Cindy, Stella recalled, was happy-go-lucky at first, nothing wrong. But she grew angry when Stella said she and Harry Swanson had considered going to Northern California to see Cindy's little girl. Though it had been more than six months, the child still didn't know her "grandpa" had died.

"Cindy didn't want her to know. She called [her foster mother] and told [her] not to let the little girl watch the news or listen to the radio or anything, don't let anything slip around her about her granddad being dead."

"I think she has a right to know about her grandpa."

"You stay away from my daughter."

"She's also my granddaughter."

"I will tell her when I think the time is right. I'll tell her myself."

"Well, I was just trying to help, because you haven't had any experience in this. If you tell her the wrong way, it's gonna scar her the rest of her life."

"You haven't had any experience in this either."

"No, but I'm a little bit older. I basically know how to break it to [her] so it doesn't scar her for life."

"I'll tell her myself! If I don't do it right, we'll just have to get over it. You stay away from my daughter. I'm going to call [her foster mother] and tell [her] that you're not allowed to go near her."

With that, Cindy Hamilton stomped off the property, leaving Stella Nickell with Harry Swanson.

As time went on, Stella later said, her daughter's belligerent behavior began to make sense.

"Because she said that I am mad at her, probably said that I now hate her, because of what she done to me and that to get even with her, I would try to hurt somebody that she loves. This was the story she was telling to try to get people to believe how vicious I am and that she had told the truth about me. And she said that I'm capable of doing anything 'cause I was mad at her, that I could even hurt [Cindy's daughter]. [She] is my granddaughter."

Years later, Stella Nickell summed up her feelings for her daughter: "Even though there were times that I used to get so angry at Cynthia that I could snap her little head off just like a grasshopper's, I don't have any hate in me for Cynthia."

CHAPTER 76

In the afternoon session Tom Hillier would cross-examine. Since he planned to clear up some of the confusing time frames, he requested that Stella's daughter have her grand jury testimony available to her for reference.

While Cynthia Hamilton agreed that the majority of the specific details of her stepfather's murder were discussed during the months at the airport, she said general discussions had occurred sporadically over several years.

"And you have no real firm time frame to offer us with respect to, for example, the first discussion you talked about which related to heroin, the date that took place, that sort of thing?"

"No, I don't."

Referring to her grand jury testimony, Tom Hillier asked if she recalled a specific event that occurred in April 1985 that she was able to pinpoint relative to the time the hit man was discussed.

"In April of '85 I received a DWI."

"Okay. So you're able to put that conversation within a context because of something specific that occurred to you?"

"Yes."

"Now, I'm a little uncertain as to when you began working at the airport. Was that in February of '86?"

"To the best of my recall right now, yes."

"And Bruce, of course, died as we all know on June 5, so most of these discussions you've related took place during that four-month period of time, would that be true?"

"Yes."

The federal public defender asked a series of questions relating to conversations the witness had with the FBI, as well as her appearance before the grand jury in March of 1987.

"Before that you had, I thought I heard you say, two major conversations with FBI agents?"

"Yes."

"And those would have occurred in January of 1987?"

"Yes."

Hillier pointed out the obvious with his next questions. Yes, she had follow-up conversations with the FBI and the prosecution. Yes, she had an opportunity to review her testimony with the prosecution before court.

Yes, she and her daughter both lived with the Nickells after she moved up in December 1982. Yes, they moved out in April 1983 over differences of opinion concerning her lifestyle.

"And when you entrusted [your daughter] to their care, you knew that your mother, in addition to caring for [your daughter], took care of other children in that mobile-home park, didn't you?"

"Yes."

"And when you returned in 1982 in December, indeed you even discovered a different Bruce Nickell than the man you had met some years previous?"

"Yes."

"In fact, years ago when you first met Bruce, you resented the fact that he and your mother had gotten married?"

"No."

"No?" Tom Hillier feigned a surprised look. "Do you recall testifying to that effect to the grand jury?"

"No, because I didn't resent their marriage." She said she was upset because her mother hadn't contacted her to let her know of the marriage.

Yes, Bruce Nickell was boorish when he was drinking. And yes, he was good-natured, loving, intelligent when she moved in in December 1982 because he had stopped drinking.

"And it's true, isn't it, Ms. Hamilton, that your mother was instrumental in bringing that change about?"

"Yes, she was."

"She helped him, supported him, and encouraged him to stop drinking?"

"Yes, she did."

"And she stood by him through that ordeal?"

"Yes, she did."

Through his cross-examination, Tom Hillier established Stella Nickell "doted" on her husband and stayed home with him because he had stopped drinking. She didn't even drink around the house as a show of support. Stella also paid all the bills and ran the household.

Cindy Hamilton admitted she didn't socialize much with the Nickells after Bruce stopped drinking. Yet, she said, she did visit now and then after moving out in April 1983.

"Now, as I understood your testimony today and yesterday, your first conversation regarding drugs with your mother occurred some four years before Bruce died?"

"Yes."

"A very generalized discussion about heroin?"

"Yes."

"She asked you where it could be acquired?"

"Yes."

"In fact, you had shared with your mother the fact of your prior problems with drugs?"

"My prior usage of drugs, yes."

"Yes. Would it be accurate to say that you moved from California in part not only to escape your marital difficulties but to disassociate yourself from that drug past?"

Cindy Hamilton bristled at the question. "No, that wasn't necessarily a major portion of it."

"You and your mom talked about that, though, didn't you?"

She said they had.

Tom Hillier prodded on. As he understood the witness's testimony, later there were additional "generalized conversations" about overdosages and drugs such as heroin, and later more discussions concerning cocaine and speed. Bruce Nickell's name was not a part of the discussions. The same was true of the hitman idea.

Cindy Hamilton agreed.

"And did there come a time during those general conversations that Bruce's name was mentioned?"

"Not that I recall."

Tom Hillier asked the witness to turn to page 26 of her grand jury testimony.

"Did there come a time that Bruce's name was mentioned specifically with regard to these numerous hit men–type plots you talked about today? The answer is yes or no to that question."

"During the general conversations—"

"No; later on. I'm not trying to trap you or anything. Did his name ever come up in relation to any of those conversations?"

"Yes, in later conversations it did."

He referred her to Joanne Maida's question:

"Q: How did your stepfather's name first get introduced into this whole business about eliminating people?"

Cindy Hamilton read:

"A: I honestly can't remember exactly when it came as far as me knowing definitely that it was my dad, and I honest to God cannot even recall if she brought up his name or if it was just that I knew, because you have to understand my mother, you know, you know it sounds strange, but my mother and I are like on the same wavelength. It's like I know what she's thinking before she says it, and vice versa. I recall . . . can't recall if it was just there and then from that point forward. I can't remember when she first brought up his name, but—"

The defense lawyer waited for the young woman to look up.

"In view of that testimony, do you remember your father's name, your stepfather's name, being mentioned at all in relation to this hit-man testimony?"

"I cannot with actual positive recall on exactly saying the name of Bruce."

Under further cross, the witness agreed her testimony had indicated that at some point she knew her mother had been talking about Bruce Nickell. And, yes, most of the conversations had taken place during the four months she worked with her mother at SeaTac.

And as convinced as she was, she didn't warn Bruce or the police. No one would believe her.

"Perhaps more importantly, you didn't angrily confront your mom and ask her to knock it off, did you?"

"No, I did not."

"You testified that this plot concerning stuffing tablets with black seeds seemed feasible to you because your father was always chewing on grass or whatever. What else did he chew on besides toothpicks?"

"He chewed on toothpicks, he would chew on matches, he would chew on anything out on the property. Sometimes he would chew on pieces of grass."

"Did you ever see him chewing on any foxglove or anything that appeared to be foxglove?"

"No. I probably couldn't point out foxglove if I saw it."

Tom Hillier described the plant in detail, but she still couldn't recall if she had ever seen it.

Cindy Hamilton told the jury that she had told her mother to divorce Bruce Nickell but Stella didn't want to lose her community property.

"And then today you testified that at the same time she was willing to walk out of the marriage and go to Mexico with regard to a bodyguard business because of dreams of richness there?"

"Yes."

"And abandon her community property?"

"Yes."

Again, as she testified, it was conversations that reportedly took place while at SeaTac, before and after her employment. She was certain of the time frame.

Tom Hillier referred the witness to her grand jury testimony indicating that the bodyguard venture fell through in April or May of 1986; "she definitely knew by May."

"So your testimony in March of 1987 was that specifically Bruce Nickell's name never came up in relation to drug overdosing until after the Mexican affair fell through?"

"Yes."

"That would have been in April or May of 1986?"

"Yes."

"And indeed, as I read your testimony here, instead of dissuading your mother, you offer her some information concerning overdosing?"

"I offered her *negative* information, yes."

Stella's daughter agreed that it was after those particular discussions that the subject of cyanide first came up.

"Did you ever see your mom with any cyanide?"

"I don't know what cyanide looks like."

"You have no idea that she ever had any cyanide. Is that true?"

"I have no idea."

Further, the witness said she never saw her mother crushing Algae Destroyer. Never saw her mother go to the library to research cyanide, either. Never saw her mother buy Anacin-3, or Excedrin capsules. Never saw her put them back on the shelves.

"She never told you she had done that, either, did she?"

"Not that she positively had done it, no."

And, as she testified, she never asked.

Tom Hillier had nothing further, and Cindy Hamilton finally stepped down.

SAs Cusack and Nichols speculated on what they had perceived to be weak cross-examination from the defense lawyer. A lot of what Cindy Hamilton had said might have been the first time Hillier had heard any of it.

"I don't think Stella told him the truth," SA Nichols offered later.

Even the defendant was surprised.

"At first he said he was really going to nail Cynthia when she got on the stand and I was making notes to help him, like he told me to. And then when it came time for him to question her, he told me he was going to go kinda easy on her because he wanted to prove to the jury that we were on friendly terms. At the time I thought it strange. But he was my attorney, and I believed he was working in my best interest—oh, the gullibility of the innocent who still believe in justice and truth win out."

A little sign in a cheap black frame in the witness room admonished those waiting: "They [witness] should not look into the courtroom and not attempt to overhear . . ." Friendship and curiosity was enough for Katy Hurt Parker and her new husband to disregard the warning. The couple watched Cindy testify through the two small windows punched through the seagrass-blue vinyl courtroom doors.

Katy told her husband it looked as if Tom Hillier was "beating up" on her friend.

Her testimony over, Cindy rushed out of the courtroom, past the Parkers. A moment later, she sent word that she wanted to see them. The three met in a courthouse room set aside for her. Cindy, who had recovered, was in terrific spirits.

"So we went down to this little room where we talked and we kidded around. We didn't talk about the trial, just different things, and we laughed. She always picked on my husband, so she just kept picking at him," Katy later recalled.

When Joanne Maida came into the room, Cindy told her to watch out for Katy on the stand.

"Katy gets all red and puffs up like a big puffer fish, and she's gonna cut loose. . . ."

Though Katy's husband said he was worried the defendant might seek revenge for his wife's testimony, Katy wasn't concerned.

"I never thought about it. Cindy was my friend and she needed me to back her, and that's the way it was," she said later.

After Joanne Maida called her, Tom Hillier requested a side bar, and Katy Hurt Parker sat on the stand wondering what in the world was going on.

Hillier apologized, but within the last day or two he had received the young woman's grand jury testimony and was concerned about her trial testimony's being hearsay.

Joanne Maida disagreed. The testimony would be offered as corroboration of a conversation between Cindy Hamilton and the witness regarding overdosages of cocaine.

"As Mr. Hillier knows and as the Court is aware, the government's case rests on the reliability of Cindy Hamilton in the jury's eyes," she said.

The Asst. U.S. Attorney wanted to offer it as a prior consistent statement to corroborate Hamilton. The government felt it would show that its star witness had made the statement long before there would be any reason to fabricate it.

The attorneys argued whether the cross-examination had challenged Cindy Hamilton with a recent fabrication, which would allow it, but Judge Dwyer ruled on the side of caution: the witness would not testify.

On direct examination, Jeanne Rice told the court how in February 1986 she became a victim of "burnout" at her job as a screener at SeaTac. Before she left SeaTac, she had worked with the defendant. It was at the airport that she told Stella Nickell about a business venture she was developing.

"I wanted to start a service in Monterrey, Mexico, to bodyguard wealthy people there. . . . And she was very interested, and after a time she was interested for her daughter, Cindy, also."

"Who made the approach about the defendant Stella Nickell then working with you in this bodyguard business in Mexico?" Joanne Maida asked.

"I talked to her about what I was doing and what the ambitions and the hopes were for this service, and at that time she broached with me the subject of possibly working for me there, and I told her at that time that I really hadn't considered female bodyguards but that I would do so."

There was money to be made, she testified, from guarding the rich of Monterrey.

"Did you discuss with the defendant how she was going to accomplish going down to Mexico with you, since she was married?"

"Well, at the time that Stella and I had talked about this, this occurred over several conversations. . . . She said to me at that time that she would just be willing to leave and no suitcase or whatever, that she would just be willing to go."

"According to her, what would happen to Bruce, her husband?"

"She never stated that to me."

Under direct, Jeanne Rice said Stella Nickell said her marriage was unhappy, but she could not recall anything specific. Joanne Rice concluded her testimony by saying she did not know anything about the cyanide deaths until she read an article in a Las Vegas paper "maybe about a week or so ago."

Tom Hillier again tried to pinpoint when specific events had occurred.

"In terms of discussions out at the airport, did you continue talking about it through early '86 or not? Do you remember?"

"I believe I talked about it maybe through January of '86, and it just was not gelling. It wasn't pulling itself together."

She thought it was in 1985 that she talked with the defendant about it, during their overlapping shifts.

On cross-examination, Jeanne Rice was unable to be more precise as to when the conversations regarding Stella Nickell's unhappy marriage had occurred. Tom Hillier was able, however, to get her to concede that the conversations were general, just two women talking about their men and their relationships.

Melinda Denton, a professor of botany at the University of Washington took the stand and under direct brief questioning told the court how she and the FBI had walked the wooded area adjacent to the Nickells' property where she identified foxglove. Seeds from the plant are dark brown or black. She also stated the seeds were toxic.

While the next witness, FBI chemist Roger Martz, took the stand, charts showing the cyanide and what had been the mysterious green crystals were displayed for the jury.

SA Martz said he had examined the bottles and determined the capsules inside had been tainted with potassium cyanide.

And there was something else.

"When I first looked at the contents of some of the capsules I noticed some green specks, what I call some green material, and on chemical analysis of this green material, I was able to identify some algicides in the green material, specifically monuron, cemazin, and atrozin. These are three algicides.

"I also identified a yellow-and-blue dye which together make the little specks green, and also sodium chloride."

Joanne Maida promised to return to the algicide after the five bottles were discussed.

One by one, the bottles and their contents, starting with Sue Snow's, were identified as the ones he had examined. SA Nichols moved the chart "Cyanide-Laced Medications" closer to the jury, and Roger Martz approached to explain the photographs. The photographs had a slight green tinge, presumably from the contaminant.

Under further direct, SA Martz stated that the capsules, which averaged 700 milligrams of cyanide, had been emptied, not methodically, cleaned with a cotton swab, but "just opened and emptied and then refilled with cyanide."

The witness identified the specks as Algae Destroyer.

Tom Hillier's cross-examination went after the FBI chemist's difficulty with the analysis of the cyanide.

"You weren't able to determine whether the cyanide itself, potassium cyanide, was the same potassium cyanide, came from the same batch or not?"

"That's correct."

"I guess if you weren't able to determine that, you weren't able to determine what the manufacturing source was either."

"That's correct."

"Did you try?"

"In my experience—"

"Is that a yes or a no?"

"I did try, yes."

SA Martz said he analyzed for trace quantities. Since sodium was the largest trace quantity in potassium cyanide, and also the largest component in Algae Destroyer, it could not be done.

"Did you analyze the contents of the various capsules including the cyanide and the algicide in determining whether there was Anacin in the Anacin capsules and Excedrin in the Excedrin capsules?"

"Yes. I was able to identify Anacin in the Anacin capsules and Excedrin in the Excedrin capsules."

"There was no Anacin found in the Excedrin capsules?"

"I did not identify any."

"The capsules themselves were filled with a mix of the Excedrin and the cyanide and the Anacin capsules were filled with a mix of the Anacin and the cyanide. Right?"

"Yes. As I testified earlier, the capsules were emptied but not methodically cleaned out, so some of the original content was left in."

"And what was left, would it be consistent to say that the mixture in the tampered capsules would have had to have been prepared on at least two different occasions, in view of what you discovered after analyzing the capsules?"

The witness had no basis for offering that opinion.

In preparation for the government's next witness, the FBI's fingerprint specialist Carl Collins, Jr., the Asst. U.S. Attorney instructed the clerk to pull the library books that had been received in evidence and SA Collins was sworn in. This was a man who had been examining fingerprints since July 1957—it was clear that he was no rookie. Stella Nickell's attorney had said that the defendant had looked at the books, so the testimony, while chilling in the context it was being placed, was not a shock to anyone in the courtroom. If there was any surprise, it was that SA Collins said none of the capsules and bottles had any fingerprints, with the single exception of a lone print left by Sarah Webb, Sue Snow's twin sister.

SA Collins testified about the eighty-four fingerprints and three palm prints on *Deadly Harvest*, nine fingerprints and one palm print on pages discussing cyanide in the *McGraw-Hill Encyclopedia*, two prints on the cyanide pages in the *New Caxton Encyclopedia*, and five Nickell fingerprints and a palm in the *Merit Student's Encyclopedia* on the pages around the cyanide discussion.

Stella Nickell just looked on, somehow detached. Maybe even confident. No one could say for sure. She had to be glad the day was over.

CHAPTER 77

Tom Hillier and Joanne Maida met before court the morning of April 27. Hillier had been thinking about the case the night before, and wanted to inform the Asst. U.S. Attorney of his intention to offer the stipulation about the reward so the defense would not need to call in someone from the Proprietary Association to testify it existed.

In that case, Joanne Maida argued that the polygraph/phone call testimony be admitted, that it, in fact, was the reason Cindy Hamilton came forward—not the reward.

Tom Hillier, testing the waters, naturally opposed the idea. Testimony about the reward should not automatically allow the prosecution to bring up the phone call. How the court would rule on the matter was critical. After all, Cindy had just told the jury she came forward because it was "the right thing to do."

Judge Dwyer had several things to consider. The testimony of Katy Hurt Parker, offered as a prior consistent statement of Cindy Hamilton in 1985, was not allowed since the government hadn't shown there had been an attack on the young woman's credibility—recent fabrication or improper motive. The government's offer was based on Tom Hillier's cross-examination but the public defender asked her only about areas already discussed in direct.

Judge Dwyer did not believe the admission of the reward stipulation would justify the admission of the polygraph or the phone call. It would be prejudicial and outweigh any value it might have in explaining why Cindy Hamilton came forward.

Joanne Maida planned to ask the Court again later.

Later that morning, Carl Collins returned to the witness stand and continued testifying to what would not be disputed by the defense.

Stella Nickell's fingerprint was on the All American Life enrollment card from September 5, 1985. He also found two prints belonging to the defendant on Bruce Nickell's Long-Term Disability Enrollment Change form dated January 8, 1986.

In preparation for more book testimony, the clerk stacked the four volumes in front of the witness. Enlargements of the prints on the pages were also set up for the jury.

Asst. U.S. Attorney Maida drove a point home. "Now, you told us yesterday that the standard that you use is one of achieving positive identification based on seven points of comparison?"

"Yes."

Enlargements of the pages from the *New Caxton Encyclopedia* were set on the easel.

"Is there a print that you have charted out on the enlargement?"

He nodded, and testified that he positively identified "on page 1742 . . . the left thumbprint of Stella Nickell."

More enlargements, from the *Merit Student's Encyclopedia* and *Deadly Harvest*, were displayed in turn as SA Collins pointed out the characteristics that matched the defendant's inked prints.

A working copy of *Deadly Harvest*, tinged with purple and mottled with labeled print after print, was identified by the witness. This copy would give the jurors a veritable road map of the travels Stella Nickell's fingers took as she read the book.

SA Collins demonstrated how Stella Nickell touched the book on page 89, the spot where she left behind forty-seven crystalclear points of comparison.

With questioning, the witness testified to the pages with prints with the greatest number of points of comparison.

Page 73, with information on cyanide, was one. Page 66 had a discussion of hemlock; 67 had a discussion about toxic seeds.

After recess, Tom Hillier stepped forward and launched into his cross-examination first on the subject of the bottles received in evidence.

"You found no prints of Stella Nickell on any of those bottles?"

"No, I did not."

None of the defendant's prints—or anyone else's, for that matter—were found on the capsules either.

"Evidently, at the time there was no perspiration or oily matter on the fingers, at the time those bottles were handled, to leave an impression," SA Collins said.

Tom Hillier also had the witness affirm that people can touch objects without leaving prints, and it was impossible to say when prints were made.

"And would it be true, based upon your testimony, that the absence of fingerprints on some pages, latent prints that you could develop and identify as Mrs. Nickell's, would not necessarily mean she didn't touch those pages?"

"That's correct."

The defense attorney turned to his prepared questions for cross, regarding the working copy of *Deadly Harvest*. He cited pages 66 and 67 and the discussion of hemlock.

"Those pages, in addition to using the word 'hemlock,' discuss the hemlock tree, don't they?"

SA Collins read the first paragraph before agreeing with the defense attorney.

He confirmed that the following paragraph contained information about yews. Tom Hillier pressed on.

"And in that same paragraph it indicates these fruits attract the attention of children, speaking of the fruits of the yew. Correct?"

The witness concurred.

Page 67 discussed the toxicity of cocklebur and hydroquinone.

"And on page 72 and 73 . . . you were directed to indicate whether or not cyanide was mentioned on those pages."

He had, and, in fact, cyanide was mentioned on page 72.

Tom Hillier asked the witness to read the first full paragraph for the record.

Next Tom Hillier asked the witness to look at page 126, the index, particularly the entries as relating to cyanide.

"Now, several of those pages, specifically 24, 54, 115, and 121, there are no prints of Stella Nickell that were developed in your examination. Correct?"

SA Collins needed to look at his records. A moment later, he agreed.

"You testified this morning that pages 88 and 89 contain the most number of prints that you found in the book."

"Yes."

But as public defender Hillier pointed out, page 88 had two prints and 89 had six. Page 119 had six prints and one palm.

"So that page had . . . standing alone, had the most identifiers of Stella Nickell. Correct?"

"By itself, yes."

"And that page discusses elderberry, lobelias, tobacco, nicotine. Correct?"

SA Collins studied the page. "I see elderberry. Yes. Yes, I see the rest of them."

Yes. Yes. Yes. The defendant's prints were found on pages concerning nightshade, pokeweed, poison ivy, poison oak, poison sumac.

"Based upon your examination and view of the book *Deadly Harvest*, would it be consistent to say that it is a book that discusses plants and their potentially toxic effects?"

"Yes, that's what the book is about."

Joanne Maida had no re-direct, and the witness was excused. The United States rested.

It was Tom Hillier's turn to present his case.

The testimony in the courtroom had been overshadowed by strange goings-on in the witness room. While Stella Nickell's character witnesses, Stan and Laurie Church and Sue and Jeff Ford, quietly waited for their turn, a woman in her twenties announced she was a cellmate of the defendant's. The Fords tried to pass the time buried in copies of *U.S. News* and *Smithsonian*, but the young woman made it known the defendant had said something to her about the killings when she was in jail. What it was was unclear.

"Her boyfriend would come in and out of the witness room from the trial and tell her what they were saying and how she was supposed to respond. He was pumping her on what these witnesses were saying, so she'd say the right thing," Sue Ford said later.

"We thought she was a witness for the defense. She'd try to talk about the case. We'd say, 'We're not supposed to talk about it.' She'd say, *'You know what they said!'* "

Later, Jeff Ford had another memory of the witness room.

"The witnesses for the prosecution were in the same room as we were. That Joanne Maida had come and saw Laurie [Church] and realized, I think, and she came unglued. She went out in the hall and talked to Cusack about it."

CHAPTER 78

Tom Hillier's list of defense witnesses was small. With the exception of the defendant, none were insiders who could refute what Cynthia Lea had told the jury.

Dr. Dennis Reichenbach, Harborview's chief of pathology, was called first. He testified that after performing a routine hospital autopsy on Bruce Nickell, which determined pulmonary emphysema as the cause of death, he spoke with Stella Nickell. He couldn't recall specifics of the conversation.

"Is it unusual that next of kin contact the hospital to discuss what the results of an autopsy were?"

"No, it is not."

Two weeks later, he said, there was another call from the defendant.

"In fact, it was at the time of the examination of the brain when she had contacted the pathology department and wanted to talk with me and had indicated that she had—This was right after Sue Snow had died and there was some publicity about the capsules, and she wanted to know whether there was any possibility that her husband could have died of cyanide poisoning."

At that point, the doctor testified, the Medical Examiner was involved. The cause of death was amended to acute cyanide poisoning.

"During your discussions with Mrs. Nickell, did you find anything out of the ordinary or odd about those contacts?" Hillier asked.

"No."

Joanne Maida began her questioning.

It was true that while Bruce Nickell did not die of emphysema, he did have emphysema.

Joanne Maida pointed out that no one picked up the scent of bitter almonds at the time of Bruce Nickell's autopsy.

"And that is one thing that ordinarily might clue a pathologist like yourself to the possibility that someone has died of cyanide poisoning?" she asked.

"Particularly, I think, if there is a large amount of it and if someone is able to smell it. Not everyone is able to smell it."

"Are you able to smell it?"

"I don't know."

Soft-spoken Bruce Stone, a social worker who was on duty at Harborview when the defendant died, took the stand next. Hillier needed someone to tell the jury his client wasn't the coldhearted, dying-husband abandoner that the prosecution had suggested.

Bruce Stone's testimony was very brief. He told how he had met with Stella Nickell in a "quiet room" at the hospital for about five minutes. She and her mother were not permitted to be in the emergency room with Bruce Nickell.

"She was very quiet, withdrawn. She was very drawn into herself," he said. Such a response was consistent with others he had seen in similar circumstances.

The witness was turned over for cross-examination.

The Asst. U.S. Attorney reminded Bruce Stone of his interview with SA Jack Cusack at the beginning of the investigation.

"Do you recall what your response was at that time?"

"I believe I told him that she did not go in to see him."

"Didn't you tell Mr. Cusack, when your memory was fresher in 1986, that someone extended the opportunity to the defendant, Mrs. Nickell, to be by her husband's bedside when he died?"

"I may have, because that again is, you know, standard procedure for the hospital."

"You talked again with Mr. Cusack this morning, did you not?"

"I did."

"And in discussing that, did you agree with him that Mrs. Nickell declined the opportunity to be by her husband when he died?"

"I don't think it was worded quite that way this morning. If, in my documentation in the chart, you know, if I could see that, I think I could clarify this."

Joanne Maida asked if he had the chart, but he didn't.

"In any event, do you have any factual basis today to dispute any statements that you made to Mr. Cusack back in 1986?"

"No, I do not."

Bill Donais, thirty years a lawyer, twenty of them spent in Auburn, took the stand. He told the court how he had met the Nickells in the early 1980s when they waged the battle over cable-TV service at White River Estates. Later, in 1983, he represented the Nickells in their request for bankruptcy declaration.

Bill Donais testified, a day or two after Bruce's death, that the defendant called and asked if she should meet with him in the event something needed to be done immediately. He told her to wait until things calmed down and get in touch with him then.

Later, she made an appointment for June 17.

"What was the substance of that meeting?" Tom Hillier asked.

"We went over the assets of the estate—the real estate was about all there was, a little personal property—and discussed the insurance that was involved, at least the two credit-card policies."

"What did you see in that respect?"

"I was a little bit concerned when I first read it. The documents she gave me indicated that there was only one policy and that she was the insured."

"Did you express that concern to her?"

"Yes. I told her we might have a problem because I thought there should be another policy, or at least a rider indicating that Bruce was an insured. However, either papers she had with her as I reviewed them further or something she brought in . . . the application had been returned by the company and the application was very clear that both of them were insured. . . . The applications were clear enough that she didn't have to worry about it. I told her to go ahead and make the application for the insurance."

"Did she ever bring to your attention a state insurance policy?"

"Yes. At that time, or perhaps subsequent to that, she brought in a number of papers. One of them was sort of an outline that the state had probably given Bruce when he got the insurance information, but one page of that was sort of a breakdown which was apparently given to Bruce as an employee, saying you have a basic $5,000 life-insurance coverage, and I think it was $5,000 accidental coverage, and you also may apply for $100,000 additional accident policy and $25,000 life."

Yes, the witness said, Stella Nickell was concerned about what coverage Bruce Nickell truly had. A missed appointment for a physical left her believing she was entitled only to $5,000 basic life.

Further, Bill Donais said, it had been his suggestion to file the lawsuit in connection with Bruce Nickell's death. The discussion occurred two or three days after the cyanide was announced.

Tom Hillier asked why.

"The legislature in the prior session had passed what they referred to as the Tort Reform Act, which very seriously affected the possibility of damages, the amount of damages that a plaintiff could receive in an action of this sort. I consulted with Sue Snow's estate's lawyer, who was also concerned about the cyanide, and we had to file the action prior to August 1."

Joanne Maida reiterated information gleaned from Bill Donais's direct.

"With respect to your testimony about the coverage of the insurance policies, you indicated that she brought to your attention that there were two other credit-card policies?"

"No. She brought those to my attention first."

"And the point of my question being, the policies were group term life insurance policies, were they not?"

"That's correct."

"Taken out on their credit cards?"

Again, correct.

"Were you aware at the time, Mr. Donais, that your client had denied the existence of those policies to the FBI?"

Tom Hillier jumped up. "Your Honor, I would object. That is not accurate."

"It's argumentative. The objection is sustained."

"Did you know whether your client had made any previous inconsistent statements to the existence of those policies?"

Another objection, and Judge Dwyer sustained it.

It was a good time for the midday recess.

Later, Joanne Maida continued to question the lawyer from Auburn.

He was aware that his former client had been interviewed by the FBI in June, and had some contact with an insurance investigator in July, and again with the FBI in November.

Each time Bill Donais answered, his testimony was marred by uncertainty and inexact recall.

Yes, he said, he and Stella Nickell discussed the two All American policies, but he didn't know if she provided information on them to the FBI or Equifax.

The clerk was asked to produce the June 16, 1986, letter from Northwestern noting the $25,000 coverage was contingent on a physical.

"At any time during this association with your client up until Mr. Hillier stepped in to represent her, did she ever bring this letter to your attention or tell you that she stood corrected about the amount—it was actually $25,000 and not $100,000 that was contingent on the medical exam?"

"No. At the time she came in to me on the seventeenth, she was not clear on what the amount of insurance was."

Next, Joanne Maida had the court clerk hand the witness the copy of the lawsuit against Bristol-Myers. Over the defense's objections, she ferreted out the status of the damages contingent on Stella's criminal case.

Bill Donais said that in the event they won damages, he'd receive one-third, plus costs.

Dick Johnson was the third witness for the defense. No longer with the Department of Transportation, Dick Johnson had retired a few months before trial. He told the court that he hired Bruce Nickell as a temporary welder in November 1984 and that Nickell became permanent in January 1986. At that point, he received full state benefits.

Dick Johnson met Stella Nickell only after her husband died.

"As I recall, on June the sixth, 1986, I received a phone call in my office, approximately seven o'clock in the morning, from Mrs. Nickell stating that Bruce would no longer be coming to work, that he had passed away the night before."

He talked to the defendant again several days later. They arranged a meeting at Johnson's office in Seattle approximately a week and a half after Mr. Nickell's death.

"I had informed Mrs. Nickell that there was certain paperwork that she had to take care of in order to collect the wages and sick benefits that were coming to Bruce Nickell."

Johnson explained he had directed her to the accountant who

handled that type of work, and consequently she was directed to
the insurance board in Olympia.

After Tom Hillier's cross-examination of Cindy Hamilton, the defendant's best chance for "reasonable doubt" lay in the testimony
of the next witness, Dr. David Honigs, an assistant professor of
chemistry from the University of Washington.

Dr. Honigs was a young and imposing man. His Ph.D. was in
analytical chemistry, and, in fact, he had written a number of articles on the analysis of cyanide as related to product tampering. He
had received $70,000 in grants to explore preventive techniques
developed in his lab.

For the record, the witness defined the "elemental fingerprints
of cyanides," as related by the experts at the FDA. He told the court
how potassium cyanide contained some trace metals that when analyzed can determine which of the three manufacturers produced it.

"They [FDA] found they could take the cyanide from the different companies and match up different lots and different batches."

With that in mind, Dr. Honigs said he set out to determine where
the Seamurs cyanide had come from.

"The analysis was performed by the FDA and submitted to the
FBI at their request. The analysis in this particular case was less
than the ideal case—that is, the cyanide was not pure. Rather, it
was mixed substantially with the Excedrin or with the Anacin-3.
This meant that you couldn't simply take the powder and do the
analysis in a straightforward fashion. You have to allow for the
dilution and also perhaps for any other trace metals that might have
been in the aspirin."

Yet, according to the chemistry professor, the FDA did its analysis in two ways. First, they analyzed the bulk powder, which did
not reveal the elemental fingerprint. Second, it analyzed individual
cyanide crystals.

"The numbers," Dr. Honigs said, "matched the fingerprint of the
manufacturer DeGasa, a West German manufacturer of cyanide."

"Did the FBI and the FDA reach conclusions similar to yours?"
Tom Hillier asked.

"No, they did not. They had a little bit of difficulty in inter-
preting the results, both in their written report and then verbally
when I contacted Mr. Martz with the FBI."

Dr. Honigs said he talked to SA Martz a couple of weeks before
the trial, and at that time he asked his opinion of the source of the

cyanide. The FBI chemist told him that the analysis was "too gar-bled" because of the presence of sodium.

But the witness insisted barium was also a fingerprint. It was his analysis of the barium concentration that led him to believe the Seamurs cyanide was manufactured by DeGasa.

"The other manufacturers of cyanide, Du Pont and ICI, which is in England, do not have any measurable levels of barium at all in their cyanide. So both the amount and the identity confirmed my analysis."

"Did you explain that to Mr. Martz?" Tom Hillier asked.

"Mr. Martz said that I could say whatever I felt was important and that he would stand up in court and say that he was the expert; he had been doing this longer than anybody else, and that in his opinion it could not be done."

The defense moved on to the green specks.

Dr. Honigs said the FDA's analysis of green particles had in fact made up approximately 190 of the 200 pages of chemical doc-umentation he reviewed.

He also said he went to the FBI office and analyzed the powder that had been dumped out of the capsules.

"Any conclusions?" Tom Hillier asked.

"The conclusion I reached was that the particles were in there not by accident, that they were put in there on purpose. The reasons I concluded this were, first of all, particles were found in almost all of the capsules. They were found in the vast majority, and in most of the cases, most of the tampered bottles, particles were found in every single one of the capsules, so it was not, therefore, in my opinion, there by chance. It was too common.

"The second thing is that the capsules had to be mixed up, the poison with the material put in the capsules had to be mixed up more than once."

There were two reasons for his conclusion.

First, the tampered Excedrin capsules contained Excedrin, cya-nide, and the green particles. The tampered Anacin capsules were filled with cyanide, Anacin, and the green particles.

". . . So they had to be mixed up at separate times in separate containers."

Of additional concern, he noted how the number of contami-nated capsules and the total number in the bottles was very consis-tent.

"In the cases that I looked at in all the evidence, the tamperer took out between eight and nine capsules, dumped out the contents of those, mixed them, and then put them back into the capsules. Since every bottle had some capsules missing, it's very likely, then, that they were all done individually, that they were taken apart, dumped out, mixed up, and placed back together," he told the jury.

The final reason he believed the Algae Destroyer was added intentionally was that it was so visible against the whitish cyanide.

"If a person is mixing these up, they can see the green particles in there. It was evident to the analyst as soon as the analyst dumped the contents of the capsules out, you could see the green particles, and so it seems to me that the person who was mixing this up had to be able to see that as well as the analyst could later on."

Tom Hillier wondered if the witness noticed a difference between the powders found in the Anacin capsules and that found in the Excedrin capsules.

"I took a look at the cyanide because of the particle size. While you can't tell chemically from the fingerprint what the material is, sometimes you can tell how it's been treated. The particle size ranged in—the particle size was different in the different bottles. In some bottles the particles of cyanide were very large, crystalline-like, larger than crystals of salt or sugar that you would see. In others they were very mossy and very amorphous, kind of a blob sort of shape, and so from that evidence as well it would appear that they were not mixed up from one batch."

David Honigs had served the defense well—even the jury seemed impressed. Joanne Maida stepped from her chair with a quick deliberateness to question his conclusions that the cyanide was mixed in different batches, deliberately and not accidentally.

"Now, you have to make a number of assumptions about the facts in order to get to that conclusion," she said.

"I have to make assumptions if I assume it was mixed up more than two times. The chemical evidence directly supports two times. There is additional evidence that supports more than two times."

"So you're telling us you did have to make some factual assumptions?"

"That's correct, to support more than *two* times."

"You made an assumption that the green specks had to have been noticed by the tamperer, and that is a factual assumption that you have no factual basis upon which to make. Isn't that correct?"

The young professor responded: "There is an assumption that the person can see. I can see those in that situation. The FBI analysis, the FDA analysis, they all saw the particles in that same situation, and I assumed that the person doing the tampering could have the same faculties of observation that I and these other people did."

"And that is an assumption that has no basis in fact, isn't it?"

"I don't know the tamperer; therefore, I am suggesting, then, that the tamperer should have the same facilities that I or these other people do."

"And, Dr. Honigs, you have no idea whether the tamperer would have noticed or could have noticed the green specks in the cyanide, do you?"

"I know that they were obvious—"

"Do you, sir?" Joanne Maida snapped, cutting him off.

Judge Dwyer stepped in, letting the witness complete his answer.

"I know that to the average person, they would be visible. I don't know if the tamperer looked at it."

"And, sir, you don't know whether the tamperer performed the tampering under as good lighting conditions as you would have in your laboratory, do you?"

He did not.

Asst. U.S. Attorney Maida inquired about the witness's statement, from a preliminary report, that there was no reason why the defendant would have a container of the green particles sitting around the house.

"That's speculation, sir, isn't it?"

"It is speculation, based upon the fact that she had a fifty-gallon aquarium, that the instructions, if she followed them, would require that she use and would drop in several of these tablets at once. She wouldn't be using fractions of tablets, and so it's based on the size of the tank and the manufacturer's instructions."

"And you speculated as to whether she kept a container with these particles lying around the house. You don't know that, sir, do you?"

"The speculation was based on the facts that I stated."

"Correct. And you don't know that was a fact, do you, sir?"

"It is speculation."

"And you used these two factual speculations to arrive at your conclusion that the cyanide was mixed in different batches, sir?"

"These are some of the speculations and some of the facts that were used. There are additional ones, which I stated."

"Sir, you are a scientist and not a detective, is that correct?"

"This is correct. My training is as a scientist."

The Asst. U.S. Attorney questioned the witness's purported analysis of the evidence in the case during his visit to the FBI office.

"Dr. Honigs, it's fair to say that you never obtained a sample of the cyanide that's in this case, in evidence, and chemically analyzed it as Mr. Martz did at the FBI?"

"Mr. Martz, as I understand it, did not analyze the samples. He sent them to FDA."

"Can you just answer the question, sir?"

"You compared me to Mr. Martz, and I don't think that was phrased so that the answer could be either yes or no."

Judge Dwyer again stepped in. "The question did include 'as Mr. Martz did.' The best procedure is to let the answer come forth and then go on to the next question."

Joanne Maida went after him again.

"You're aware that Mr. Martz did handle the capsules in this case, the contents of those capsules, and chemically analyzed them, aren't you?"

"The reports that I have document the analysts as other than Mr. Martz."

"Aren't you aware that Mr. Martz analyzed the substances in question and concluded it was potassium cyanide with traces of Algae Destroyer?"

"The conclusions that I have say that the person drawing the conclusion is Mr. Martz. The documentation on who run the chromatograms, who run the flame ionization and the like, some of these analyses was done at the Food and Drug Administration. In every case, Mr. Martz's name did not appear as the analyst."

It was true, he said under further cross, that he did not chemically analyze the contents of the capsules.

"From your gross observation of the way in which these capsules were mixed, it doesn't take any level of special expertise for a layperson just to sit down and mix them in the same way, does it?"

"The capsule showed no special expertise in terms of mixing."

Compact, with her soft brown eyes and brown hair, Vicki Bagby Moen was next. She told the court how Stella Nickell had taken care of her little boy when they lived at White River Estates. The Nickells seemed happy.

"It was a normal marriage. We went camping. We had birthdays together with my little boy. It was as normal as my marriage or anyone's."

Tom Hillier brought up Cindy Hamilton's name. The look of recognition and disdain on the witness's face was clear.

"In my own opinion? Very unstable. She didn't—Bruce and Stella helped her very much when she came up.... They helped her through beauty school. She wouldn't stick with that. Stella took care of [Cynthia's daughter]... If she needed anything, Stella would do it. [Cynthia's daughter] went camping with us. Her mother wasn't very responsible, in my opinion."

Did the witness have any opinion about Stella Nickell's character for truthfulness?

"She's always been very truthful. Very aboveboard with everything."

The defense turned over Vicki for cross.

She told the court that the Nickell marriage was happy, normal. As far as she knew.

Joanne Maida asked the witness about her interview with SA Stone.

"And did you tell Agent Marshall Stone that you could not tell whether or not Stella Nickell was happy in this marriage because she was a very difficult person to read, did not show her emotions very much?"

"We never really talked about it. Stella wasn't the type of person that if there was a problem she would talk about it."

"The question was, if I could direct you back to it, did you ever tell Marshall Stone other than what you've testified to in court today?"

"No."

"You don't recall telling Mr. Stone that you couldn't tell whether or not Stella Nickell was happy in her marriage simply because you couldn't read her?"

"No."

"Ms. Moen, Stella Nickell did not confide in you, did she?"

The witness didn't understand what the prosecutor actually meant.

"In such a sense that you would be close enough to be able to determine whether the marriage was a happy one."

"We talked about our children. If our husbands did something stupid or dumb, that to me is confiding in friends about things that you do."

"Finally, Ms. Moen, in observing the interactions between Stella Nickell and Bruce Nickell, did you ever see Stella Nickell feed Bruce Nickell any capsules, medications?"

"If he had a headache, yes."

On re-direct, Tom Hillier followed up on the government's last question, a question that had made the witness's face redden with anger.

"Mrs. Moen, with respect to that last question, was there any— Did you observe Mrs. Nickell, for example, handing her husband, upon request, medicine if he had a headache or the like?"

"I do the same thing."

"Okay. Was there any question about what it was she was handing him in those instances?"

"No. He asked her, if he had a headache, give it to him, you know. If your husband asks you to do something, you do it. No question at the time."

"There may be some people that disagree with you on that."

"I'm sure," she said, nodding.

Some spectators chuckled at the remark. Even the defendant broke a smile.

Sal Ramos helped a trembling Laurie Church, dressed in her best suit, a gray and maroon pinstripe, to the stand to give some rudimentary testimony on her background and the fact that she and the defendant had a very close friendship.

Laurie Church told of a good friendship, one of dinners out, CB radios, visits at one another's homes. She and her husband saw Bruce every weekend up until he died. Laurie Church saw Stella at least once during the week.

Hillier asked how the witness learned of Bruce Nickell's death.

"My daughter was married June 7 and that evening, later that evening, Stella came over and told me that Bruce had died on the fifth."

Tom Hillier asked why Stella Nickell had waited.

"She didn't want to let us know beforehand because my daughter had made these great plans for her wedding and Stella didn't want to ruin her day. She wanted that to be her day and so she told us later."

Joanne Maida went after one of Church's last answers, which was that Stella and Bruce "had a very good marriage."

"To you it appeared on the surface that they had a happy marriage?"

"I thought all the way around they had a happy marriage."

Yet under cross, Laurie Church admitted she was unaware of any financial or personal problems the Nickells might have had. Stella never told her she was unhappy in her marriage. Never said she was going to leave Bruce and run off to Mexico or Texas.

"Oh, no. No."

"Did your friend Stella Nickell tell you at any time about plans that she had to open a fish store?"

"She said she wanted to open it and have—she wanted to have Cindy work it with her, yes."

Judge Dwyer allowed the defense to recall Dr. Honigs for a question Tom Hillier had neglected to ask during direct. He wanted to know if there was any reason for the green particles to be "sitting around in a dish or elsewhere." There was not. No instructions on the package suggested such a possibility.

If there had been such instructions to crush and dissolve the tablets in warm water, Tom Hillier wanted to know what effect the practice would have on the green particles.

"If the green particles were first crushed and then water was added, those could not be the same green particles that were found in the mixed cyanide. The particles in the cyanide had very, very perfect match, the amount of sodium, the amount of inert ingredients, the amount of the active ingredients, to exactly that same material out of the algae killer, Algae Destroyer, tablets. If you took one right from the package and the particles, they were identical in all the different aspects.

"Now, if you added water, things dissolve, and they dissolve at different rates, especially sodium. Sodium goes into water very fast, and so if those particles had been anywhere near any reasonable amount of water, if they had had water placed on them or had been mixed up with water, the sodium would have gone out, almost all of it if not all of it, and so that ratio that was observed in the capsules was not the ratio that you would see if they had ever had water added."

Dr. Honigs was excused for the final time.

Stan Church took the stand to do battle for his best friend's wife. Looking at Stan was like looking at Bruce Nickell—blue-collar, working stiff.

He was asked to describe the Nickell marriage.

"I was . . ." Church stammered for the words, not because he couldn't think of an answer, but because he was nervous as hell. "I would say that they had a good marriage, you know, just like my wife and I do, and that it was no—I mean, there was no arguments or nothing, at least not during our presence or when we was out."

Tom Hillier ended his direct with the question of Stella Nickell's veracity.

She was always truthful, Stan Church said. "*Very* truthful."

With one question, Joanne Maida basically impugned any relevance of Stan Church's testimony. Anything he knew about Stella Nickell, it was likely he learned through his wife.

"Do you know the defendant Stella Nickell better than your wife does?"

"No, ma'am."

CHAPTER 79

"Call Stella Nickell!"

The woman flanked by Ramos and Hillier, her bearing stoic, took the stand. The tone and cadence of her voice matched her appearance—stiff and earnest.

Stella Maudine Nickell gave her version of her life story—born in Colton, Oregon, moved to Washington in late forties, Seattle, then California, back to the Northwest in the early seventies where she met Bruce Nickell. She sketched a simple life of CBs, bowling, working on the property.

She told the court how she had helped her husband to stop drinking in 1979.

"Did you find a change in the lifestyle you and Bruce had as a result of his decision and yours not to drink?"

"Yes. Our life together improved considerably because he did not have the aftereffects of the alcohol. He was easier to get along with. His temper was not quite as quick as it used to be."

When Tom Hillier asked if she had found the new life boring, Stella offered an emphatic "No."

At no time, Stella testified, did she tell Cindy she was bored with her marriage and resented that she could no longer go out and drink. In fact, her love for her husband grew.

"Well, we got along a lot better. We were at home more often. It wasn't a constant running uptown or going here or going there.

We were able to settle down, catch our breath, and get to know one another more easily."

Next, the defense focused on the Nickell finances. According to Stella, they had their ups and downs. She, of course, did not deny the bankruptcy filing, but reported that they had been fortunate enough to be able to pay off the creditors.

Yes, they had "discussions" or arguments over finances—Stella pointed out that any couple did. Yes, there was stress over money. No, there had been no physical altercations.

Under direct, the defendant said Bruce had been "climbing the walls" during the summer and fall of 1984 when he was unemployed. He had things to do on the property, but he wanted a real job. He finally started working for the state in October.

Tom Hillier asked if Stella's employment at SeaTac was a source of contention for the couple.

Stella Nickell said it wasn't. Her husband "realized what I had been trying to tell him about my inactivity around the house, being he went through it for six months."

Steady employment for both of them eased the financial problems, she said. But in early 1986, there was another "slump" in their finances.

"We had gotten behind, and the banks and our other companies that we owed were sending us letters, wanting us to make our payments."

Stella referred to the April 25, 1986, letter to the bank.

"The purpose of that letter was in answer to the letter that I had received letting our creditors know that we were having financial difficulties. We were having a little bit of family difficulties because of arguments in discussion over finances, and that I was trying the best that I could to pick up the payments and keep them current."

"You mentioned in the letter that 'your marital problems are about to be solved.' What marital problems were you talking about?"

"Our marital problems as far as finances go."

"What did you mean by 'about to be solved'?"

"Bruce had taken over the finances for a short time. He was— dictating is not the right word—but he was telling me what bills that we were to pay, what ones he wanted paid. That was the ones that I paid and we were falling behind. I had contacted these people and told them that this problem was about to be solved because I was taking the finances back over again."

"When you say 'Bruce is no longer involved and I would like a chance for me myself to prove my word to you,' what did you mean?"

"That meant that I was not at that particular time listening to Bruce. We had had a discussion about it, which was part of our marital problems, and told him that I was taking the finances back over and trying to catch us back up to date where we should be."

"Were you meaning to suggest anything sinister by that letter?"

"No, I was not."

Tom Hillier asked if finances were improving immediately prior to Bruce Nickell's death.

They were, she said, "because we had finally gotten on permanently with the State of Washington."

Prior to her husband's full-time insurance benefits with the state, Stella Nickell told the court, she and her husband satisfied their insurance needs with policies purchased through credit cards.

Stella said she had filled out applications, even to the point of signing her husband's name. Anyone who knew Bruce knew he "despised paperwork."

She identified the insurance enrollment forms from Bank Cardholders of America and admitted filling them out.

When Tom Hillier asked about the defendant's meeting with SA Nakamoto, the defendant said it was after her meeting with Bill Donais. She was uncertain about who was covered on the credit-card policy. In addition, her attorney thought it was a single policy "because both policies that were in the envelope looked exactly the same."

Stella Nickell told the court that since she didn't have the certificates of insurance, that Bill Donais had them, she turned over a wallet card to SA Nakamoto.

Yes, he asked if there were any other policies and the witness told him no.

No, Bill Donais did not process the claims, but he might have made some phone calls on the witness's behalf.

"I did try to contact him to find out if he had found out, and he told me that it looked like it was a clerical error and for me to go ahead and process them and see what the company sent back to me."

Next up were the letters to All American on October 20, 1986. Stella did not deny writing them, nor sending them to the same place on the same date. Based on a letter from All American, the defendant said she filled out the claimant's statement.

She identified her original and the photo copy, but she could not recall submitting two claimant statements.

Concerning the All American letter from October 29, 1986, Stella Nickell said she had written "both policies are the same."

"What do you mean that they were the same?" Tom Hillier asked.

"There was the same contents in them. They were the same all around. They were identical."

"Did you think there was one policy?"

"Yes, I did," she said.

Stella said that it was her husband who filled out the state policy while the two of them sat at their kitchen table. At that time, they discussed the kinds of coverage they should have. Bruce had wanted $25,000 optional life and $100,000 supplemental.

Just before Bruce's death, there "was a foul-up with the insurance company's communication and us. They had sent out a packet for Bruce to have a medical examination, and we did not receive that package in the mail in time because there was a dated letter in it saying he had fifteen days to take a physical."

The letter, she said, was received about a month after they were supposed to get it.

When Tom Hillier turned to the amount of insurance Stella Nickell said she believed her husband was covered for, she stuck with the $25,000 figure from the state.

Prior to the All American policies, Stella Nickell said, she and her husband had applied for Firemen's Fund insurance through their American Express card, but premiums got out of hand and they canceled.

Tom Hillier switched the defendant's direct to tropical fish. The witness said she had been interested in fish for some twenty years. Her husband enjoyed the fish too, she said. At the time of his death they had one tank, down from two. Her daughter was also interested in fish.

"Her knowledge is more technical than your own?"

"Yes. She had quite an advanced knowledge. To me it was advanced. It wasn't professional or anything, but she had quite a knowledge of fish tanks."

Tom Hillier asked how she handled her algae problem. The defendant said she preferred scavenger fish over chemical remedies.

Stella Nickell said she shopped for fish ninety-nine percent of the time at Kent East Hill Fish Gallery and Pets, so yes, she recognized Tom Noonan. But she did not recall any particular conversation about algae control in October of 1985. She could not recall a particular conversation about Algae Destroyer, but conceded it "could have entered into our conversation."

She said she did not buy the product from Noonan.

"Do you recall ever crushing Algae Destroyer and using it in your aquarium?"

"No."

"Do you recall receiving advice from Cindy concerning a different kind of algae control, a liquid product, through Aquatronics?"

"Not to the best of my recollection. She could have mentioned about me controlling the algae in my tank, because it's very unsightly. We discussed several fish products."

After Sal Ramos released the Fords, they stepped into the courtroom in time to catch some of Stella Nickell's direct.

Sue Ford thought Stella was "hanging herself" with her hard-core, tough-lady demeanor.

"She just came off as a real hard person. She could bite nails," she told her husband.

When Stella later broke down and cried, it surprised Sue Ford. She had never seen that kind of emotion come from Stella before. She seemed to be hurt, seemed to truly miss Bruce.

In the courtroom Stella Nickell did not refute her daughter's claim that she had read up on poisonous plants. It was her concern for the children she baby-sat at White River Estates that prompted the reading. A girlfriend told her dieffenbachia, a houseplant she had, was poisonous.

Concern for her granddaughter led her to do more reading after they moved to the wooded property east of Auburn. She identified poisonous plants there—foxglove and nightshade.

"Did you ever mention foxglove or any of those observations to Cindy?"

"Yes, I did. I told her that I thought these plants were out there and that I had to check to find out if there was any other type of plants out there, because for fear of my granddaughter getting into them, because when she came out, we told her she had the run of the property and she was only six years old."

"Did you ever research cyanide?"

"No, I haven't."

The response surprised Tom Hillier. He asked again. "You've never researched it?"

"Before Bruce died when we moved on the property, no. After Bruce died, yes."

It was in late June, after her husband's death had been discovered as having been caused by cyanide poisoning, when the defendant said she did some reading about it. She did not dispute that she touched any of the books in evidence.

Stella Nickell's next answers were a succession of "No"s. She never discussed poisoning Bruce with her daughter. No, she never wondered where she could get cyanide. No, she didn't talk about photography stores. And she never discussed poisoning Bruce with seeds she found on the property.

Tom Hillier had the defendant describe Bruce's death. The witness painted a scene of blue-collar normalcy. A kiss, a glass of iced tea, and the tired working man sat in front of the TV before showering.

"When he finished his shower he came back out of the shower, walked through the kitchen, stopped at the end of the cook table, reached up into the cupboard above the counter, and he took some Excedrin."

Stella said her husband had been suffering "tension" headaches caused by the hectic nature of his job. He had also injured his foot. The evening he died, he took four.

"I asked him, 'Why four?' " she recalled. "He said, 'That's what I need.' "

Bruce walked into the den and sat down and finished watching TV.

Tom Hillier's questioning would later be described as "gentle." The defendant choked back tears. She didn't seem to be the antifreeze-veined killer her daughter had contended.

"He went back into the living room and sat down to finish watching TV. He had on his bathrobe. I was finishing fixing dinner for him. Pretty soon he got up and he walked out onto the patio. I thought that he had spotted a hawk that we have out there on the property and that he was watching the hawk.

"He stood there for a few minutes with his hands on the railing. I was still working in the kitchen. Pretty soon he turned around like he was going to walk back into the house. He stooped at the doorway and he said, 'Babe.' I answered him. He didn't answer me for a minute, and I said, 'What do you want?'

"He was leaned over. He said, 'I feel like I'm going to pass out.' I went to him. I asked him what was wrong. By that time he had squatted down in the doorway and he just shook his head. He didn't answer me again. I told him to come in the house and lie down on the couch. We had a couch in the den right by the glass doors.

"When he stood up he started to walk off of the steps to the patio, and I got a hold of his arm and I pulled him back towards the door, and I said, 'Come in the house and lay down.' He followed, pulled on my hand, and got back into the house, and he started to reach for the couch. He put his hands on it to brace himself. As he put his hands on the couch to lay down, he collapsed."

"What did you do?" Hillier asked sympathetically.

"I tried to get him to get up, and he did not respond. I went immediately to the telephone and called 911."

Stan and Laurie Church drove their yellow '72 Chevy pickup home mostly in silence. Laurie cried part of the way to Pacific. She felt she had let her friend down, hadn't done her job. Her husband was angry over the whole trial fiasco.

"Why didn't he let me say something?" she asked about Tom Hillier.

It was so brief, so pointless.

"I will ask these questions and you will say yes or no."

"She wanted it factual and she wanted it now, and that's it," Laurie Church later said of Joanne Maida. "There was no caring about her at all."

And there had been nothing about Cindy Hamilton. Nothing about the way she lived, how she had acted, nothing at all. Stan Church wondered why Tom Hillier hadn't pushed Stella's no-good daughter harder. His wife gave an answer.

"She testified for the government. They're not going to let her testify, then slap her down!"

Vicki Bagby Moen left the courtroom feeling that Tom Hillier didn't have the right people up there on Stella Nickell's behalf.

She also wondered why Tom Hillier didn't tear apart Cynthia Lea.

"She went after the money, that's all she was interested in," she said later.

CHAPTER 80

All eleven benches in Bill Dwyer's courtroom were wedged tight with spectators on the morning of April 28. Air-conditioning systems worked overtime to keep the heat of the courtroom in check.

Tom Hillier had his client pick up her testimony at the point when she was en route to the hospital with her mother. She said she and her mother waited in an area outside of the emergency room because hospital personnel had preferred it. It was there they learned doctors didn't know what was wrong with her husband, and "they did not know if they were going to be able to save him or not."

Bruce Nickell was moved to another area for more tests—an EKG, she recalled. A social worker said she and her mother could go to the ICU and wait.

"We waited there to be notified that he had been brought up so we could be with him. The social worker came back in and said the doctors wished to see us downstairs, and he took us back down to the same room that we had been waiting in."

"What happened next?"

Again, Stella Nickell choked with emotion.

"The doctor came in and informed us that they had not been able to save him."

She said a doctor asked if she wanted to be with her husband, but the teary-eyed defendant declined because "I didn't think that I could at that time."

Every now and then Tom Hillier paused to allow his client to get a grip on herself, underscoring her emotional delivery.

"The doctor said that they would like to perform an autopsy on him to find out the cause of death and asked me if I would sign the papers, and I told him yes, because I wished also to find out why my husband had died."

She told the court she went home, tried to sleep, and made the trip to Wenatchee to tell Bruce's folks the news. She told the jury that since the Nickells were quite elderly, she asked Bruce's cousin Dick Nickell break the news.

"When did you meet with Cindy?"

"I don't know the exact time, but I met with Cindy that same day after I got home and relaxed from the long drive, trying to get myself together to go over to a friend's house where my daughter was staying and tell her that her dad was gone."

Stella said she had been concerned about telling her daughter. Cindy and her stepfather had become close.

"I was concerned on how she would take the news because shortly before that, right at Bruce's death, Cindy and Bruce were not getting along very well because she had, in his mind, shirked her responsibility and sent her daughter to California to stay with a friend of hers, and Bruce was upset because our granddaughter was in California."

"Do you remember what you told her?" Tom Hillier asked.

"I had set down at the table and I asked her to sit down because I had something to tell her, and when she set down and she saw the condition I was in, she asked me if something was wrong with Mom or Dad Nickell. I told her no, that it was not them. I said, 'It's your dad.' I said, 'He's gone.' "

Her daughter looked at her in a state of shock, then cried, even though the defendant said she had tried to make "things as easy on her as I could."

Stella Nickell said she could not specifically recall making the "I know what you're thinking; the answer is no" statement.

"If I made the remark it was because, knowing Cindy, she was feeling bad about her and her dad not having made up before he died."

She told the court how, after seeing a TV report on Sue Snow and calling 911, King County police came out to pick up the bottles. Later, the FBI and FDA called for an interview. She recalled the meeting with Ike Nakamoto and Kim Rice.

She provided all the information they requested, including where she shopped—Albertson's North Auburn, the Pay 'N Save South Auburn, and Johnny's on the East Hill of Kent. She had shopped in about "every store in Auburn."

When asked about the third bottle found in her bathroom, Stella said she didn't know anything about it. She could not recall if she had purchased it or not.

"Do you know who else had access to your house during that time period—say, from May to early June?"

The defendant rattled off the names: Jerry Kimble, Cindy Hamilton, Wilma Stewart, A. J. and Jim Rider, Cora Lee Rice.

Further, the defendant said she met with the FBI *after* she had met with her lawyer. She said she did not know Bruce had died of cyanide poisoning until after she and Bill Donais discussed problems with the insurance policies.

Tom Hillier brandished the June 16, 1986, letter from the state concerning the physical exam Bruce was to take.

"Did you receive that letter before or after meeting with the FDA and the FBI on June 19?"

"I received that letter afterwards."

"What action, if any, did you take in response to that letter?"

"I didn't take any action, because there was none to take because it had to do with a physical examination that Bruce was supposed to take, and by that time he was already dead."

Stella Nickell told the jury how she had met with Dick Johnson and others at the Department of Transportation to learn what was required to file a claim. She said she was told it would be easier for her to go to Olympia in person. She was also told to bring a certified copy of the death certificate, "and they said that if I had any, to bring with me some newspaper clippings."

The defendant further testified that she made follow-up calls to the state, but it was because the "lady in the office" told her the insurance board would make a decision on the policy and when she didn't hear from them, she called. She also made other follow-up calls, because she had been told to do so in the event she didn't hear from them.

The defendant said that while she might have mentioned the ongoing investigation to the SEIB, she could not recall mentioning the names of anyone from the FBI.

It was time for Hillier to focus on SAs Cusack and Nichols's interview of November 1986.

While the defendant admitted the subject of her late husband's state insurance policy had been broached by the FBI, "it never went into any detail."

"I told them that as far as I knew, the only coverage that he had was approximately $25,000 in coverage."

She said the FBI had never indicated it might be worth more.

"I told them that there was no other policies because there wasn't, other than what Ike and I had already talked about, which was the credit-card policy and Bruce's state insurance."

When Tom Hiller pointed out that she had written to All American prior to her FBI interview, the defendant said she still hadn't heard back from the company until *after* the interview with Cusack and Nichols.

It was time for the defense to go back to the daughter.

Regarding Cynthia's move from California in December 1982, Stella Nickell said her daughter "was having problems down there with the gentleman that she was living with. She wanted out of the area, and I told her to come up. Bruce and I talked about it. She could stay with us because she was my daughter."

The defendant testified she did what any mother would do, despite finances that "were not the greatest."

Tom Hillier asked why she allowed Cindy to live at the Nickells' for four months.

"Because Cynthia had had a rough life when she was younger. We were trying to make it better for her. I was quite young when I had Cynthia. I know that I wasn't the greatest mother, as most young girls are not, but we wanted to help Cindy as best we could to get her feet under her and get her situated up here where she was close to us and we could be together."

Stella said her daughter had a "natural talent for being a beautician" and so they enrolled her in a beauty college. They bought her a car.

"We knew that she was still young and she needed to do her running around, meet new friends, get herself situated, and go back and forth to beauty college."

Why did the living arrangements change in April 1983?

"Cindy and I had gotten on the outs a little bit because of the way that she was doing. Because I had volunteered to take care of [her little girl], she was taking advantage of that situation and she was coming in at all hours. The only restriction that we really put on her, we requested that she call if she was going to be extremely late so that we would know that she was safe. She was ignoring that point, and Cindy and I had a few words about it.

"Then, Bruce had also stepped into it with me and told me that I was not going to be taken advantage of and be a built-in baby-sitter for her. We decided that it was time that she start looking for an apartment of her own."

Stella said after she "calmed down and after Cindy got over her mad spot, we became close again like we were, mother and daughter."

The federal public defender brought up the subject of drugs.

Stella claimed she and her daughter had first discussed drugs during Cindy's teen years in California. The discussions continued after she moved to Washington. Drug use, the defendant said, was one of the reasons Cindy moved back to the Seattle area. Friends in California would leave her alone when she tried to give up drugs. After a while, the defendant said, her daughter got back into cocaine through one of her boyfriends. Beyond that, the two did not discuss drugs.

Next, Tom Hillier hauled out Cynthia Lea's testimony checklist.

No, Stella Nickell said she never discussed hiring a hit man to kill her husband.

No, she did not tell her she wanted to get someone to run him off the road.

"Run him into a semi truck or some sort of head-on collision?"

"No."

"Shoot at him during rush-hour traffic?"

"No."

"Did you ever discuss anything remotely connected with that testimony Cindy offered here?"

"No. I have never discussed anything of that sort."

Stella Nickell shook her head with great certainty.

"The thought had never entered my mind and never would, because I loved Bruce too much. There is no way that I could even possibly think of getting rid of him."

She denied telling her daughter she was going to Texas as an alibi.

Tom Hillier asked his client a series of questions about the phone call she and Wilma Stewart shared in May 1986. The defendant "vaguely" recalled it. She was angry and upset with Bruce at the time, and told Wilma she might end up on her doorstep one day. It was fleeting, not a real threat. And, she said, she had no intention of making it a permanent split.

"When two people are upset and as angry as I was, I figured if we had a week or two of separation to make us realize what we actually had, that things would straighten out and we'd calm down and become closer."

The defendant concluded that by the end of the call her "mad spot" was gone, and of course, she never went to Texas.

"Did you ask her not to tell Bruce about that talk?"

The defendant nodded. Her husband was "extremely jealous," she said.

"I told her not to mention it to her uncle Bruce because I didn't want him to probably get the wrong idea that I was talking about leaving him, which I wasn't. It would have been a little bit hard to explain to him why I was so angry."

Though she recalled Jeanne Rice's frequent conversations about the bodyguard venture, the defendant also denied discussing it with her daughter. She never considered the job as something she'd like to do.

"I could not picture me in that at forty-one years old and never having any physical training at all, which I'm not an exercise person."

Tom Hillier asked about Jeanne Rice's testimony citing confessions of an unhappy marriage.

"It's possible that we could have mentioned having problems in our marriage, because when you get two women together and they have a few problems in their marriage to begin with, you end up starting to grumble and gripe about your men in common conversation."

Was it true, as her daughter had testified, that she wanted out of her marriage but didn't want to lose community property?

The defendant again made a flat denial.

She never told her daughter she hoped to end the marriage by poisoning her husband.

"Did you ever tell Cindy that perhaps you would simulate the Tylenol-type murders that occurred back east because that would be easy?"

"No."

"Did you ever tamper with the capsules that were in fact tampered with that have been introduced into evidence through the five bottles that are in court here today?"

"No, I haven't."

"Did you kill your husband, Bruce Nickell?"

"No, I did not."

"Are you responsible in any way for the death of Sue Snow?"

"No, I'm not."

"Did you place the bottles that were found at Johnny's and Albertson's and that are in evidence today on those shelves?"

"No, I have not."

"Have you ever touched or come in contact with cyanide?"

"No, I haven't. Not to my knowledge."

"Are you responsible in any way for the crimes charged?"

"No, I am not."

Stella Nickell later told a friend that she had been battling for composure.

"If I hadn't tried to keep a big hand on my emotions, we'd have never made it through the trial. If my emotions had gotten loose of me, I wouldn't have been able to testify, because every time I started to testify, I would've started blubbering. I had problems enough as it was."

CHAPTER 81

As expected, in her cross-examination, Joanne Maida hammered question after question as the defendant's rigid posture stiffened to near breaking.

"Mrs. Nickell, you told Wilma Stewart two weeks before Bruce's death that you were sick and tired of fighting with him. Correct?"

"Yes, I was sick and tired of fighting with him. I did not like to fight."

"And that you were very angry at him. Correct?"

She was angry, she said, but she wasn't going to leave her man.

Next, the prosecutor hauled out the April 25, 1986, letter to North Pacific Bank.

"The earlier letter that you wrote to them that came out to them between March and April 1986, do you remember telling them in that letter not to push?"

"If you just have patience . . . I will eventually catch up. Just don't push . . ."

"By May 1986, you were almost $1,900 behind in payments to North Pacific Bank, weren't you?"

The defendant couldn't recall the amount. To refresh her memory, Joanne Maida had pulled the government's exhibit, the North Pacific Bank letter from June 1, 1986.

The defendant was asked to read the last sentence into the record.

"Thank you for your patience in this matter. My payments will stay current."

"This letter was written four days before your husband's death, was it not?"

"Yes, it was."

"And at the point in time that that letter was written and on the day that Bruce Nickell died, your financial situation was steadily deteriorating, was it not?"

"No, it was not steadily deteriorating."

"Was it steadily improving?"

"Not very fast, but it *was* improving."

Again, to refresh the defendant's memory, Joanne Maida pulled three more government exhibits: the Visa and MasterCard accounts, the delinquency letter from Pacific Coast Investment on the land, and the North Pacific Bank debt on the mobile home. All delinquent, with a total topping $8,500 and escalating rapidly the day Bruce Nickell died.

"Mrs. Nickell, in April to May of 1986, your financial situation had not been improving. It was steadily getting worse, was it not?"

"No, it wasn't."

Just as Joanne Maida had sized up Stella Nickell before her cross-examination, the defendant would be damned before she'd give an inch.

"The thing that got her angry was the fact that I wasn't looking away from her, I wasn't looking around the courtroom. When she asked me a question, I looked her square in the face and answered it. And she tried to outmaneuver me a couple of times," Stella said later.

Time for the books. Stella was presented with a copy of *Deadly Harvest.*

Joanne Maida pressed: "Did pages 88 and 89 of the book particularly interest you, Mrs. Nickell?"

"That is included in the book. Yes, it was of interest to me."

The Asst. U.S. Attorney sought an explanation for the large number of prints found on the two pages.

"From what I understand from your fingerprint expert, the fingerprints are not always left on the pages you look at. I do not know which pages have the most fingerprints and which ones don't because I looked at the whole book."

The defendant was asked to read a passage on the odor of bitter almonds.

"Did the thought occur to you how it is that the pathologist missed the scent of bitter almonds during your husband's autopsy?"

"No."

When asked how cyanide works, the defendant could only offer that "it messes up the oxygen getting into the body."

"It poisons an enzyme that is required in the human body to process oxygen and it renders it functionless, does it not?"

Stella Nickell said she didn't know.

Maida asked her to read from the book again.

"Cyanide poisoning is asphyxiation at the level of the body cells . . ."

Joanne Maida asked if the defendant knew if cyanide had an odor.

When Stella Nickell said she did not know, she was asked to read.

"But cyanide itself has no odor. The odor of bitter almonds is that of benzaldehyde."

After morning recess, Joanne Maida focused a great deal of attention on the encyclopedias, and more critically, her contention that the defendant had read the volumes as a guide to killing her husband.

She zeroed in on a palm print.

"Were you holding the page down, Mrs. Nickell?"

"Yes, I was."

"So you could take notes?"

"No."

Again, Stella Nickell didn't deny she read about foxglove.

"Is foxglove poisonous?" Joanne Maida asked.

"I don't know how poisonous, but it is dangerous, especially to children."

"It's very poisonous, ma'am, isn't it?"

Stella Nickell repeated her answer.

"What kind of seeds does foxglove bear?"

"I don't know."

"Little black seeds, Mrs. Nickell?"

"I have no idea. Except for the testimony that has already been given, of my own knowledge, I don't know."

"Does foxglove grow on your property?"

"Yes, it does."

"And you were familiar with it prior to June 5, 1986, were you not?"

"Yes, *we* were."

The "we" was an interesting choice of pronouns. Did she mean Bruce? Cindy, perhaps?

The overdue book, *Human Poisoning from Native and Cultivated Plants*, was discussed next. Stella Nickell did not deny reading that book either.

"Do you recall what the symptoms are of ingestion of the fox-glove plant?"

"No, I do not recall."

"Do you recall that the book talked about children being placed in danger from sucking the flowers or eating the leaves or seeds of the foxglove plant?"

"Yes, I do."

As cross continued, Joanne Maida returned to *Deadly Harvest* and its passages on Indian tobacco, page 119 and its seven finger-prints. The defendant acknowledged that the text indicated lobelia, or Indian tobacco, was chemically similar to the nicotine of tobacco. And, in fact, nicotine was a powerful alkaloid.

Asst. U.S. Attorney Maida read a passage: *"Overdoses brought serious illness and sometimes death. Thus, lobelia received a reputation as a poisonous plant."*

It was clear where the line of questioning was headed.

Stella did not refute that Bruce was a chain-smoker and there had been the presence of emphysema in his lungs, but she did deny a nicotine-overdose murder plan.

Now to put all of the defendant's interest in plants into some kind of context that would lead the jury to conclude murder. Joanne Maida questioned the defendant on her financial difficulties around the time she checked out the book *Deadly Harvest*, due June 16, 1983.

Stella Nickell said she could not recall any.

To jog her memory, Joanne Maida presented the Chapter 13 petition filed two weeks after *Deadly Harvest* was due back at the Auburn library.

The second time Stella Nickell checked out the book, it carried a due date of May 22, 1984. Bruce Nickell had been laid off the month before.

"Mrs. Nickell, do you recall complaining to your daughter that your husband wasn't trying hard enough to find work and you were unhappy with him just being around the house?"

"No."

"You weren't happy with his unemployment status, were you?"

"Nobody is happy to be unemployed. He was trying his best."

"I'm not talking about Bruce's unhappiness. You weren't happy with your husband's unemployment, were you?"

"That's a hard question to answer."

"Well, were you or weren't you?"

"No. Neither one of us were happy over the fact that he had become unemployed."

Joanne Maida had the clerk show the defendant the Nickells' 1984 tax return, showing $13,502 in total income. Of that amount, Maida pointed out, some $1,100 was earned by the defendant at Eddie Bauer.

"Mrs. Nickell, you weren't happy to go to work at Eddie Bauer; you did so because you had to, didn't you?"

"No, I did not have to. I did it to help relieve the financial situation we were in."

Joanne Maida turned to the Firemen's Fund/American Life Insurance application.

"And was it applied for on January 20, 1984, a couple of months before Bruce was laid off from McDonald Industries?"

"Yes, it was."

The Asst. U.S. Attorney presented the form letter from Firemen's showing the $50,000 death benefit.

"And throughout the life of that policy, you actively tracked its progress, did you not?"

"What do you mean by 'actively tracked its progress'?"

"When the premium payments went up, you immediately made a note of that and tried to call the insurance company, did you not?"

"I noticed it coming in on our bill, yes, and I wanted to find out what it was for."

"And you sent a letter to the insurance company after you received this notification of an increase in premiums, didn't you?"

"I do not recall receiving a notification of an increase."

"Nevertheless, you sent a letter to them asking about why the policy payments had increased?"

"Yes, I did."

Yes, the defendant said, she canceled the policy, signing her husband's name. The cancellation acknowledgment was dated July 19, 1985.

"Mrs. Nickell, a month and a half after you received that acknowledgment letter of cancellation from the insurance company, you signed Bruce's name to another insurance policy, did you not?"

"I do not recall."

The clerk was asked to hand the defendant the All American exhibits.

Now Stella remembered. It had been filled out and signed September 1985.

"A month after you signed Bruce's name to that policy, you signed his name again to another one, didn't you?"

"Yes."

It, too, was for $20,000.

"So you knew by October 14, 1985, that you had submitted and were in the process of submitting two different applications for two different life insurance policies, did you not?"

"I did not remember applying for the first one. I had not received a policy yet in the mail."

Joanne Maida was skeptical. "You had forgotten that?"

"I did not recall it in my memory."

"You did not recall that a month prior you had signed your husband's name on another $20,000 group term life insurance policy?"

"There was a lot going on in our life at that time."

"Do you recollect telling your niece, Wilma Stewart, that part of the life insurance total that you were tallying up was comprised of two $20,000 life insurance policies with a total amount of $40,000?"

"No, I do not recall that, and I never tallied up what I expected to receive from my husband's death."

Stella said her niece could have been confused, "because when she was talking to me at one time and said the FBI agents had been over to question her, they told her that the life insurance that I could expect from Bruce's death was over $200,000."

When asked, Stella said she could not recall Bruce's staying home ill in January, February, and March of 1985. Joanne Maida again jogged her memory with an exhibit, this the sick-leave records from work. On January 21, Bruce Nickell was "sick to his stomach." On February 11, 1985, Bruce Nickell had written "stomach flu." On March 18–20, 1985, he wrote "sick to my stomach."

The defendant found the last entries, October 30–November 1. Her husband had written "flu."

"Mrs. Nickell, you heard Dr. Denton from the University of Washington testify about the effect of ingesting foxglove, about nausea and fatigue. We've talked about what that *Human Poisoning* book says are the symptoms of foxglove poisoning."

"Yes."

"Have you ever observed anyone who's exhibited these symptoms?"

"Not to my knowledge, no."

Under more cross, the defendant said that she could not recall, telling SA Nakamoto she had called the insurance company's toll-free number and had been told there had been a clerical error.

Though the defendant had remained steadfast, her friends were glad it was time for afternoon recess. Some didn't think her defiant stance was doing her case any good.

At 1:30, the trial resumed with Joanne Maida picking apart Stella Nickell's claim that when she was asked by Equifax's Lynn Force, she declined to tell him of other policies, when, in fact, she knew of them.

"And that was a lie, wasn't it?"

Tom Hillier objected; this time he was overruled.

"A lot of people look at it in a different way. I did not consider it an out-and-out lie, because I did not see where it was any of his concern that I had other insurance policies because he gave me no reason as to why he needed to know."

"It was a little lie, Mrs. Nickell?"

Another objection from the defense, and Judge Dwyer sustained it.

"It was not an out-and-out lie, Mrs. Nickell? Is that what you just told this jury?"

"Yes, it is."

"So although you had been—You tried to be helpful when you first visited the state insurance people who had asked you to bring some news clippings with you, when you talked to this insurance investigator the following month, you just chose to tell him something that was not an out-and-out lie?"

"I chose to tell him the way that I felt."

The defendant said Lynn Force did not give her "any reason to need to know about any other insurance."

Again, Stella Nickell denied hearing Lynn Force say that her husband had been covered for $136,000 under the state insurance.

Joanne Maida moved to the "third time" anyone asked about insurance policies—November's meeting with SAs Cusack and Nichols.

"The only policy you told them about was a policy that you describe to have a $25,000 base coverage. Correct?"

"No, that's not the only policy I told them about. On that particular day they asked me about that particular insurance and asked me what the coverage was on it. I told them. They asked me if there was any other insurance policy, and I told them no."

She said she did not tell them about the two $20,000 policies because she thought they were referring back to Mr. Nakamoto's notes, where she had already told about them.

"When they asked you what other interest you might have with regard to your husband's death, what did you tell them?"

The defendant bristled. "What do you mean by 'what other interests I might have'?"

"Did you make an affirmative statement about any interest you might have or might not have in your husband's death?"

"I do not recall a question being put to me in that manner."

"And yet, Mrs. Nickell, six days prior to that interview in November of 1986, you had filed a claimant's statement against both of the All American Life insurance policies, had you not?"

The defendant admitted she had, but she was very confused at that time.

Joanne Maida challenged her. "You completely forgot, it completely slipped your mind, that six days before you had mailed in a claimant's statement against both of the life insurance policies on Bruce Nickell's life?"

"I told you I did not remember exactly what time I sent them in. I had sent in references to those policies, yes."

The defendant was reminded that she had testified the day before that she believed she had only one All American policy. The Asst. U.S. Attorney wondered how that could be. She asked the defendant to study the documents.

Stella Nickell looked up and conceded there were two specification schedules and two different policy numbers.

"That's correct. And you sent in both of those personal specification schedules attached to the claimant's statement, did you not?"

Stella Nickell said she was confused so she had copied the contents of both envelopes and, yes, sent in two specification schedules.

She stuck with her story.

When Joanne Maida asked the defendant about her call to SEIB two days after seeing the FBI, she said she could not recall telling Pam Stegenga the investigation was over.

"I cannot say yes, I did, and I cannot say no, I didn't. I do not recall making that remark to the lady."

The witness was asked to review the statement of insurance from the state.

"Now, you've indicated to us that there was some amount of confusion on your part about the $100,000, the Part E that's referred to on this statement, accidental-death and dismemberment coverage. Is that correct?"

There was.

Joanne Maida had the defendant read from the document.

"The following optional life insurance coverages are available and you have selected the coverages that are indicated."

"Is there anything in that statement that leaves it in question about what the coverage was?"

"No, not on this statement."

Joanne Maida referred to the $100,000 optional life insurance.

"The statement says that these coverages are available and that you have selected the coverages indicated below. Correct?"

"Yes."

When asked how much money the defendant thought she was going to inherit after her husband died, Stella Nickell said from what she learned in court she thought the total was $125,000.

Joanne Maida approached the defendant and totaled the figures one by one for a grand total of $176,000.

The June 16 letter referred to $25,000 supplemental life coverage.

"To your understanding, the letter refers to the $25,000 coverage that was incompleted due to a failure to take a medical examination. Correct?"

"I did not have that understanding. According to the letter, yes."

The $25,000 was not even figured into the grand total.

"That's pretty close to the statements you made to Wilma Stewart about getting close to two hundred grand, isn't it?"

Tom Hillier objected to the argumentative question, and Judge Dwyer sustained it.

"Mrs. Nickell, you were preoccupied with getting paid on these policies, weren't you?"

"No, I was not."

"Isn't that why you called on September 26, September 29, October 10, and November 20th of 1986?"

"No. I was following directions from the insurance board to call back."

The defendant fumed when the prosecutor made mention of "a briefcase full of clippings," as had been seen by SEIB's Sandy Sorby.

"I had some clippings in my briefcase. It was not *full* of clippings."

Stella said there were approximately fifteen to twenty clippings in her briefcase—nowhere near the number Sandy Sorby had said she'd seen.

"You were keeping a pile of them for proof when you filed your insurance claim?"

"I took them with me, yes, because they needed them. I didn't know what kind of clippings they might possibly need, so I took all of them."

"In fact, you told Sandy Sorby once you got down there that you waited to come in until you had gotten the revised death certificate showing cause of death of your husband of acute cyanide poisoning, didn't you?"

"I do not remember the exact phrase that I used, but I did wait for the death certificate because I was informed by Ms. Fligner that it would be sent out to me immediately."

"Didn't you wait until the authorities would catch up with their error and finally put the true cause of death on that certificate?"

"No, I did not wait for that purpose."

"Mrs. Nickell, you waited, didn't you, because you always knew that acute cyanide poisoning was the only true cause of death behind your husband's sudden collapse at home?"

The defense again objected to the questioning as argumentative.

"Overruled."

"No, I did not."

On questions of the book research, Stella again remained firm.

"Didn't your research, didn't your reading prior to Bruce Nickell's death tell you that the odor of bitter almonds could be smelled, and wasn't it your expectation based on that that any doctor would have found it during the autopsy, it would have been that easy?"

"There was no way I could have known that, because I did not read about it before my husband's death."

Joanne Maida wouldn't give up so easily on the smell of bitter almonds. It was in *Deadly Harvest*, and the defendant had checked that book out twice. She suggested the defendant must have been surprised about the initial emphysema ruling.

"There was no way that it could have surprised me at the beginning of these autopsies. Later, yes, it did enter my mind why they didn't know of it."

Stella Nickell did not deny making calls to the pathologists on June 7, and again a week later. Yes, she asked her family doctor about the plausibility of emphysema as Bruce's cause of death.

"Mrs. Nickell, you were trying, were you not, to reopen a closed file on your husband's death because you knew that the insurance paid out more than four hundred percent for accidental over a natural cause of death?"

"No, I was not trying to open anything."

"Mrs. Nickell, when you weren't getting the autopsy results back from the authorities on June 7 when you called, and again on June 13, isn't that why you mixed up another batch of potassium cyanide and planted those bottles on the store shelves in the Auburn-Kent area?"

Tom Hillier objected that the question was argumentative and inappropriate for cross-examination, but Judge Dwyer allowed it.

The defendant answered with an emphatic "No."

"I have never mixed up anything of that sort."

Next, Maida fired off questions concerning the placement of bottles on store shelves.

One claim after another was denied by the defendant.

"If it could appear that someone else had died from acute cyanide poisoning by random chance, that was the only way that you could directly inform the authorities of your husband's own death without casting suspicion on yourself, wasn't it?"

"No."

"Mrs. Nickell, you knew that if you had suggested acute cyanide poisoning as the cause of your husband's death, that that would cast too much suspicion on you, didn't you?"

"There was no way that I could suggest that, because I had no idea what had killed him."

"When Sue Snow's death was first broadcast on Monday, June 16, 1986, you knew it at that time, didn't you?"

"No, I did not."

"You waited twenty-four hours before calling the police to turn in your two bottles of Excedrin so that you would not appear too anxious to turn those bottles in as to your own husband's death, didn't you?"

"No. I called the 911 number on the seventeenth, the same day that I saw it in the news report on TV."

"By the way, Mrs. Nickell, you do shop at the Pay 'N Save North?"

"I do periodically, but it is not a common place for my shopping."

"Do you recall, when you talked to Ron Nichols and Jack Cusack on November 18 of '86, that you told them you did not shop at the Pay 'N Save North store because you didn't like the physical layout of the store? That's why you shop at Pay 'N Save South only. Do you recall that?"

"I did not say 'only'. I said that is why I shop at Pay 'N Save South. That is my regular place of shopping."

"Incidentally, for the record, Pay 'N Save North store was where the Anacin was found."

Tom Hillier stood. "Your Honor, I would object to something for the record. I think it's improper for the prosecutor—"

The objection was sustained.

The Asst. U.S. Attorney asked about the third Excedrin bottle, the one Stella Nickell claimed to know nothing about.

The "Cyanide-Laced Medications" chart was moved to the easel.

"We're talking about a third bottle of Excedrin that was recovered in your house, the bottle that you indicate you knew nothing about—Lot no. 5H102 expiration 8-88, the bottle recovered from Johnny's Market.

"Mrs. Nickell, on June 3, 1986, two days before Bruce's death, you shopped at Johnny's Market, did you not, and purchased over ninety dollars' worth of groceries?"

"To the best of my recollection, yes, ma'am."

"That particular bottle has the same number of capsules as the one found in your house. Referring your attention to another sixty-capsule bottle, Excedrin 5H102, expiration 8-88, taken out of the Snow residence, and referring also to her purchase of that bottle from either Albertson's North or Safeway, ma'am, you shopped at Albertson's North, didn't you, from time to time?"

The defendant said she did.

When Joanne Maida asked if she had shopped at Safeway, the defendant said she hadn't in "a long time."

"When we found the bottle that's marked by the arrow, Mrs. Nickell, it still had sixty capsules in it. Mrs. Nickell, didn't you purchase that bottle as one of several bottles that you bought for the purpose of tampering with it?"

Another flat no.

"And when you had enough bottles that you had laced with cyanide, that bottle turned up to be an extra bottle and you placed that under your bathroom sink."

"No."

The defendant denied she purchased the Anacin-3 with her ninety dollars of groceries from Johnny's. She had no idea how the Anacin-3 wound up on the shelves at Pay 'N Save North.

"And as I understood your testimony from yesterday, you have never purchased Algae Destroyer for use in killing algae in your aquariums. Is that correct?"

"To the best of my knowledge, I have never purchased it."

Stella Nickell continued her denials concerning Tom Noonan's purported recommendation to crush tablets.

"I have never used a solid algae destroyer. Whether we ever discussed an algae destroyer or not, I do not recall, because we have had far too many conversations about our fish tanks."

There was more legal bickering as the defendant sat glumly in the witness chair.

"Mrs. Nickell, can you think of any reason why Tom Noonan would be mistaken about your purchases of Algae Destroyer?"

"I have no idea why Tom Noonan would be mistaken as to referring to that conversation with us. We may have talked about Algae Destroyer in our extensive conversations that we have had."

"Can you think—"

Stella interrupted: "I do know that I have been mistaken for another lady that does go in there. The only way they have separated us is when I speak or when I write out my checks and they see my name on the check."

Joanne Maida looked incredulous.

"This is the first time you have ever made a remark in that regard, isn't it?"

Stella Nickell said she had told her attorney, but she didn't know who the woman was.

"Can you think of any reason why your daughter would be mistaken about your using Algae Destroyer?"

"As far as I know, she has never said that I used it. I have never used a solid algae destroyer. If she was mistaken and made that remark, I have no reason why she would."

"Mrs. Nickell, at home you kept a container or containers with some residue amounts of Algae Destroyer still left over from before you switched to liquid algicide, did you not?"

"No, because I have not used it."

The prosecutor asked if the defendant had used the same contaminated container when she packed the capsules with cyanide.

Stella Nickell again denied it.

The litany of denials went on.

"You knew that you could get potassium cyanide from a photographer, didn't you?" Joanne Maida asked.

"The only way that I knew you could get it in photography was in the solution you develop film in, because there was an article on the front of the paper up at the airport that she and I both read that said it was very easily accessible to the public because it was used in developing film."

Yet, as Joanne Maida pointed out, the *New Caxton Encyclopedia* said the same thing.

Stella Nickell did not, however, deny discussing the Tylenol poisonings with her daughter. She said it was "one of the common conversations up at the airport." But she denied talking about the ease of putting things back on store shelves.

"Mrs. Nickell, do you personally know of any reason why your daughter would go through the ordeal of trial to testify the way she has?"

Tom Hillier objected. "Your Honor, I'll object. It's argumentative."

"Sustained."

After some thought, the question was rephrased: "Can you think of any reason why your daughter would have said all these things that you have now denied on the record you discussed with her?"

Stella paused; this answer slower in coming than the others. And of course, there was good reason for that.

"I have no reason to believe what she said. I have no idea as to why she would say the things that she has said to put herself and me through this situation."

Over Hillier's continued objections, Maida broke down the next question.

"The Mexico idea fizzled out when Jeanne Rice left town. Correct?"

"As far as she was concerned, yes. I never had the idea."

"This was a couple of months prior to your husband's death that she left town. Is that right, as far as you know?"

"I do not know. I do not even know that she had left town, because she had quit working at the airport."

"By April 1986, a couple of months before your husband's death, you had made a decision that you would stay with the house in Auburn because you were committing yourself to the bank to make the financial payments they wanted, didn't you?"

"I was always committed to staying with my husband and the house and the land."

"That's why you wrote that letter under date of April 25 to North Pacific Bank saying that you had had marital problems, they were just about resolved, Bruce was no longer involved, and you had taken over the payments."

"What reason are you referring to?" Stella asked.

"The reason that you had committed yourself to pay off the delinquency payments on the property in Auburn."

"The reason I was committed to that was because Bruce and I needed to catch our payments up to date."

The jury departed down the steps to the right of the jury box for afternoon recess, and Stella Maudine managed a smile for her sisters. She felt she was holding her own.

Stella Nickell and Joanne Maida resumed their little drama after recess, with the Asst. U.S. Attorney running through the status of the Nickell marriage according to the defendant. It was a marriage getting better, not worse, when Bruce Nickell died.

Stella Nickell agreed.

"You recall that I directed your attention to the chart earlier and showed all of your credit-card balances and how much you owed?"

"Yes."

"And that it had not changed in April–May 1986 from what it had been anytime earlier?"

"Those particular bills had not changed that much, no, but our financial situation was up the uphill grade."

"And yet by April you were telling the bank that Bruce was no longer involved. Correct?"

"Yes."

Joanne Maida distilled the letter's content for a reminder.

". . . The second-to-the-last sentence indicates that *'My payments will be on time in the future.'* Correct?"

"Yes."

"What does the last sentence say?"

"It says, *'Thank you for your cooperation until I can get my feet under me again.'*"

"'My feet under me'?"

"Yes."

It was shortly after Stella Nickell sent the letter that she phoned Wilma Stewart.

"You were very angry with Bruce and you were thinking about just packing up and leaving and coming down to live with her in Houston?"

Stella denied the idea of a Houston move.

"I don't recall her saying that I had thought about packing up. . . . She had been trying for quite a long time to get us to move down there, and she was hoping that I might possibly stay."

"The reason why you called Wilma Stewart in May of 1986 was to ask if that was possible, if you could come and live with her. Correct?"

"No. If I had had any plans whatsoever of going to live with my niece, I would not have had to ask her if it was possible, because I knew it was."

By June 1, the prosecutor charged, Stella changed her plans.

The defendant denied any plans to live anywhere else. She had gotten over her anger by the time she was off the phone.

The prosecutor directed the defendant's attention to her June 1 letter to North Pacific.

"And throughout this letter, you're talking in the first person. I, I, my my, all the way down, and what do you say in the very last sentence of that letter?"

"It says: *'My payments will now stay current'.*"

"Mrs. Nickell, by June 1, 1986, you wrote that letter four days prior to your husband's death, you had already decided that this property was going to be all yours, hadn't you?"

"No."

"Three days after you wrote that letter dated June 1 of 1986, you set out to execute a plan by which the property would become all yours, didn't you?"

"No, I didn't."

By June 5, 1986, Joanne Maida pointed out, Bruce Nickell was "no longer involved."

Tom Hillier's re-direct was damage control. It was clear that while his client hadn't budged from her story, things still looked bad for her.

He went over the bank letter.

"Because you used expressions such as 'I would like a chance for me myself to prove my word,' did you mean to imply that you were intending to kill Bruce?"

"No. I phrased that letter—I have a bad habit of saying 'I' and 'me' as an individual because I wrote the letter. I cannot speak for somebody else."

She said she never meant to suggest that it was her property alone, or that it was about to be so.

"Ms. Maida talks about your financial situation in April and May, and we have an illustrative chart here. As evidenced by the April 26 letter, you enclosed a check for $800 to North Pacific, and then on June 1 you wrote again, indicating another payment and that by the end of that month you would be all caught up. So this figure by the end of May was not $1,892 in debt, was it?"

"No," she said, the figure would be less. In fact, she and her husband, both employed at the time, were trying to catch up as fast as they could. That was what she had meant by an improving financial situation.

Concerning the April 26 letter to the bank, the defendant said she was not suggesting she'd leave her husband.

"Did you ever think of leaving him?" Tom Hillier asked.

"No, because Bruce was like a part of me."

By the time she hung up the phone, she said her niece had talked her "out of being angry" and put her "back into a good mood."

"Did you—again, are you responsible in any way for the crimes charged in the indictment the government has brought against you?"

"No, I am not."

Tom Hillier was finished. He thanked his client, who sat glumly, drained of any of the little color she had.

Joanne Maida said she had three more questions.

The defendant again denied telling her daughter of any cyanide research before Bruce died.

"Did you not tell her that you had learned that potassium cyanide could be obtained from photography?"

"No, I didn't. We read that in the newspaper."

"When you told your daughter the day after your husband died, 'I know what you're thinking, but the answer is no,' the import of what you were saying to her was clear, wasn't it, in light of these prior conversations with her?"

"I don't understand what you're getting at. If I made the remark, which I have no recollection of most of the remarks I make to her, I was trying to comfort her over a death in our family."

"Based on your prior conversations with your daughter about your husband, nothing more needed to be said between you."

Tom Hillier objected, argumentative.

Judge Dwyer agreed, and there were no more questions.

Stella Nickell stepped down as the defense rested.

The jury was excused, while over Tom Hillier's continued objections Joanne Maida reargued the admissibility of Katy Hurt Parker's rebuttal testimony. Judge Dwyer agreed that the testimony of the defendant, and even Vicki Moen's, was enough to suggest recent fabrications. He cited the defendant's denials and Vicki's charge of Cindy's "unstable" personality.

Katy Hurt Parker would be allowed to testify.

Tom Hillier had lost that battle; he pulled the reward from his threadbare bag of tricks. It was agreed the reward stipulation would be read to the jury before the government's rebuttal case.

The Asst. U.S. Attorney Maida made another play for the polygraph/phone call, but Judge Dwyer held firm—the jury would not hear it.

The jury returned, and the judge read:

"Stipulation: The parties agree and stipulate that the Proprietary Association and Over-the-Counter Drug Trade Association advertised a $300,000 reward for information leading to the arrest and conviction of the person or persons responsible for the deaths involved in this case, and that information about the reward was published in both The Seattle Times *and* The Seattle Post-Intelligencer *on June 20, 1986."*

Katy Hurt Parker took the stand for the second time. The government's sole rebuttal witness told the jury she had lived with Cindy Hamilton in the mid-eighties. Prior to that time, she said, she knew Cindy for about a year.

"About a year?"

"About a year, year and a half."

"Did you meet her in 1985?"

The defense objected. The witness was being led. Judge Dwyer agreed.

Katy looked flustered, without a clear path to follow.

She told the court she met Cindy in 1985 when they worked at 7-Eleven. The two women became roommates.

The witness figured they had lived together off and on for "approximately six months" since March or April of '85.

"Did there come a time, Ms. Parker, when Cindy Hamilton came home and shared with you a conversation she said she had had with her mother?"

"Yes, there was."

Her time frames were less than precise. She thought it was "about November" of 1985, reasoning:

"Because she spent holidays with us, Thanksgiving and Halloween."

The specific conversation occurred at her kitchen table. It was Cindy who broached the subject.

"She says, "Katy, do you know what my mom asked me today?" "

Her voice was so soft, the jury strained to hear.

"She asked me how much cocaine it would take to kill a person, and I asked her why. She said that her mother had been talking about getting rid of her father and this was one way."

Joanne Maida asked if a reason had been mentioned as to why Stella would want to kill Bruce.

"That she was getting tired of him."

The witness stated further that Cindy had told her that Stella was worried that her own mother wouldn't have a place to go if she lost her property.

"Did you talk immediately at that time to Cindy about whether there was a possibility of that happening?"

The witness said she had.

The judge interrupted the testimony to remind the Asst. U.S. Attorney that questioning be confined to the conversation between mother and daughter.

Maida promised clarification.

"Was that the end of the conversation, or did it go on?"

"It went on."

"Did you pursue the subject with her?"

The witness said she did. She said she asked if Cindy thought that her mother would really do it.

"What did she say?"

"She said—"

Again, Judge Dwyer interceded and Tom Hillier objected.

"Did you continue your contact with Cindy Hamilton the year later, after Bruce Nickell died?"

"Yes, we did."

Joanne Maida switched tracks and asked if Cindy and the witness discussed her going to the authorities back in November of 1985. She said they had. A few questions followed, and the witness was turned over to Hillier for cross-examination.

Tom Hillier had a chance to discredit the witness. She had been extremely vague in her recollections.

He asked if she had been contacted and asked to come forward by Cindy Hamilton prior to her appearance before the grand jury.

She said she had.

He continued, but was unable to further pinpoint when Cindy Hamilton moved in and how long she had stayed.

Katy didn't agree that her friend had "an unstable lifestyle."

"Do you know whether or not she was using cocaine during that time frame?"

Katy didn't care too much for Hillier, and it showed. She admitted Cindy drank, but that was the extent of her drug use.

"In all the time that I have known Cindy, I have never known Cindy to use any drugs."

"When you say she was visiting with you during the holidays, was she living with you?"

"I know that she stayed with me during, like, Thanksgiving, and she was there on Halloween because we got our kids together and got them dressed, but I don't recall if she was actually living there. But her and [her daughter] did stay with us on Halloween Night and on Thanksgiving Day night."

Further questions showed only that the conversation didn't take place on either of those nights.

"Didn't Cindy Hamilton tell you that her mom and her stepfather enjoyed a good relationship?"

"She never really said anything. Just, whenever she talked, it was 'my mom and dad.' "

Katy Parker stepped down madder than hell at Tom Hillier.

"I wanted to get off that stand and knock his teeth down his throat. I did. The way he held himself. It was like: You're a liar and I'm gonna get you! That's the way I felt—like he was attacking me. Fuck you! Take a walk, bud!"

With no more witnesses from either side, testimony was over. The next day, the attorneys would meet to go over the exhibits to go to the jury. Final arguments would wait for Monday.

Some stories never made it to court. Maybe it was because they didn't fit, or they impugned a witness's credibility. Katy Hurt Parker held one in her memory. It was a phone call she received from Cindy back in June 1986. The two women seldom saw each other during that time. Some would say the contact was infrequent because Cindy no longer needed Katy's babysitting services—Cindy was living with Dee Rogers, and her little girl was off in Northern California.

It might have been a nice surprise when Cindy phoned if her news hadn't been so terrible.

"Katy, my dad died a couple days ago," she said, sounding shaky.

Katy gave her condolences, then blurted something that even surprised herself.

"Did your mom do it?"

"No. He dropped something on his toe at work, and it caused a blood clot and it went to his heart."

"Well, I don't think your mom could have something to do with that," Katy offered.

" 'Course not. No way."

If Katy didn't question her friend because she seemed so upset by her loss, there was also another reason.

"I didn't want to know any more than I already knew," she later said.

CHAPTER 82

If Stella Maudine Nickell was a rawhide pioneer gal, as Jack Cusack liked to consider her, May 2 and closing arguments was to be her final roundup. Her fate was now delivered into the hands of seven women and five men who had studied her every move, every gesture.

Joanne Maida started her closing with expressions of empathy, an emotion she seldom displayed throughout the trial. She said Sue Snow had died because Stella Nickell's plan depended on it and depended on her husband's death appearing just as random.

"But the so-called random killer made three fatal mistakes in the execution of an otherwise flawless scheme. The scheme was flawless because of its simplicity. It was flawless also because of its anonymity," she said.

The first mistake was the Algae Destroyer-contaminated bowl. The defendant, she said, had switched from the tablets to a liquid, leaving the bowl aside to dissolve the hard tablets. The bowl was used for cyanide.

Stella Nickell's second mistake was not leaving the autopsy well enough alone. She had committed the perfect crime, and her husband's file had been closed. He had died of emphysema.

"Stella Nickell had read that potassium cyanide gave off the odor of bitter almonds, she was surprised when it had not been detected. . . . She needed the authorities to discover the cause, so she could collect on accidental-death benefits."

But they hadn't, and Stella Nickell was forced to bring the bottles to the authorities' attention.

Joanne Maida went through the evidence. The Anacin-3, found at the Pay 'N Save store the defendant claimed she did not shop—yet checks were written there. Pay 'N Save North did not stock that particular count-size of Anacin-3 found on their store shelves. A price sticker on the box showed it had originally been stocked by a member of Associate Grocers.

Johnny's in Kent, where Stella Nickell purchased almost a hundred dollars of groceries on June 3, 1986, stocked Anacin-3. Johnny's was an Associate Grocer.

Only five of the 15,000 bottles examined by the FDA were laced with potassium cyanide. Of the five, Stella Nickell produced two.

That, Asst. U.S. Attorney Maida said, was her third mistake.

"The staggering odds were multiplied further because the defendant purchased them at different stores, at different times."

Her husband dead, the defendant applied for the benefits . . . money, money, money. . . .

First the state policy, then two All American insurance policies. There were two letters, two claims made by the defendant.

"It's crystal clear, ladies and gentlemen, that Stella Nickell is filing a claim against each of the two policies. She sends in two different specification schedules, two death certificates, and the two applications which she made separately in September and October 1985."

The defense's professed misunderstandings were dismissed as flat-out lies—to Ike Nakamoto, to Lynn Force, to Cusack and Nichols. The defendant was not confused; she knew the state insurance was $136,000.

Joanne Maida also spoke about the defendant's daughter, first acknowledging her background, the drugs.

"Cindy Hamilton was working and trying to keep two jobs at the same time. She also had a very active social life. She got involved in speed, or otherwise called methamphetamines, and she used a lot of it. She tried to shield its use from her daughter, and the reason why she moved up to the state of Washington, one of the reasons was to move away from a social circle of friends who used drugs, and also she wanted to temporarily leave California because of a bad marriage down there."

The move was followed by a close relationship between mother and daughter.

"Throughout this period of several years, Ms. Hamilton became aware of financial and personal problems that plagued the Nickell marriage. She was aware that the Nickell marriage to the outside world appeared to be a happy one to most people."

Happy or unhappy marriage? Joanne Maida told the jurors to use their common sense. Bonnie Anderson had said the defendant liked her work hours because she didn't have to deal with her husband. Jeanne Rice told the court of Stella Nickell's interest in packing up and leaving for Mexico—with her daughter, not her husband.

She covered Tom Noonan's testimony.

"The reason he says he remembers further advising Stella Nickell to crush up the hard tablets of Algae Destroyer was because it was his recommendation that she use the liquid form of algicide called Algaegon—in his expert opinion, a more effective form of algicide. But since Stella Nickell preferred the hard tablets in Algae Destroyer, he said he told her to crush them up."

Joanne Maida went on, dredging up Cynthia Lea's charges against her mother: the hit man, Katy Parker and the cocaine, the Firemen's Fund insurance, Bruce's layoff, *Deadly Harvest*, the little black seeds, the bodyguard business, the Tylenol murders . . . the comment "I know what you're thinking, but the answer is no."

"Nothing more needs to be said between mother and daughter for the significance of that comment to be grasped. It is not lost on Cindy Hamilton."

She reminded the jurors that Cindy Hamilton came forward six months later and told her story to the FBI, providing information that suggested her mother researched the cyanide plan at a library.

The jurors were asked to examine the library books carefully, the positions of the prints, the number of prints on pages dealing with cyanide.

After four hours of closing, Joanne Maida put her case to bed.

"Two people died because Stella Maudine Nickell, with cool, chilling deliberation, set out to eliminate them because it behooved her interests to do so. Her acts reflect a human being without social or moral conscience; a hard, icy human being who was willing to adopt a horrendous course of action as was convenient to accomplishing her purposes. She has attempted to explain away all of her words and conduct just as she has attempted to explain away every shred of physical evidence in this case presented against her. But she attempts to deny and she attempts to explain away too much. Stella Maudine Nickell attempts to escape accountability for decisions which she made which had irrevocable consequences to Sue Snow and to Bruce Nickell."

The courtroom clock read 1:10 when Tom Hillier stepped up to begin his closing and immediately attacked the government's "close-minded" view of the case. Joanne Maida's opening remarks suggested Bruce Nickell died alone, without his wife at his side. The prosecution assumed Stella Nickell was lying and not confused. The prosecution assumed there was a bowl that was used to crush cyanide and algicide together, and that that bowl had been lying around Stella Nickell's house for up to six months or a year—depending on whether Tom Noonan's or Cindy Hamilton's version was believed.

Further, Tom Hillier said, the prosecution assumed the defendant called the pathology department in mid-June 1986 to press for autopsy results, when the pathologists suggested it was a reasonable concern.

"The prosecution, without scarcely acknowledging the lies and inconsistencies of Cindy Hamilton, doesn't talk about her character at all," he said.

The prosecution had argued that Stella's daughter in no way could have known about the cyanide research without Stella's having told her about that sometime prior to Bruce's death.

Yet, as Tom Hillier pointed out, Cindy Hamilton stayed with her mother *after* Bruce Nickell died. It was then, he said, that his client researched both cyanide and emphysema.

The government's case rested on Cindy Hamilton's shoulders.

As the defense lawyer saw it, Cindy's time frame concerning the insurance was at odds with the government's theories.

"She testified first that late in 1985 or early 1986, 'My mom talked about overdosing Bruce with cocaine, but I told her that she couldn't do that because it might show up in his blood stream, and he might flunk his physical. Then I won't get any insurance.'

"So the best we have is a vague time frame of late December, early January, which doesn't tend to mesh very well with the government's proof, because it was January 2, 1986, that Bruce took his physical."

Tom Hillier further suggested that the time frame was vague by design, so it would mesh with the government's theory concerning the insurance motive. Her testimony was contradictory—she said May or April 1986 during cross-examination.

Hillier referred to Cindy Hamilton's grand jury testimony.

"*Q: How did your stepfather's name first get introduced into this whole business?*

"*A: I honestly can't remember exactly when it came as far as me knowing definitely that it was my dad, and I honest to God can't even recall if she brought his name up or if it was just that I knew, because you have to understand, my mother and I, you know, it sounds strange but my mother and I are on the same wavelength.*"

Another passage was recalled.

"*A: Prior to her disappearing with the bodyguard thing—*

"This is Cindy testifying," said Tom Hillier.

"*—I don't recall that she had actually said at that time—I don't think she did say at that time that the reason she had been asking about the hit man and the drugs was to eliminate my dad, but she wanted, she wanted out of the marriage one way or another. And then the bodyguard thing fell through. Jeanne Rice was terminated from the airport.*

"*Q: When did it fall through?*

"*A: About May or April.*

"*Q: Of which year?*

"*A: May for sure. Definitely knew by May.*

"*Q: Of which year?*

"*A: '86.*

"*Q: So a couple of months before your stepfather died?*

"*A: Uh-huh.*

"*Q: After she decided, then, that there was no way, then after the bodyguard business fell through, that she was going to leave this marriage, what conversation did she have with you, if any, about eliminating Bruce Nickell?*

"*A: She started on the cocaine thing first. This is March of '86, the first time Bruce's name is mentioned. She wanted to know how much it would take to O.D. a person on cocaine.*

"*Q: Overdose a person?*

"*A: Uh-huh.*

"*Q: Was this the first time she talked about cocaine?*

"*A: No. She had talked about it before when she had asked me about acquiring some for her.*

"*Q: But this is the first time she talked about it in a specific context with your stepfather concerned?*

"*A: Yes. I told her I didn't know, and she said that she would do some, you know, would look into it, and I told her, I says, 'Well,'*

*I says, 'an O.D.' I says, 'You can't just do. I do know for a fact
you can't just do a one-time O.D.' "*

Tom Hillier looked up from his reading, his face full of seriousness.

"April or May of 1986, the first time. In testimony last week
she changed that to a vague time frame. Why did she change it to
a vague time frame? Because this doesn't fit with the government's
theory as to how the insurance policy played into the motive that
they allege was what caused this financial obsession on the part of
Stella Nickell."

There was no way for the defense to challenge a vague time
frame, he said.

It was also at odds with Katy Hurt Parker's vague testimony.
Katy was unable to say exactly when Cindy Hamilton moved in,
or when she told the cocaine story.

"We also learned from Katherine Parker that Cindy Hamilton
brought her forward to the FBI in August of 1987. A suspicious
mutual vagueness is shared between the two."

The third reason to question the insurance motive, Tom Hillier
claimed, was that ample testimony suggested Stella Nickell did not
know what her husband's policies were worth.

He pointed out that no one had told Stella Nickell the amount
of the insurance, with the exception of Lynn Force. Yet Stella didn't
hear him. When the FBI interviewed the defendant in November,
they knew of the correct figure, but they didn't clue the defendant
in.

"Because the government would choose to hold these cards close
to their vest and then argue a conflict that they create because they
don't have the courtesy or forthrightness to confront Stella Nickell
with information that they think they have to try to get some clarity
to this situation.

"The fact is, ladies and gentlemen, that there was confusion on
that policy, and it was documented from day one and you heard it
from witness after witness after witness, and from that fact reasonably follows the fact that Stella Nickell believed that the policy was
worth $25,000."

He cited the All American policies. Stella Nickell was confused
about their value, but she didn't conceal that she had them. She
told SA Ike Nakamoto of the policy, even gave him its number.

Tom Hillier disputed the prosecution's claim that Stella continued to conceal the existence of the polices when she met with SAs

Cusack and Nichols. When asked if there were any other polices, she said no.

"She said, 'I said that because I assumed he meant beyond the information I had already provided.'"

"Heck, ladies and gentlemen. Several days before, Stella Nickell had just sent in her claimant's form to the insurance company. Obviously she's not going to try to conceal that kind of information, having already provided the insurance numbers to the FBI."

The jury was asked to put themselves in Stella Nickell's chair as the FBI interrogated her.

"Are you going to try, when a week [earlier] you sent in an application for insurance proceeds, to lie and conceal, knowing these gentlemen have been investigating the heck out of the case for the last five months?"

Concerning the letters to North Pacific evoking the Nickells' financial problems, Tom Hillier sarcastically dismissed the prosecutor's insistence that they were confessions of murder.

"We're having problems in the marriage. Don't worry about it. I'm getting rid of Bruce. Boy, I'm going to get the life-insurance policies to you in a hurry, so hang in there, please."

Such talk, as evident in her letters, suggested Stella Nickell was a direct person, a take-charge woman. She was upset with her husband and she was pretty vocal about it, but she had taken the bull by the horns and would get caught up on their bills.

Tom Hillier suggested that Joanne Maida's cross-examination on the Nickells' financial problems, beginning in 1983 and followed by books on poisonous plants, were an attempt to "bootstrap" and "shore up" Cindy Hamilton's time frame on her story "that Stella Nickell was going to poison Bruce anytime she's got a problem with the money."

Tom Hillier shook his head. The facts were, he said, that Stella Nickell was spending time baby-sitting in 1983, and when the Nickells moved to the property two years later, she was concerned about her granddaughter's getting into poisonous plants.

"The time frame concerning the checking out of the book is absolutely consistent with what Stella Nickell said as to why she checked them out."

He pointed out that the government's testimony concerning the foxglove was placed in the context of sick-leave records from early 1985. But Cindy Hamilton said the seeds conversation occurred at the airport, within six months of Bruce Nickell's death.

"So according to Cindy's own testimony and the government's strained theory as to the significance of these physical papers, Bruce was sick in January and February of 1985, and if Cindy Hamilton is believable at all—and she's not—this occurred in January and February of 1986, a full year later, according to the only basis for even making that argument, and it's a strained argument to begin with. Flat contradiction by the government's star witness. Flat contradiction because Cindy Hamilton is not telling the truth."

The prosecutor had cross-examined the defendant at length about the problems in 1983 and '84 with finances and about Indian tobacco and emphysema. "What are we supposed to guess here? That Stella was going to roll up some Indian tobacco and give it to Bruce and to use the emphysema as a cover for that? Or that she would cause his death and argue that he had emphysema?"

What of the notes Stella Nickell had allegedly taken as she plotted to kill her husband?

"Who among you didn't expect some notes to appear in evidence in front of Stella Nickell in a dramatic proof that she is lying?"

But there were no notes in evidence.

"The prosecutor planted seeds in your minds without proof in the hope that you will abandon your common sense, your experience, and your reason and join the prosecutor in her murder mystery. . . .

"The government puts a lot of emphasis on the smell of almonds. What in those books said that twenty to ninety percent of the people can't smell that smell? *Nothing*. It contradicts the government's theory of the significance of the smell of the almonds."

Tom Hillier had never given a more lengthy argument, and he told the jury so. Yet he had more. The details of the case alone would free his client.

He brought up the algicide and Tom Noonan. Tom Noonan said he sold the defendant Algae Destroyer beginning in October 1985, before moving to a new store by January 1986.

"Cindy Hamilton says that twelve months before Bruce died, during the summer of '85—and again, your recall is critical, twelve months before Bruce died—she told her mom to use a liquid algae killer produced by Aquatronics Products, and that her mom had used tablets before. Cindy Hamilton never mentioned a brand name. *Never mentioned a brand name*. To the extent that Ms. Maida suggests otherwise, she's wrong. She wasn't questioned about it, and

I mentioned this in sort of my rebuttal remarks earlier this afternoon. She wasn't shown 12-1, the picture of Algae Destroyer, and asked is this it? That's telling proof that even Cindy Hamilton wouldn't have confirmed the prosecutor's theory."

Public defender Hillier also emphasized that the FBI's Roger Martz couldn't offer a reason for the algicide's presence in the cyanide. His witness, Dr. David Honigs, insisted the green particles were not placed in there by accident.

Tom Hillier invoked Tom Noonan's testimony about Stella Nickell's first purchase of Alage Destroyer.

"Remember what he said? He paused. He looked up. *Paused.* October 1985. October. Right out of the blue, out of nowhere, we came with October. Is that the quality of information that a woman's liberty depends upon? Right out of the blue!"

The testimony was at odds with Cindy's testimony. She said she talked with her mother about algae problems caused by sunlight, a problem of the summertime. Not October.

Stella Nickell said she never discussed crushing any tablets with Tom Noonan.

"Who do you believe? Out-of-the-blue-October Tom Noonan? Or Stella Nickell?"

After chiseling away at Tom Noonan, Tom Hillier went after Cindy Hamilton's testimony.

He questioned if his client's actions were consistent with her daughter's characterizations. Greedy? When she had little or no money she helped Hamilton buy a car, offered free daycare for her granddaughter, school tuition.

Bored with her husband? When Bruce Nickell hit rock bottom, it was the defendant who helped him dry out.

"Does it make sense that a strong woman, a direct woman, would cater to every whim of her husband to the point of obnoxiousness, by some standards of liberation, if she hated him?

"Does it make sense, ladies and gentlemen, that Stella Nickell would ask Cindy Hamilton where she could acquire heroin, cocaine, speed, and other drugs for, as Cindy Hamilton figured, the purpose of resale because, as Cindy Hamilton testified, it could supplement her mom's income? Is that reasonable? Is that reasonable? Or is it more reasonable that Stella, knowing Cindy—as Cindy admitted, quote 'been known to use cocaine'—of her daughter's problems with drugs, would talk to her about her drug use?"

He called Cynthia Lea's reasoning on why she didn't do anything to save Bruce Nickell "absolute insulting nonsense, and suggests how truly detached from reality that troubled young woman is."

"Why does the prosecutor change its theory three and four times during this case from Stella going to poison her husband Bruce back in '83, to going to leave him, going to divorce him, going to go to Mexico, going to kill him, going to Texas, going to kill him? The reason is they've got to keep up with Cindy Hamilton and her oscillating details.

"We're talking, from the prosecutor's theory, of a woman driven to kill. Where is there anybody other than Cindy Hamilton? We've got a lot of people saying, 'Yeah, Stella had her gripes.' She voiced those gripes to Wilma and Jeanne Rice. That's consistent with the normal marriage, ladies and gentlemen, with the usual ups and downs, with some frightful financial stress?

"Don't buy into this theory that there's just too much there. Analyze each piece of evidence one by one. What are you left with? Cindy Hamilton."

After fifty more minutes, Tom Hillier was finished.

A ten-minute break allowed Joanne Maida to prepare a rebuttal.

She defended Katy's and Cindy's time-frame testimony.

"Both of them have approximately the same time frame. No one two years ago was taking notes at the time that certain conversations occurred."

The Asst. U.S. Attorney addressed the reward.

"It is too late now to hurl that charge or any insinuation against any witness who has testified, who has not been given the opportunity to respond to that accusation. Without that, the record is absolutely bald that any witness called by the United States has testified for any other reason than to report the facts as facts must be reported."

In defense of Cindy Hamilton: "If you bring to your deliberations your commonsense perceptions of human behavior, based on your collective life experiences, you will find that Cindy Hamilton would not have put herself through the anguish of the last two years and the ordeal of this trial unless she speaks the truth. She has no motive to incriminate her mother, and the fact that the discussions with her mother were too important to disregard were reason enough for her to come forward, and come forward she did."

The prosecutor told the jury that Cindy did not stand alone.

Physical evidence and the testimony of others backed up her story.

"Not a single witness, not a single witness has disparaged her ability to tell the truth or any reputation for doing so except the defendant, who has a direct interest in the outcome of this case," she said.

"When the whole picture is put together, piece by piece, detail by detail, there is undeniably only one person who had the motive, the inclination, and the opportunity to commit these crimes. The real killer, who Mr. Hillier suggests is still out there on the loose somewhere, is sitting within the four corners of this courtroom, and she knows it."

It was four o'clock, and rather than have the jury deliberate for an hour, Judge Dwyer sent them home.

Whether he was sending a heroine or an accomplice home, when SA Jack Cusack put Cindy Hamilton on a plane headed for California, he did so with relief. Though he had kept his promise to watch out for her and see her through the ordeal, many times it had gotten old. Yes, there was anguish, or what seemed to be, but there was also the tiresome personality of a young woman out of control. Cynthia Hamilton enjoyed the experience. Friends said she likened it to the Secret Service. She loved to throw her weight around the men in suits.

"Stop the car! I need a pack of smokes!"

He waited for her plane to leave, then returned to Seattle to phone Joanne Maida with the word that Cindy was on her way back to Garden Grove.

"You know, Joanne," he said, laughing. "I've never been divorced before, but I have a hunch the way I feel right now is pretty close to the feeling."

CHAPTER 83

The Nickell trial jurors filed into court single file. It had all come to this moment on May 3, 1988. Some were eager to get going, others somewhat excited by the culmination of their responsibilities. Most were concerned that whatever came from the deliberations, it be the right decision. After instructions from Judge Dwyer, they were excused to the jury room. It was time to get busy.

Being on a jury is not a life of courtroom drama. It can be quite dull. Twelve jurors and two alternates had been thrown together to weigh the evidence. Fourteen people with little in common.

The waiting game between rulings had been boring, and the fact that the case could not be discussed had been excruciating. Small talk passed the time for some, reading for others.

The Seattle newspapers were brought into the jury room, though the big windows cut from them indicated the Nickell case was getting major local press.

Jurors talked about their jobs—at Boeing, a law office, the state, real estate . . . even unemployment. Those who had them, discussed their kids and grandchildren.

Some days little groups sporting "Juror" badges would break and lunch together at the Chinese restaurant not far from the courthouse. Others never did, preferring to brown-bag it. A refrigerator had been provided for that purpose.

It was all so quiet, so anonymous.

And yet within that group known as the jury, one would emerge during deliberations. Once in the jury room it was apparent, nearly immediately, that one person had broken from the feeling that Stella Nickell was guilty.

It was the real estate saleswoman, Laurel Holliday.

Yes, the defendant came off as glacially cold. But that didn't mean anything, most of the jurors agreed as they sat at the table to begin deliberations. Most knew a courtroom was hardly the most comfortable venue for the accused.

"She was under max control, everyone was watching her. . . ."

"She *did* cry."

"Right. So what?"

"She's innocent, I tell you."

The last comment was made by Laurel Holliday.

And as they went over the evidence, a juror asked if the defendant had been so innocent, why had she lied about shopping that particular Pay 'N Save when checks proved otherwise?

Laurie Adams took it further: "It was the closest to her house . . . she didn't have to deny going to the store. It would have been very reasonable to say she went there."

Others agreed.

"They had those canceled checks. Did she forget about them?"

The argument resumed the next day.

Yet Laurel Holliday maintained such a response pointed to innocence. Her reasoning confused other jurors.

Juror Adams later recalled Laurel Holliday's conclusion: " 'The woman is innocent, the end justifies the means.' It is okay for her to lie on the stand to get herself off, to get a not-guilty verdict. She even said, 'I'd do the same thing.' "

Hands went up in the air and jurors stood away from the table as a show of protest. Sighs were as loud as screams.

The foxglove was another case in point. The defendant's prints were on the books, on *passages* about foxglove. She told the court she had read about dangerous plants to protect her granddaughter.

One juror said that it would have been totally reasonable for Stella Nickell to say she recalled information about the plant.

"Why deny it now?"

And so it went, the clock counting the hours, the jurors waiting on the holdout to get with the program. If she had a valid point, it would have been likely made things different.

"Laurel had this totally different agenda," a woman juror said later, though she didn't know what it was.

In time, all would.

Five and a half hours in the jury room had passed as the group considered evidence and listened to recollections and views on the evidence, and at 4:30, the jurors gathered their things to leave. Clear in their minds was Judge Dwyer's precise admonishments to avoid the news and any discussion of the case.

Laurie Adams took the bus to her home in Redmond. Those single drove home alone. They were lucky. No one would ask them any questions.

Jurors spent some of their time trying to prove to Laurel Holliday that Stella Maudine Nickell had a reason to kill her husband.

But she just didn't seem to get it.

"It was almost like she was playing dumb. It was very clear to all of us that this woman took out insurance policies on her husband that he knew nothing about," Marcheta Cruse said later.

Yet Laurel Holliday questioned them.

"What do you mean?"

"I don't understand."

She gave the same response when the jury reviewed the flurry of checks presented by SA Marshall Stone.

Jeez, the poor thing. She hasn't been out in the world, Marcheta thought.

Murray Andrews kept things going as smoothly as he could, as some of the older men in the group grew agitated when the real estate agent went over the same thing again and again.

One of the women suggested a flip chart be procured to help organize questions about cyanide-laced bottles, the stores where they had been purchased, and the proximity to places frequented by the defendant.

A couple of the men rolled their eyes upward. *Why bother?* They knew Stella Nickell was guilty. *Jesus, a flip chart!*

At 11 A.M., Murray Andrews wrote out a note on a slip of paper for the bailiff.

We would like to request a large note pad (for easel) and marker pen, if available.

Signed, Murray M. Andrews, Foreman.

After clearing it with counsel, neither of whom had any objections, Judge Dwyer had the materials sent to the jury.

Later, the foreman would point to the unassuming Anna Wong as the juror who helped to defuse a potentially combustive situation. It seemed clear to her that Laurel Holliday wasn't going to be satisfied until every single avenue of escape had been refuted by the evidence.

Andrews kept his mouth shut, not wanting to dominate the proceedings.

Laurel is looking for that one needle in the haystack that would allow her to say Stella was innocent, he thought.

A patient Anna Wong spoke up.

"The way we're going to get this solved is to just go through the evidence," she said, offering no bitterness, no judgment, of the juror.

And so they did.

"Are you satisfied that it all points to the fact that she's lying?"

"Or do you have any more questions about the checks?"

"What else would you like to look at?"

It was obvious that something was off with juror 7, Laurel Holliday. Nobody knew what it was. Laurie Adams, a young woman who preferred the country and rode her Appaloosa every evening after trial, was shaken by what she saw during the second day of deliberations.

Laurel Holliday had told everyone she had been writing up notes at the Seattle Public Library just across the street from the courthouse.

"It helps me keep my thoughts organized," she said.

With that in mind, Laurie Adams thought nothing of the file folder Holliday kept in front of her during deliberations. And as people tend to do, jurors Holliday and Adams both sat in the same seats both days.

Laurie Adams noticed that the title on the folder had something to do with real estate taxes, which seemed like such an odd subject to read during deliberations. As Holliday sat reading one of the single-spaced typed pages, a curious Laurie Adams looked over her shoulder and read. Later, she recalled the gist of what she saw. It made her recoil as if she had seen a rattlesnake. Laurel Holliday had written:

"And these jurors, one of them reads the National Enquirer!"

"And the only one that's close to my intellectual equal reads a Robert Ludlum novel!!"

"And that Vietnamese guy . . ."

Appalled, Laurie Adams quit reading.

Later she summed up what the notes had meant to her: "It just spoke volumes of her negative attitudes of everyone who was on the jury. It said a lot in terms of why she was so difficult. . . . She was there with a major responsibility, it wasn't something to be taken lightly. You leave your preconceptions, emotions behind. You need to do the job."

Laurie Adams took a couple of deep breaths and moved to a seat away from Holliday and her little folder. The young woman told herself she wasn't going to say anything to anybody. She didn't want to harm the deliberations.

But it was only the beginning.

At 5 P.M. it was time to call it a day. Again, the twelve left after being dismissed by Judge Dwyer in his courtroom: Frustrated, 11, and Isolated, 1.

Juror Laurie Adams changed the way she related to Laurel Holliday after she read the notes concerning the jury. By May 5, it was clear Laurel Holliday had some other agenda. But to call her on it would be a mistake.

That day the jury focused on Cindy Hamilton.

Murray Andrews considered the daughter's testimony to be the most damning. The case was circumstantial, but Cindy had put all the pieces together. He spoke for the majority of jurors on this.

But though she believed much of it, Laurie Adams, for one, was somewhat leery of the daughter's testimony. She considered the sometimes volatile dynamics of the mother-daughter relationship when she weighed what Cindy had told the court. Yes, they had problems in the past, but she knew of a lot of instances where such relationships improved as a child grew.

Marcheta Cruse didn't think Stella's daughter was a hundred percent believable.

"I'm sure there's a lot of things we don't know," juror Cruse said later. "Why did she wait to come forward?"

Murray Andrews later summed up his recollections on Laurel Holliday's questions about the defendant's daughter's motives.

"If the FBI contacted Cindy and forced a confession out of her, it would be different than saying 'we're offering a reward, then she decided to come forward, which makes it very questionable.' Then she was obviously doing it for the money, was what Laurel was alluding to," he said later.

" 'We're hung, aren't we?' " Murray Andrews recalled Laurel Holliday asking. " 'Because we don't know.' "

"Let's ask the judge," the foreman said.

Laurel Holliday was stuck, unable to back down, unable to move forward. She needed answers to some questions, and no one on the jury was certain.

Just after three o'clock, Andrews sent a note to Judge Dwyer:

> 5-5-88.
> Please provide the testimony that will help clarify (1) Did Cindy come forward voluntarily to the FBI or did they contact her at which time she offered information about Stella's conversations with her. (2) What date did Cindy provide this information to the FBI?
> Signed, Murray M. Andrews, Foreman.

Judge Dwyer knew such questions are routinely answered, but a better approach would be to refer the jury to their collective memories. His note, under Maida and Hillier's approval, responsed:

> To the jury:
> It is not feasible to try to locate, select and read back the parts of the trial record that bear on these subjects. The jurors must rely on their collective recollection of the evidence presented during the trial.

Back to deliberations, and no one, it seemed to the foreman, was more disappointed than Laurel Holliday.

The reward was discussed, but most didn't feel it had been the motivation. While it was true the daughter was in line for some of the reward, she also had much to forfeit.

One juror considered how difficult it would be to turn a parent in when, no doubt, it would lead to an irrevocable estrangement.

"She had a lot to lose if she was making all this up."

By five o'clock, Judge Dwyer dismissed the jury again, reminding them not to discuss the case outside the jury room.

"As time goes on, it might seem difficult to abide by this instruction, but I must keep giving it. It is very important that you comply with it one hundred percent."

That might, *The Seattle Post-Intelligencer* readied its edition for the next day.

JURY REBUFFED IN BID TO REVIEW
TESTIMONY OF NICKELL'S DAUGHTER

> ... Speculation immediately arose that the jury is deadlocked over the issue of the credibility of the 28-year-old daughter, Cindy Hamilton, whose testimony was challenged on the witness stand by her mother ...
>
> —*The Seattle P-I*

Many had lost sleep over the difficult case, but still Laurel Holliday seemed to feel she was alone in that regard.

Just as deliberations were getting underway on May 6, the real estate agent nervously said she had something to read for the group. Laurel Holliday pulled out a letter she said she had written at her word processor the night before.

Later, jurors would remember the tone of its content, if not the exact words.

"I think she felt we were all against her, making life difficult for her," foreman Andrews recalled. "I don't think she was a strong person, couldn't come up with that extemporaneously. She needed to write it down."

Marcheta Cruse was put off.

"It was a letter voicing her opinion more or less of all of us as being against her. She didn't like the tone we used with her during deliberation. I think she resented the men's attitude against her more than the women's. I think in her mind they were badgering her."

Juror Carolyn Bidleman was frustrated by the letter. If Laurel Holliday had truly felt other jurors weren't as serious about the case as she, why didn't she go through the evidence?

Was the holdout coming around, or just jerking their chains? No one in the jury room seemed to know. Juror Holliday wanted another definition of reasonable doubt.

Marcheta Cruse asked Laurel Holliday to tell the others what her personal definition was.

The woman said she had some doubts; she was only at fifty percent sure that Stella Nickell was the guilty party.

"I have to be ninety percent sure."

Some wondered how in the world someone could measure their doubts in percentages.

"That's awfully strange when eleven of us are ninety percent sure," Marcheta Cruse answered back. "How can eleven of us be ninety percent sure and only one of us fifty percent sure? And every one of us the same thing?"

It went on and on. Finally, peacemaker and foreman, Murray Andrews said he'd write another note to the judge.

5-6-88
> *May we have more detailed explanation on what constitutes "reasonable doubt"?*
>> *Signed, Murray M. Andrews, Foreman.*

He knew a mob scene in the jury room was not the way to get a conviction.

That afternoon, the judge and counsel met over Andrews's note. Stella Nickell interpreted the words as an indication that things were going her way.

The federal judge was reluctant to offer clarification, preferring that the jury review the instructions he had already provided.

"Experience has shown it doesn't add anything really to pile on more definitions; that these words mean what they say and they should decide the case accordingly . . ."

A supplemental instruction was a possibility, but Tom Hillier objected to its wording.

Judge Dwyer said he would send a note back to the jury telling them to consider the instructions they had already received.

Further, he told counsel that should circumstances suggest the jury is deadlocked, he might make available Cindy Hamilton's testimony regarding the FBI and the timing on her coming forward. It would be a lot of work, but, of course, it would be worth it. Nobody wanted a retrial.

The jury got their answer in the form of a typed response on a page with their original note affixed. As Murray Andrews read it, he thought he noticed Laurel Holliday slump a bit.

"Experience has shown that to try to expand upon the meaning of 'reasonable doubt,' as expressed in Instruction No. 13, is ordinarily not helpful to juries in reaching their verdicts. Please con-

tinue your deliberations under the instructions as given, bearing in
mind that all the instructions are to be read together in arriving at
your verdict."

And around they went. Another vote was taken, and again there
was the lone dissenter.

"I'm not convinced," Laurel Holliday said.

"If you want to see a smoking gun," the foreman said, "it is
here. It is the total evidence and testimony that shows us Stella
Nickell is guilty."

One of the men cursed and walked away from the table. Laurel
Holliday said nothing further. She held firm.

"She didn't do it," she said.

Again there was hope. For Stella Nickell, there was a chance that
the jury had not believed Cynthia Lea's tales of cyanide and murder.

She hoped they had believed her.

At 3:15, Judge Dwyer read the note without a trace of resigna-
tion:

> 5-6-88, 2:50 p.m.
>   "After three votes taken over the last three days, we have
> been unable to reach a unanimous decision. No juror has
> changed his/her vote during this time. We await your instruc-
> tions.
>
>   Signed, Murray M. Andrews, Foreman.

The judge was adamant that deliberations continue. It was pre-
mature to give up and accept a mistrial, and the expense of the
inevitable retrial. He proposed that the jury retire early for the weekend, rest up, and resume deliberations on Monday.

Further, Judge Dwyer said he proposed to read them the supplemental instruction he prepared on reasonable doubt, and offer an
explanation concerning the "technical difficulties" of searching
Cynthia Hamilton's testimony when a transcript didn't exist. Counsel agreed to meet early Monday to discuss the court reporter's
findings, in advance of the jury's continuing deliberations.

The jury returned and Judge Dwyer offered a supplemental definition of reasonable doubt. He was clear, however, that it was not
meant to replace the existing instruction.

*"A reasonable doubt is one for which a reason exists and may
arise from the evidence or lack of evidence. It is such a doubt as*

*would exist in the mind of a reasonable person after fully, fairly
and carefully considering all of the evidence or lack of evidence.
If after such consideration you have an abiding belief in the truth
of the charge, you are satisfied beyond a reasonable doubt."*

Regarding their request for clarification of Cindy Hamilton's
testimony, the court reporter would look for the proper passages
over the weekend.

Though the jurors had gone around and around with Laurel Holliday as they tried to get her to see what they saw, it was clear by
Friday afternoon she was not going to make a decision to convict.
Murray Andrews thought she was simply unable to make the decision. It was something personal.

She was trying to get out of it.

They agreed to go home and start fresh Monday.

Berta and her husband could not stay in Seattle any longer. They
were needed home in Michigan. So, as hard as it was, Stella's sister
had to say good-bye to both her jailed sister and her hospitalized
mother. She was worried sick about both.

She needn't have worried about either.

When Berta saw her mother at Harborview, Cora Lee was feeling much better, cursing a blue streak and demanding a cigarette
and some news about the trial.

Awaiting the verdict, Stella Maudine again demonstrated her
strong resolve.

"It'll be fine," she said when Berta told her good-bye.

CHAPTER 84

Stella Nickell looked better after her weekend of hope than she had in the three weeks of trial. Her black hair was shiny, the gray streaks appearing more like highlights than an indication that she had run out of L'Oreal soft black long ago. She wore a maroon skirt, floral blouse, and a knit acrylic sweater vest. It was May 9, 1988.

U.S. marshals escorted the defendant to her chair as Tom Hillier, Joanne Maida, and Judge Bill Dwyer remained embroiled in hammering out the scope of her daughter's testimony, based on the notes taken by the court reporter.

Tom Hillier's preference was that a stipulation be made to simply give the answers to the jury's questions. He considered the court's ruling when the questions were first asked to be the best tack—reliance on collective memories. He was uncertain that all the appropriate references could be found, given the lack of a complete transcript.

And though Joanne Maida had no problem with a stipulation, Judge Dwyer had told the jury they were going to get the testimony, and that is what was going to happen.

By 9:00 the testimony was ready for the jury.

Of course, none of those in the courtroom could have foreseen what was about to happen that Monday morning—eleven jurors, however, wouldn't have been surprised. They knew something was up with Juror Holliday when she abruptly left the jury room with a bailiff. She did not say a word.

In the courtroom, moments later, Judge Dwyer read a note the troubled juror had written on Sunday and submitted to him through the court clerk.

> *Dear Judge Dwyer:*
>
> *I am a juror in Stella Nickell's trial. Something happened on Friday which I must tell you about. A woman called me at home about 7 p.m. and said, "Don't you [all] know that she failed the lie detector test." (I can't remember whether she said "all" or not.) She hung up before I even had a chance to realize what she was saying. I have tried to think who it could have been but I did not recognize the voice.*
>
> *It frightened me that someone sought out my home number and called me like this. I told my roommate about it shortly after this woman called but I haven't told anyone else. I left a message for you on the phone machine for jurors Friday night, but then I remembered that we are only supposed to write to you.*
>
> *Sincerely, Laurel Holliday*

While the defendant sat confused and quiet, unsure of what to make of the letter, Judge Dwyer proposed to question the juror to discern whether she should continue deliberating or be excused.

Tom Hillier didn't see how the issue of the polygraph could be covered at all. As far as he was concerned, Stella Nickell never failed the polygraph—he saw only a summary, never a full report.

The judge planned to tell the juror that polygraphs are inadmissible, and nothing on the record indicated she took one anyway.

Joanne Maida, who clearly could see a verdict in jeopardy, was concerned that other jurors might have heard about the phone call.

It was agreed that each would be questioned after Laurel Holliday.

As Laurel Holliday was seated in the witness box, Judge Dwyer reminded her that her oath from her original impaneling still applied. He started off asking her if she had told any other jurors about the phone call.

She said she hadn't.

"It's very important that you not do that. Don't mention anything about it at all. Are you willing to undertake that?"

She agreed.

The juror told the court she had no idea who made the call. It happened too quickly.

Judge Dwyer told the juror that nothing in the testimony, the court record, or the exhibits indicated that Stella Nickell had taken a lie-detector test. She was to decide the case solely on the record. Further, he offered a comment that would have put Jack Cusack in another line of work:

"Also, you should know that in any case the law provides, and has provided for many years, that the results of these polygraph tests, if a person has taken one, are not admissible in evidence, and the reason they're not admissible in evidence, or one reason, is that their scientific reliability has never been established."

Laurel Holliday was emphatic when she told the court she could go forward and decide the case.

After talking with his client, Tom Hillier made the surprise announcement that juror Holliday could stay on the jury. Joanne Maida pressed for an alternate to replace her.

"I would ask the Court to give very serious consideration to that, simply because it is a matter that is of absolute inadmissible nature and we get into the problem of the bell being rung that I am not sure a juror, with every good faith, could unring. I would like to believe that she could, but humanly I'm not sure that that's possible."

Judge Dwyer suggested another option: using a jury of eleven.

He recessed to think it over.

Laurel Holliday returned to the jury room in silence. She looked straight ahead, presenting a stoic front.

When they convened later, Joanne Maida asked that the juror be excused and deliberations continue with eleven. It was too risky, considering what might happen "in the heat of deliberations." In addition, there was the concern of future calls.

If both sides wanted her off the jury, the judge said, it would be done without hesitation. But Tom Hillier wanted her to stay on.

"What we have here is a situation in which a juror has been exposed to an outside influence about the case but has also given very firm and clear and emphatic commitments in answer to questions that she can and will decide the case strictly on the evidence and the instructions. Under those circumstances, I think it is required that I keep her on in light of the defendant's request that she be kept on. The information—*alleged information*—to which she was exposed in the telephone call ordinarily would be information that would cut against the defendant, and as I say, if counsel for both sides requested it, I would certainly excuse the juror. But under the circumstances, I am satisfied that her assurances should be accepted and she should continue deliberating with the other eleven."

Tom Hillier was reminded that counsel are not permitted to interview jurors after a verdict. Hillier found the rule "offensive" to the First Amendment. He said he wasn't willing to abandon any rights.

"Well, let me put it this way," Judge Dwyer said, "do you still want the juror on the panel, knowing that this incident that we've been talking about this morning will not cause the Court to make an exception to the usual rule about postverdict interviews?"

Tom Hillier said yes.

When the jury returned, the judge announced that one among them had received an inappropriate anonymous phone call concerning the case. Yet the juror stated she could put the call out of her mind and decide the case based solely on the evidence.

"Neither side in the case was responsible for this incident, and it has nothing whatever to do with your deliberations," he said.

When asked for a show of hands from other jurors who might have received a communication outside of the courtroom, no one raised a hand.

That said, the Court moved on to Cynthia Hamilton's testimony.

The court reporter was sworn as a witness and instructed to read from his shorthand notes:

"Q: (by Ms. Maida) You have told us that when you were first questioned by the FBI shortly after your dad's death, that you denied any involvement your mother had in your father's death. Did we understand you correctly?

"A: Yes.

"Q: Did there come a point in time after that that you came forward with information to the FBI, basically what you've testified to in court today, that information?

"A: Yes.

"Q: The second time that you talked with the FBI, was that in January of 1987?

"A: Yes, it was.

"Q: That's about a six-month lapse between interviews, is that correct?

"*A: Yes.*

"*Q: Did you do a lot of serious thinking in those six months?*

"*A: Yes, I did.*

"*Q: Just answer yes or no to this question. By January 1987 had you thought it over? Had you decided to tell the FBI what you knew?*

"*A: Yes, I did.*

"*Q: After you told the FBI what you knew, did you tell the grand jury?*

"*A: Yes, I did.*"

Next, the court reporter read from Tom Hillier's cross-examination:

"*Q: (by Mr. Hillier) In addition to that conversation with the grand jury—well, let me back up. You were sworn and took an oath to tell the truth during that testimony?*

"*A: Yes, I was.*

"*Q: Before that you had, I thought I heard you say, two major conversations with FBI agents?*

"*A: Yes.*

"*Q: And those would have occurred in January of 1987?*

"*A: Yes.*

"*Q: So about two months before you testified before the grand jury?*

"*A: Yes.*"

At 10:30, the court reporter stepped down and the jury resumed deliberations.

Of course, the attorneys and the judge didn't know it, but some of the jurors who had been deliberating with Holliday seriously doubted there had been a phone call to a juror at all. Outside the people in the jury room, who really could have known that the greatest trial in the Federal Courthouse occurred after the government and defendant rested the Nickell case?

Marcheta Cruse didn't say anything to any other jurors, but inside she was angry.

"When this deal about a phone call came through, then things started clicking in my mind . . . this lady has just been bamboozling us all the way through here," she said later.

Juror Cruse worried that the jury would end up hung because it was probably the oddball real estate saleswoman who had received the supposed phone call.

What is going on in this woman's mind? Cruse thought, while returning to the jury room.

No one knew who the holdout had been. It seemed suspicious that no one else had been called.

Murray Andrews thought it was just another ploy the troubled juror was using to get out of making a decision. He figured she was hoping the judge would excuse her, but he didn't.

SAs Cusack and Stone thought the phone-call story was ridiculous.

"There is no way she could have gotten a call. No way anyone would have known she was on the jury. No goddamn way!" Cusack told the younger agent.

The courtroom was full, with media cameras outside its doors ready to pounce on jurors as they left. It was 3:35, and the verdict was in.

Stella Nickell was expressionless. She closed her green eyes for the verdict. Tom Hillier put his arm around her.

Murray Andrews gave the verdict to the clerk, who stood and read:

"CR87-276WD, United States versus Stella Maudine Nickell. We the jury find Stella Maudine Nickell guilty of the crime as charged in Count I; guilty of the crime as charged in Count II; guilty of the crime as charged in Count III; guilty of the crime as charged in Count IV; guilty of the crime as charged in Count V of the indictment."

Stella Maudine clenched her hands slightly, lowered her head, and bit down on her lower lip. It was over. It had been mother against daughter, and daughter had won. She looked down as the jurors were polled.

What had promised to be a day of hope ended with *guilty on all counts*.

Tears fell from juror Holliday's eyes, and another juror, Rick Patterson, clutched his chest.

Tom Hillier asked for a sidebar. In light of the unusual events of the morning, the defense wanted to question the jurors to find out if Laurel Holliday had been the holdout.

"I think that raises the probability beyond any possible odds that we have a juror-misconduct issue that ought to be ferreted out in the interest of justice," Tom Hillier said.

He wanted to know if it had been another juror who had made the call.

Joanne Maida balked.

"Their verdict should remain inviolate; and I would oppose any attempt of counsel to go behind the verdict at this point."

The judge sided with the Asst. U.S. Attorney. He refused to "violate the sanctity of the jury's deliberations."

The judge moved on to thank and excuse the battle-weary jurors. Sentencing would take place on June 17.

Bright sunshine and microphones assaulting his face, Murray Andrews was the only juror to speak to reporters on the courthouse steps. Others were still reeling from the experience of deliberations, not to mention the theatrics of crying juror number 7. At least one hoped she'd never have to serve again.

"When did you find out she failed a lie-detector test?" a reporter asked.

"Right now," he said. "You are the first one to tell me that . . ."

The foreman was quoted in an article in the following day's Auburn edition of the *Valley Daily News* headlined:

NICKELL GUILTY IN CYANIDE KILLINGS

"Cindy's testimony obviously was the key that brought things together," Andrews said. "We felt we had to link together a whole chain of circumstances to get beyond a feeling of reasonable doubt. Without her [Hamilton's] testimony, there was not the thread that carried through all the evidence."

When Fred Phelps saw Stella after the verdict, she seemed all right. Upbeat even.

"She was planning her appeal," he said later.

SA Dave Hill drove over to the Tri-Cities to break the news to Wilma Stewart over drinks at Clinkerdaggers. Somewhere between friend and adversary was Dave. Wilma still didn't know where.

While Paul Webking stood on his doorstep and spoke to the media on his emotional reaction to an expected verdict, Sarah Webb, reached in Cairo by telephone, could find few words for a reporter: "Oh, my God. Oh, my God. Oh, my God. Oh, my God."

Hayley Snow cried when she got the news. It was supposed to be over, but she knew now it wasn't. The verdict didn't make her feel any better.

In Garden Grove, Cindy Hamilton surely must have been a mire of mixed feelings of relief and worry. It was true the verdict was guilty, but what of the mess with the juror?

She called the FBI to talk with SA Cusack for reassurance on May 10.

Her stepfather Bob Strong also had mixed feelings.

"After watching TV, listening to the FBI and Cindy, reading the papers, I've come to my conclusion: I don't know who did it," he said later.

CHAPTER 85

If it hadn't been one of the jurors, could someone from inside the courthouse have passed on the information that Laurel Holliday was the Nickell holdout? News reports suggesting someone who knew of the jury's split during deliberations had added to the legal maelstrom. In advance of court with the convicted and her attorney, Judge Dwyer made a check of his own staff—from law clerks to courtroom personnel.

No one knew anything.

Other court staff denied any knowledge.

The U.S. Marshal's office queried all eight of the court security officers under its jurisdiction.

Again, nothing.

At 2:30 on May 11, 1988, Stella Nickell sat quietly in her seat while Tom Hillier argued his motion for an order granting permission to interview jurors. His original concern was over whether Laurel Holliday, who had received the phone call, had been the holdout. Since news reports now stated that with absolute clarity, he no longer needed to query the jury on that point.

Instead, he requested the court to hold an evidentiary hearing to determine the case of juror misconduct.

Joanne Maida disagreed. The jury had followed their oaths, and it was pure speculation they had not. Juror Holliday reported the call in good faith, and the court accepted it.

"In spite of information learned by this juror that was prejudicial to the defense, Mr. Hillier insisted on her remaining on the panel. I can think of only one acceptable reason why an experienced defense counsel would do that, knowing that she has learned prejudicial information to the defense, and that is that he was not ignoring . . . what was very apparent to all of us who would have had to ignore what our eyes and our ears and our common sense were telling us when we saw the jury panel come out on Friday afternoon to tell us basically that they were deadlocked.

"Mr. Hillier took an awful risk, but not only did he not object to her remaining as a juror, he adamantly objected to her excusal. He did this after consulting with his client. At that time I believe I advised the Court that we had a real mess on our hands, but in the event of a verdict sending this woman back to continue deliberations with the rest of the jurors, that Mr. Hillier, the first thing that he would be asking is for an interview of the jurors, or something to that effect, something that would be tantamount to that effect."

The court's ruling was clear, then, Joanne Maida said, that neither counsel be permitted to interview the jurors. Tom Hillier was seeking the same thing now—except now with judicial supervision.

"It seems to me that the defense took a gamble and they lost, and that's as far as it should be pursued."

Joanne Maida suggested that Tom Hillier set aside his second-guessing and learn to live with his decision to keep Laurel Holliday on the jury. The U.S. Attorney's office would not sanction any jury inquiry into the verdict "based on pure speculation and conjecture."

Though he doubted any juror had made the call or that any had told someone outside the court where they stood, Judge Dwyer had no choice but to question the jurors under oath. The claim of juror misconduct had to be investigated. The jurors would return to court Friday morning. Questions from counsel would need to be in his chambers by the next afternoon.

Tom Hillier ended his appearance with a play for juror phone records and a subpoena for an appearance of Laurel Holliday's roommate.

Assistant U.S. Attorney Joanne Maida returned to an office buried in stacks of media messages and flowers from Paul Webking.

She sent off a thank-you: *"I was grateful for the outcome, especially for you and your family. . . ."*

*   *   *

Jeff Ford was among the many who tried to sort it out after the verdict. He still wasn't sure Stella Nickell was the killer. He knew Bruce and Cindy had had run-ins over drugs, and wondered if the crime had been Cindy's doing. But that was fleeting.

He figured it had to be simpler than that.

"My impression of the whole thing was somebody took a dislike to Stella and said, 'You're it!' . . . Come hell or high water, they are going to get you."

Others figured the problem was the defense attorney.

Laurie Church thought Tom Hillier was "a very nice man" but was intimidated by Joanne Maida.

"I don't think that he thought that 'Okay, I'll get up there and make a good show.' He thought, 'I don't know how I can stand up to her type thing!' "

Stella's sister Berta was less charitable.

"To me he wasn't like a lawyer, he was like a spectator. Just like he didn't know anything about Stella. The whole thing that really aggravates me, I just really believe that this is a setup. Stella is a nobody. She has no power behind her. There is no money in the family."

Of course, no one outside of the Nickell jury knew of Laurel Holliday's strange behavior during deliberations: the letter she read, the journal entries she made, the professed feelings that all were against her, the tears during the verdict. No one talked about it. It had been bad enough.

And it was about to get even worse.

A *Seattle Times* reporter who heard about the mysterious phone call late the afternoon of the verdict bolted over to the courthouse a half hour before closing, just to see if there was anything on the Holliday woman. It was the kind of thing a good reporter does as a matter of course. It seldom paid off so big.

A quick records search indicated a single case, a civil suit, with her name.

He learned that juror Holliday had filed a lawsuit against Pepperidge Farms. It stemmed from an incident occurring on the last day of July 1986.

A thirty-eight-page deposition she gave in *Laurel Holliday* v. *Pepperidge Farms* on August 19, 1987, detailed how Laurel Holliday claimed to have bitten into a Goldfish cracker during a bro-

ker's open house. The crackers were hard, the taste bitter, followed
by a burning sensation. She spat them out.

"I saw a pill inside the cracker."

Panic ensued, and she called poison control.

"I pretty much figured I was dead. This was right after the cyanide poisonings in Auburn."

Right after the poisonings in Auburn! It was unbelievable that
she could ignore a lawsuit in which she cited the very case she is
impaneled for! Most prospective jurors go out of their way to tell
the court of incidents that are even remotely suspect.

Laurel Holliday, for some reason, hadn't.

Later, FDA labs identified the pill as ibuprofen. If it had been
cyanide, as Laurel Holliday's mind had first flashed, she would have
been dead.

On May 12, 1988, the *Seattle Times* ran a copyright story:

NICKELL JUROR HAD ACCEPTED
SETTLEMENT IN PRODUCT CASE

She sued after eating pill in cracker in 1986

In the article, she told the reporter she never told the judge about
the case because "I was never asked . . . there was no reason to . . ."
The case was assigned to arbitration and settled out of court, with
Laurel Holliday getting only $500.

She told the reporter she had discussed the incident just before
impanelment, but felt it didn't apply to the Nickell case. It was a
manufacturer's error, not product tampering.

Talk around Seattle was that Pepperidge Farms' attorney had
questioned whether the incident ever took place in the first place.
A pill could not survive the steel rollers cracker dough was forced
between.

Jurors were aghast after they saw the news report.

Marcheta Cruse felt betrayed. Holliday could have had the whole
thing end in a hung jury. And for what purpose?

"How did she ever get on that jury?" Cruse asked.

Carolyn Bidleman couldn't come up with an answer. It seemed
to her, however, that Holliday's civil suit should have been revealed
by the prospective juror.

"I think her priorities were for her benefit, not for the trial, the jury, or for Stella Nickell, as far as that's concerned. I think she was there for her own gain," Cruse said later.

While the FBI and the U.S. Attorney were investigating the Holliday phone call and other bizarre revelations, the call brought both hope and confusion to the defense.

Tom Hillier told Stella Nickell that it was debatable whether the call had even been made.

"I mentioned to him, who had the phone numbers?" Stella Nickell recalled later.

" 'The U.S. Attorney and the FBI.'

"And I said, 'Who's to say the FBI didn't make this phone call? There's enough female staff in there.'

"He says, 'I don't even wanna think about that.' He said, 'Don't think it hasn't crossed my mind, but I don't even wanna think about that.' He said, 'Because that means our judicial system has gone down even more than what I thought it was.' "

The defendant also wondered if her daughter had somehow made the call in a desperate bid to ensure a guilty verdict. She studied the wording of Holliday's note to the court.

"Cindy says 'ya'll and you all' all the time."

CHAPTER 86

It was not a happy reunion for the Nickell jurors. They had given their time and dedication, and now many felt betrayed by one of their own. They were being questioned yet again by Judge Dwyer, a part of an investigation hearing into juror misconduct. Some were flat out insulted.

Before filing back into the courtroom on the afternoon of May 13, they waited in familiar quarters, the jury room. Laurel Holliday, dressed in a dark V-necked garment and a white longsleeved blouse, looked physically ill. She told a fellow juror her answering machine had been jammed with phone calls from media the past couple of nights.

Talk about creating your own problems, Laurie Adams thought.

Joanne Maida, Tom Hillier, and Stella Nickell, a loose tendril of dark hair hung over her forehead, listened as Judge Dwyer went over the afternoon's plans. The jurors would be brought in as a group, resworn, then individually questioned from the bench.

Laurel Holliday was first.

Judge Dwyer opened the hearing by asking a pale and nervous Laurel Holliday if she had indeed received the call.

She said she had, and she still had no idea who made it. She did not tell the other jurors about the call.

In a voice just barely audible, juror Holliday told the court she had not told anyone where she stood, innocent or guilty.

"I suspect my feelings were obvious to everyone who knew me, but I said nothing about my intended verdict," she said.

Concerning notes she might have made indicating how the deliberations stood, Laurel Holliday said she took them home most days, though there might have been one day she did not.

"Was there anything in your notebook that would have shown anybody, if anybody read it, how the jury stood?"

"I didn't bring it with me. I don't think that—It's possible. It's possible."

Judge Dwyer turned to the subject of the impanelment process, reminding the juror that she was placed under oath at the time she was first questioned. He pulled Court's Exhibit 1, a copy of Holliday's voir dire.

"Q: Have you yourself, by chance, or anyone you know been the victim of a product-tampering incident?

"A: No."

She maintained her answer was true, despite news reports about the Pepperidge Farms incident.

The judge pulled Exhibit 2, Laurel Holliday's August 19, 1987, lawsuit deposition.

He read the passages where the juror had cited the Auburn poisonings.

"Now, at that point—that is, when you bit into the cracker and had that thought—did you believe you were a victim of product tampering?" the judge asked.

Laurel Holliday said that at that point, she did think she was a tampering victim, but she wasn't sure.

"And when was it, then, if you recall, that you decided this was not product tampering but something else?"

"We never even considered it. I knew within seconds. Poison control said I wouldn't be calling them if it were cyanide, and the FDA report came sometime later—I don't remember exactly when—but then we knew that it was just actually a pill that I take for headaches myself."

Judge Dwyer moved on. Had she considered mentioning her lawsuit?

"It occurred to me, but I was trying to be very exact and to the point, and listening to your question, and I knew this had nothing to do with the federal tampering law, which is the law that you had just read us, I believe."

She told the judge she had mentioned the Pepperidge Farms case to reporter Kristen Jackson of the *Times*, the day before impanelment.

"I said, you know, I wondered if it would matter, but I just listened to the questions and if it didn't come up, it wasn't important to me and it would have no impact at all on my feelings about this case."

"Can you recall what, if anything, she told you when you asked her?"

"She said that she thought the important thing was to answer directly to the questions, and that only I would know whether anything in my life had biased my ability to be on the jury."

"Then, when you were asked the question I just read, did you believe that the 1986 incident and your lawsuit did or did not come within the scope of the question?"

"I thought that it was completely outside the scope of the question."

The judge read from Exhibit 1, questions from impanelment:

"Q: Can you think of anything in your life experience that you feel would affect your ability to be anything other than an impartial juror?

"A: I can't. My job involves having two sides see each other's point of view when I negotiate an offer, so I think I would be fair."

Laurel Holliday stuck by her answer.

Judge Dwyer returned to the lawsuit deposition, reading juror Holliday's professed "paranoia" concerning packaged products and her anxiety, less trust in the world.

Why hadn't she considered those feelings when Tom Hillier asked his question concerning life experience?

"I don't see the relationship. To me the anxiety I felt at that time was over, for one thing. This took place, I believe, the last day of July in '86. This deposition was taken in August, I guess, of '87. I eat Pepperidge Farms Goldfish now. The feeling had changed, and I still don't understand . . . no one has explained to me how that relates to Stella Nickell and any feeling I might have about whether she would be guilty or innocent."

Again, from the Exhibit 1, he cited the question concerning potential jurors' having read or seen news reports on the Auburn cases.

Holliday had said she'd seen only one, the Sunday before impanelment. She said she'd been out of the state caring for her ill father during the time the tampering happened.

"Q: Have you heard or learned anything about this case from

any other source such as hearing other people talk about it?

"A: Not really. I just don't know much about it."

"Now, were those answers true?"

"I didn't hear anything about the case. I didn't know Stella Nickell's name, but I did know that there had been a cyanide problem in Auburn."

The judge wondered how she could know about the Auburn cyanide poisonings when she gave her civil deposition, if she hadn't read anything about the case up until the jury-impanelment article in the Sunday *Times*.

"I guess I just had heard from other people or—I really don't know. I just was aware of it. I probably had read something, but I can't remember specifically what."

She also told the judge that she did in fact recall his telling the jury not to discuss the case at the beginning of impanelment. But she talked with the *Times* reporter again.

"I told her it was the jury, you know, that it was the one."

Laurel Holliday also admitted she had talked with others about writing about the case. One was a San Francisco—based literary agent.

Had any discussions concerning writing about Stella Nickell's case occurred between impanelment and her discharge as a juror?

"Well, yes. As I said, I think I did mention that I did consider writing an article if anything came. I probably mentioned it to three or four people."

"During the trial?"

"Just—yeah, probably I did say that. You know, I was thinking about it."

She did not, she insisted, reveal anything about jury deliberations.

"Any other conversations you've had with anybody on the subject of books or articles?"

"Well, I can probably name some more names of people who—because I know that I keep a journal every day and that I do write—that I might have mentioned it to, close friends."

"During the trial or after?"

"Probably both."

Judge Dwyer followed up with a series of questions concerning Holliday's ability to be an impartial juror.

Her lawsuit had no effect.

The conversations about writing about the case had no effect.

"I listened very carefully. I paid extreme attention to everything."

Through the judge, Tom Hillier asked if the manufacturer raised the possibility of product tampering.

Laurel Holliday said they did not.

"They just felt that the crushing of it wasn't in keeping with what would be possible, in their baking process, but they never said anything about product tampering."

After Laurel Holliday returned to the jury room, the others, one by one, were called in. None knew anything about the phone call. And certainly none had told anyone where individual jurors stood for conviction or acquittal. All were excused.

Drained by more than an hour of questioning, Laurel Holliday left the courthouse by the back door, declining to talk to the media. And that, for once, seemed like a good idea.

SA Ron Nichols put in a gentle jab at Joanne Maida. He reminded her that he had wanted to challenge Holliday as a juror during voir dire. He didn't think she'd be right for the prosecution.

"I should have listened to you," the Asst. U.S. Attorney said.

SAs Cusack and Stone shared a sense of disbelief back at the FBI offices down the hill from the courthouse. They had come so far in the two years since Seamurs began, and now this juror might screw it all up.

A week later, Tom Hillier filed a sixteen-page brief seeking a new trial for Stella Nickell, citing that juror Holliday "willfully concealed material information during jury selection . . ." The brief was convincing. Talk circulated around the courthouse and the jail that in the event of a mistrial, murder charges might be filed, in King County, with Joanne Maida named special prosecutor. "Ice" Maida would go after the death penalty.

There was one hitch: would Cindy cooperate if called on again? She had told Dee Rogers she couldn't do it if her mother might be executed.

Maybe now such sentiment didn't matter. Push had come to shove.

Friends who visited Stella Maudine in jail during this time reported that the woman was doing great considering all she had been through. It was true she didn't have her hot rollers, but now she had a chance for freedom. She was even upbeat, as she had been when Harry Swanson kissed her good-bye the day she took the polygraph a year and a half before.

"Just great! Super! Gonna beat this!"

Stella shared her hope with Wilma Mae that the Laurel Holliday fiasco might be the answer. Stella's niece prayed alongside her. Her aunt might go free after all.

Just before lunch on June 3, the players sans jury met in Judge Dwyer's courtroom for brief oral arguments on the defense motion for a new trial. The focus was Tom Hillier's argument that Laurel Holliday had withheld information during voir dire and therefore should not have been seated on the jury.

"Was her withholding inadvertent, a mistake, or otherwise innocent withholding? Your Honor, I submit it was not."

Joanne Maida disagreed and stood behind the juror.

The hearing ended with the distribution of copies of a letter written to Judge Dwyer. It was from Laurel Holliday. Holliday claimed *Times* reporter Kristen Jackson called her when she saw her name on a list of potential jurors—provided to the *Times* by the court.

Kristen Jackson later denied any such list.

Laurel Holliday blasted the media for their "witch hunt" tactics.

She wrote about voting guilty and whether she made the right choice.

"I'll never know for sure ... I am constantly agonizing over whether I was correct in my assessment of 'reasonable doubt.' "

CHAPTER 87

Wilma Stewart cried a Northwest downpour when her aunt Stella was finally sentenced on June 17. Joanne Maida had done all she could to ruin an innocent woman, and Tom Hillier had failed miserably in getting a mistrial out of the Laurel Holliday debacle.

And there was nothing Wilma could do about any of it. She felt disgusted by the sea of betrayal that had swallowed her aunt. The FBI and Cynthia Lea had done a big number on everyone. Cynthia Lea was going to get reward money and the FBI agents were able to stand proudly and give Americans everywhere the all-clear signal—a madwoman was going away for a long time.

After brief oral presentations from both sides, Judge Dwyer pronounced a sentence of ninety years, with parole a possibility at thirty years.

Aunt Stella would be at least seventy-four before she had a chance for parole.

Tom Hillier announced he had filed an appeal, as Stella Nickell looked on stoically.

Judge Dwyer agreed to recommend that during the time of the appeal, Stella Maudine would be incarcerated at the women's prison in Purdy, Washington.

Some time after sentencing, Wilma heard from SA Dave Hill. He told her there had been some talk around the U.S. Attorney's office that Joanne Maida might seek perjury charges against her.

Stella Nickell's niece blew a gasket.

Why don't these people leave me and my family alone? she thought.

"I told Dave Hill, 'Go for it. My son had been gone a month when I testified at grand jury. I was nervous and scared at grand jury. There was no perjury."

Charges were never filed.

Stephenson girls never give up. And Stella Nickell did not disappoint her tribe. Just as mother Cora Lee had bucked up time and time again when trouble befell her, so did her youngest daughter.

After sentencing, Stella Maudine continued to place collect calls to Wilma whenever possible. A new trial was the usual topic of discussion. Both women held great hope that the Laurel Holliday affair would eventually win a new trial. Other times the prisoner even suggested that maybe Cynthia Lea would "come to her senses and say she lied."

Stella asked her niece to call famed San Francisco attorney Melvin Belli to see if he'd take the case. Wilma made the call, only to learn he wouldn't even take a look at the case unless she could come up with a $5,000 retainer. Of course, there was no money for that.

"What we need is an attorney who'll earn a name for himself out of this," Wilma told her aunt.

"You got that right, babe."

One time, she asked her aunt if she had heard from Cynthia Lea.

"No, but I'd like to."

"How can you want to still see her after what she's done to you?"

"She's still my daughter."

On her own, Wilma Stewart pursued other avenues. She tried to find out if maybe Sue Snow and Uncle Bruce were having an affair, but that led nowhere.

Her aunt wasn't dead, but as the weeks passed people sometimes made it seem that way.

With the Nickell mobile home about to be hauled away, Wilma had been charged with the responsibility of storing her aunt's belongings. She wanted to save the mobile home from repossession, but she simply didn't have the money.

Fred Phelps, the dutiful boyfriend who had been to every day of the trial, hadn't helped matters. Stella claimed Fred hadn't paid a bill since she was arrested in December.

Wilma had to move fast, or there wouldn't be anything left.

Stella said Fred could have a few items—the wall unit, the davenport, and some other furniture. Wilma wanted the Commodore 64 computer and asked for the refrigerator and some of her aunt's Corningware, and her aunt Stella said she was glad to let her *use* it.

"I'll need some of those things back when I get out," she said with utter conviction.

Wilma Stewart's heart ached for her aunt . . . framed, set up, somehow either by an overzealous FBI desperate to solve a tampering case or, even worse, by a daughter hypnotized by dollar signs. The way she saw it, there were three victims in this case: Uncle Bruce, Sue Snow, and, now, Aunt Stella.

Wilma rented a 4 × 8 trailer in Richland and pulled it behind her Datsun. Her estranged husband Mel and their toddler came along to help and keep her company.

When she got to the Auburn mobile home she noticed the Commodore 64 was already gone. Fred Phelps told her Stella had given it to Jim McCarthy.

Surrounded by boxes in the middle of the living-room floor, while Mel and Fred loaded the trailer, Wilma dismissed her aunt's considerable collection of bric-a-brac into containers. Among the boxes was a safe. Inside, there was a shoe box. Inside the shoe box Wilma found a denim-blue five-year diary, the kind young girls often use. It was fastened with a tinny gold-colored lock. Also inside the shoe box were several small bottles.

She scooped all of it into a box bound for Eastern Washington.

It took a week and three trips over the Cascades to bring all of the Nickells' belongings home for storage. Stella's loyal niece stacked it all in the garage and a bedroom closet. She planned to go through it later.

The next time her aunt called from prison, Wilma Mae asked about the computer. Stella told her that she had, in fact, let Big Mac have it.

"He'll give it back to you," she told her niece. "He'll call and get it to you."

Wilma wondered why she had given it to him in the first place. She was family; Jim McCarthy was just a friend.

As she came to and from the property, it crossed Wilma's mind that it might have been her grandmother and aunt who had done the crime. Cora Lee had said little, if anything, about the case—at least not to Wilma Mae. It seemed as if she was holding back—not because she was ignorant about it, but because she knew something.

"Grandma stood to lose more than Aunt Stella did—her whole investment."

When Stella Nickell finally came to believe Fred Phelps had taken her for a ride, there was very little she could do. He was on the Outside, and she was in prison. She wanted Bruce's guns back, but Fred said he had sent them out to be cleaned. She even asked Wilma to hot-wire the truck and steal it back, but she refused.

Wilma Stewart had learned a lot of things at the Maple Lane reformatory; hot-wiring, however, was not among them.

Later, with a trace of regret, Stella Nickell spoke about her last man.

"I cared about Fred. I won't say I loved him. But Fred also happened to be there when I was still at loose ends and looking for something and not knowing what I was looking for. From different things that have happened, the thought has run through my mind that I think Fred was using me, that he knew more than he let on he knew about me and that he kind of made it a point to meet me."

A handful of the Nickell jurors gathered at Murray Andrews's Vashon Island waterfront getaway for a picnic on a hot summer day. Since Laurel Holliday was not among the group, she was naturally a key topic of conversation.

"What was she thinking? What was really going on?" Laurie Adams wondered.

No one really knew.

"I think she wanted to be there to write the story . . . but not to have to make the decision. She all of a sudden realized, 'My God, I've got to be part of the decision process.' She was basically stalling for time, because she didn't want to do it," Murray Andrews said later.

CHAPTER 88

No one disputed that Cora Lee was never the same after her fall during her baby girl's federal product-tampering trial. The old woman, as formidable as she was, couldn't put all the pieces together again. Neither could the other Stephenson girls. After the trial, after she lost everything she had, Cora Lee split time between her daughters, living in spare bedrooms, basements. It was a useless, defeating end for a woman who had worked so hard everywhere, from sawmills to pea fields. Her knotty hands were idle. Her mind was frail.

By July the year after Stella Maudine was sent to prison as the nation's first convicted federal product tamperer, Cora Lee could last no longer.

Though doctors said it was cancer, her youngest daughter had other ideas about the cause of her mother's death.

"For me to end up in a prison and my daughter's the one that put me there and her favorite grandchild on top of that, it's part of what killed Mother. Basically, if you look at it in all perspectives, Cynthia was the complete cause of Mother dying," Stella Nickell said later from prison.

"I can't prove it," Stella later went on, "medical science might not be able to prove it. Nobody has said anything about it. But in my own mind, I'm sure that when Mother fell and hit her head and bruised the brain, somehow that upset the body to the point where it started the cancer in the top part of her lung. Because Mother had no traces of cancer before that. None. Mother fell in April, hit her head, she contracted cancer in October, and by the following July, she was dead. And when they found the cancer in October, it was only the size of a quarter.

"But see, if she hadn't have been at the courthouse to begin with, she wouldn't have fell on those steps. So when you come right down to the knotty nitty-gritty, all circumstances involved, Cynthia is basically the reason for our mother's death."

There was a big media brouhaha over the idea of the cyanide killer going to her mother's funeral. But Stella phoned Stan and Laurie Church and told them she wasn't going to go. She wasn't going to let anyone take pictures of her.

"I'm not going to glorify it for those newspaper people. I'm not going to my mother's funeral in shackles and chains," she said.

Her sisters wanted her there, though they understood her presence would alter the mood and meaning of the service.

"We all agreed," Berta said, "that if she wanted to be there, we would surround her and be there. We'd be there for her."

Cynthia Hamilton talked with Dee Rogers around the time of her grandmother's death.

"Dee," she said, "the thing that hurts me most is my grandmother died hating me."

Dee told her that couldn't be true. She insisted Cora Lee would have backed up her favorite granddaughter if she had known the truth.

Years later, Berta recalled her mother's feelings about Cynthia Lea.

Cora Lee, in fact, had talked about her favorite grandchild the week before she died.

" 'When Cindy gets off these drugs, if she's on drugs . . . she's going to have to live the rest of her life with these memories,' " Berta recalled her mother saying.

Hate her? *Never*. Cora Lee loved her granddaughter.

"I don't want to give her any relief," Berta said years later. "I wouldn't want to tell Cindy, but mother did not die hating her. She kept the picture in her wallet. I love the kid too. But she's done wrong."

In July 1989, Cora Lee was laid to rest in a grave south of Tacoma. She wore the pretty, full-length dress she had planned to wear for her last wedding. With her went family secrets. And, Stella Nickell later said, all of her hope.

"Mother knew for a fact that I didn't do this," she said. "She knew it."

It was late summer–early fall 1990 when officials from some-where—Bob Strong never caught exactly who they were—called the house on Ranchero Way in Garden Grove, looking for Cindy Hamilton. Despite Laurel Holliday's shenanigans, 6th Circuit Appellate Court had upheld the conviction in the *United States of America v. Stella Maudine Nickell*. There was money to be handed out.

Bob Strong didn't know where Cindy Lea was. He wished he did. He and his stepdaughter had had a falling-out over drug paraphernalia he claimed she brought into their house. Cindy said a set of scales she had was used to weigh gold chains she was selling. Bob wasn't anybody's fool and told her he didn't think so. Cindy left in a bitter huff, and never came back to the house. When the folks from up north called about the money, he didn't have a clue where to find her.

"It took them a long time to locate her just to give her the money. That itself seemed kind of strange to me," he said later

The Nonprescription Drug Manufacturers Association's dispersion of the money following Stella Maudine Nickell's failed appeals in 1989 and 1990 brought joy and disappointment to its recipients. Cindy Hamilton got the lion's share, $250,000; Tom Noonan, $15,000; Bonnie Anderson, $10,000; Dee Rogers, $7,500; Sandy Scott, $7,500; Katy Parker, $2,500; Melinda Denton, $2,500; Gerry McIntyre, $2,500; Lynn Force, $2,500.

It brought outrage to those like A. J. Rider who had been left out in the cold.

"I never got shit! They never even gave me an application. Jack had told me on several occasions that after it was done I'd probably get something for it. I didn't get shit," A. J. Rider said, unable to disguise her bitterness.

She smelled a rat named Cindy Hamilton.

"They had to have done something drastic to get her to testify, as much as she was trying to hide and evading them. Somebody made some deep promises somewhere."

Jack Cusack was uncomfortable with the split. He felt it should have been divided among the witnesses more evenly. But it had not been his decision.

A woman reporter from Los Angeles called Tom Noonan with her congratulations and to ask if he knew the whereabouts of Cindy Hamilton.

He did not.

"Well, Auburn's a small town, isn't it?"

"Yeah, but it's not that small. There's thirty thousand people here; I can't know everybody."

"You didn't stay in contact after trial?"

"We didn't stay in touch during, before."

Like just about everyone, the woman reporter wanted to talk only to Cindy.

Tom Noonan later complained, though he didn't want to come off as a money-grubbing individual. He was glad for his windfall, but . . .

"I look at the way the reward was dispersed and I always have questions in my mind. She got $250,000, you know . . . I mean, granted she had the most incriminating testimony, and I had of all the money that was left and split up between everyone else, I got the most. Fifteen thousand dollars. It's not that I'm unappreciative . . . it took five years to wind through its course and Sue Snow had to die."

Going into it, he figured that the ten or so witnesses he was told were going to split the money would share in it equally—$30,000 each. He was going to put the money down on a house.

When he found out Cindy Hamilton got almost all of it, he thought there had been a "conspiracy."

"I think somebody got behind closed doors with her and said, 'Here, if you'll say what you know, we'll promise you X amount of money for saying it. To me it would be the only viable reason why she would do it," Tom Noonan said.

While others also speculated on what they'd get for their share of the reward when it was finally divvied out, only one did not. Cindy Hamilton told people she was coming into a great sum of money, but she never felt compelled to call any of the officials associated with its disbursement.

Maybe it was, as Tom Noonan suggested, because she already knew how much she was going to get?

The letter from the association made it clear: figures were determined by the FBI and the Seattle office of the U.S. Attorney.

The greatest surprise to some observers was the fact that Dee Rogers had been awarded so little. No matter what anyone thought of her out-there-in-your-face personality, her somewhat pumped-up stories, the fact remained undisputable—without her, there would have been no Cindy. And without Cindy, there would not have been a winnable case.

Dee Rogers paid some bills and blew the rest of it on fun stuff. The trust funds for the kids and the country farm without men was a dream that was not to come true.

Although Sandy Scott was glad to get her share of the reward, and had come to accept her neighbor as some kind of Cyanide Stella, some of the convicted's actions still confounded her.

Why hadn't Stella disposed of two of the bottles of Excedrin capsules recovered from her home? It was easy to reconcile why she kept one—to prove her story that Bruce had been the victim of a tampering—but why the others?

Stella clearly hadn't known the third bottle was under the sink.

"I knew it was in there," Sandy said later. "Why wouldn't she have known it was in there? She wouldn't have left it sitting there. Why have evidence against yourself? It had to be a plant."

Sandy also wondered about Cindy's behavior the day the FBI and FDA came out to the Nickell place.

"Why are they accusing my mother?"

"The thing that got me about Cindy from the very start was that attitude she had when she came that day, automatically assuming that they were accusing Stella. That would lead me to believe she knew something ahead," she said later.

Later, Sandy Scott came to believe Cindy Hamilton was an accomplice.

"It makes me angry beyond words. It's not right. Cindy not only got away with something, she got paid a quarter of a million dollars! Who says crime doesn't pay?"

Stella Nickell's neighbor had wanted to ask Jack Cusack that very question, but held back. She didn't want to bother him with things she knew had probably been investigated to the core. Even though he was so damned good-looking, she had learned to trust him, too.

Sandy also wondered if Stella's motive really had been money. Why hadn't she waited until Bruce had his physical for the additional $25,000?

"You would have thought that someone planning a murder for

insurance money would have been clued in to how much money she was going to get when she did it."

She also considered the idea that Stella Nickell's daughter had become frustrated with her mother's lack of initiative to get the job done, and took care of it herself.

"Could it have been 'I'm sick of you dinking around. I'll do it'?"

Bonnie Anderson was floored by her share of the reward. She hadn't expected much, if anything. Ten thousand dollars was a major and wonderful windfall.

She stuck up for her friend, who, thankfully, didn't hear the comments made about her cashing in her mother.

"Everybody said, 'God, she got $250,000!'"

It made Bonnie mad. "But you have to remember, she lost her mother and her father. Is that worth it?"

She summed it up later. "The money didn't make any difference to her. She didn't do it for the money."

Stella Nickell, of course, made note of the money her daughter received. In a letter she wrote to her girlfriend Shirley Webbly, she wrote:

"There was a news article on Cynthia getting $250,000 for her part in my being here. I wonder what they are going to do when they find out I'm not guilty?"

Once Stella Nickell's daughter got her bundle of money, she was gone.

The California woman who had cared for Cindy's daughter off and on for years was heartbroken when, after two years, Cindy came one December day and took the pretty little dark-haired girl away. Before Cindy came, the woman had asked for permanent custody papers. The foster mother, whom Dee Rogers said the girl called her "other mommy," was under the impression the papers were on the way.

Instead, the little girl left with her birth mother.

She has not seen her since.

"I still have her pictures on my wall," the foster mother said in 1991. "I wasn't a blood relative, I simply took that baby because somebody needed to. I loved her. . . . Cindy used me as a dump. Dropped me."

Leah Strong has not heard from her sister either.

"I've been thinking about Cindy. It makes me mad because she's not wanting no one to know where she's at, it's like she's doing it on purpose. Like, to hell with you all. I ain't done nothing to her. She don't even know I'm pregnant.

"That's why when I went out there Christmas [1990] before last, I tried working things out with her. I thought things were worked out. As soon as I come back out here, I haven't heard nothing from her. It hurts me. I wonder why? I thought things were worked out. We were talking. Getting along. It made me feel good. It was like I did it all for nothing. She don't call me anymore to let me know where she is. She could at least call me or write me something. It wouldn't hurt her to call me."

Bob and Pat Strong haven't seen Cindy in years, though now and then they hear she's living somewhere in Orange County.

Rumored sightings are their only link: *"So and so saw Cindy at 7-Eleven! She didn't say nothing! But it was her!"*

It has been years since Katy, Bonnie, or even Dee has heard from Cindy.

"Last time I saw her was right around the time of the trial," Dee Rogers said. "It wasn't good-bye, but it was different. This chapter is closed, now it's done. I don't know that I will ever see her again, I might not ever. It's okay too. I know I'm always in her heart. I know if Cindy needs me, she'll call."

She clings to the hope the cycle of abuse and neglect has been broken and Cindy and her daughter are living on a ranch somewhere in Oregon, raising animals and never thinking about Stella Maudine.

Wilma Mae stood by her aunt, bitter beyond words over Cynthia Lea.

"I can understand her being angry at her mother for raising her the way she did. I'm trying to understand that she could be so angry that she could turn against her and put her in prison."

The money was insignificant when the Snow/Webking out-of-court settlement with drug giant Bristol-Myers was paid. No amount could replace Sue Snow. Hayley and Exa both used some of the funds to pay for schooling, and for airfare to and from their aunt Sarah's in Cairo. Paul Webking went on with his life too. He had the greatest bitterness to set aside. Few could imagine the stress and pain of being accused of killing a loved one, by the very people to whom he was closest.

CHAPTER 89

Stella Maudine Nickell: lone killer, or did she have an accomplice in her daughter? SA Jack Cusack had been troubled by the idea from the very beginning. So had most others on the case. But after the conviction and the reward, he could only wonder about it. Though the law can only focus on the hard facts that merit a conviction, what was the right thing here?

His children watching television, his wife clearing the dinner dishes, Jack Cusack took his place in his trophy-filled office. His old ham radio sat idle. He knew that only Cindy Hamilton knew what really happened and what was really said between her and her mother.

Only those two knew what the hell they had said out on the concourse, or when they rode to work. When conversations ranged from screwing with Bruce Nickell's brakes, to hiring a hit man, to reenacting the Tylenol murders, it wasn't likely that it was a one-way conversation. There had to be a dialogue of some sort going on.

What had Cindy Hamilton omitted from her story to the FBI?

It seemed doubtful that someone would discuss the utopian outcome of a murder plot—the insurance money, the fish or ceramic store—without having been involved in it more than Cindy maintained she had been.

The question SA Cusack later posed was "just how deep was Cindy into it?"

No one knew. Nothing tied her to the actual plots, no evidence, no testimony.

Two things stuck in his mind. Here's a woman that was privy to a lot of inside information about a murder she says she wasn't involved with. She testifies against her mother and rides out in the sunset with a quarter of a million dollars.

"That's a big jump," he said later.

Why had Stella's daughter turned her mother in? Some close to the case suggested it was far from her story of doing "the right thing." Cynthia Hamilton also might have come forward to save herself. The FBI investigation was not going to go away. No stone was going unturned, and after a few months of watching the feds get closer, closer . . . *dangerously closer* . . . she decided to tell her story.

Stella Nickell might have done the same thing and saved herself. All of her arguments could have been believed—she always signed Bruce's name, she was confused about the insurance amounts, she researched the cyanide after Bruce died. Who had the contacts with drug dealers? It was Cindy, not Stella. There are plenty of reasons why Stella Maudine would never point the finger at Cindy. A mother's love was possible, though farfetched. One scenario could be that if Stella and Cindy had in fact done it together, Stella might entangle herself by implicating her daughter. And Stella Maudine was too smart for that. She took her chances that Cynthia Lea would change her mind; she gambled on her daughter's love and loyalty. And she lost.

With her beloved and maligned aunt Stella incarcerated for a crime she felt sure she didn't commit, Wilma Stewart began the lonely task of going through her aunt's belongings, mementos of a life: a set of *Star Trek* collector's plates, refrigerator magnets, two Tri-Chem liquid embroidery kits, tropical-fish paraphernalia. Her bowling ball, her leather tooling kit, even her aunt's saddlebag purse with its jingling cat bell were sorted into piles for Goodwill, for posterity, and for the garbage man.

Some things struck Stella's niece as odd or telling. Every bathing suit Aunt Stella owned was a bikini. Wilma, lovely figure that she had, wouldn't even dream of wearing a bikini. Yet that was Aunt Stella.

As a child would save Little League articles featuring his name, for some reason her aunt had saved clippings from her forgery conviction in Southern California: "Woman Held for Forgery," "Welfare Fraud Sentence Given" ...

Box by box, Stella Maudine's niece hauled things from the storage closet to her bedroom in the little duplex on Jadwin Street. Her son Michael was coming for the summer and she needed to make room for some of his things. She and Mel Stewart were divorcing, and she was unemployed. It was the perfect time to think miserable thoughts.

Aunt Stella is never getting out of prison ... never.

She began to wonder who knew what. What did Big Mac know? His photographs kept coming up in her aunt's belongings. It was strange he never testified *for* Aunt Stella.

Wilma also came to believe even more strongly that her grandmother knew more than she had let on. But what? Cora Lee, like Stella Maudine, never talked about anything specific.

Late one night, while smoking a cigarette and sucking on her usual eucalyptus cough drop, Wilma Stewart sat in her upstairs bedroom and pored over the legal papers that had filled the box whose contents had come from the minisafe out at the property in Auburn. Divorce papers, insurance papers about Stella's claims on Bruce's policy, even military records suggesting Uncle Bruce's discharge had been without honor.

Among the papers she found items that would break her heart.

Several small amber prescription bottles, stripped of any pharmacist's labeling, were in a clutch in a shoe box. A couple of the bottles were full of small, blackish seeds. A single bottle was marked: "Foxglove." Wilma couldn't discern whose hand had written the label. Stella's? Cynthia's? Cora Lee's?

But there was more. She picked up the five-year diary, the one she had seen back at the property when she moved her aunt's belongings but hadn't had time to read. Seven or eight pages had been filled out. What Wilma read then would haunt her forever.

"I'm getting strange phone calls ..."

"There's a strange man watching me from across the street ..."

"Left work the other day and there was a car parked across the street ... it followed me ... I ditched him ..."

Then the writings simply ended.

At first, she thought the entries had reflected something that was happening to her aunt when she was with Fred Phelps. There had been several media creeps hanging around for a story. She looked at the date again.

1986.

It had been written before Bruce Nickell died.

When she first read it, however, nothing really clicked. It was as though she had two pieces of a puzzle without the interconnecting piece. She couldn't put it together. Wilma Mae kept thinking about it.

"There's a strange man watching me from across the street . . ."

Where had she heard the story before?

The answer that came later was Cynthia Lea. It was Stella's daughter, the apple of Cora Lee's eye, the woman who betrayed the family, who had said Stella Maudine had been planning a kidnapping and had poisoned Bruce with seeds she gathered on the property.

Wilma's discovery added credibility to someone she chose not to believe.

"I had heard during the trial Cynthia Lea testified Aunt Stella had originally schemed at this idea of a kidnapping," Wilma said some years later. "She was going to journal that someone . . . was kidnapping. It was confirmation of what Cynthia Lea was saying about Aunt Stella being kidnapped and going to Mexico."

The discovery puzzled her, too. Aunt Stella was not stupid, and she surely had time to get rid of anything so incriminating. How could she have forgotten the diary and the seeds? She had more than a year and half, why hadn't she destroyed them?

In the pile of mementos was also Aunt Stella's white leather-covered Bible.

Fred Phelps had claimed Stella found more time for Bible study after she took her leave from Burns. She was private about it, not saying what she was really looking for. Yet a slip of paper she kept inside the Bible betrayed her search. On it she wrote:

Death in family
Ps 29
1 Cor 25
Lying detected
Ps ci
Acts 5, Rev 21
Repentance:
Ps li, xxxii, lxxxiv, cxxx, cxxxix
Babtism [sic]: Mark X, 39, Etc;
Acts ii 37 Etc.

Marriage:
John ii, Eph V
Thanks: 2 Sam vii

Stella Maudine also pressed Bruce's obituary between the pages: *"Bruce Edward Nickell, 52, a former Winthrop, Peshastin and longtime Seattle area resident, died at Harborview Medical Center . . ."*

Wilma Mae threw away the diary and the little black seeds. If there was another trial, she was not going to give anyone the chance to force her into testifying. One time had been more than enough. The Bible, of course, could not be burned. She stored it in a box in her adopted father's basement.

Guilty or innocent, her aunt was a woman she loved. She never told Stella about her discovery, even though they wrote and had frequent phone contact. What Wilma had discovered helped to make some things seem more plausible, but in the end, who but God knew if Stella Maudine really had killed Bruce Nickell and Sue Snow?

Or if she had done it alone.

AUTHOR'S NOTES
& ACKNOWLEDGMENTS

This is a work of nonfiction and as such it is only as good as the author's sources. I have been very fortunate. Nearly all of the people cited in these pages were interviewed specifically for this book. Two names have been changed. Where possible, verbatim testimony was used to reconstruct conversations. In other cases, I relied on the recollections of sources directly involved in such conversations.

I regret I was unable to reach Cindy Hamilton. None involved in the case, her life, her family knew—or would say—where Stella's daughter was living. I tried every legal means available, but could not locate her.

Over the years of researching and writing this book, I have had the pleasure of meeting and getting to know dozens involved in this tragic American drama. I appreciate the time and effort given so freely by so many seeking the answers to questions of their own.

I have also been inspired by some, in particular, Sue Snow's survivors—Hayley Snow, Cindy "Exa" Snow, Sarah Webb, and Paul Webking. Hayley's anguish and confusion over family loyalties, as written in her diaries, shaped the book tremendously. Sarah Webb's devotion to her twin sister's memory and her pain over her loss touched me profoundly. Guilty of nothing but the kind of personality that might rub some the wrong way, Paul Webking was always honest, thoughtful, and direct. I thank him for all of that.

The many contributions Wilma Stewart made to this book are

immeasurable. Stella's niece, now happy and successful in her career, put me in touch with relatives and friends who filled in the gaps. Whenever I had a question, Wilma was always ready to search for an answer. Wilma, in many ways, is my hero, the hero of this work.

I also wish to thank the FBI, especially Seamurs Case Agent Jack Cusack, and the many others who assisted me throughout the project, including Ron Nichols, Dave Hill, Dick Thurston, and Bobbi Cotter.

Others I am indebted to: literary agent Janice Gordon of Black, Inc.; the wonderful Anne Milburn, my editor at Warner Books; Dawn Anderson, Paula Bates, Barb Meyer, Larry Venable, Dee Rogers, and, of course, the ever-resourceful Sandy Scott.

Then there is Stella Maudine Nickell. As the only writer to ever interview Stella, I met her several times at the federal prison near Pleasanton, California. It is one of those prisons invariably described as resembling a college campus or a country club. Of course, it is neither. Here are some notes on the first of several visits:

She surprised me in both her appearance and demeanor. I had seen only her driver's license photograph; this Stella Nickell looked better than ever. Blue jeans flattered her 49-year-old figure and her trademark long wavy black hair, now streaked with gray, was pulled back in a barrette. Earrings she made herself dangled.

Despite her reputation as a human iceberg, the Stella I met exhibited a full range of emotions: laughter, anger, tears. She was pleasant and polite—and adamant about everything. Stella never wavered from her position of innocence.

"It is not in me to kill anyone," she told me several times.

Destined to be the grande dame of the federal prison system when, and if, she is paroled in her seventies, Stella told me she was the victim of some kind of a plot or a frame-up. Though she had several years to conjure one up, she had no pat answer to explain why she was arrested and convicted of five counts of product tampering.

But part of the puzzle, she said, rested with her elder daughter. Though she never came out and said it, the implication was always that Cindy had set her up. The betrayal hurt her deeply, but Stella always knew it would end that way.

"Everybody was sure she'd back off, change her mind and change her story. I said no. Once Cynthia starts something she will not back off. Because Cynthia is not one to admit that she's wrong. Even though she might know that she's wrong, she will never admit it. She's been that way all of her life."

To pass time, in addition to a prison job, Stella reads quite a bit and crochets afghans for her grandchildren and niece. She avoids television—MTV is a favorite of Pleasanton inmates and Stella has always been a little bit country.

Under the sink in her cell is a box of legal papers from her 1988 trial. She says she has other appeals to file but is unable to come up with the money for an attorney. She won't give up, and someday, she insists, she will prove her innocence.

"I am not a killer," she repeated.

Though I could see the indications of a hard life on her face and in her manner, I left Pleasanton feeling sad for her and angry at her at the same time. I couldn't forget the anguish and tragically altered lives of Sue Snow and her family. But I also felt torn. I liked Stella Maudine. I never expected that.

—G.O., April 1993

P.S. I'd like to thank the following who helped make this updated re-issue possible: My agent Susan Raihofer of the David Black Literary Agency; the editorial staff of St. Martin's Press—Charles Spicer and Joe Cleemann; and lastly, Tina Marie Brewer and her mother, June Wolfe, for their much appreciated help.

—G.O., September 2002

UPDATE: 2002

Investigators like to roll up their sleeves, put their feet up and talk about a case that haunts them. They replay the case over and over as if by doing so they'd be able to find missing pieces. As a writer, I understand that kind of exercise. I'm guilty of it myself. Whenever the product tampering case that took the lives of Sue Snow and Bruce Nickell comes to mind, I rerun the same movie. For me, there are just as many unanswered questions today as there were when I first wrote *Bitter Almonds*. Most of those questions are posed within the last few paragraphs of the book you've just read.

The biggest question I had was always about Stella's daughter. What did she know? How much of what she said was the truth? Why hadn't Stella's lawyer pushed her harder on the stand? How come she got all that money? And where did she go?

In January 2001, after more than a decade of nothing, things started stirring in the Nickell case. CBS News' *48 Hours* was working on a piece profiling a couple of private investigators and a lawyer who were about to proclaim Stella Nickell's complete innocence and file for a new trial. Their premise was that an overzealous government, led by FBI agent Jack Cusack, had railroaded their client. The private investigators wanted to find Cindy and had been searching for her for the past year, but with no luck. I told one of them to join the club.

About that time, I got an email through my Web site. It was

Cindy's daughter, whom I didn't name in the book and I won't name here. She had heard bits and pieces of the product-tampering story that put her grandmother in prison and her mother on the run. She wanted a copy of the book and I gladly sent one to her address in Southern California.

She also wanted to tell me about her life. She told me of a childhood marked by a five-year abandonment by her mother; of a mother who appeared to put her own needs well ahead of her daughter's. It was so much a retelling of Stella's own techniques it reminded me of how Bob Strong had said how daughter and mother walked in the same tracks, the same way. Cindy's daughter said she was abused and had a baby at sixteen, whom she gave up for adoption. She said that her mother "was in competition with me" when it came to men. Sounded just like—Stella.

The young woman told me how Cindy never wanted to talk about the case or her mother. She also said that her mother kept her isolated from the rest of the family.

And the money? It was long gone, victim to bad choices, drugs and an IRS bill. Her mother had a series of men and marriages and dead-end jobs. According to the daughter, Cindy even worked at a fast food place. She was no longer the trailer park babe in the spandex pants. Her weight had ballooned.

She didn't know much about the case, except she did know of the existence of the diary that Wilma said she found. Her mother told her about it.

"It is a little nagging voice in the back of my head that I learn to trust," she said.

Investigators used "more than 1,000 pages" of previously undisclosed FBI and FDA lab documents related to the case to tentpole their argument that the government had been in cahoots to put Stella Nickell behind bars for the product tampering case. Some of the documents purported to show that the chemical composition between the Snow and Nickell tainted capsules was NOT a match. Famed FBI whistleblower Frederic Whitehurst suggested that chemist Roger Martz, who had testified at trial, had mislead the jury. Whitehurst wrote how Martz "cut many corners" and testified to things he did not do.

Stella went on camera on *48 Hours*. It was the first time I'd seen her since my interviews. It was the first interview she had given anyone since we met four times when I researched the book. The song hadn't changed, only now she had momentum. Part of that momentum was wrapped up in the motion filed in the Ninth Circuit Court of Appeals, seeking a new trial. The primary basis for the trial would be new evidence. As far as I could tell, there wasn't much of that.

Various declarations provided exact or very similar themes as to what had been discussed so many years ago. Stella wrote how her hands had been tied by the court when she was not permitted to bring up the reward money—the reason why her daughter said the "terrible things she did." She also attacked Cusack over the polygraph, putting the word *polygraph* in quotation marks to underscore how phony she believed the whole thing was. She was right, now as back then, the polygraph report was lost and her defense council never had a chance to review it.

Cindy's sister **Leah** weighed in with her assessment on whether her older sister's testimony should be believed. In the court documents, she wrote: "In addition to drug use my sister was one of the biggest and best liars I have ever known . . . She was one of the best actresses I have ever seen when it came to lying." Cindy's daughter shared similar thoughts, "My mother was what I would describe as a pathological liar."

In the fall of 2001, the court rejected the plea for a new trial. The case was closed with a resounding thud. It was a good effort, but it would take something far more extraordinary for the court to order a new trial. What the investigators had was a rehash, most of which appeared in *Bitter Almonds*. It was good stuff, just not *that* new.

Life goes on for Sue Snow's family. Her youngest daughter, **Hayley**, has been married to a local boy, Kevin Klein, for a couple of years and is living on a cattle and sheep ranch 75 miles southeast of Artesia, New Mexico. Thirty-one-year-old Hayley's mother has been gone longer than the time they had together. Sue probably would have laughed at the idea of her daughter living in Artesia, when she had worked so hard to escape the place. She would have loved how her daughter and twin sister had remained so close. After four years as a reporter for the Artesia Daily Press, Hayley now runs a nonprofit organization called Artesia MainStreet that is revitalizing the city's downtown. She is a smart and beautiful young woman. Sue would have been so proud.

The private investigator working with Stella and CBS stirred things up and for some probably caused more hurt than illumination. It not only brought up old memories, but it brought some confusion, too. "It bothered me that for so many years I had this organized story in my brain about what happened," Hayley told me. "And now that was being questioned. It really hurt. If Stella weren't guilty, I wouldn't want her in prison. Who would?"

Now, that is past. Hayley feels that the jury reached the correct verdict. And the case has been closed for good. At least for her.

Hayley sees her aunt Sarah and uncle Rodney often. Rodney still owns his oil business, and the ranch the Kleins run. Sarah misses her twin and always will, but her focus remains on her husband and daughter—now a student at Boston University.

Exa Snow, the oldest of Sue's girls, is engaged to be married. She'll make her home with her new husband in London.

Still married to the same woman, **Paul Webking** lives in Tacoma. The CBS show cast a shadow of suspicion on him, and Hayley feels bad about any part she might have played in that. She invited him to her wedding, but Paul didn't make it. He, did, however, send a gift later. Since the show aired in June 2001, she began to wonder if she'd ever hear from him again.

Sandy Scott still lives in her house just up the hill from Bruce and Stella Nickell's property. If Stella still owned the property, she'd find that it would be worth more than the insurance money she might have collected after Bruce's death. A lot more. Over the years Sandy appeared on several television shows. She hasn't changed her story.

A.J. Rider, now single, lives in the southern part of the Puget Sound region in Washington state. Of all the people associated with the case, Rider remains the most troubled. She feels that the FBI misled her and that her friend should not be in prison. She says Stella feels betrayed by her. "If they had just taken the straight road and looked at the evidence they would have found that Cindy and another person was responsible but they didn't do that. That didn't make a big enough headline for them. It has cost Stella fourteen going on fifteen years of her life and for me the best friend I ever really had." Over the years, A.J. has been involved with Search and Rescue and has been an advocate for the ethical treatment of animals.

Wilma "Willie" Stewart, now forty-nine, is raising her daughter Melissa, now fifteen, in eastern Washington, where she remains one of the area's top real estate agents. She dates occasionally, but has not remarried. Her focus in the years following her Aunt Stella's conviction has been on raising her daughter—and breaking the cycle that has harmed so many of the Stephenson girls. She enjoys camping and boating at her riverside recreation property and plays a little golf when she finds the time. She has not heard from her Aunt Stella in several years. She still loves her aunt, but she stands by her story of the diary and the seed bottles.

Special Agent **Jack Cusack** has retired from the FBI and is leading the security department for a major northwestern institution. **Ron Nichols** has also retired.

Dee Rogers moved from the Seattle area to the Midwest in the early 1990s. She's not living out in some Podunk town because she was afraid of Stella, as she had once worried. It was a better job offer and a chance to start over that brought her there.

Hold out juror **Laurel Holliday** finally got her wish and became an author—something she so desperately wanted during the Nickell trial. She's published a number of children's diaries.

A few have died in the years since the case went to trial. Among those are **Bob Strong** and U.S. District Court Judge **Bill Dwyer.**

Almost 60, **Stella Maudine Nickell** continues serving her sentence at the federal women's prison near Pleasanton, Calif. She reportedly has a good job in the facility and is well liked by inmates and the staff. She has never wavered on her innocence. "I am not guilty," she recently said. "And I won't quit fighting until I prove it."

About every other year, I receive a Christmas card from Stella Nickell. She wishes my family well and signs her name.

Gregg Olsen,
Olalla, Wash.
Spring, 2002

Dear Reader:

If you're a true crime aficionado, you know that these stories never really end. With the exception of a murder victim, of course, life goes on for the players in the dramas that make the news—sometimes in the pages of true crime books, like mine. I thought I'd take a moment here to update you on some of the people that I've written about in the five books St. Martin's Paperbacks has honored as "True Crime Classics."

My update for you on the players of *Bitter Almonds* is short and sweet here (please refer to the previous pages for more detail). Willie Stewart, Stella's niece, has made a wonderful life for herself and her daughter in Washington. She's selling scads of real estate, traveling the world, and somehow finding time to serve as president of the Scuba club. Says Willie: "I love my aunt very much and wish she would write. But that's our family for ya. Once they shut you out, it's all done." Wonderful news comes out of Artesia, New Mexico, Sue Snow's hometown—and now her daughter Hayley's home. Hayley was just 15 when her mother was poisoned by the tainted Excedrin capsules. She's now manager of a downtown revitalization organization. But even better news is that she's now a mother. She and her husband have a three-year-old son. Her sister, Cindy/Exa, is also a mother of two. When I heard this news, I couldn't help but think how proud Sue would have been. She was such a "mom" herself.

Tanya Thaxton Reid, the focus of my book, *Cruel Deception*, is nearing the end of her prison sentence for the Munchausen's-by-Proxy murder of her baby girl, Morgan. Family members have stood by Tanya—her daughter and former husband, among them—and visit her when they can. They also write frequently. Tanya had an ovarian cancer scare not long ago, but is reportedly fully recovered at this writing. Tanya's son, who was also seen as a Munchausen's-by-Proxy victim, is one of the few family members with no contact with Tanya. He suffers permanent hearing loss that he believes was caused by his mother's abuse. The good news for both of Tanya's children is that they have found the loves of their lives. Back-to-back (almost) weddings are planned for the fall of this year. When Tanya's released in the fall of 2008, a family member says, she plans to move to California where she hopes she can make a "fresh start."

In my book, *If Loving You is Wrong*, I wrote about sixth grade school teacher Mary Kay Letourneau, who was convicted of child